THE STORY OF THE JAMAICAN PEOPLE

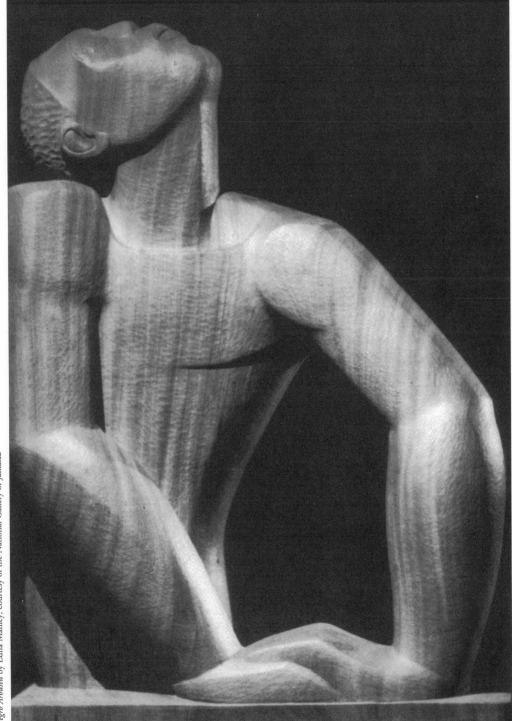

The Story of the Jamaican People

PHILIP SHERLOCK
& HAZEL BENNETT

 IRP IAN RANDLE PUBLISHERS
KINGSTON

MARKUS WIENER PUBLISHERS
PRINCETON

in collaboration with the
Creative Production and Training Centre Ltd, Kingston, Jamaica

© Philip Sherlock and Hazel Bennett

First published 1998 by

Ian Randle Publishers Limited
206 Old Hope Road, Box 686
Kingston 6, Jamaica

In collaboration with the Creative Production and
Training Centre Ltd (CPTC), Kingston, Jamaica

ISBN 976-8123-09-5 Cloth
      976-8100-30-3 Paper

A catalogue record for this book is available
from the National Library of Jamaica

and

Markus Wiener Publishers, Inc.
114 Jefferson Road
Princeton, NJ 08540

Library of Congress Cataloging-in-Publication Data
Sherlock, Philip Manderson, Sir.
      The story of the Jamaican People / Philip Sherlock and Hazel
Bennett
Includes bibliographic references and index.
   ISBN 1-55876-145-4 (hc : alk. Paper). — ISBN 1-55876-146-2
(pb : alk. Paper)
   1. Jamaica—History. 1. Bennett, Hazel. 11. Title.
F1881.S5 1997
96.45648 CIP
972.92—dc21

Book and cover design by ProDesign Ltd, Red Gal Ring, Kingston

Set in 11/13 Adobe Garamond with Casablanca Antique display

Printed and bound in the USA

Cover painting *Mannings Hill Market* by Alexander Cooper
The Hardingham Collection

This book is dedicated to
the People of Jamaica, the gallant makers of our history;
the Youth of Jamaica in whose hands the nation's future rests; the
Promoters and Custodians of the nation's history.

CONTENTS

Acknowledgements

The authors acknowledge with gratitude the interest and support of Sir Alister McIntyre, Vice-Chancellor of the University of the West Indies and of Mrs Jean Smith, Director of Special Programmes Division of the Vice-Chancellor's Office.

Special thanks are due to the Creative Production and Training Centre Ltd (CPTC) which gave its sponsorship to the book and to Mr Wycliffe Bennett, the Chairman and Chief Executive Officer, for his invaluable advice and guidance throughout the writing. The CPTC is producing a companion series, ten one-hour documentaries entitled "The Story of the Jamaican People". Developing the parameters for these documentaries inspired the authors to write this book. We thank the Hon. Burchell Whiteman, Minister of Education, Youth and Culture, for his early encouragement.

We acknowledge our indebtedness to the Institute of Jamaica, to Mr Aaron Matalon, Chairman of the Council of the National Gallery of Jamaica, and to the Hon. Rex Nettleford, O.M., who was both guide and inspiration. In addition we are indebted to the University of the West Indies Library, the National Library of Jamaica, the National Gallery of Jamaica and the Jamaica National Heritage Trust for providing access to scarce material.

The authors record with pleasure the help of Miss Luletta King, who typed and retyped the manuscript and continued to smile.

The authors hope that this book will serve as a useful first step towards new approaches to the study of the Jamaican people. The authors take full responsibility for the contents.

We would also like to acknowledge our indebtedness to the following organisations and individuals who also gave permission for the use of the photographs in this publication:

The National Library of Jamaica
The Jamaica Information Service
The Creative Production and Training Centre Ltd
The Jamaica Library Service
The National Gallery of Jamaica
The Jamaica National Heritage Trust
The Institute of Jamaica Publications
The Gleaner Company
The University of the West Indies, Mona, Library
Kingston Publishers
Mr A. D. Scott
Miss Suzanne Issa
Miss Nellie Chin
Mr Cedric McDonald
Mr and Mrs Easton Lee
Mrs Sheila Barnett
Mr Wycliffe Bennett
Mr J. Tyndale-Biscoe
Mr Oliver Cox
Mr Tom Willcockson
Mr. Wallace Campbell

Introduction

In this book the authors tell the story of the Jamaican people from an African-Jamaican, not a European, point of view.

The story begins in West Africa, with many different African peoples, but chiefly with the Akan, Ashanti, Yorubas, Ibibios and with nations from the region of the Congo.

The Jamaican people have never accepted what was presented to them as the history of Jamaica. The heroes of the British Empire are not their heroes. Their battlefields are in African-America, in Palmares in Brazil, in Accompong, the Great River Valley of Hanover and St James, in Morant Bay, wherever African-American freedom fighters struggled for liberty.

Africa is at the centre of the story. Africa is motherland not only for all African-Jamaicans, but for African-Americans throughout the Americas.

By claiming Africa as the homeland, Jamaicans gain a sense of historical continuity, of identity, of roots. With this perspective they also claim a remarkable heritage of achievement on a hemispheric scale across four centuries, from the beginning of the Atlantic Slave Trade in 1518. African-Jamaicans, not Europeans, built into the story the love of liberty, and a passion for justice and equality–witness Cudjoe, Nanny, Sam Sharpe, Gordon, Bogle, Garvey, Norman Manley and Bustamante.

Africans and their descendants, the African-Jamaican people laid the foundation for a rich national culture by retaining their sense of spiritual values, by creating a vivid creole language, preserving their natural love for drama, music, song, drumming, for laughter, sympathy and wit. They created religious cults and modes of self-expression and developed Jamaica's internal marketing system based, in the early years, on provision grounds on marginal land, and on a network of Sunday markets and higglers.

In the nineteenth century others joined us, partners in the struggle for nationhood, from India, China, Lebanon and Syria, in addition to those who chose to make Jamaica their home when the Spanish colonists left. Loyal Jamaicans, they also treasure their own cultural heritage. They understand the need of the African-Jamaicans to do the same.

This book is a beginning. We hope it will carry further the work already begun by our artists, poets, writers, carvers, sculptors, athletes, reggae musicians, the dub poets, the rastafarians, the scholars, members of the public and private sectors and political parties who are dedicated to building a better Jamaica. A better Jamaica will come if the African-Jamaican people know and treasure their story.

Their history confirms Norman Manley's words, spoken towards the end of his life: "I affirm of Jamaica that we are a great people. Out of the past of fire and suffering and neglect, the human spirit has survived – patient and strong, quick to anger, quick to forgive, lusty and vigorous, but with deep reserves of loyalty and love and a deep capacity for steadiness under stress and for joy in all the things that make life good and blessed."

CHAPTER I

Honour the Ancestors

This history begins with a tribute of loving respect for the Jamaican and West Indian people, achievers of our freedom and independence.

George Lamming sets the opening theme with words from the introductory essay to his novel *In the Castle of My Skin*. He speaks there of his desire to bring,

> this world of men and women from down below to a proper order of attention; to make their reality the supreme concern of the total society.
>
> Along with this desire there was also the writer's recognition that this world, in spite of the long history of deprivation, represented the womb from which he himself had sprung, and the richest collective reservoir of experience on which the creative imagination could draw.
>
> This world of men and women from down below is not simply poor. This world is black and it has a long history at once vital and complex. It is vital because it constitutes the base of labour on which the entire Caribbean society has been built; and it is complex because plantation slave society (the point at which the modern Caribbean began) conspired to smash its ancestral African culture, and to bring about a total alienation of man, the source of labour, from man, the human person.

The story of the Jamaican people includes accounts of the coming of the Jews in the sixteenth century and of the East Indians, Chinese, Syrians and Lebanese in the nineteenth and twentieth centuries. These all became valued partners in the movement towards nationhood and independence. But our story centres on the historical experience of Jamaicans of African origin, who constitute the overwhelming majority of the population. Their ancestors were in Jamaica 150 years before the English arrived and their long struggle for freedom and justice forms an epic chapter in the story of African-America. Their ancestral links are with various West African countries. Africa, not Britain, is their motherland.

Africa is present everywhere in Jamaica. She has been here for five centuries. She walks the dark valleys and sun-baked savannas, the coastal plains and sculptured mountain slopes. She reveals herself in the physical appearance of nine out of every ten Jamaicans, in their body language, everyday talk, in their way with words, their crafts, customs, cults, in their attitudes and modes of self-expression. She is the homeland of a vigorous creative people who, out of a past of fire, exploitation and suffering, preserved a passion for freedom and justice and built these values into the Jamaican way of life.

Britain also is present. She was dominant in Jamaica for three centuries. She is present in churches and schools, in the institutions and forms of law and government. Her presence lingers in old great houses, around broken fortifications and in eighteenth-century sugar ports. Today she lives in her powerful, supple language, an open sesame to one of mankind's great treasuries of literature and to communication with countless millions of people throughout the world.

The Taino is slowly becoming a reality. For long, cassava and tobacco, the hammock and polished stone tools in museums, broken pieces of pottery and worn grinding stones provided proof of his presence in the island before Europe arrived five centuries ago. To most of us the Taino presence remains no more than shapes and shadows seen through a light evening mist, mute witnesses to the demonic force of European colonisation and to the genocide of millions of the indigenous people of the Americas. But recent studies have shown that the Tainos survived longer than was thought. Few though they were, they resisted forced labour and the last survivors established a base in the Dry Harbour Mountains of St Ann and another in the Blue Mountains, probably at Nanny Town. Three important Taino carvings have recently been found and authenticated. The story of the Tainos is woven into the story of the African-Jamaicans, the "old indigenous" melding with those who became the "new indigenous".

Europe brought Africa to the Caribbean early in the sixteenth century. Europe came as victor, dispossessor, exploiter. Africa came as victim, dispossessed, exploited. For five centuries the two shaped Caribbean history, Europe through the sugar-and-slave plantation, colonialism and the doctrine of white superiority, and Africa through the African-Jamaican's rejection of slavery, his triumphant struggle for freedom and justice, his resilience of spirit and his creativity. From the start the story of the Jamaican people is one of a stubborn defiant courage that would not be denied the final triumph.

The greatest agony the imported African slave endured was not physical, terrible though that was, but psychological. He suffered the trauma of being captured or betrayed, of being sold by men of his own race, of being transported in festering slave ships to a strange land, of being bought as a piece of property and of being set to work at new tasks for masters of another race and colour who spoke a strange language. He lived under laws which, in the English-speaking Caribbean and North American colonies, stripped him of the rights of personality and denied him a sense of destiny, of a future. What a catalogue of immeasurable woes and irreparable wrongs! This was in very truth the severest deprivation of all, this surgical severing of the ties with community, with ancestors, with one's history, with one's land.

The Ancestor by Edna Manley

Even at this distance in time it is painful to recall this Gethsemane agony, to enter, as the Haitian poet Jean Briere does, into the experience of uprooting:

> Together we knew the horror of the slave-ships
> and often like me you feel cramps
> awaking after the murderous centuries
> and feel the old wounds bleed in your flesh.

Briere was addressing Haitian blacks but his words find a home in the hearts of the Jamaican people and of all African-Americans. Their story begins with the African men and women, the ancestors, who came in these slave ships from Africa, and with their positive response to deprivation and penalisation. To grasp the significance of their achievement it is necessary to place their history in the context of plantation America, a vast region that extends from North-East Brazil through Suriname, the Guyanas, the Caribbean to the deep south of the United States. These people, coming though they did from different language groups, from tribes with different cultures, from widely separated kingdoms and empires in Africa, and having been distributed as "pieces of India" throughout this region, were as one in their rejection of slavery. Wherever in the Americas the slave plantation was, there also were the African-American freedom fighters. Their defiance lives on in the American civil rights movement, in the dream of Martin Luther King, in the vision of Marcus Garvey and in the words of African-American writers such as Claude McKay, Langston Hughes and Alain Locke.

This defiance was not a passing mood. It was what

Courtesy of the National Gallery of Jamaica

Sam Sharpe said, that he preferred death to slavery. It was what Paul Bogle said: "It is time for us to help ourselves, skin for skin. The iron bar is now broken in this parish . . . War is at us, my black skin. War is at hand."

This central empowering theme of the struggle of the African for liberty, justice and political power gives coherence and purpose to the story of the Jamaican people and links them with other African-Americans.

The struggle took many forms. One was marronage, flight to the forest and mountains and the formation of maroon communities. In a later chapter we will give a more detailed account of the founding of these free autonomous communities in Jamaica by Cudjoe, Nanny and the Trelawny and Portland maroons. There were other African freedom fighters on the plantations, nameless and forgotten men and women who struck a blow for freedom by sabotage, go-slows, damage to property, deliberate misunderstanding of instructions. Without realising it, the Jamaican sugar planter William Beckford paid tribute to them for their success in making slavery unpleasant for the owner: "They were so very capricious, so hardened and provoking that the best tempers may be soured by opposition and be made severe by obstinacy . . . the tricks that are constantly practised by the former, who are worthless and idle, are sufficient to make their superintendents cautious." (Beckford: 1790) These also were among the freedom fighters.

Sam Sharpe, leader of the largest of the many uprisings and rebellions in Jamaica, carried the struggle for freedom and the rejection of slavery further by claiming freedom as a human right and by making the issue one of morality: "The whites had no more right to enslave the blacks than the blacks to enslave the whites."

The struggle did not end with emancipation. The Jamaican people preserved a passion for justice, equality and for a voice in the management of their affairs. In 1865 George William Gordon and Paul Bogle led the demand of the St Thomas peasants for social justice. In the words of Samuel Clarke, at a Kingston Rally in 1865, it was "time for the negro to throw off the yoke and seek your liberty . . . there was one law for the black man and one for the white man". Heroes and martyrs, Gordon and Bogle rejected the doctrine of white supremacy and claimed equality for all before the law.

Up to this point freedom had been achieved, but freedom without an economic base, without social recognition, without the provision of medical and educational services. By 1850 free villages had been established but in ten grim years, from 1855 to 1865, cholera, small pox, floods and drought ravaged Jamaica. The coffin makers and grave diggers were busy. The people endured but they were in great distress. In their affliction a group of St Ann peasants petitioned the Queen for help in 1865. They would work with heart and hand but they needed land. These men and women, poor and in distress, by sheer courage and determination, were bringing into existence a black peasantry and an economy based on small-holdings. They did not ask for charity but for help in obtaining land. In reply the Queen gave them a sermon on the virtue of hard work.

History vindicated the peasants of St Ann, and with them the Jamaican people. In 1897 a Royal Commission endorsed the programme the people and the Baptist missionaries had initiated in the 1830s and that the petitioners of 1865 had put forward. For the first time in their history the achievement of the Jamaican people was officially recognised. The Commission reported: "It seems to us that no reform offers so good a prospect for the permanent welfare in the future of the West Indies as the settlement of the labouring population on the land as small peasant proprietors as the only means by which the population can in future be supported."

But the mass of the people had no voice in shaping government policy. That was shaped by British officials and a legislative council of which only five of the members were Jamaicans; and these were elected by a small èlite. There were no African-Jamaicans on the council; and as for the peasants, heavy taxation and land of poor quality soon led to a fall in the number of peasant freeholds. It was in this period that the black peasantry turned to emigration as a solution for perpetual poverty, and left in their thousands for Panama, Costa Rica and Honduras.

The royal commission's words did not bring any significant improvement in the life of the peasant, as the steady flow of emigrants indicates. But two highly significant developments were taking place amongst the Jamaican people. Marcus Garvey challenged them to make freedom a reality by emancipating themselves from the shackles of white imperialism, by claiming their African past, by pride in their race and by striving for political power. His trumpet call, "Up, you mighty race" inspired racial pride, a sense of purpose and of self-esteem. As George Cumper points out, "In 1865 the new class which was pressing for recognition and partnership in the society was the peasantry. In 1938 a similar role was played by the 'proletarian' wage workers." (Cumper: 1954) The anger of the black peasants and of the black working class boiled over, with eruptions of violence in 1935 and 1936 in St Vincent, St Lucia, St Kitts and British Guiana; with riots at the docks in Falmouth and Kingston in May and October 1935 and with the Frome riot of January 1938. Once more the Jamaican people became the agents of change. In this period of confrontation and conflict Alexander Bustamante and Norman Manley began the transformation of Jamaican society, Bustamante by organising a labour movement and the Jamaica Labour Party, Norman Manley by leading a campaign for universal adult suffrage and freedom from colonial dominance and by organising the People's National Party. These two leaders, opponents but never enemies, became the architects of Jamaican independence; and the Jamaican people have demonstrated that people of the African race are as capable as the people of any other race of founding and maintaining democratic systems of government.

These changes began in the minds of grassroots blacks who realised in a natural pragmatic way that, as Sam Sharpe insisted, freedom was a right for which those who wished to be free had to be prepared to die; that freedom was not an end in itself, a static condition, but a never-ending process of preserving and enlarging the gains that had been won.

The people did these things with little government help. The cost in human suffering was heavy. In 1850 a stipendiary magistrate declared that the country had done little or nothing for the blacks. In 1860 an American journalist, William Sewell, described the mortality rate among children as frightful, and pointed out that the government provided, in 1859, the sum of £2,950 for the education of children between the ages of ten and 15. This worked out at one shilling per child for the year. The churches and the teachers, not the government, not the privileged, stood by the people, guiding and counselling them. Short of capital, the people shared their labour by "day for day", "morning digging", by "pardner" or "susu." Their burial scheme societies, lodges and benevolent and friendly societies added fellowship, a measure of social security, and social recognition to their lives.

From the homes of the people, from board houses roofed with cedar shingles or zinc, wattle and daub thatched roof cottages, each set in its yard, each surrounded by fruit trees, mango, avocado, pear, ackee, soursop, star apple, banana, coconut, coffee, each in dry parishes with its square tank or its "kick-and-buck", each with its lean-to kitchen or covered fireplace, from these came many of the primary school teachers, the black clergy, the policemen, the emigrants who went overseas to Panama, Central America, the United States and, in the 1920s, to Cuba. From these yards and from the "eight by ten" rooms of landless tenants came the urban wage-earners who emerged in the 1930s as the Jamaican working class. Theirs was a monumental achievement, but up to the 1920s "Quashie" remained a term of derision for those who so decisively shaped our history.

Our poets, our artists, recorded our story. Edna Manley revealed the strength and meaning of our history in "Negro Aroused", while George Campbell transformed that history into a psalm:

> For the old roads
> Lead to new ones

And our fathers are our sons
And our sons are our fathers.
No part of our past that is not
Part of our memory
No death in our past
That is not resurrection unto us.

We pay honour also to those who cast in their lot with us; to the Portuguese Jews who chose to stay when Isasi and the Spanish colonists left and who, like blacks and browns, were denied civil rights up to 1829; to the East Indians who loved Jamaica and chose to stay after the indenture period although they had been humiliated and unjustly treated; to the Chinese who so often, throughout the country, made it easier for the poor to buy bread and won a place in our affection; to the Syrians and Lebanese who expressed their dedication to Jamaica by public service, industry and philanthropy. For more than a century these have contributed to Jamaica's progress and to the quality and diversity of Jamaican culture. Their devotion to their own homelands and their knowledge of their own history enabled them to enter fully into the effort of African-Jamaicans to move toward self-government and independence. African-Jamaicans have learned much from these fellow citizens about pride in one's history.

In the chapters that follow we discuss the distinguished hertiage of achievement which African-Jamaicans inherited from the people, the makers of our history. We move on from the story of this heritage and the perception of our history as a source of inspiration to Africa the homeland, and then we turn to the great turning point in human history when mankind turned from hunting to agriculture and from a nomadic way of life to a sedentary one.

And in this change we come face-to-face with the pioneers of urban civilisation, with Chinese people in the valley of the Yellow River, with Indians in the Indus River, with people from the Middle East and from the valley of the Nile. In these early chapters we find unexpected, exciting linkages with other heirs to great civilisations and ancient cultures.

CHAPTER 2

On claiming our great heritage

How does the Jamaican see himself or herself? Has he or she developed the self-pride, self-respect, the sense of self-esteem for which Marcus Garvey pleaded and which history justifies?

The second question is linked with the first and with our theme of Africa as the original homeland. What is the Jamaican's world picture of Africa and of the standing of people of African descent in a world that is no longer dominated by white power? Does the African-Jamaican's world vision begin, as Europe affirmed, with barracoons and slave ships leaving a savage, black country, a land where "the heathen in his blindness bows down to wood and stone"?

In our search for the answers we come to a third question which is at the very heart of our subject. Why do Jamaicans avert their eyes from their history, when in all countries the teaching of history is an opportunity to build up a basic nationalism and patriotism in the mind of a child. And in the minds of the people also, for as Norman Manley said, "It is out of your own minds, out of your own faith in yourselves, out of your own conviction about the future of the country that the spirit of national unity and of patriotism will be built." The African-Jamaican people left to their children, and their children's children, a great heritage. The challenge is to use that heritage for building a sense of self-worth and for national unity and achievement.

Richard Hart, in *Blacks in Rebellion*, put the challenge in these words:

> One of the problems confronting the pioneers of the new popular movements was the formidable historical legacy of a widespread lack of racial self-respect.
>
> Garvey's oratory in the late 1920s and early 1930s had struck a responsive chord and the experience of participation in this movement had provided many thousands of people with a founda-

tion for self-assurance. But even so the task of inspiring national self-confidence was a formidable one.

The historical legacy of self-denigration was only partly attributable to the objective circumstances of generations of enslavement and cruel exploitation. It was also the contrived effect of a system of education and indoctrination designed to promote a loyalty to the prevailing imperialism and an acceptance of the domination of whites over blacks.

Many peoples who have been subjected to alien domination have been able to draw strength from their own legends and history. The Jamaican people were at a disadvantage. The imperial power had largely succeeded in erasing from their memory their African cultural heritage. Jamaica had no legends but it did have a history. And there were aspects of that history which, if brought to the people's attention, could provide abundant inspiration for future struggles against oppression.

Africa and Britain provide ennobling examples of ways in which they used history for empowerment. Many African societies see to it that the young learn the genealogies of their descent. As John Mbiti explains this gives "a sense of depth, historical belongingness, a feeling of deep-rootedness and a sense of a sacred obligation to extend the genealogical line".

Also, many African tribes see God as participating in human history. "They do not sever man from his total environment, so that in effect human history is cosmic history . . . God is not divorced from this concept of history; it is His universe, He is active in it and apparent silence may be a feature of his divine activity." (Mbiti: 1970)

African folklore, an important part of African history, emphasises the universality of the human spirit, overcoming the barriers of race: "Are the dreams of other men so different from those of Africans? It is difficult to speak of a black or a white soul. Souls are seen to be the same in their aspirations."

And where can a nobler tradition of freedom and justice be found than in English history, with its dedication to just and ancient fundamental rights and its record of the progressive safeguarding of the folk, the common people, against the tyranny of rulers.

This tradition was deep-rooted, for as Ernest Rhys points out in *The Growth of Political Liberty*, "the islands bred a notable people, already showing a marked bias and stout temper, before any Angle or Saxon had landed. We read in Tacitus that they would bear cheerfully the service of government if they were not ill-treated, for their subjection ran to obedience, but not to servitude."

In later generations rulers such as Alfred the Great and Saxon King Edgar strengthened the tradition of just laws. King Edgar stated: "This is what I will – that Every Man be worthy of folkright, poor and rich alike, and that righteous dooms [judgments] be judged to him." (Rhys: 1921) Alfred, for his part, by insisting that English history should be set down in an English book, ensured that law by law, record by record, the prescriptive right of the folk to safe conduct in their life and work and justice at the hands of their rulers and governors, is asserted and reasserted.

There followed in 1215 the Magna Carta, the great cornerstone of English liberty, which safeguards the tenant, the heir-at-law, the king's labourer and the common man against feudal abuses: "No man is to be put in prison, outlawed, punished or molested, but by the judgment of his equals, or by the law of the land." (Rhys: 1921)

It could have been Osei Tutu of Kumasi speaking, or the West African creators of the great empires of Ghana, Mali and Songhai, which were organised before the formation of states in northern and eastern Europe.

The Britain that cherished this glorious tradition of "folk right" and "folk moot" betrayed that heritage when it became a coloniser and slave master. In contrast, the enslaved Africans proved to be "a notable people of marked bias and stout temper" who rejected European tyranny.

The Africans and the British saw themselves as the makers of their history. Jamaicans have averted their eyes from their past because they know only that of their history which told of the victories of Nelson and Rodney, which portrayed Europe as model, Africa as a land of savages and the African as an inferior sort of human being. African-Jamaicans know deep within themselves that this is not their history. They refuse to accept or to recognise it.

Also, and this distressed them greatly, they have felt ashamed of being the descendants of docile slaves, who accepted enslavement and European domination and never achieved anything, never created anything, had no past of which to be proud, no history that empowered their descendants and gave them a feeling of self-worth.

The existing system of education, having been taken over from the coloniser without fundamental changes, reinforces their self-doubt, their uncertainty about affirming their blackness, their African heritage, their standing in the world.

Outraged at the utter neglect of African history and at the distortions in British colonial history, Marcus Garvey challenged the black majority to "affirm your ancestry, claim your history", but 300 years of that history had been blotted out; and those 300 years contained the distinguished record of black achievement throughout plantation America, a liberating record of African-American triumph.

Poet/singer Jimmy Cliff, took up the protest, accusing the British coloniser in bitter words:

> You stole my history
> Destroyed my culture,
> Cut out my tongue
> So I can't communicate

He protested against the purpose of the coloniser as being the destruction of his self-esteem:

> You mediate
> And separate,
> So myself I should hate

Jimmy Cliff's message was that for three centuries they had lived like people without being certain who they were, people without a past, without a present, with little prospect of a future; the theft was part of a planned assault on the mind of the black majority so that "myself I should hate". George Lamming reinforced Jimmy Cliff's words.

> If people are shaped by the view that they are made into history by some chosen few who are the real makers of history, you stablize the relation of dominant and dominated . . . If we could ever succeed in planting in people, not only the idea but the fact, in their consciousness, that they are the makers of history, then you alter the relationship between them and those who hold them in their hands. (Lamming: 1983)

We come here to the fact that the African-British conflict had two dimensions, one taking the form of liberation wars for freedom and justice, and the other being the even more difficult resistance to the doctrine of white superiority. It is one of the great achievements of Robert Love and Marcus Garvey that when it appeared that Europe and the governing class in Jamaica were on the point of capturing the African mind they turned the tide; and in that critical period the emerging national movement, coupled with the worldwide anti-colonial movement, brought about the defeat of colonialism. But through the system of education the colonial stereotypes and principles survived.

Only by ridding the mind of the colonial stereotypes and of attitudes of dependence, only by seeing that the African-Jamaican people are the makers of their history, can African-Jamaicans find in their historic achievements the inspiration they need for rekindling the national spirit, for building a united Jamaica, and also ways of using the collective intelligence and wisdom of the Jamaican people to meet the imperatives of the twenty-first century.

The basic colonial principles were: the doctrine of the superiority of the white race and the inferiority of the black. Europe was civiliser and Africa was savage. Skin colour was a badge of status, with blackness denoting slave labour and the gradations of colour moving downwards to degradation. These ideas were clearly stated by British intellectuals such as Thomas Carlyle and James Anthony Froude.

In his highly neurotic and unpleasant *Discourse on the Negro Question* and in his later writings Carlyle maintained that "supply and demand . . . have an uphill task of it with such a man [the Negro]. Strong sun supplies self gratis, rich soil in those unpeopled or half-peopled regions, almost gratis; these are his 'supply' and half an hour a day directed upon these will produce pumpkin, which is his demand".

J. A. Froude insisted that "it is as certain as any future event can be that if we give the negroes as a body the political powers which we claim for ourselves, they will use them only to their own injury. They will slide back into their own condition and the chance will be gone of lifting them to the level to which we have no right to say that they are incapable of rising".

Froude said: "Nature has made us unequal, and Acts of Parliament cannot make us equal. Some must lead and some follow, and the question is only one of degree and kind." Should political freedom be forced on this child or on this race, they would be driven back into "the condition from which the slave trade was the beginning of their emancipation". Blacks had not demonstrated any capacity for civilisation except "under European laws, European education and European authority . . . and the old African superstitions lie undisturbed at the bottom of their souls. Give them independence and in a few generations they will peel off such civilisation as they have learnt as easily and as willingly as their coats and trousers".

These were the attitudes of the ruling class. Even the liberal-minded royal commission of 1897 saw "black economic and moral progress as depending on white guidance and control". (Holt: 1992)

Slavery and the slave trade were justified, as Carlyle and Froude indicated, because Europe, as benefactor and civiliser, rescued the African from savagery.

Isaiah Berlin, one of the great British philosophers of our time, has pointed out that in the nineteenth and twentieth centuries European thought has been astonishingly Eurocentric and that even the most radical political thinkers of this period, speaking of the inhabitants of Africa and Asia, have some curiously remote and abstract ideas. They think of Asians and Africans almost exclusively in terms of their treatment by Europeans. "The peoples of Africa and Asia are discussed as wards or as victims of Europeans, but seldom . . . in their own right, as people with histories and cultures of their own, with a past and present and future which must be understood in terms of their own actual character and circumstances." (Berlin: 1981)

Eric Williams considered that for the West Indian people: "the most pernicious effect of colonialism . . . for the West Indies has been that many black people have internalised this value system and have come to believe in the deepest recesses of their minds that black is in fact inferior to white".

To this day another product of British racism is the split society, with political and economic control in the hands of a white and brown èlite, and with limited educational opportunities for a large, predominantly African, or African and East Indian underclass, trained to serve as cheap labour: "The whole policy of the colonizer is to keep the native in his primitive state and make him economically dependent."

Already we begin to realise that the Africans, thrown as individuals into a society governed by these principles, must have felt utterly alone. Consider the nature of Jamaican society and the odds appear insuperable.

Jamaican society, mirrored the principles of colonialism and revealed their impact in all its crudity. One of Jamaica's distinguished sociologists, Orlando Patterson, described it as lacking any sense of concern for moral values and for the welfare of the community. Britain created in Jamaica a society that was wholly dedicated to making money by producing sugar, exploiting the land and the African.

> As the island reached its period of greatest prosperity, toward the end of the third decade of the eighteenth century, the wealthiest land-owners, possessing well over three-quarters of the island's property (including slaves) were all absentees, living in great style in Britain, where they married into the petty aristocracy and made up the greatest part of the West India lobby, the most powerful interest group in British politics at that time (Williams: 1944).

Orlando Patterson points out that as a result the core of the white ruling class in Jamaica consisted of the attorneys or agents of the absentee proprietors, the few resident large-scale owners, and leading echelons of the appointed officers. Unlike the slave systems of the American South or of the Iberian colonies there was here no ruling class who, infused with the pioneer spirit, were committed to the social well-being and cultural development of their community.

That was not all. In Jamaica England institutionalised violence and legalised injustice by establishing a system of negro jurisprudence which the clerk of the English Committee on the Slave Trade (1789) analysed in these terms:

> The leading idea in the negro system of jurisprudence is that which was the first in the minds of those most interested in its formation,

namely that negroes were property, and a species of property that needed a rigorous and vigilant regulation.

To secure the rights of owners and maintain the subordination of negroes seems to have most occupied the attention and excited the solicitude of the different legislatures . . . the welfare of these unhappy objects was left to the owner . . . The provisions therefore, for the protection and for improving the condition of the negroes make a very small portion of the earlier policy respecting slaves.

In discussing a slave's rights in a court of law, Michael Craton wrote: "Very little measure appears to have been assigned, by any general laws, to the authority of the master in punishing his slaves. It appears that any degree of severity in the way of punishment, though it went even to the life of the slave, was looked upon as an object not deserving public consideration and that even murder was not marked with any very heavy penalty." (Craton: 1976)

Europe created a society that was totally immoral. Legislation made the African slave, male or female, property, a chattel, no longer a person. In so doing, the concept of the family as a basic social unit was destroyed. The white owner exercised the functions of the father as protector, provider, source of authority, counsellor and model. The natural father was downgraded to progenitor and the woman from mother to breeder.

In law, "The young of slaves stand on the same footing as other animals." The master was owner, not the parent. Women "were breeders, animals whose monetary value could be precisely calculated in terms of their ability to multiply their numbers". An absentee proprietor, Monk Lewis, wrote: "The concerns of the family must be to a slave woman matters of very inferior moment compared with the work of her owner. He insists on all the prime of her strength being devoted to his business; it is only after the toils, the indecencies, the insults and miseries of the day spent in the gang that she can think of doing anything to promote the comfort of her household." (Lewis: 1834)

Philip Curtin in *The Atlantic Slave Trade,* states that in the period 1518-1874 about 10 million Africans were brought as slaves to plantation America. Just under 2 million were brought to Jamaica. This book tells how these people made our history: not the British government, the white ruling class, not the powerful, the privileged, but the black majority who had been stripped of all possessions, even of their names and of their status as persons. They and their descendants initiated every movement towards freedom and justice. They built the foundations of nationhood.

The chapters that follow tell the story of the Africans and of their descendants, but we will point here to three of the major achievements of the enslaved Africans and African-Jamaicans. First, we come face-to-face with the greatest achievement of African-Jamaicans and of African-Americans. From the years of their first landings in plantation America, more than a century before the Mayflower arrived in New England, the enslaved Africans set about founding free and independent societies wherever in the Americas. Big Massa had his backyard. The African resistence to enslavement went beyond rejection to creating models of free, just and independent societies. By doing this the African pioneered all the liberation movement of the Americas, with the Palmares Republic, the Suriname Bush Negroes and with the establishment of Haitian Independence in 1807.

This achievement is all the more remarkable because the Africans arrived in America as individuals from different language groups, tribes and kingdoms, who had been removed by force from their kinsfolk, from participation in beliefs, ceremonies, rituals and festivals. They had been severed from their roots, from the security of their tribe and "from the entire group of those who made them aware of their own existence. To be without one of these corporate elements is to be out of the whole picture".

Europe, as explorer, coloniser, slave master brought the African by force to the Americas. She did this with the assistance of some Africans, a fact that many African-Jamaicans find it hard to think of or to accept. But the supreme achievement was that the African-American responded immediately to the challenge of freedom by becoming a liberator and a champion of justice.

African-Jamaicans began the struggle for freedom and justice more than a century before the *Mayflower* arrived and a century-and-a-half before liberty, fraternity and equality became the battle cry of the American War of Independence and of the French Revolution. The African-American struggle for these rights which began early in the sixteenth century and continued up to the time of Martin Luther King, the Alabama bus boycott that began with Rosa Parks, the United States Civil Rights Act (1957), the Unites States Equal Opportunity Act, and a claim for equality that found powerful expression in the Black Power Movement of the 1960s.

The story of the African-Jamaican and African-West Indian people is a significant part of that larger hemispheric struggle. It was global as well as hemispheric, for in the process of time African-West Indians such as Marcus Garvey, George Padmore, C. L. R. James, the Haitian founders of Négritude and its principal exponent Aimé Césaire of Martinique, contributed to the nationalist and liberation movements led by Nnamdi Azikiwe, Kwame Nkrumah and Jomo Kenyatta.

This hemispheric perspective extends across 500 years and reveals the magnitude and significance of the liberation movements which began with scattered, uprooted groups of African fugitives seeking freedom in the forests and mountains of the Americas.

The first Africans to come to the Americas were brought by their masters to Hispaniola in Ovando's fleet in 1502. One of them "escaped to the Indians" soon after arriving. This solitary African's rejection of enslavement set a pattern that was followed by enslaved Africans in Jamaica and throughout plantation America. The word "maroon" is from the Spanish *cimarron*, the name originally given to domestic cattle that had taken to the hills in Hispaniola. It was given also to Indians who had escaped from the lowlands and by the 1530s it referred also to African runaways.

Marronage became a regional movement in which the Africans planted in the slave masters' own backyards visible, tangible reminders of freedom, justice, and independence. Mexico, Colombia, Brazil, the Guyanas, Jamaica, Peru, Haiti, Cuba, the French islands, bear witness to the hemispheric scale of these liberation movements.

In these terms the African-Jamaican heritage ranks with the affirmation of the inalienable rights of man in the American Declaration of Independence and with Abraham Lincoln's declaration at Gettysburg that government was of the people, by the people, for the people.

It was the supreme achievement of the African-American peoples that they transformed slavery into freedom, initiated the longest, most extensive liberation movement in the history of the Americas, and recorded decisive triumphs over European enslavement, colonialism and racial prejudice.

In the process they enriched the cultures of the various countries in which they lived, creating creole languages, a distinguished range of folk cultures and producing world-recognised masterpieces in music, sculpture painting and the dance.

In the history of the Americas three leaders command veneration and evoke profound feelings of gratitude. The three are: white George Washington who defeated the English tyranny and led the North American colonists to independence as citizens of the United States; brown Simón Bolívar, who defeated the Spanish troops and started various independence movements throughout America; and the black ex-slave, Toussaint L'Ouverture, who defeated the armies of Napoleon and took Haiti to independence.

CHAPTER 3

Africa, the original homeland

Marcus Garvey was the first African-Jamaican to make Africa a reality to middle-class and working-class Jamaicans. But many well-educated middle- and upper-class Jamaicans saw both Africa and Garvey through European eyes. This was because

> colonial ideological policy consistently debased Africa as well as peoples and things African. The future, the colonizer claimed, belonged to Europe. Hence colonial subjects were made to identify progress with the ideals of their master. In the process of the formation of Jamaica as a nation the negation of Africa and blackness has been constant. And so has the resistance to it of black people. (Lewis: 1987)

Garvey saw that the reaction of Jamaicans to the name of Africa and to people of African descent defined how Eurocentric they were, how completely they had been transformed into Anglo-Jamaicans. They saw Africa as savage, and Africans as savages. "The image marked the colonial mind, so slavery was portrayed as civilizing." (Lewis: 1987)

Lewis said that in a predominantly black society in the 1920s, as far as Jamaica's leading journalist and novelist, Herbert George DeLisser, was concerned,

> insofar as Jamaica was civilized, it was English . . . DeLisser said that Jamaica bore the indelible impress of English influence and that Jamaicans were proud of their connections with the British empire . . . so when DeLisser came to write Jamaican history through his novels, he portrayed that to be black was to be savage at heart. Paul Bogle, leader of the 1865 rebellion and later a national hero, was described as being a brave man, but underneath the veneer of his religion lay deep the superstitions of the African savage.

The story of the Jamaican people reveals how essential it is to see that history has to do with processes as well as events, with ideas, aspirations, religious beliefs, self-concept, the way in which we see the standing of our nation and people in the world. This means that self-esteem and unquestioning pride in racial ancestry are powerful motivating forces.

The historical experience of the African-Jamaica people shows that only Africa can evoke this response. Garvey emphasised the centrality of Africa, not of Europe, of blackness, not of whiteness, of affirming an African identity, as essential steps to power, and in the first instance, to self-determination. He lamented the fact that in his day West Indians had developed more of the white psychology than of the black outlook, "for the greatest hope lay in the outlook of the Negro toward independence".

In the period 1920-45 some Jamaicans began to see themselves and Africans through African-Jamaican eyes. The change was radical. We have shown how middle- and upper-class Jamaicans saw Africans and the black working class up to the 1920s. In contrast, let us look first at the response of the bush negroes of Suriname who had removed themselves for generations from close contact with colonial authority. From them we move to the first voices of Jamaican nationalism and of the centrality of Africa, this being the generation that followed after the Anglo-Jamaicans. Our purpose in doing this is to show that the story of the African-Jamaican people begins with Africa as the cradle of mankind and as their original homeland. This is why we focus on the story of mankind and not of an empire; and why the perspective includes the emergence of centres of urban civilisation in Mesopotamia, the land between the Tigris and Euphrates; Egypt and the valley of the Nile; the valley of the Indus and the valley of the Yellow River in China. These do not speak of racial superiority. They speak of the basic unity of human beings and of membership in one family, the human race.

We begin with the emotional reaction of the four paramount chiefs of the bush negroes of Suriname when they visited Ghana and Nigeria in 1970. When they arrived in Ghana, Granman Gazon, in vivid imagery, declared that "the same wind that drove us against our will from Africa has now aided us to find our way back". The granman spoke of the emotional shock of returning to their homeland. At their meeting with the Asantahene in Kumasi, each stood close to the ruler of the Ashanti people and addressed him with great emotion. "Granman Aboikoni, trembling with emotion, sang a Kromanti song while kneeling before the Asantahene . . . They declared that finally they had found their true king again. On another occasion Granman Aboikoni concluded with a prayer in Kromanti (a sacred language of the Bush Negroes) in which the Almighty, Nana Kodiapon, is invoked. This caused great emotion for the same Supreme Ruler is invoked in Ghana."

African-Jamaicans share the emotional attachment that Granman Aboikoni and his fellow chiefs felt for their ancestral homeland. They were outraged by Benito Mussolini's attack on Ethiopia. In response, some proudly took the name of Ras Tafari, denounced the white world as Babylon and chose to worship a black god, the emperor, Haile Selassie. In recent years they poured out their love for Africa in the welcome that they gave to Nelson Mandela. Africa provides the sense of racial identity and of self-worth which the white world for so long denied them.

Through the work of Garvey and of the rapidly growing national movement, Jamaica moved to the wonderful daybreak of the late 1930s, when they began to discover themselves. One of the earliest was black Hiram Vaughan of Barbados, who said to the black girl he loved,

> Turn sideways now and let them see
> What loveliness escapes the schools,
> Then turn again and smile and be
> The perfect answer to those fools
> Who only prate of Greece and Rome
> The face that launched a thousand ships
> And such like things but keep tight lips
> For burnished beauty nearer home.

In the same period George Campbell, thought of in Jamaica as the poet of the revolution, in the closing lines of his poem in celebration of Edna Manley's carving, "Negro Aroused", cried:

> the heart shouts, Freedom,
> I lift my face to heaven, awakened,
> Shouting louder, louder,
> With triumph, with a new found strength
> Freedom! We cry only freedom – we were dead when
> Sleeping, now we live! We are aroused.

In his poem "Last Queries" he asks

> Say is my skin beautiful —
> Soft as velvet
> As deep as the blackness of a weeping night . . .

In those electric years of self-discovery and self-emancipation, Victor Stafford Reid wrote one of Jamaica's greatest stories, *New Day*, giving to the English Language new cadences and passionate rhythms. In 1981 Vic Reid said of his historical novels: "The whole reason for my writing is to have the black people proud of themselves, and their history."

Alongside the poets and novelists are two historians, C. L. R. James with *Black Jacobins* and Eric Williams with *Capitalism and Slavery* who revealed in all their starkness the savagery, greed and intellectual dishonesty of European colonialism. History was their abeng, signalling the beginning of the intellectual emancipation of the West Indian people by their own historians. Rupert Lewis and Robert Hill followed with research studies and books that reveal the heroic stature of Marcus Garvey as thinker, black leader and emancipator, who called on African-Jamaicans to take pride in and to cherish the African-Jamaican people, the makers of the history of the Jamaican people who "from the beginning have had to fight their own way up to where they are today. Some have done well but the great majority are almost where they were when they came off the plantations. They are propertyless and almost helpless". (Garvey)

It is for this generation also to claim their great historical heritage and to acknowledge Africa as motherland, as the cradle of mankind and the launching pad for the dispersal of the human beings, the nomadic hunters and food-gathering people who gradually, throughout half-a-million years, established hunting grounds and dwelling places in all the continents save Antarctica.

We begin with Africa because that is where the history of the African people and the human race begins. In contrast, imperial Europe saw the history of the Americas as beginning with the arrival of her pathfinder, Christopher Columbus, in 1492, followed by the colonisation of the New World in the following century. As for the African people, imperial Europe considered that their history began when they came under her rule. This was like saying that the history of the English people begins with the Norman Conquest in 1066.

So, on to Africa, whose political, cultural and racial diversity is bewildering. Our African ancestors came from West Africa, from the region that extends south from Senegambia to Angola. This is only a part of a continent that includes one-tenth of the world's population. These 300 million in number are divided into 50 nations, the majority belonging to about 1,000 tribes, each with its own distinct language, culture and territory. John Mbiti, one of Africa's most distinguished theologians and philosophers, points out that Africa has all the main races of the world and that each group can rightly claim to be African. Ethnologists and anthropologists have classified them broadly as follows: Bushmanoid people with light yellowish skin are found in parts of eastern and southern Africa; caucasoid people, with light to medium brown and pink skin in southern, eastern and northern Africa; mongoloid people whose skin pigmentation ranges from black to brown, yellow and pink; negroid people, black to dark-brown and brown, who are found almost everywhere in Africa; and pygmoid people with light-brown yellowish skins.

Imagine that in order to form an impression of the size and antiquity of

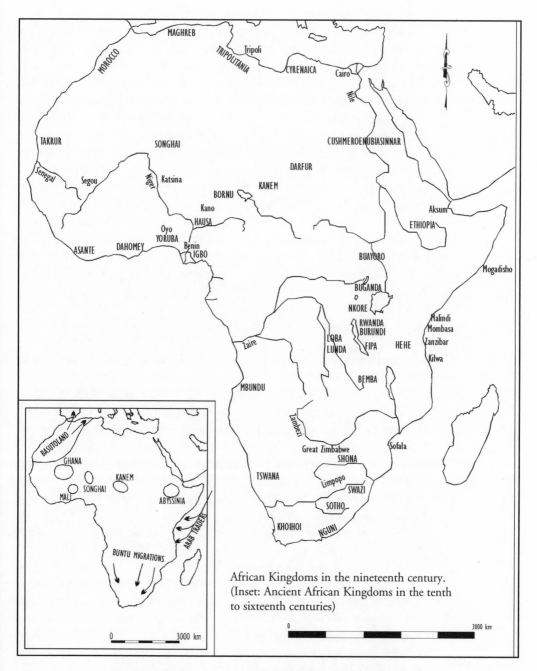

African Kingdoms in the nineteenth century.
(Inset: Ancient African Kingdoms in the tenth to sixteenth centuries)

Africa, we set out by plane from Cairo to Cape Town, 7,000 miles away at the southern end of the continent. Soon, following the Nile Valley, we are looking down on the pyramids. The oldest was built 2,600 years before Christ.

Further south, around Khartoum and the Nile Valley, we fly over areas in the Sudan where scholars have found evidence that negroid people contributed to the growth of Egyptian civilisation and that they were using tools and planting grain 6,000 years ago; that by 4,000 years BC, African people bordering on the West African forest area had developed a system of agriculture based on cereals and that another system based on stock-raising had been established in the highlands of East Africa.

Later, in the sixth century BC, iron-smelting and the making of iron tools and weapons came to the Nile Valley from the eastern Mediterranean and then percolated south. Skills in iron-working travelled by another route also from the Carthaginian cities on the Mediterranean coast of Africa to Nigeria (450 BC at Taruga). Iron technology led to iron tools and these, in turn, led to the expansion of cereal production. During the same period traders, using the Indian Ocean as a pathway to India and Indonesia, promoted cultural contacts and brought to East Africa the banana and yam. Better tools and new types of food seem to have produced a population explosion and to have made possible the emergence of the Bantu-speaking family of African people who now dominate the central and southern region of Africa. By AD 1000 peoples of black Africa were living in settled agricultural communities and were becoming politically organised.

Our southward journey from Khartoum takes us over the Olduvai Gorge in Tanzania, near Lake Victoria, where in 1959 Lewis Leakey found fragments of bones and stone tools that attest to the existence of early man. In 1967 a fragment of jawbone was found at Lothagm Hill in Kenya that dates back to an even earlier period. Africa was the cradle of mankind. The Olduvai Gorge and Lothagm Hill discoveries date back 5 million years, to a period before early man adopted his ground-living habit and an upright posture that freed his arms for using tools.

Other marvels and mysteries lie ahead. The ruined city of stone called Zimbabwe, in the Bantu language "stone houses", was found in 1870. The city dates back to the third century. Some believe that this was the site of the biblical city of Ophir, a seaport from which King Solomon's ships brought gold, jewels and ivory. Still further south, beyond the Zambezi, rock carvings and engravings testify to the growth of an artistic tradition that may date back 8,000 years BC.

With the help of twentieth-century technology we have watched the almost boundless landscape of a continent unroll before us, and we have travelled backwards through millennia to the period of palaeolithic man when Africa was the centre of human activity, technical invention and development. Not until the evolution of the neolithic civilisation in western Asia some 10,000 years ago did Africa cease to occupy the central

African artifacts, *clockwise from the right;* weaving loom – Ghana; woman with braided hair – Sierra Leone; carving representing dead twin; head mask, third tier missing; child's toy – Ghana

position. Today, it is important to develop a sense of the long perspectives of the past to free oneself from the glib convictions of the "natural superiority" of one people over another.

Those perspectives enable us to watch light-skinned, caucasoid people moving from South-West Asia, 10,000 years ago, into Africa. We can picture ideas and technology flowing from brilliant centres of civilisation in the valleys of the Euphrates and Tigris, with their great temples, their skills in smelting and working iron, their domestication and use of the camel, the horse and other animals, into the valley of the Nile and across the Sahara; and in a later period, six or seven centuries after the birth of Christ, we see Phoenician traders founding towns along the coast of North Africa and sowing amongst the Berber people the elements of urban civilisation. In that period semitic colonists from South Arabia were establishing settlements in the north-eastern highlands of Ethiopia. Later in the fourth century AD, Syrian missionaries grafted the new religion of Christianity onto the elaborate civilisation that developed in the Ethiopian Kingdom of Axum.

From Asia also, in the sixth century AD, the armies of Islam swept from the Arabian lands across North Africa, spreading the Muslim faith, and with it the Arabic language, new concepts of law, government, social and economic organisation. Hallett has described how Islam, carried not by the sword but by wandering merchants and scholars, gradually penetrated along trans-Saharan trading routes into the western Sudan, to Gao, Jenne, Timbuctu; across the Red Sea into Ethiopia and the Horn of Africa, where the pastoral Somali continue to preserve genealogies that go back to Arabian origins and to the lineage of the prophet Mohammed; and south along the east coast of Africa to Madagascar and the archipelago of the Comoros.

Pondering over Africa's antiquity and diversity, we draw closer to these ancient peoples and to the tribes to which many of our ancestors belonged. The Yoruba people of the savannas and forests that lie between the lower Niger and the Gulf of Guinea are established in kingdoms that are among the oldest on the continent. Tradition said that their origin was Ile Ife, where God let down a chair by which their founder Oduduwa descended bringing with him a cock, some earth and a palm kernel. Not far away are the Ibo people, made up of over 200 groups, each one a separate society of villages or communities. They all speak a common language, Ibo, one of the Kwa languages of the Niger Congo family. Well to the north, scattered over the western Sudan in the savanna belt from Senegambia extending east to parts of the Central African Republic, are the pastoral Fulani. They are a racially mixed Caucasian and negro people, with their close-knit clans, kinship systems and families and domesticated herds of cattle. Far to

Similarities between African and Jamaican sculpture

*Joined Couple
– Ghana*

Male and Female Created He Them – Mallica "Kapo" Reynolds

Africa, the original homeland

the south the Kung bushmen of the Kalahari Desert live in small, independent nomadic widely scattered groups, a people unique physically, linguis-
tically and culturally, whose time and energies are devoted almost entirely
to survival, but where families remain responsible for dependents. The off-
spring support old dependent relatives, who may choose with whom they
wish to live. Skillful hunters, the Kung bushmen developed cooperative
patterns of sharing in order to survive in the 8,000 square miles of desert
that they inhabit. In their environment these are highly developed people.

We have mentioned but four of the 1,000 or so tribes of Africa, each with
its own distinct language, its own religion, political system, territory, traditions
and culture. Here indeed is an extraordinary diversity of cultures and of political systems.

Yet despite the diversity, with the help of African scholars we will
identify some of the special features that characterise many African
societies. They reveal to us the ethical values that shape their way of life,
the moral principles and codes of behaviour that guide them.

African life is rooted in religion. Religion forms the whole system of
being. Life is not divided into secular and sacred.

> Wherever the African is, there is his religion: he carries it to the fields
> when he is sowing seeds or harvesting a new crop; he takes it with
> him to the beer party or to attend a funeral ceremony . . . Traditional
> religions are not primarily for the individual but for his community
> of which he is a part . . . To be human is to belong to the whole
> community and to do so involves participating in the beliefs,
> ceremonies, rituals and festivals of that community. A person cannot
> detach himself from the religion of his group, for to do so is to be
> severed from his roots, his foundation, his context of security, his
> kinsfolk . . . to be without religion amounts to a self-excommunica-
> tion from the entire life of society, and African peoples do not know
> how to exist without religion. (Mbiti: 1970)

Prayer is the African's commonest act of worship. He talks to the Supreme
Being at all times, often only in a sentence or two, with great simplicity
and naturalness. Mbiti provides us with examples. When Abaluyia old
men rise in the morning they kneel facing east and pray to God, spit-ting
and asking him to let the day dawn well, to pour on them the medicine of
his health and to drive away the evil divinity. The Bamburi pygmies, terrified of thunderstorms, pray: "Good father, Great Father, let all go well
with me for I am going into the forest." If they are already in the forest
when the storm breaks, they pray:

> Father, thy children are afraid; and
> behold we shall die.

The Galla people pray to God in the morning and at evening time,

> O God thou has given me a good day,
> Give me a good night;
> Thou has given me a good night
> Give me a good day.

In times of drought they come together and invoke God,

> Come to us with a continued rain,
> O God, fall.

If men on a hunting expedition do not kill anything they sit down around the oldest man in the group, who prays:

> Oh Mutalabala, Eternal One . . . we pray thee,
> Let us kill today before sunset.

The hunters fall to the ground saying: "O Chief, today let us kill."

When they succeed, they cut up pieces of the meat and the oldest man offers a piece to God, saying:

> I thank thee for the meat
> which Thou givest me,
> Today Thou has stood by me.

The Nuer people pray at any time, for they like to speak to God when they are happy. One of their typical prayers runs:

> Our Father, it is Thy universe, it is Thy will, let us be at peace, let the souls of Thy people be cool. Thou art our Father, remove all evil from our path.

God is everywhere. So are the spirits of the ancestors, and the spiritual world can be seen or felt through the natural, physical world. This is the message of a Senegalese poet, Birago Diop:

> Listen more often to things rather than beings.
> Hear the fire's voice
> Hear the voice of water.
> In the wind hear the sobbing of the trees,
> It is our forefathers breathing.

From religion we move to social organisation, and first of all to the tribe, the unit or grouping in which most of the indigenous people of Africa have lived for centuries, and in which many continue to live. Some tribes like the Swazi of Swaziland number about 200,000 people, and others, such as the Yoruba, about 12 million. Each tribe is a community into which a member is initiated. "Physical birth is not enough; the child must go through rites of initiation so that it becomes fully integrated into the entire society." In the words of the South African novelist, Peter Abrahams, African tribal man's society is exclusive and not, like Western society, inclusive. "The lines are drawn very clearly, very sharply. Anybody not an 'insider' is an enemy, actually or potentially someone to distrust, someone to fear, someone to keep at bay. The tribal society is therefore possibly the most exclusive society in the twentieth-century world. If you are not in the tribe, there is no way into it. If you are in it there is no way out of it except death."

Within the tribe and the clans into which the tribe is subdivided are the kinship groups, the family and the household. In these are rooted the individual African's sense of identity. "What does matter to the tribal African, what is important, is the complex pattern of his position in his own group and his relations with the other members of the group." (Abrahams: 1969). The view is reinforced by Mbiti: "Kinship is reckoned through blood and betrothal. It is kinship which controls social relations between people in a given community. This sense of kinship binds together the entire life of the tribe . . . this it is which largely governs the behaviour, thinking and whole life of the individual member . . . the kinship system is like a vast network stretching laterally in every direction to embrace everybody in any given local group." (Mbiti: 1970) This means that each individual is a brother or sister, father or mother, grandmother or grandfather, or cousin or brother-in-law, uncle or aunt or something else, so that a person literally has hundreds of "fathers", hundreds of mothers, hundreds of "uncles", hundreds of "sons" and "daughters".

In these critical years, many Jamaicans stand beside Africa with affection, as she searches for new values, identity and security. As John Mbiti says:

> Africa is caught up in a world revolution which is so dynamic that it has almost got out of human control. It is a revolution of men as a whole, and therefore no people or country remain unaffected by this new rhythm of human history. In Europe and North America, this revolution goes back three to five generations. But in Africa we are nearly all in the first generation of the change . . . Without warning and without physical or psychological preparation, Africa has been invaded by a world revolution . . . The man of Africa must get up and dance, for better or for worse, on the arena of world change. His image of himself and of the universe is disrupted and must make room for the changing 'Universal' and not simply 'tribal man'. This is the general worldwide revolution affecting African societies. (Mbiti: 1970)

In Abrahams' words, "tribal man" is the man who raised Nkrumah to power. He is the man whose pressure led Jomo Kenyatta to the Mau Mau and then to his lonely prison exile in a barren and isolated spot. He, tribal man, will have a crucial say in the future of Africa.

The people of the English-speaking Caribbean form the largest cluster of independent non-white nations in the Americas. In terms of population, size and material resources they are small, but in terms of international politics and cultural achievement they exercise an influence beyond what their size would lead one to expect. They take pride in the close relationships they have established with the African nations and in rendering such assistance as they have been able to render to their homeland.

The relationship will flourish if African-Jamaicans understand that they are foreigners. In a penetrating passage, Peter Abrahams points out that whereas "blackness" unifies African-Americans, the tribe is the binding force in Africa. It is also in today's world, as Jomo Kenyatta and Kwame Nkrumah found, an isolating, dividing force.

CHAPTER 4

From a colonial to a world perspective

Africa, not Europe, is where the story of the Jamaican people begins;
Africa, the cradle of mankind, where human history began; Africa, the
original homeland of the groups of nomadic hunters and food gatherers
who first moved into Asia and Europe and whose descendants moved from
Siberia into the Americas many millennia later; Africa, where black people
from the southern regions of the Nile Valley helped to found one of
mankind's earliest centres of urban civilisation.

To begin with Africa is to affirm that the African-Jamaican people are
the makers of their history, and to reject the notion that their history began
with the arrival of Columbus in the 1490s or with the entry, under
compulsion, of African slaves into plantation America in the sixteenth
century.

English colonial rule in Jamaica began in 1655. Twenty years later the
sugar-and-slave plantation economy took over the colony. We begin by
showing how the colonial perspective demeaned and psychologically
damaged the African-Jamaican. We conclude by rejecting that perspective
in favour of the broader, uplifting one of Africa and early human history.

The Africans who were brought to Jamaica were distributed throughout
the island's sugar estates and pens. Each, by law, was the property of a
master and was tethered to a particular property. The African's world view
was limited to that property, to Golden Grove, for example, which was
bounded by the Plantain Garden River to the north and by Duckenfield
Estate to the east; or Lucky Valley Estate in Clarendon, which belonged to
Samuel Long,

> with the hills in canes, Pinder's River, tops of plantations in the
> foreground, buildings from the left, old overseer's house where the
> doctor resides, new overseer's house concealed by trees, trash house,

corn store, shed and cattle pen, cooper's shop, hospital, Mr. Miller's house, works, mill house, boiling and still house, rum store, piggery etc, poultry house with sheep pen, wagon with 12 steers and load of sugar going down. (Higman: 1976)

The aim was to control the enslaved African labour force, immobilise it, blot out any sense of identity save that of "belonging to the owner Samuel Long", or Daniel Lascelles at Williamsfield, or any other.

Even so cultivated a planter as the historian Bryan Edwards saw the African people as property, not people:

From the late Guinea sales, I have purchased altogether twenty boys and girls, from ten to thirteen years old. It is the practice, on bringing them to the estate to distribute them in the huts of creole negroes, under their direction and care, who are to feed them, train them to work and teach them their new language. For this care of tending and bringing up the young African, the creole negro receives no allowance of provisions whatever. He receives only a knife, a calabash to eat from and an iron boiling pot for each.(Edwards: 1793)

These teenagers were condemned to a lifetime of dictated routines and prohibitions; to an existence without a future, and to a brief life, for the average life expectancy of a slave was seven years. The world view was that of a tunnel that had no light at the end.

Barry Higman's description of the typical slave village shows the narrow boundaries within which, for 150 years, generations of enslaved Africans were confined.

The second major element of the sugar estate's settlement pattern was the workers' village. In the period of slavery, every estate set aside an area for slaves' houses but after 1838 there was a gradual drift away from residence sites on estates . . .in general the site of the estate labourers' village was determined by the location of the works. Workers were required to spend long hours in the factories, especially during slavery when the mills frequently worked around the clock over a crop season extending through six months of the year. Field slaves were required to labour in the mills at night, following a day cutting and carting canes. Artisans laboured in shops near the works for the greater part of the year. Thus the desire to minimize the time involved in the movement of labourer meant that the estate village tended to be tied to the works rather than being located at a central site. (Higman: 1976)

This was a world of constant surveillance. Thus William Beckford, writing in 1790, observed that:

The negro-houses are, in general, at some distance from the works, but not so far removed as to be beyond the sight of the overseer. And Beckford advised that during crop the overseer should be required to sleep at the works, in a room in the curing house with a window into the boiling house. Roughley, in the 1820s, recommended only that the overseer's house should be located near the boiling house with a clear view of all the works buildings and specified that the slave hospital and mule stable should be placed behind the house in order to ensure an unimpeded view.

Emancipation brought some relief, but no substantial change. The plantocracy took no responsibility for enlarging the horizons of the newly freed people. "No general system of public instruction has been introduced in Jamaica, and it is surely unreasonable to expect that this people, or any other people, could acquire a knowledge that has never been placed within their reach." (Sewell: 1968).

Crown colony government undertook responsibility for the education of the Jamaican people, but only to primary school level for the black majority. It provided, instead of a tunnel, a ten-by-ten room with a home-sweet-home kerosene lamp. As late as 1937 Marcus Garvey protested:

> the labouring classes of Jamaica have never had anything to be loyal about; they have been among the most brutally oppressed people of the British Empire. The employer has no sympathy for the poorer classes . . . The classes in the island are visibly drawn. The man with money is on the top and the man without can easily be seen as the unfortunate human being that he is. Money and colour count for more than anything else.

In 1938 Arthur Lewis emphasised that social discontent and actions taken by the people had forced the British Government to appoint a Royal Commission to investigate social conditions and that West Indian governments had been forced "to adopt all sorts of measures to meet the grievances of the workers . . . a revolution for hitherto West Indian governments have not regarded measures of this sort as of primary importance. But even more important is the fact that the working classes have become organized politically and that their interests have been forced into the foreground".

The perspectives and purposes of British colonialism and of Eurocentricity demeaned and diminished the African-Jamaican people. Independence and the new age into which mankind has moved call for relevant inspiring approaches.

Another reason for developing longer perspectives that show man in the setting of his culture, his religion, his ideas, is that the "imperial model"

turned out to be a recipe for disaster. In his book *The Great Transformation*, the Austrian-born economist Poliany, shows that the European civilisation which collapsed in the 1920s was "economic" in "the distinctive sense that it chose to base itself on a motive never before raised to the level of justification of action and behaviour, namely gain". This was the justification for the partitioning of Africa by the European powers between the 1870s and 1890s, an act that led to the global anti-colonial movement of the 1920s and 1930s.

The European coloniser's perspectives apply to European imperial history and not to the history of the Jamaican people. The coloniser made his history and stamped on it his figure as slave master, destroyer of millions of the indigenous American people, and as the creator of an economic system and an imperial philosophy that carried within themselves the seeds of the their own destruction. The collapse of the imperial system in the 1920s and 1930s confirms this.

We turn now to the long view of African and human history, and we begin with the hunters and food-gathering people of the early period. We stay with them briefly and then move to the emerging centres of urban civilisation in Egypt, Mesopotamia, India and China some 5,000 years before the birth of Christ.

This approach liberates us from the fracturing influence of imperial Europe, engenders a sense of the essential unity of mankind and of a deep reverence for each human being as a uniquely precious combination of mind, body, spirit; as a restless, creative being who, through countless millennia, found ways of surviving by manipulating the physical environment. In the process, by analysing and using their individual and collective experience, the hunters and food gatherers developed methods of social organisation for meeting their material needs. From the beginning they also developed forms of worship that kept them in touch with the Great Spirit, with God, the Creator of Life, the Great Eye, the One before whom "Majesties bend".

Fragile, skin-clad, for long without the knowledge of how to kindle a fire, armed only with crude weapons of bone, shells and stone, these early nomadic hunters survived in a long contest with glaciers and great sheets of ice that periodically spread across large areas of the temperate zone, limiting human beings to the tropical zone, the only warm place on earth. The survival of these early people rested on their skills as hunters, as makers of tools and on their intellectual capacity. They developed to the full the hunting and food-gathering way of life and achieved a level of social and technical development quite different from that of other hunting mammals. "Only during the last few thousand years has the practice of agriculture, the domestication of plants and animals, replaced the earlier way of life; only in this brief period had man been able to make use of materials other than stone, wood or bone, or harness sources of energy other than those of the human body." (*Times Atlas of World History*)

After many millennia, although the hunters and food-gatherers had greatly extended their hunting grounds to Siberia, and in later ages south-wards into South America as far as the continent's southern tip, the sources of food began to run short. Throughout the world hunters and food gatherers were driven by hunger to plant food crops rather than to chase food which galloped away from them.

Throughout the subtropical region of the world, without prior consultation or planning, the hunters and food gatherers began to develop improved varieties of cereals. These became the staple crops on which their survival depended. Farmers in the Near East developed wheat and barley, which became the basic cereals there as well as in Europe and India. In China and in South-East Asia farmers developed millet and rice into staple crops.

In the subtropical regions of the Old World there was a rapid and widespread exploitation of animals: cattle, pigs, the horses in the region of the steppes north of the Black Sea, the ass, camel, goat, sheep in Arabia and the Middle East, the two-humped or Bactrian camel of Central Asia, the yak in the Himalayas and native cattle in South-East Asia. By domesticating these animals human beings obtained a more varied supply of meat and milk and greatly increased their productivity by harnessing animal power to agriculture and to the transport of goods.

In Central America Indian tribes cultivated cotton for clothing, as well as a variety of food plants, including lima-beans, runner-beans, squashes, peanuts, sweet potatoes, tomatoes, peppers, white potatoes, manioc, and in some areas the avocado and cocoa, but the only animals that were domesticated were the llama and alpaca of Peru.

Gradually, in response to the many diverse demands of agriculture, nomadic man began to follow a different way of life based on villages, not camp-sites, homes built of more lasting materials such as bricks and rocks instead of tents, centralised services such as the storage of crops, irrigation and flood control, rearing and protecting flocks, establishing trade routes, developing new technologies for tilling the soil, such as using ploughs, creating a wheel with spokes, inventing the art of writing and record-keeping.

As the villages grew in size so the social and economic needs increased, for the process of change generated by agriculture and trade had its own built-in dynamism, and with each generation the pace of life quickened. Every advance provided the foundation for further progress.

We stand at a point in history where we are able to look back across the 10,000 years that have passed since the agricultural revolution set these forces of change in motion. We see that every change in the source of power speeded up the pace. When human muscle power was reinforced by horse-power and cattle-power, production increased; when wind-power took the place of oars, travel times were shortened; steam power and electricity packed 100 years of production into five or ten years. These prepared the way for scientfic and technological advances that have moved mankind into a new age, with satellites, nuclear power and computers. But what was the form of social organisation, what the social unit that released the creative energy, directed the collective undertakings, exercised control and authority, brought into being a bureaucracy, a specialised legal system, a standing army, and that created also the supporting social structure such as a hierarchy with a king, a high priest, a literate class?

The period from 6000 to 4500 BC contains the answer. In that period there emerged in four widely separated, very fertile river valleys the earliest centres of urban civilisation. Africa with the valley of the Nile, Mesopotamia (the land between the Tigris and Euphrates Rivers), the valley of the Indus in India, in the region around Harappa and Mohenjo-Daro, and the valley of the Yellow River in China around Anyang.

Chinese, Indians, Syrians, Lebanese, Arabs and Africans all share the patrimony of ancestors who took the first steps toward urban civilisation. This was not the act of any one race. They all share the distinction of having created the city as the dominant social form that provided the "complex division of labour, literacy and a literate class (usually the priesthood), monumental public buildings, political and religious hierarchies, a kingship descended from the gods, and ultimately empires". (*Times Atlas of World History*)

We find that the advances took place in a setting of confusion and strife. This ceaseless warring of city-states then of royal alliances, and finally of empires in the Near East was a prime source of human suffering. Wars were waged for booty, tribute, slaves, raw materials, control of trade routes and imperial ambition. As a Sumerian proverb puts it,

> You go and carry off the enemy's land;
> The enemy comes and carries off your land. (Eban)

This perspective, which takes us back in time to the birth of civilisation, gives to our history a sense of continuity and enlarges our understanding of the central role that Africa and the Mediterranean region played in the history of civilisation. By beginning with Mesopotamia and Egypt, by focussing on areas that provide links with our way of life, we are discovering the proper path to understanding our history and to learning how to use past achievements to galvanise the national spirit and to reinforce national unity.

Using the criteria of relevance to the historical experience and way of life of the Jamaican people, we have selected three leaders from this early period of emerging urban civilisation who, by their actions, achievements, ideas and beliefs, still influence our lives. Their names are Sargon, king of the city of Kish, Abraham, the father of the Jewish people, and Moses, who led the Jews out of bondage.

We begin with Sargon, who greatly strengthened and enlarged the city-state in a very formative period. He stabilised the political and religious structures in Kish, with himself as head of state and of the political hierarchy and with the high priest at the head of the religious hierarchy. Then he turned his attention to his neighbours and is recorded as having been victorious in 34 campaigns and having dismantled (all) the cities as far as the shore of the sea. Sargon's rule extended from South West Persia to Syria, and he extended his empire's sea-trade along the Persian coast possibly as far as the mouth of the Indus River.

His empire collapsed under the attacks of fierce fighting tribes from the hills, but the rival city-state of Ur of the Chaldees turned with zest to the task of empire-building. It had a well-developed bureaucracy and a more stable base. In the course of time Ur also collapsed, but the pattern of empire-building had by then been established. It was followed by the Assyrians, by Babylonians, Egyptians and the Hellenes, and then gradually became worldwide.

Towns, city-states, empires are the most powerful forms of social and political organisation. The growth of cities, for example, has made twentieth century urbanisation a major cause of concern to mankind. Before many decades pass one-quarter of the world's population will be living in towns. Already in Jamaica every fourth Jamaican lives in an urban area. To drive along the north coast road, or the central highway from Morant Bay through Kingston, Spanish Town, May Pen, Mandeville to Black River and Savanna-la-Mar, is to see that Jamaican society is for the most part urban, not rural.

The change is even more evident along the eastern coast of the United States where metropolis has become megalopolis, "great city".

Abraham takes us away from the world of growing cities jostling for trade and leads us into that inner world in which we reach out for some contact with God. He was born and grew up amongst people who had many gods: cosmic gods, local gods, gods who were at war with each other, gods whose names were changed. He observed that this multiplicity of gods sometimes caused fear and confusion, for often people were not sure to which gods they should make offerings so as to keep well or to prosper. Often, when in trouble or distress, they felt utterly helpless and deserted because, as a Sumerian wrote:

> The god whom I know or do not know has oppressed me.
> The goddess whom I know or do not know has placed suffering
>   upon me.
> Although I am constantly looking for help, no one takes me by
>   the hand;
> When I weep they do not come to my side. (Eban)

Going against all the religious beliefs of his time, Abraham rejected the desolating polythesim which reduced religion, the communion of God with man, to a magic that could be manipulated. His vision was of one God who was both cosmic and local, and of a special covenant or agreement between a people who agreed to worship and serve Him, in return for His protection and for land that He would give to them.

Abraham was greatly concerned about the relationship between God and his people. He believed that God listened to their prayers and communicated with them. He was convinced that repentance and atonement were possible. When calamity overtook a Sumerian he could only accept it as being the will of the gods which was irreversible. Abraham and his kinsfolk believed that their God was a just God, and that if one repented there was the possiblity of forgiveness, for God was merciful as well as just. Repentance and salvation were possible. Good deeds opened the way to atonement and were a shield against punishment. The mission of the Israelites and of their first patriarch and founder was to be unto God "a Kingdom of priests and an holy nation".

Somewhere about the year 2000 BC, the city of Ur, at that time the centre of Mesopotamian culture, fell. After that calamity God spoke to Abraham, saying: "Get thee out of thy country, and from thy kindred, and from thy father's house unto a land that I will show thee." (Bible)

Abraham obeyed. His obedience symbolised another rejection of the current Sumerian way of life. The general trend was away from a nomadic way of life to city-dwelling. In contrast, Abraham and his kinsfolk became semi-nomads, a pastoral people, shepherds and herdsmen who were always moving in search of green pastures and still waters; living in tents, going without great possessions, developing a sense of solidarity, of belonging together, as compared with the often fiercely competitive way of life in the city. So it came about that the imagery of the Bible includes frequent references to a pastoral culture in which rainfall and water meant life and the shepherd's rod meant protection and comfort.

To Abraham, in the plain of Mamre, near Hebron, there came a vision of an agreement or covenant with God: "Fear not, Abraham, I am thy shield and thy exceeding great reward." On the same day, the Lord made a covenant with Abraham, saying: "Unto thy seed have I given this land, from the river of Egypt unto the great river, the river Euphrates." (Bible) So profound was Abraham's faith, so excellent an example did he set of a close relationship with God, that: "Both Christian and Muslim traditions admit Abraham as their spiritual ancestor. To the Jews, he is the first and unique patriarch, the model of Hebrew excellence." (Eban).

Throughout the generations that followed the death of Abraham Egyptian civilisation flowered and then, for a time, it came under the rule of Asian people, the Hyksos. Later, Rameses II came to power and restored Egypt to its former greatness. He was the tyrannical pharaoh who oppressed the enslaved Hebrews.

Moses, who had been born and bred into the Egyptian way of life, but who also felt deeply for his oppressed brethren went out to speak with his brothers, the enslaved Hebrews. "Moses was greatly angered when he saw an Egyptian beating an Hebrew. He looked this way and that and when he saw there was nobody in sight, he killed the Egyptian and hid him in the sand." (Bible)

News of the killing reached the pharaoh and Moses had to leave Egypt and take refuge with the Midianites in the land of Sinai. There, at Horeb, God spoke to him from a burning bush that was not consumed, saying: "Behold the cry of the children of Israel is come unto me and I have also seen the oppression with which the Egyptians also oppress them. Come and I will send thee unto Pharaoh, that thou mayest bring forth the children of Israel out of Egypt." (Bible)

At this moment, Moses, the liberator of the Hebrews and leader of the

Exodus, transformed the history of the people of Israel and – some 3,000 years later – the history of the Jamaican people.

The Bible reached the African-Jamaican people in the 1790s when two black Baptist preachers who had been freed by their masters came to Jamaica, George Lisle and Moses Baker. They built up large followings, Lisle in Kingston and Baker in western Jamaica. Their congregations grew rapidly, and they appealed to the newly-founded Baptist Missionary Society in England for help. By the 1820s white Baptist missionaries, troublesome dissenters in the eyes of the plantocracy, had begun to arrive.

Never before had the enslaved people held a book in their hands, and certainly not the Bible, for it was not regarded with favour on the Jamaican sugar-and-slave plantation. All school doors were closed to African-Jamaicans, so they could not read. Church doors were closed to them, for in the eyes of the plantocracy God was white and there was a colour line. The African-Jamaicans, a very religious people, sought what comfort they could find in communion with Obi, Myalism, Cumina, in Haiti with Vodun, in Trinidad in a later period with Shango. Barred from the church, the school and any form of marriage, the African-Jamaicans were derided as being superstitious, stupid and immoral.

Now, with the missionaries as their teachers in Sunday school, the Bible became their holy book that contained the word of God, their comforter and beloved companion in the Valley of the Shadow of Death. It was their certificate of identity which confirmed their status as God the Father's children, their guarantee of a future in the Father's company and above all their blessed assurance that each one was a worth-while somebody for whom Massa God gave His only son. They were no longer the only ones who had been slaves. They shared the Jewish experience of having been an oppressed people. In the prophets, patriarchs, psalmists they found comfort and hope. The Jewish story had for them an almost unbearable, piercing relevance.

This is how it came about that Daddy Sharpe, deacon in Parson Burchell's church in Montego Bay, and Thomas Dove, Johnson, Dehaney, Linton and all the people walked the Great River Valley tracks together to Retrieve, Lethe, Seven Rivers, Montpelier with Father Moses. This is how it came about that in the time of execution in Montego Bay, they passed through the Valley of the Shadow with such courage, for their Shepherd was with them. This is how, up to the time of Bogle and of Bedward, the shepherd and the shepherdess were trusted leaders among Jamaican working class people.

In recent years scholars from different disciplines have carried out studies which prove that African people played a more important part in establishing Egyptian civilisation than was originally thought. There is increasing evidence that major elements in that civlisation flowed from the southern region of the Nile, from the Sudan, Ethiopia and parts of central Africa, north to Memphis, the capital of the pharoahs.

The murals of the early periods show the Egyptians as black, brown and yellow-skinned people. It appears that about one-third of the population was black.

Ethiopia was closely involved with Egypt and Ethiopian kings ruled Egypt for more than a century. History records that the greatest of these was Taharka, who became pharaoh at the age of 42, an able, energetic ruler, so powerful that he called himself "emperor of the world". By contributing so significantly to the growth of Egptian civilisation and power, Africa was participating also in founding Western civilisation.

In this chapter we have rejected the notion that the story of the Jamaican people is merely a footnote to the story of British imperialism, and we have illustrated the crippling effects of the colonial or Eurocentric perspective.

We have placed our story in a new, historically validated setting centred on the human being, not on a system but on early man's way of life. We have linked this with Africa, where human history began. We have told of the agricultural revolution of 10,000 years ago which set the feet of mankind on the road to founding cities, establishing urban civilisation and, through Abraham, creating a monotheistic religion as an alternative to the polytheism of that age. With monotheism Abraham linked the concept of a covenant between God and a special people, which replaced the fatalism of idolatry, with its doctrine of the irreversible will of the gods, with a theology rooted in belief in a just God, in repentance for sins and in atonement. We then turned to Moses, to the African-Jamaican people of the 1820s and to the liberating, ennobling and hope-kindling impact of the Bible.

The criteria that guided us to this new approach to our history had historical validity, relevance and continuity. Relevance meant considering the present circumstances of the Jamaican people and also taking into account the total racial experience, which had its beginnings in African cultural and religious traditions and included the psychologically damaging effects of colonialism and the sugar-and-slave plantation; continuity meant establishing linkages with Africa as the homeland and at showing that the Africans' creation of free communities in response to the twin penalisation of uprooting and of enslavement was a product of their own cultural traditions.

This is a fact of central importance. Enslavement and political subjection to an alien people were painful interruptions, so extensive and damaging that they became a harsh form of penalisation. The response of

African-Americans throughout the hemisphere to that penalisation was comprehensive and creative. It included liberation movements that were ultimately successful, and cultural contributions that ranged from language and folklore to the performing and creative arts and the creation of democratic, non-racist societies. This was the towering achievement, that it was the African who, out of his earlier experience of civilisation, created in the Americas the first models of free and independent democratic societies – in some cases 200 years before Washington.

The sense of continuity reveals two aspects of the history of the African-Jamaican and the African-American people which have not been fully recognised. The first is that the diaspora was spread out across some 350 years or more; in Jamaica, across the period 1675-1807, when Britain abolished the slave trade. Uprooting and dispersal were interruptions that caused discontinuity but the annual inflow of new Africans made survival possible and transformed the diaspora into a continuing revitalising of the African response.

Also, the very rejection of enslavement, the insistent demand for freedom, the insistent demand for justice, built into African-American and African-Jamaican history elements that were ennobling and inspiring because they represented, in Jefferson's words, disobedience to tyranny and therefore obedience to God. Few responses to penalisation in human history have been so sustained or so far-reaching in their results.

CHAPTER 5

The Asians colonise America
and the Caribbean

Hunters and food gatherers from Asia, not Europeans, were the first colonisers of the New World. More than 40,000 years ago, following the migrating caribou and the hairy mammoth, they crossed over a narrow land or ice bridge into North America at the point where the Bering Strait now divides the two continents. Over many millennia, as they spread slowly over the two vast continents of North and South America, groups of individuals kept branching off to form independent tribes. In the process, they adapted to changing environmental conditions and developed distinctive characteristics, lifestyles and languages.

In their wanderings they left behind imprints of their presence, as at the Bluefish Caves in the Yukon, where caribou and mammoth bone tools unearthed there have been traced to about 25000 BC. In the Orogrande Cave in New Mexico, a flint spear point stuck in a horse's toe bone dates from about 38000 BC. and in the same area, a fireplace estimated to be about 30,000 years old reveals human fingerprints impressed upon clay.

When conditions permitted some communities remained for long periods in one locality, preferring to live off the roots and crops nearby, rather than to keep on the move behind fleet-footed animals. From these more stable communities, town dwellers, city-states and eventually empires evolved.

As early as 3372 BC, at the time that the Egyptians were developing the use of numerals, the Mayas of Central America, whose empire then covered modern Belize, were beginning to record their history. The Inca empire of South America extended from Ecuador in the north to Chile in the south. The Inca built imposing structures decorated with drawings and incisions which tell their story. The Toltecs and later the Aztecs of Mexico established educational and religious institutions and left accounts of their activities on bark and on stone, using a form of picture writing. After centuries of examination, these monuments are beginning to yield the secrets of their skills and technologies and possibly of their collapse. The *Codex Montezuma*, compiled at the time of the Spanish invasion of Mexico, is a horrifyingly graphic record of Europe's encounter with the Americas and the atrocities committed against the native people.

Both the Incas and the Aztecs developed mathematics early and refined the theory of geometry. Thus huge rocks employed in the construction of Inca edifices are cut so precisely that they appear to be cemented together. The Aztecs were also applying the concept of zero 1,000 years before the Europeans acquired this knowledge from India.

All these major civilisations had centralised governments ruled by god-kings, with a hierarchy of priests and functionaries to carry out the daily religious, commercial and military activities. Although none of these civilisations developed the wheel, the keystone arch, or an alphabet, magnificent stone structures survive even after many centuries.

Not all the first nomads chose to settle in villages or towns. Some continued to roam the great grasslands and tropical forests in search of food. Today small numbers of their descendants are still to be found in the forests of Central and South America where they live very much as their ancestors did. Sometime between 2000 BC and 300 BC, groups of these nomads left the tropical forests and river valleys of Venezuela and Guyana and the Yucatan Peninsula. Using fire and stone implements, they fashioned canoes from giant softwood trees and in these they explored nearby coastal waters and the islands of the Caribbean archipelago. Unlike the mountain-dwellers of Central and South America, they left no monuments of their civilisation.

They hunted, raided, captured their weaker neighbours, moved on or settled if conditions were to their liking and food was easily available. The Caribs chose the southern islands of the archipelago while the Tainos, who it is believed evolved in the region, inhabited the larger islands of Puerto Rico, Hispaniola, Cuba, Jamaica and the Bahama Islands. It was in the Bahamas in 1492 that they encountered Europeans for the first time, an encounter that began and ended tragically for them.

The Caribs were more warlike than the Tainos. When they captured girls and women they kept them as wives and slaves. The men they starved and sacrificed to their gods. Both groups of people spoke a common language, Arawakan, so that they could communicate with each other and share practices. Because of the common language they are frequently called Arawaks.

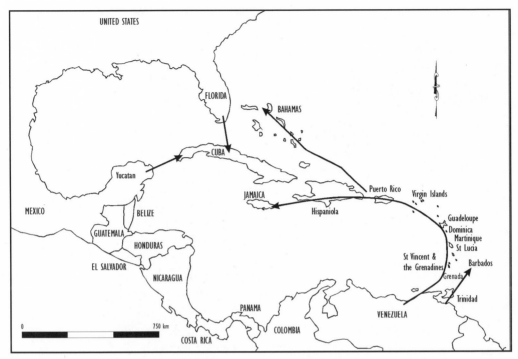

UNITED STATES

FLORIDA

BAHAMAS

CUBA

Yucatan

JAMAICA

Puerto Rico

Virgin Islands

MEXICO

BELIZE

Hispaniola

Guadeloupe
Dominica
Martinique
St Lucia

GUATEMALA

HONDURAS

EL SALVADOR

NICARAGUA

St Vincent &
the Grenadines

Barbados

Grenada

PANAMA

Trinidad

VENEZUELA

COLOMBIA

COSTA RICA

0   750 km

Probable routes of Taino migration through the Caribbean

Jamaica was inhabited by the Tainos somewhere between AD 600 and 900. However, until the beginning of the twentieth century these original inhabitants seemed a shadowy people who had left no impact on the Jamaican way of life. Nevertheless, research shows that they lived an ordered existence and had a philosophy which compares with that of other polytheistic societies. They respected law and order and were in fact Jamaica's first freedom fighters. When the Spaniards conquered the island and began to enslave them, they resisted to the death. This happened before the arrival of the first African slaves. Some committed suicide rather than lose their freedom while those who could, escaped to the mountains. They established hideouts in the densely forested interior, particularly in the Blue Mountains where they provided refuge for later runaway African slaves. Because their numbers were reduced, mostly by European diseases, and there were therefore few replacements to boost their numbers, they were gradually absorbed by the more numerous African resisters who became known as the maroons. It is no doubt as a result of this resistance that a few of their *zemis* or deities and other artefacts have survived in caves in the mountains. Within the past 200 years two of these caves have been located. One is in the Carpenter's Mountain in Manchester where the first two *zemis* were found, and the other is near Aboukir in the Dry Harbour Mountains in St Ann, where three others were found.

Opposite, Stone implements; *below left*, Metate or grinding stone with head of a John Crow; *and below*, a bowl

The Tainos' foodstuffs and fruits included delicacies such as the exotic pineapple and cocoa. Naseberries, star apples, guavas, sweet and sour sops found growing in most West Indian gardens today were first enjoyed by these early peoples. Maize cultivation was established on the American mainland and brought to the islands by the first inhabitants. The bammie or cassava bread, regarded as a delicacy by most Jamaicans, is prepared in almost the same fashion as it was more than 600 years ago. Tobacco, now shunned by many because of its addictive and carcinogenic properties, was one of the most popular products that the Europeans introduced to the rest of the world.

Taino communities were loosely grouped and democratically organised, each with its own chief who in turn owed allegiance to a paramount or regional chief. They lived together communally, sometimes several families to a hut. Men and women shared administrative and domestic activities equally, but danced and played games separately.

Taino philosophies of creation and of eternal life are similar to those held by most societies. They believed in a superior being, a creator of the universe, just as most other human beings do. This life-giving force they called the Ancient One or Yucahu, just as modern native Americans refer to the Great Spirit Chief and Christians speak of God, the creator of heaven and earth. They also engaged in a form of ancestor worship, as many people in Asia and Africa do.

They deified a number of lesser gods (*zemis*) which were expected to watch over their daily lives and protect them from harm. They painted their impressions of the *zemis* on the walls of caves or carved them out of wood, stone or bone. Some they wore as ornaments and others they kept in special niches in their huts and caves. Yucahu, the life-giving force, represented sea and cassava because both are constant elements and never-failing sources of food and sustenance.

The Tainos believed in immortality and in life after death. When an individual died, the spirit journeyed north to purgatory, to a land of ice-and snow-covered mountains, then south again until it reached the happy hunting ground, *Coaybay*. The evil spirit was forever damned and sent to purgatory. *Maquetauri Guayaba*, whose image sometimes formed the handles of utensils, was Lord of the Underworld.

The Tainos lived from day-to-day in a world that knew no change. They feared only the man-hunting Caribs and the fierce god Huracan who sometimes brought storms in summer, who whipped up the sea and drove mountains of water against the land, who tore branches from giant trees. When old men and women died, younger men and women took their places and continued in the way of their fathers before them.

Sometimes resting under giant trees or in the shade of their houses, the native people sang songs accompanied by musical instruments; one was stringed and was shaped like a gourd, another was hollowed out of wood like a trumpet. They smoked tobacco and other addictive plants, and told tales of the first people to come out of two caves on the island of Hispaniola, men out of one, women out of the other; and of their forefathers who had left their homeland in the region of the Orinoco River and made their way to these new lands. They told of the Ancient One who

Taino house

Taino in a hammock

lived in the heights; of the Sun Spirit Arawidi who sometimes fished in the rivers of Guyana; of the giant coomaka tree, so tall its branches touched the sky, and of the happy hunting ground where their spirits went after death.

Their favourite game, *bato* or *batey*, played on a rectangular or open court, required a ball that was bounced by a wooden girdle worn round the body and was not to be touched by the hand. Sometimes a community organised players either among themselves or against visiting teams. On occasion the game was used to decide the spoils of war, as in 1504 when Diego Méndez, one of Columbus' crew members, was captured in the eastern end of the island while on his way to Cuba to seek help for his marooned comrades. Fortunately for him he escaped before the game ended.

The foundations of a house unearthed at White Marl near Spanish Town give us first-hand knowledge of what Taino houses were like. This one was 14 feet in diameter, with nine posts planted in the ground in a circle and one in the centre to support the roof. The top and sides would have been covered with leaves to protect the occupants from the elements. This type of building is still used today by Tainos in the Venezuelan forests.

On their *conucos* (a raised mound approximately 3 feet high and 9 feet in circumference), the Tainos planted food crops including cassava, sweet potato, maize and, pepper. When the sun parched the land and fruits were scarce, the conucos saved them from starvation.

With the passing of time, Taino settlements in Jamaica spread along the north coast from Priestman's River in the East, through Maima (overlooking present-day St Ann's Bay) and onwards to Montego Bay and Negril. They settled along the south coast at Savanna-la-Mar, Bluefields (Oristán), Portland Bight (Cow Bay), on the Clarendon Plains along the course of the Rio Minho, at Morant Bay and further on to Morant Point. They lived in small communities on Jacks Hill, on Long Mountain and on Red Hills, where at day's end they relaxed in the cooling breezes and looked out across their fishing grounds on to the plains below and to the blue Caribbean Sea beyond. They settled on dry ground amidst the swampy Liguanea Plains, at White Marl just above the flood plains of the Rio Cobre River near modern Spanish Town, inland at Ewarton along the course of the Rio Cobre River, over the mountains and close by the shores of the Moneague Lake. So far more than 400 Taino villages, caves and burial sites have been located. The island had no precious metals that they could extract or they would have used them for ornamentation as their neighbours did in some of the other islands. As a result only one small piece of gold has been found.

It is estimated that there were 50,000-60,000 Tainos in Jamaica at the time of the arrival of the Spaniards. A village like Maima in the vicinity of Seville, where Columbus first landed in 1494, and where he was later marooned for a year, is estimated to have been settled by about 150 persons.

The two wooden *zemis* found in the Carpenter's Mountain in Manchester in the eighteenth century were taken to the British Museum in London. The three found in the twentieth century in the Dry Harbour Mountains in St Ann are at the National Gallery of Jamaica. The largest and most imposing may have formed the head of a ceremonial staff and once carried a sphere extended above the warrior's head. The figure is dressed in a cloak of plaited leaves, which protected him from the sharply pointed spears of his enemy, cover the head and shoulders as well as the shins. This form of dress was worn by early Africans, in particular the Akan people and may well have been what the eighteenth-century maroon chieftaness, Nanny, used to ward off the English bullets.

The second figure, a small statuette which probably represents *Maquetauri Guayaba*, once formed the handle of a "cleansing" spoon. The third figure, a pelican, carries a flat sphere extended by a rod above its back. On ceremonial occasions snuff was placed on the sphere and worshippers inhaled it through a forked tube. Before participating in this act, worshippers purified themselves by fasting or by inserting the cleansing spoon in their throats to cause vomiting. The snuff, sometimes made from the seeds of the piptadenia tree, created hallucination and in this state worshippers claimed that they communicated with their *zemis*.

Once a year the whole village turned out to pay homage to the chief's *zemis* and to their departed chiefs. The ceremony began with a procession of villagers "wearing their ornaments, carrying baskets of cassava bread, and singing songs about the *zemis*. The chief sat at the entrance to the temple, beating a drum, while the priests entered and dressed the *zemis*". The temple could have been a cave or a hut built for that purpose. After the villagers had purified themselves, the women presented cassava bread which the priests offered to the *zemis*. After that there was merrymaking in which the villagers danced, sang and drank the intoxicating fermented cassava juice. The ceremony ended with prayers offered for the protection and prosperity of the village, after which the priests distributed pieces of cassava bread to the heads of families who kept them throughout the year for protection against accidents. (Rouse: 1992)

One of the Tainos' prophetic songs told how in some far distant time strangers would come amongst them covered with garments and armed with thunders and lightnings of heaven. This may have induced the Tainos on Jamaica to feed Columbus and his more than 100 stranded crew

Zemis found in Dry Harbour Mountains

Pelican

Maquetauri Guayaba
(handle of
cleansing spoon)

Youchahuma
(head of
ceremonial staff)

members for over a year. The legend is not unlike the Aztec legend of white gods coming from the east, which probably led Montezuma to accept Cortés and his soldiers.

CHAPTER 6

Europe: Explorer, coloniser and slave master

In the boisterous decade of the 1490s Europe broke into the Indian Ocean and opened up an Atlantic pathway to India, China, Indonesia and the Pacific Ocean. In the same period Europe also broke into the world of the Americas and opened up Atlantic pathways to these two vast and hitherto unknown continents. These voyages changed the course of human history by propelling mankind into the Age of Europe, in which Europe eventually rose to world dominance.

We prefer the term "Atlantic Age" to the "Age of Europe", because it recognises the geographic and historic unity of the Atlantic Basin which later came to include western Europe, Africa and the Americas. It recognises also the close involvement of the African-American and Euro-American people in every aspect of the political, economic and cultural development of what has become the Atlantic community. This term complements the more recent development of the Pacific Basin, and it is also appropriate to the multiracial, multicultural world community of which all human beings are members.

This larger perspective makes it clear that the African-American contributed significantly to the achievements of the Atlantic Age. The colonial perspective concealed this. As Orlando Patterson and Franz Fanon both emphasised, the historians of the colonising societies narrowed their perspectives because "the settler makes history and is conscious of making it. And because he constantly refers to the history of his mother-country, he clearly indicates that he himself is the extension of that mother-country. Thus the history he writes is not the history of the country which he plunders but the history of his own nation in regard to all that she skims off, all that she violates and starves."

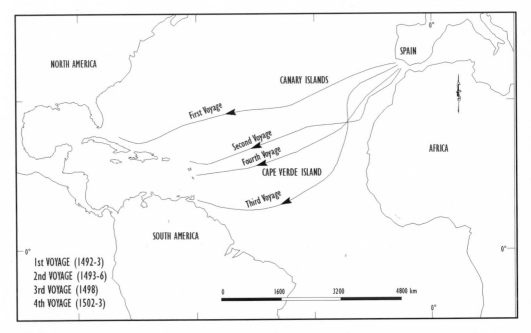

The four voyages of Colombus

NORTH AMERICA

SPAIN

CANARY ISLANDS

First Voyage

Second Voyage

Fourth Voyage

CAPE VERDE ISLAND

AFRICA

Third Voyage

SOUTH AMERICA

1st VOYAGE (1492-3)
2nd VOYAGE (1493-6)
3rd VOYAGE (1498)
4th VOYAGE (1502-3)

0   1600   3200   4800 km

The concept of the Atlantic Age reveals the pioneering role of Portugal in "the cosmic upheaval generated by the geographical expansion of Europe at the end of the fifteenth century. Portugal was the detonator of an explosion which reverberated around the world. This was her finest hour." (Braudel: 1982).

Instead of focusing our attention at this stage on Columbus and Spain, we begin earlier in the fifteenth century with the Portuguese and their development of a trading monopoly along the western coast of Africa. Portugal kept her eyes fixed on the glittering prize of the spice trade, which awaited the nation whose sea captains found an alternative route to Ceylon, India and other spice-producing lands. However, we soon perceive that the driving forces generated by a demand for gold, labour and, in growing measure, for sugar were determining Portugal's policy and leading it to seek the support of bankers and investors.

That Portugal's interest in the West African trade and the development of the offshore islands indicated a long-term commitment is shown by the establishment, under the leadership of Prince Henry the Navigator, of a centre for the study of oceanic navigation at Cape Sagres, on the Portuguese coast near Lisbon, where the wind systems and currents of the eastern Atlantic were studied.

The presence of Portuguese traders along the African west coast attracted the attention of some African traders in gold dust, but the West African gold producers of the great bend of the Niger river concentrated on the trans-Saharan trade. Regularly Arab caravans brought luxury goods, salt, which was a dietary necessity, and firearms and returned to the Mediterranean ports with gold. The power and splendour of the empires of the western Sudan – Ghana, Mali and Songhai – were achieved by the gold trade, for this region supplied Europe with about one-quarter of its requirement. The profits from the trans-Saharah trade, which was facilitated by the introduction of the camel from Arabia into North Africa 1000 BC, enabled these three empires to dominate the political, economic and cultural development of West Africa.

The capture by the Portuguese of the important gold-trading city of Ceuta in Morocco in 1415 was their first major step towards exploring the West African coast to find out if there was any point of entry into the Indian Ocean. Portugal had only recently regained its territory from the Moors. It was a small country with a population of about 70,000 persons, impoverished but bred to battling Atlantic rollers with sturdy fishing-boats. It recognised that it was outside the Mediterranean world, since to travel from Lisbon to Venice took some 40 days. On the other hand, Portugal held a few Atlantic islands, Madeira and the Azores, that had potential as sugar-producers.

Portugal's only prospect of wealth lay in finding a sea route down the African coast to the spice-producing countries of Asia and in developing a trade in gold with West Africa and in sugar with its own plantations in Madeira and the Canary Islands.

The bankers and traders of Genoa were interested. A city of between 60,000 and 80,000 people, it depended entirely on its inhabitants' entrepreneurial skills. They lived by their wits. Genoa "manufactured goods for other people; sent out her shipping, for other people; invested, but in other places. Even in the eighteenth century, only half of Genoese capital remained in the city. The rest, for want of local investment openings, went abroad. The constraints of geography sent it on foreign ventures". (Braudel: 1982) The Genoese are of special interest to us because they were among the first of the European bankers and traders to invest in commodities and in ventures that prepared the way for the Atlantic Age. They had organised Sicilian sugar production and there were Genoese settlements in North Africa, Seville, Lisbon, Bruges and Antwerp. Genoese investors saw that there were profits to be made in Portugal, and soon they were handling some of Lisbon's wholesale and retail trade, although the latter was generally kept in the hands of Portuguese citizens.

Between 1433 and 1482 the Portuguese occupied Madeira (1433), rediscovered the Azores (1430) and discovered the Cape Verde Islands (1455), Fernando Po and São Tome off the coast of Africa (1471). They also built up a profitable trading area on the African coast that supplied ivory, a pepper substitute called malaguetta, gold dust and slaves, the number of which rose from about 1,000 in the 1450s to 3,000 annually in the 1480s. By signing a treaty with Spain in 1479 and building a fort at São Jorge da Mina on the Guinea coast in 1481, Portugal established its monopoly of trade with the western coast of Africa.

The Genoese played a substantial part in this expansion of Portuguese power and of its monopoly of the West African trade. So did the Florentines, but the Genoese were Portugal's chief partners. They promoted the spread of the sugar plantation from the eastern Mediterranean to Sicily, southern Spain (whence sugar moved to Hispaniola), Morocco, the Portuguese Algarve, Madeira and onto the Cape Verde Islands.

Through these efforts Portugal established a profitable, coherent economic zone that included bases for trade along the African coast. At the same time it continued its search for control of the spice trade. Success came when Bartholomew Diaz rounded the Cape of Good Hope in 1488. Ten years later, in 1498, Vasco da Gama returned to Lisbon with the news that Portugal had won the race for the spice trade.

The impact on Alexandria and Venice was disastrous. Braudel reports that in 1504, when the Venetian galleys arrived at Alexandria in Egypt, they found not a single sack of pepper waiting for them.

But Portugal lost an even richer prize. In 1484 the Genoese-born Christopher Columbus put his proposal for a westerly route to the Indies to the King of Portugal and his advisers. Understandably, they rejected the proposal for by then they were sure that the Atlantic led into the Indian ocean and control of the spice trade was within their grasp. What more could Columbus offer than, possibly, a shorter sea route and therefore a less expensive one?

Columbus turned to Spain and in 1492, the Spanish sovereigns, having completed the reconquest of Spain, commissioned him to discover a western pathway to Cathay and the Indies.

Before daybreak on the morning of Friday, 2 August 1492, Columbus ordered his fleet of three ships to weigh anchor and leave the sheltered waters of the Rio Tinto for the Atlantic. Soon the wind filled their sails and the ships came to life with creaking timbers and billowing sails: the *Santa María* of 100 tons, the low, swift sailing *Pinta*, a caravel, and the midget *Niña*. There were 90 men aboard the fleet, most of them from the villages and townships around Cadiz. Columbus made first for the Canary Islands, took water and other supplies aboard and then set out on a westerly course, making for the kingdom of the Great Khan in Asia, which by his reckoning was about 3,000 miles away. By 1 October he had covered that distance but there was no sign of land. The crew grew mutinous for they noted that the winds blew constantly in a westerly direction, always away from home. On 7 October, they saw flocks of birds and in the water the branch of a tree, still green and with berries on it.

Suddenly, at 2 o'clock on the morning of the 12 October, a sailor, Rodrigo, who was on watch on the *Pinta* shouted, "Tierra, Tierra." Ahead appeared something gleaming white. On the orders of Columbus they lay offshore, waiting for daylight. After 31 days at sea, they had arrived at a small island in the Bahamas which was inhabited by Tainos, and which bore the name of Guanahani. Columbus named it San Salvador (Holy Saviour). He was sure that he had come to an island off the coast of Japan. He was sure that gold lay ahead, and pepper, cloves, cinnamon, nutmeg, mace, aloes, ginger, the riches of the world and great glory.

Constructed replicas of the *Niña, Pinta* and *Santa María*

Japan and China were some 10,000 miles away across the Pacific, but to the day of his death in 1506 Columbus believed that he had discovered a sea route to Cathay. He never realised that he had come to the Americas, the western coastlands of the Atlantic Basin, that he had put the old world of the Americas in permanent contact with the older world of Europe and had prepared the way for a shift of power from the Mediterranean to the Atlantic. These things became known when other explorers began to reveal the magnitude of an achievement that he was never able to comprehend.

With Columbus as pathfinder and explorer, Europe entered the Americas. When he landed on Guanahani later that morning, he was greeted by a group of friendly Indians. He wrote in his journal:

> All I saw were youths, none of them more than thirty years of age. They were very well made, with very handsome bodies and very good countenances – they are of the colour of the Canareans, neither black nor white . . . they neither carry nor know anything of arms, for I showed them swords, and they grasped them by the blade and cut themselves through ignorance. They have no iron.

Columbus also noted that they ought to be good servants, and of good skill, for they repeated very quickly all that was said to them.

On that small, sandy island, surrounded by uncomprehending friendly indigenous Americans who had discovered and settled it centuries earlier, Columbus affirmed Europe's mission of conquest, dispossession and enslavement. He lost no time in unfurling the flag of Spain. To the bewildered Tainos he was saying, "This island is no longer yours. Now it belongs to Spain." He followed this up by claiming for Spain, Cuba, Hispaniola and in 1494, Jamaica.

The Tainos, stone-age people, marvelled at the swords the Europeans carried. The shedding of blood when they grasped the blade signified what was to happen. The entry in his journal, "They ought to be good servants, and of good skill," foretold the enslavement of the Taino people. He hoped that a trade in Indian slaves would prove as profitable as the market in African slaves that the Portuguese had already established in Lisbon.

Territory, gold, spices, slaves, the demand for which had driven the Portuguese to storm Ceuta and begin their long exploration of the African coast, had driven Columbus to cross the Atlantic. Market forces had him in their grip. A proud, fiercely ambitious man, he dreamed of wealth and a coat-of-arms, as clauses in his proposal to the Spanish rulers reveal. He proposed:

> Firstly, that your Highness . . . appoint from this date the said Don Cristóbal Colon to be your Admiral in all those islands and mainlands which by his activity and industry shall he discover . . . That of all and every kind of merchandise, whether pearls, precious stones, gold, silver, spices and other objects of merchandise . . . Your Highnesses grant . . . to the said Don Cristóbal, the tenth part of the whole, after deducting all the expenses.
>
> That in all the vessels which may be equipped . . . the said Don Cristóbal Colon may . . . contribute and pay the eighth part of all that may be spent in the equipment, and that likewise he may have and take the eighth part of the profits that may result. (Columbus)

From Guanahani Columbus set out to explore the north cost of Cuba, for although he had completed his voyage, the search for gold had only just begun. Always the question came, "Have you gold?" Columbus found none along the north coast of Cuba. Not until he landed on the northern coast of Hispaniola did he see ornaments made of the precious metal. He left some of his crew behind in a small fortified settlement at La Navidad, with instructions to collect gold, and hurried back to Spain with exhibits and samples of gold and Indians.

In September 1493 Columbus, laden with honours, returned to Hispaniola. He had been made Admiral of the Ocean Sea, and was in command of an armada of 17 vessels. He and his successors had been ennobled and potentially were very wealthy.

This voyage was for settlement. Aboard were 1,400 men, including armed footmen and horsemen, smiths, carpenters, "all kinds of pulse or grain and corn, as well for food as to sow; besides vines, plants and seeds . . . and sundry kinds of artillery and iron tools . . . as bows, arrows, crossbows, broadswords, pikes, hammers, nails, saws, axes". (Martyr)

At Gomera in the Canaries the fleet had taken aboard,

> goats and ewes and eight sows . . . From these eight sows have multiplied all the pigs which to this day have been and are in the Indies, which have been and are numbered and this was the seed from which all that there is here of things of Castile has [sic] sprung, whether pigs and seeds of orange, limes and melons and all kinds of vegetables. Horses, sheep, cattle, vines, wheat barley, rye, citrus; and from Hispaniola many of them spread and grew. (Las Casas: 1875)

This *armada* was followed in 1502 by an even larger one of 30 ships and 2,500 people under the command of Nicolas de Ovando. They were sent to reinforce the 300 or so surviving from the earlier settlement. There were in the fleet a few African slaves who accompanied their masters from Spain. Soon after arriving, one of the Africans escaped to the Indians in the mountainous interior, and so became the first African maroon in the Americas.

In this early period of the Spanish settlement of Hispaniola, one of the more enterprising and better-off settlers, Gonzalo de Velosa, started Hispaniola's sugar industry:

> Now sugar is one of the richest crops to be found in any province or Kingdom of this world and on this island there is so much and it is so good although it was so recently introduced and has been followed for such a short time . . . Every one was blind until Bachelor Gonzalo de Velosa, at his own cost and investing everything he had and with great personal effort, brought workmen expert in sugar to this island, and built a horse-powered mill and first made sugar in this island; he alone deserves thanks as the principal inventor of this rich industry. (Oviedo)

The *armadas* under Columbus and Ovando marked the beginning of a global redistribution of races, cultures, languages, technology, animals and plants which continues to this day. The sugar cane, citrus, and people – Europeans, Africans, East Indians, Jews, Lebanese and Syrians – are constant reminders that West Indians are imported people in a largely imported environment. The roots of the West Indian community are to be found across the Atlantic, in the Old World. There also most of the useful plants and all the domestic animals had their origin. Many of the social institutions, religious beliefs, languages, various skills and technologies travelled with Old World people to the Caribbean and to mainland America. In consequence, Africa, Asia and Europe give historical continuity to the story of the various racial and cultural groups that make up the West Indian community.

The movement we have described should be seen as a redistribution, or transplanting, and not as a complete severance. The story of the African-Jamaican people begins in West Africa, whereas the recorded history of the West Indian community begins with an abrupt event, the arrival of Columbus in the Caribbean.

Unseen, in silence, mankind's constant and feared companions also crossed the Atlantic. Smallpox, typhoid, influenza and measles decimated the New World populations and in exchange syphilis, endemic among the Tainos, journeyed to Spain and raged with extraordinary virulence among Spanish armies fighting in North Italy.

This redistribution began at the dictates of money and of imperial ambitions, which caused the land-enclosed Mediterranean to give way to the Atlantic and Venice, Genoa and Florence to give way to Lisbon, Antwerp, Amsterdam, London, Paris, all financial and banking centres that had direct contact with the Americas.

We turn from these global movements to Hispaniola, where enslavement and savagery wiped out the Tainos in less than a century. Columbus, Nicolas de Ovando and Juan de Esquivel led the way.

Columbus, a great explorer and sea-commander, knew that he had enemies among the colonists. Many regarded him as a foreigner, the son of a Genoese artisan, tricked out with an empty title and a new coat of arms. Socially, in Spain's rigid hierarchy, he was an upstart. Only by discovering a source of gold and other precious metals could he consolidate his standing with the Spanish sovereigns. Following their instructions, he set out from Hispaniola to explore the south coast of Cuba and, from there, went on to Yamaye (Jamaica) where, according to the Tainos, gold was plentiful. His greedy, questing eyes found no evidence of gold in Jamaica. Greatly disappointed, Columbus returned to Hispaniola empty-handed, only to find that the dissatisfied and angry colonists were sending a stream of complaints to Spain.

Frustrated and insecure, Columbus decided to pacify the colonists by supplying them with Taino slaves and to prove that Hispaniola was a source of wealth by sending Tainos to Spain for sale as slaves. He sent a detachment of armed colonists into the countryside to hunt down the Tainos with horses and fierce dogs. The colonists brought in some 1,500 captives. The Torres fleet of three caravels returned to Spain that autumn with 500 of these captives who were to be put up for sale. About 600 were claimed by the colonists. An eyewitness, Michele de Cuneo, reported that the remaining 400, "Many of them with infants at the breast, in order better to escape us, since they were afraid we would turn to catch them again, left their infants anywhere on the ground and started to flee like desperate people, and some fled our settlement of Isabella for seven or eight days beyond the mountains and across huge rivers."

Two hundred of the Indians died before the Torres fleet reached Spain. Their bodies were thrown into the sea. Half of the survivors were sick when they disembarked in Cadiz. Cuneo's comment was "they are not working people, and they very much fear cold, nor have they long life". Queen Isabella ordered that the pitiful remnant should be sent back to their homes. The hope Columbus had cherished of a profitable trade in Taino slaves came to nothing.

Under Ovando and his successors Hispaniola became the stage on which the first tragic act in the destruction of many millions of the indigenous American people was played out. Even at this distance in time the story is one of horror and heartbreak. In a long and shameful catalogue of savagery, one of the most horrifying was the invitation to 80 Taino *caciques* to assemble for a meeting in a building, where Ovando's soldiers tied them to the wooden posts supporting the roof. The building was then set on fire and they were burnt to death. Anacaona, wife of the chief *cacique,* Caonabo, was then taken to Santo Domingo and hanged for plotting against the Spaniards. Architect of the massacre was Juan de Esquivel who later became the first Spanish governor of Jamaica.

Many of the Tainos were soon wiped out, some by imported diseases, others by forced labour in the mines and yet others by starvation, for they had little time to devote to tilling their food plots. "I sometimes came upon dead bodies on my way," wrote Las Casas, "and upon others who were gasping and moaning in their death agony, repeating hungry, hungry." It is thought that there were 300,000 Tainos in Hispaniola when the Spaniards first arrived in 1492. There were only 60,000 in 1508. By 1512 the number was down to 20,000. Oviedo, the Spanish historian, doubted if there were 500 left in 1548. In 1586, when Francis Drake sacked the city of Santo Domingo, he reported that there were no Indians left in the island.

While the Tainos of the islands were being enslaved and destroyed, the Europeans subjected the American Indians of the mainland to forced labour and enslavement. In Braudel's words, "America, lacking population, could only become something if man was shackled to the task: serfdom and slavery, those ancient forms of bondage, appeared once more . . . The everlasting problem in this boundless landscape was consequently a shortage of labour." (Braudel: 1982)

In the search for labour, Europe as conqueror ravaged the indigenous people. Diseases brought in from Europe and Africa, added their destructive force to that of the conqueror and coloniser. In many regions

> the indigenous population collapsed on this first impact of the white conquests, . . . Central Mexico, which once had some 25 million inhabitants, was reduced, it is estimated, to a residual population of

one million. The same abysmal demographic collapse occurred in the island of Hispaniola, in the Yucatan, in Central America and later in Colombia . . . The word genocide is not too strong to describe what happened to the American Indians or the black people of Africa, but it is worth noting that white men did not survive entirely unscathed and were sometimes lucky to escape at all. (Braudel: 1982)

Eric Williams, in his seminal work *Capitalism and Slavery* showed how one form of enslavement followed another. White enslavement followed on Indian enslavement, followed by the system of English and French bond servants, who were virtually slaves, but for a limited period of five or seven years.

Their lot barely differed from that of the Africans who were now beginning to arrive. In England and in France every trick was tried to meet the demand for bond servants. Misleading advertisements were coupled with violence. From Western England after Monmouth's rebellion, hundreds of rebels were transported to Barbados. In France, press gangs would swoop down on certain districts of Paris. Men, women and children were kidnapped into emigration in Bristol, or heavy criminal sentences were passed to increase the number of volunteers.

Wherever the European colonisers went they pressed ahead with great cruelty in their relentless search for labour. How was it that they were so insensitive to human suffering and killed other human beings so easily?

In Spain centuries of fighting against the Moors, with raids in which no quarter was given, and centuries of grinding poverty had produced a tough, ruthless people, as events in Hispaniola showed. But violence prevailed in many other parts of Europe as well as in Spain. In his work *Of Arms and Men*, O'Connell points out:

ultimately it was the inhumanity which Europeans applied to themselves which caused the period from 1562 to 1648 in Western European history to be such a horrific one. Just why it is that predation and technology were turned inward with such wilful malevolence is hard to pin down . . .pressures created by fundamental economic, cultural and spiritual change played a significant role.

In his historical analysis of weapons in Western culture, O'Connell suggests a definite relationship between "the drive for transnational dominion, the promiscuous use of weaponry and very brutal and costly wars". He paints a nightmare picture of northern Europe, in which a massive increase of firepower and the pressure upon local food supplies "turned the armies of the day into rapacious, ill-disciplined swarms . . . For eighty years these armed bands were destined to stagger about the Netherlands, France and Germany destroying all before them . . . a contemporary might well have wondered if northern Europe had not taken up killing largely for its own sake".

Using the military technology at their command, the *conquistadores*, Hernando Cortés, Francisco Pizarro and those who followed in their footsteps quickly overwhelmed the stone-age people who opposed them with spears tipped with shell, bone or, as in Mexico, with obsidian. Horses and hunting dogs, animals they had never known, terrified the Indians. But more than anything else, "it was the gun which paralysed them. There were reports of Aztec warriors fainting at the sound of cannon . . . firearms served to epitomise the conquistadores military advantage, imparting to it a magical quality which made resistance so much more manifestly hopeless." (O'Connell: 1989)

Within a few years after Cortés conquered Mexico and Pizarro subdued the Incas, American silver, gold and precious metals began to flow from Panama and Vera Cruz, by way of Havana, to Cadiz, to supplement the royal income by about one-quarter to one-third of the amount squeezed out of the heavily burdened 6 million inhabitants of Castile. Many of these were impoverished peasants.

> Even the development of agriculture was retarded by the privileges of the Mesta, the famous guild of sheep owners whose stock were permitted to graze widely over the Kingdom, with Spain's population growing in the first half of the sixteenth century . . . The flood of precious metals from the Indies, it was said, were to Spain as water on a roof – it poured on and then was drained away . . . While the coloniser ravaged the Americas, Spain's rulers used the loot they plundered to ravage large parts of Europe in 140 years of warfare, to the point where Spain herself, exhausted and drained of energy, fell into a decline and became but a shadow of her former self. (Kennedy: 1987)

The voyages of exploration and the conquest we have described mark the beginning of Western Europe's rise to world dominance, but there were few signs of this ascendancy in the Europe of the early 16th century. In the decade of the 1520s when Cortés was conquering Mexico, Europe was an embattled continent, internally a confusion of warring principalities and powers, with Ottoman galleons raiding Italian ports and with the armies of the Ottoman Turks thrusting north from Constantinople, which they had captured in 1453, towards Budapest and Vienna.

The European of that period thought of China under the Ming dynasty, which emerged in 1368 and held power for four centuries, as being the world's leading centre of civilisation. In that period, "The most striking feature of Chinese civilization must be its technological precocity." Printing with moveable type had appeared some two centuries earlier. "There were great libraries, paper money was in circulation, the flow of commerce had increased, markets had multiplied and a large iron industry had been established which produced about 125,000 tons a year, more than the British iron output in the early stages of the Industrial Revolution seven centuries later." Gunpowder and cannon were in use and had helped the Chinese to defeat their Mongol rulers in the fourteenth century.

Ming China was also active overseas. Under this dynasty the Chinese greatly extended overseas exploration, invented the magnetic compass, traded with the Indies and the Pacific islands, developed a prosperous coastal trade, maintained an army of one million men and in 1420 – a navy of 1,350 combat vessels,

> including 400 large floating fortresses and 250 ships for long-range cruising. In addition there were many privately managed vessels that traded with Korea, South-East Asia, Japan and even as far as East Africa. Among the most famous voyages in history are the seven long-distance voyages made by Admiral Cheng Ho between 1405 and 1433, that involved hundreds of ships and tens of thousands of men.
>
> It must be noted, however, that the Chinese apparently never plundered nor murdered – unlike the Portuguese, Dutch and other European invaders of the Indian Ocean. According to the Confucian code, warfare itself was a deplorable activity and armed forces were made necessary only by the fear of barbarian attacks or internal revolts. (Kennedy: 1987)

Gradually, under the Ming dynasty, burdened and paralysed by a conservative bureaucracy, China became a country turned in upon itself. But in the fourteenth and fifteenth centuries, through a combination of the Confucian code of ethics and significant technological advances, this non-white nation set an example of humane civilised behaviour that is in sharp contrast with the record of Europe as coloniser and also at home, a record that compelled an eyewitness, Hugo Grotius, the Dutch legal philosopher, to declare: "I saw prevailing throughout Europe a licence in making war of which even barbarous nations would have been ashamed."

CHAPTER 7

Spanish Jamaica

On his second voyage to the Americas Columbus charted a more southerly route, and ended up in the Eastern Caribbean, where he spent several weeks exploring the islands before reaching Hispaniola in September 1493. He found La Navidad, the fort he had built to accommodate 39 men left behind from the shipwrecked *Santa Maria*, in ruins, and all its inhabitants dead. It turned out that some of the men had been killed by the natives in retaliation for stealing and violating their women; others had died at the hands of their own comrades and the remainder had succumbed to various illnesses.

The overriding ambition of these early explorers was to acquire great personal fortunes at any cost, and having fulfilled their dream, to return home to Europe to live out their days in comfort. But the game of life is not always played out as men would wish. The majority of those who followed Columbus' dream over the next 200 years, found early graves in the Americas and comparatively few ever saw their native land again.

With La Navidad destroyed, Columbus was forced to locate another site and it took him several months to do this and to lay out the town. It was not until the following April, 1494, when the town of Isabella was beginning to take shape that Columbus resumed his charting of the surrounding seas. On the afternoon of 5 May, 1494, after 11 days at sea, his three vessels, the *Pinta*, the *San Juan* and the *Cardera* came in sight of towering blue-green mountains. It was the island of *Yamaye* (Jamaica), which he had first learned about in January 1493.

Taino eyes followed the strange vessels as they slowly made their way in a westerly direction along the island's north coast, and when towards evening they turned towards shore, at a place which Columbus later named Santa Gloria, native warriors leapt into action to protect their territory. But they were powerless to alter fate. The prophecy that one day strangers would come amongst them covered with garments and armed with thunders and lightnings of heaven was about to be fulfilled.

The tragic encounter of those Taino warriors at Santa Gloria, near St Ann's Bay, and Rio Bueno (misnamed Puerto Bueno), as they faced gunpowder and steel blades for the first time, is well-documented and need not detain us here. However, it should be remembered that next morning, these trusting and forgiving Tainos fed the ungracious foreigners who had so cruelly wounded and abused them the evening before. Later many took their own lives rather than endure abuse and enslavement at the hands of the European invaders.

So little is recorded about the Jamaican Tainos that we are grateful to Andres Bernaldez for the brief account of the people Columbus met in August 1494, when he skirted the coastline for a second time. Bernaldez was palace curate at Seville in Spain and travelled with Columbus on his second voyage of discovery. He probably heard the story of that visit from the admiral himself.

The Tainos whom Columbus met in their canoes at Cow Bay on the south coast, demonstrated by their behaviour that they belonged to an ordered society. Bernaldez describes the *cacique's* entourage which included his wife, daughter, sons, brothers, attendants, guards and musicians. He describes the head coverings of the men, some made of feathers, some fashioned like a helmet; the facial and body paintings of the group, ornaments of beads and beaten metal worn on their foreheads, ears, necks, waists, arms and feet as well as the elaborate ceremonial dress of some of the attendants. He makes mention of musical instruments being played at the time – two wooden trumpets "well worked with patterns of birds and other objects" fashioned from very dark and delicate wood, and also "a kind of musical instrument which they plucked". As was their practice, the visitors traded worthless curios and trinkets and even broken pieces of glass for Taino ornaments before sailing away.

Nine years passed before Columbus reappeared on Jamaican shores. On this occasion his two badly leaking vessels, with one anchor between them, barely limped to shore at the place he had named Santa Gloria. The natives of Maima and the surrounding villages found no joy at sight of them, and soon became disgruntled when they were called upon to provide regular supplies of food for an additional 140 individuals. Stone-age farming practices could not meet such demands indefinitely. Iron fish hooks traded by the newcomers may have helped somewhat, but the Tainos seemed unable to satisfy the enormous appetites of the Europeans.

While the shipwrecked Spaniards waited to be rescued, they roamed the countryside searching for gold and trading their worthless trinkets and curios for precious food and fish. One chief, called Ameryo, at the village

Courtesy of Tom Willcockson

**Spanish Place- Names
in Jamaica**
(Present -day names in brackets)

of Ameryo near Morant Point, unaware of the value of his goods, gave one of Columbus' captains, Diego Méndez, a laboriously hand-carved canoe in exchange for a cheap brass basin and a used shirt and coat.

When the Tainos began to show signs of disenchantment Columbus had to find ways of keeping them under control. From books in his possession, he knew that an eclipse of the moon was about to take place. On the appointed day, he gathered some chiefs on the decks of his rotting vessels and then told them that the moon would rise "inflamed and angry" because of their intransigence. At the height of the eclipse he told the terrified natives that if they repented he would ask his god to call off the punishment, and they would see the sign begin to disappear slowly from the heavens. After that terrifying experience, the Tainos reluctantly agreed to continue supplying the Spaniards with food.

Weeks passed and there was no sign of rescue so he decided to send captain Diego Méndez and a small company of men to seek help in Hispaniola, some 170 kilometers to the north. The first attempt failed because of heavy seas. On the second try they succeeded but their shipmates in Jamaica had no way of knowing this. Eight months later there was still no word from them, and concern heightened among the stranded men. It had taken Méndez' crew three days, battling perilous seas and blazing sun, to make the crossing. They had run out of food and drink and one Taino had died from hunger and exhaustion. They eventually reached their destination but experienced great difficulty in trying to contact the governor, Ovando, who had no liking for Columbus. After many weeks they made contact with him but he refused to help.

Spanish Jamaica   65

Weeks turned into months and the men in Jamaica waited in vain for word from Hispaniola. In his despair, Columbus recorded his own worries in the following letter to the Spanish Crown (dated 1503):

> It is visible enough how all methods are made use of to cut the thread which is breaking, for I am in my old age, and loaded with unsupportable pains of the gout and am now languishing and expiring with that and other infirmities among savages, where I have neither medicines for the body, priests nor sacraments for the soul. My men mutinying, my brother, my son, and those that are faithful, sick, starving, and dying. The Indians have abandoned us; and the governor of Santo Domingo, Obando, has sent rather to see if I am dead, than to succor us, or carry me alive hence, for his boat neither delivered a letter nor spoke, or would receive any from us, so I conclude your highness' officers intend here my voyage and life shall end. (Williams: 1963)

Governor Ovando had refused to rescue the shipwrecked men or to offer them supplies and in the end Méndez had to hire a boat and arrange the rescue himself.

The men on the island of Jamaica had by this time lost all hope, and on 2 January, 1504, some of them, led by Captain Francisco Porras and his brother Diego, mutinied. Their attempt to sail for Hispaniola failed because of rough seas. They turned back and in their frustration they wandered across the island wreaking havoc on the native people, before setting up their rebel camp in the village of Maima. There they were eventually defeated by men loyal to Columbus.

During the empty months of waiting, the Spaniards, guided by the native people, are believed to have crossed the densely wooded mountains from the north to the southern plains. The village of Porus, situated where the central mountain range meets the Clarendon plains, is supposed to have been named after the Porras brothers, and the nearby Don Figueroa mountain range, takes its name from Columbus' son. It is almost certain that they were in search of minerals, for it is unlikely that such hardy men would have expended so much energy cutting through dense jungle in search of cassava, which was easily available from villages all along the north shore.

On 28 June, 1504, one year and four days after they had been marooned on Jamaica, Diego Méndez's rescue ship arrived, and on the following day Colombus and the surviving crew of just over 100 men left for Hispaniola. Méndez's dying wish was to have a ship inscribed upon his tombstone and underneath, the word "canoa".

Columbus owned the island of Jamaica on which he was marooned. It was one of the rewards he had received from the Spanish Crown in 1494, but Ferdinand and Isabella quickly regretted this as a rash decision, and not long after took back control of the island. In 1508, two years after Columbus' death, they returned it to his heir, the viceroy, Diego. Shortly after that the Crown once again exerted control. On this occasion it granted permission to two generals, Alonzo de Ojeda and Diego de Nicuesa, to use the island as a provision base for their armies in Central America. Fearing that he was once more about to lose his patrimony, Diego Columbus quickly appointed as governor, Juan de Esquivel, the organiser of the massacre of Anacaona and the other natives at Higuey, and dispatched him with 60 men to "subdue and colonise" the island. Their arrival on 9 December, 1509, sounded the death knell for the Tainos.

The settlers hunted the native people mercilessly, enslaved those they caught and worked them to death on farms and in unproductive mines. Chiefs who resisted were either killed or sold to the other islands to work in mines and to pan for gold in the rivers. Soon the leaderless people gave up the resistance.

Other settlers who came were equally cruel as Bartolomew de Las Casas, who was then living in Hispaniola, reported. According to him the settlers who proceeded to San Juan and to Jamaica had the same aim as that which had governed their presence in Hispaniola, "to add more notorieties and excessively great cruelties, killing, burning, scorching and throwing people to wild dogs and afterwards oppressing and harassing them in the mines and other areas of economic activities". (*History of the Indies.* Book III)

Las Casas' father was a former merchant of Seville who had travelled on the second voyage and took back a Taino slave for his son, Bartholomew. The elder Las Casas returned to Hispaniola and in 1502 Bartholomew joined him there. Together with one Pablo de la Renteria, Bartholomew de Las Casas acquired several large estates (allotments) which they operated under the *encomienda* system. This system allowed colonists to employ native families on their ranches provided they were converted to Roman Catholicism and were treated humanely. The natives were deemed to be the property of the Spanish Crown, and were not to be worked more than necessary; but this was at the discretion of the Spanish settlers. The settlers were not allowed to exchange, sell, gamble or give away the possessions of the natives except for food and alms, without the prior approval of the priests or the island administrator. Nor were the colonists allowed to take away their lands. When a native family died out, the land was to pass over to the Crown. An Indian Sacristan was to be appointed if possible, "to serve in the church and teach the children to read and write until the age of nine, especially the children of the caciques and other important people of the village, and to speak Spanish". It was probably on these instructions that the Dominican friar, Fr Duele opened a school at New Seville. He had travelled on the second voyage, and had come to Jamaica with the first colonists in 1509. The school was short-lived for the friar died in 1511, and nothing more was heard of it.

In that same year Las Casas' conscience was jolted when Dominican friars began attacking the immorality of slavery under the *encomienda* system. The friars questioned the right of one set of individuals to enslave others less fortunate. They further asked if the Indians were not human beings, whether or not they had rational souls, and if the colonists were not bound to love them as they loved themselves. They warned Spanish Christians holding Indian labour under this system that they were in danger of mortal sin.

In 1514, after three years of soul-searching, Las Casas entered the priesthood. His change of heart is supposed to have occurred while he was reading a passage in Ecclesiastes, "stained is the offering of him that sacrificeth from a thing wrongfully gotten . . .". This led him to examine ethical questions such as predetermined "natural capacity" and "higher capacity" which justified the right of those with greater intelligence to rule over those of a "lower natural capacity". Based on his experience in Hispaniola, Las Casas concluded that the native people were being "unjustly" enslaved according to the moral and legal system of Latin Christianity. On the other hand, he felt that the African was "servile by nature" and so was "justly" enslaved.

His conscience was not disturbed when, in 1517, he petitioned the Spanish king for African slaves to replace the dwindling Taino population in the region. The royal contract or *asiento* was prepared and it seemed to have passed through several hands before it was sold to Genoese merchants who were authorised to import 4,000 slaves from West Africa. There is no proof that the shipment ever arrived but it opened the way for the infamous Atlantic Slave Trade – a traffic which resulted in unspeakable atrocities against millions of people from Africa. Slavery was an institution condoned by the Catholic Church, provided the slaves were held by specifically defined "just titles" for some 1,400 years. The "fallible ordinary magisterium", or the instrument which sanctioned this approval, remained in force until 1965, when it was repealed by the Second Vatican Council.

Once it was obvious that Jamaica had no mineral wealth, about half of the original 60 settlers who came with Esquivel left within a year or two to seek their fortunes elsewhere. A number of those who remained set up ranches on the plains of St Elizabeth, Westmoreland, Clarendon, St Catherine, St Thomas-in-the-East and in the vicinity of New Seville. In 1534, when the capital was removed to the St Catherine Plains and renamed Villa de la Vega, it was estimated that only about 20 of the original settlers remained in the old capital.

Pedro de Mazuelo, the Island Treasurer, was the main architect behind the removal of the capital. He owned a sugar estate on the St Catherine Plains, and realised the economic potential of sugar cultivation on flat lands as well as the greater convenience of shipping from the southern ports. The new capital, Villa de la Vega, was conveniently sited near to Mazuelo's estate.

Most settlers had by now given up hope of finding minerals, and had turned to logging and farming – growing cassava, sweet potato, grapes, oranges, cocoa, and rearing cattle, horses, pigs and other domestic animals introduced from Europe. Almost everything flourished including a new industry using cotton which the Spaniards found growing on the island. They found the native people twisting the cotton fibres into ropes, which they then used in the making of hammocks. Governor Esquivel, who went into partnership with the Spanish king to develop commercial farms and ranches, expanded cotton cultivation and in a short while began exporting shirts and hammocks to Cuba and to towns on the Spanish Main. The project was greatly aided by a royal decree that required each individual to possess a hammock.

Jamaica was ideal farming country and quickly acquired the reputation as a supplier of domestic animals and ground provisions to the armies of conquest on the American mainland, as well as to other islands in the region. For instance, in 1514, Las Casas and his partner, Renteria, stocked their new estate in Cuba with animals and cassava from Jamaica, and in 1521, the governor, Francisco de Garay exported 50 cows, 50 yearling calves, 200 sheep, 1,000 pigs and 2,000 *cargas* of cassava to Panama. Annual shipments of cassava were also sent to Cartagena.

Jamaica could have sustained a viable trade in ground provisions, meat products, hardwood and the new-found spice, pimento, had adequate shipping facilities been available, but in those first years, a convoy of only two vessels made the annual trip from Spain to Central America, carrying European foodstuffs and manufactured goods. Rarely did they call at Jamaica although it was en route. On their return journey they usually carried minerals and other valuables plundered on the mainland and were not inclined to fill their holds with bulky and comparatively inexpensive agricultural products from Jamaica. Colonists were therefore forced to purchase necessities such as oil, vinegar, wine and manufactured goods from Cartagena, at exorbitant prices. Martin Vásquez writing to Columbus' heir in June 1556, noted the commercial isolation imposed by the establishment of the convoy system and by state centralisation, which hampered the growth of commercial relationships. Droughts and plagues of locusts also laid waste the farms and severely affected the island's economic prosperity during the early years of the sixteenth century. (Padron: 1952)

Soon after his arrival in December 1509, Esquivel began sending glowing reports of the numbers of natives that had been converted to Christianity, but other accounts of the atrocities taking place also reached Spain and he was charged with misdemeanours, negligence in his administrative duties and indifference to the conversion of the natives. An *audiencia* was ordered to enquire into these charges and Esquivel was recalled in disgrace in 1512. He had spent little more than two years on the island.

Controls had to be instituted at the highest level to stem the decline of the native population, then the main source of labour. In 1511 instructions were issued to the Jeronimite Reform Commission to visit the region, beginning with Hispaniola and Jamaica. They were to take a census of the native populations, note the treatment meted out to them, the numbers under the control of individual settlers and whether or not these settlers were in a position to take proper care of them. A royal decree which was designed to prevent the settlers overworking the natives, stated that neither in San Juan nor in Jamaica should Indians be forced to carry heavy weights. It set out the conditions under which they should be employed in the mines and in households. For instance, each household was limited to not more than six servants, and these were not to be used in the mines. The natives were to receive two-thirds of gold smelted and their share was to be used to pay for the lands, cattle and other expenses incurred in establishing settlements for them. "From what is left the administration was to buy them clothes, shirts, 12 hens and one rooster for each household" and the transactions should be recorded. However, as there was no gold, it is doubtful if the instructions were ever implemented.

Farms were to be bought for the settlers who were appointed to administer the native settlements. They were to be paid a miner's salary in addition to being allowed to mine for themselves. Anyone failing to comply with these instructions would be fined. For a second offence the fine would be doubled. For the third offence it would be tripled and the offender would lose the natives under his control. This may have had a sobering effect for a time, but nothing could halt the decline of the population who were dying off at a rapid rate from European diseases and ill-treatment.

Other regulations were also put in place. The *repartimiento*, introduced by Esquivel, enabled a colonist to apply for, and receive special permission to use the indigenous people for limited periods of time, in such endeavours as planting, reaping, logging and rounding up cattle. Francisco de Garay who became governor in 1514, introduced another set of regulations, the *requerimiento* (the requirement). Under this system colonists were to convert the natives to Christianity. The hope was that they would be "always tractable, would be properly maintained and would live and greatly multiply". Taino slaves were expected to acknowledge the supremacy of the Pope and the Spanish sovereign, but as the majority of them did not understand the language of their captors and had no idea of the significance of these personages, they were deemed to be disobedient and consequently were punished.

Under Spanish supervision, Taino slaves built Jamaica's first Spanish settlement, New Seville. They cleared the primeval forests for farming, hauled timber and probably built the first log cabins occupied by the first colonists, as well as the 25 more substantial houses said to have existed along a one-mile stretch of road in the town. They quarried limestone blocks from a hill one mile away, hauled them to the building sites and carried out most of the heavy construction work. The size of some of the cut stones used in the building of the governor's palace, which was the most imposing stone structure in the town, explains the necessity for the controls.

The Spaniards soon learned to appreciate the excellence of Taino crafts-manship. A Taino *cacique*, baptised and renamed Juan de Medina, and members of his family, were said to have been skilled masons and crafts-men. They are known to have worked on the governor's palace and may also have worked on the elaborate stone church begun in 1525 through the efforts of Peter Martyr, first Spanish abbot of Jamaica. Martyr died in

Aerial photograph of the site of the town of New Seville, left of the town of St Ann's Bay

Courtesy of Jack Tyndale-Biscoe

Sixteenth-century carving from New Seville

1526 before he could take up his appointment but construction continued although at a greatly reduced pace. In 1533 the Spanish king called for an accounting on the church but the following year the capital was transferred, and the church was never finished.

It is believed that native craftsmen carved some of the limestone lintels found on the New Seville site, as they bear distinctive Taino features. These and other carvings found in the old capital are credited as being among the finest of contemporary workmanship in the Americas and on the Iberian Peninsula.

Later in the sixteenth century, an attempt was made to bring the surviving natives together on a reservation, ostensibly to protect them from extinction. However, neither the colonists nor the Tainos supported the move. The colonists feared that they might lose the slaves already in their possession, and only three Tainos seemed to have agreed to the proposal. The project was dropped because trackers claimed that they could not capture the Tainos hiding in the forests.

A physical survey of the island reveals extensive flat, fertile plains to the south of the main mountain ranges which run from east to west, almost all the way across the island. These grassy plains, watered by many rivers, made better farm lands than the steep, wooded hills on the north and the harbours on the south coast were easier to navigate. Those mountain ranges, difficult to traverse except by experienced woodsmen, have through the centuries, provided cover for all who struggled to escape enslavement and imprisonment. The very fertile Guanaboa Vale, securely hidden among the steep almost inaccessible Clarendon hills, have sheltered in turn, Tainos escaping enslavement, freed Spanish slaves and also maroon resistance fighters. In the eighteenth century it protected the maroon leader, Juan de Bolas (Lubolo) and his band of fighters, until they succumbed to the inducements of the English. From these mountains, escaped slaves made nightly raids on the plains below, stealing cattle from the Spanish plantations, and with the coming of the English, weapons and supplies from the sugar plantations.

The cockpit country of Trelawny and St Elizabeth is very close to the savannas of St Elizabeth, Westmoreland and Trelawny. Among these precipitous hills, during the eighteenth and nineteenth centuries, the Trelawny Maroons kept the English at bay for a long time, until their leaders were tricked into submission, and deported. The northern ranges of the Blue Mountains hid the first Taino freedom fighters in their bid to escape enslavement. At Seaman's Valley, Windsor, Moore Town and Comfort Castle on the Portland side of the great Blue Mountain chain, Taino hideouts predate maroon strongholds.

When the Spanish settlers found their labour force depleted they turned to Africa for replacements. Until then the only Africans on the island, were personal household servants of a few settlers. Esquivel had two or three as well as two children, two years of age whom he received as gifts. These servants did not come directly from Africa but from European countries where African slavery was already institutionalised. Then slavery did not carry the stigma which came to be attached to it in the West Indies and in Jamaica, in particular, after the end of the seventeenth century.

Under the Spaniards, slaves who had "converted" to Christianity, could receive sacraments of the Church and were permitted the basic rights of marriage. They could obtain their freedom so long as the proper condi-·tions were met: this meant that they could be freed by their owners or by the State or they could purchase their freedom. The State occasionally rewarded a slave for valour in war by granting him his freedom – a life "full of tranquility". At the time of the transfer of the capital to Villa de la Vega, former slaves were given lands on the edge of town to build their houses and to plant their gardens.

There is no certainty that the first field slaves requested by Las Casas in 1517, or another consignment approved in 1523, ever arrived. On another occasion the Portuguese king was approached to supply 5,000 slaves to the region, of which 300 were earmarked for Jamaica. Women were supposed to be included in the shipment as they were expected to produce children and increase the slave population.

Cheap cane sugar was by then becoming popular in Europe, and Spanish farmers in the Americas were set to take advantage of these new developments, except they lacked the know-how to turn sugar cane juice into sugar crystals. Pedro de Mazuelo was possibly the first Spanish colonist in Jamaica to acquire the necessary expertise. In 1534 he imported 30 Africans from the Canary Islands who may have been knowledgeable in sugar manufacture. He also brought a number of Portuguese indentured servants to his plantation on the southern plains who may also have had similar expertise. Although these Portuguese were not accepted socially by the Spaniards, in time they came to be influential commercial traders and also continued their trading activities under the English.

From time-to-time rumours of gold being found on the island surfaced, but mostly these were without foundation. Gold was the prime motivator for Spanish expansion in the Americas, and as Jamaica lacked this commodity, it was never able to attract large numbers of settlers. The situation was not helped by the local priests who extorted property from dying unmarried colonists, using the fear of eternal damnation to get them to sign over their property to the Church. A royal *audiencia* eventually stopped the practice and made it easier for relatives of deceased persons to take up residence in the island.

Throughout the period of Spanish occupation the island's white popula-tion fluctuated between a few hundred and a few thousand souls. At the end of the sixteenth century one report noted 120 "very respectable" Spanish inhabitants on the island. This was probably a fair assessment as at one time the Spanish Crown was obliged to ship 400 destitute individuals from Puerto Rico to boost the local population. The Spanish colonists were in such straitened financial circumstances that they could not accommodate all the newcomers, and Governor Melgajero had to keep 50 of them in his house for a time. The first extant census, undertaken by Abbot Bernardo de Balbuena, in 1611, shows 523 Spaniards, 558 slaves, 107 free blacks, 74 Taino herdsmen, and 75 newcomers. The figures are supported by the fact that in 1635 the military could only muster three companies of 200 men each with the possibility of another 1,000 available in an emergency. In 1643, twelve years before the English invasion, there were four badly under-equipped companies of 500 men each along with a cavalry of mulattoes, free negroes and servants. All they had among them were eight pieces of artillery of which only one was functional. The situation was not much better at the time of the English conquest when the Spanish commander could only find about 120 men to defend Port Caguaya. Settlers living near to Villa de la Vega had been so harassed by French, Dutch and English freebooters over the years, that at first sign of approaching ships they fled to the shelter of the surrounding hills, taking their few possessions with them.

Jamaica's slave population also remained small, probably not more than 1,000 at any one time, because slaves were not only expensive but difficult to acquire. Sometimes years passed before a slaver from Paria or Guinea or Angola called to replenish their supplies and to dispose of their contraband cargo. Money was usually in short supply and the colonists could not always take advantage of the opportunities when they arose. Once a shipment of 150 Africans left behind by a French vessel had to be disposed of by credit. Although payment was accepted in provisions, eleven years later the debt had not been cleared. The problem was compounded by the Spanish Crown and the Columbus heirs haggling over who should receive payment for the slaves. The colonists blamed their financial situation on poor administration, and the loss of their produce to frequent enemy raids.

If Balbuena's 1611 census is to be accepted there were probably not more than about two or three slaves to a farm or ranch. The holdings were not extensive and did not require large numbers of field-hands to maintain them. Farm animals needed little care as they were let loose and left to forage on the open range. Once the fields were prepared and planted it was a matter of weeding occasionally and waiting for the crops to come to maturity. This could take several months as in the case of cassava and plantains, or as long as seven years in the case of cocoa. Master and slave worked at close quarters with each other, and eventually a trust developed between them to the extent that on occasion slaves were allowed to carry arms in defence of the island. Jacinto Sedeño, governor of the island from 1639 to 1640 mentions the use of black divisions and two garrisons comprised of "mulattoes on horseback and free blacks with scimitars".

Spanish trade monopoly continued to restrict Jamaica's economic progress. The colonists could only transport their goods in Spanish ships and as they had no way of knowing when a vessel was likely to call, or whether it would take on goods prepared for shipment, spoilage was heavy. It is said that skins rotted on the docks and logs were attacked by termites.

Hardly any reports appear of runaway slaves in Spanish occupied Jamaica. The maroon phenomenon came about after the capture of the island by the English, as many of the former Spanish slaves elected to hold on to their newly acquired freedom. The fact that in 1655, at the time of the English invasion, some 300 of them remained with Don Cristóbal Arnaldo de Isasi to defend the island against the invaders indicates that their treatment could not have been bad. Former Spanish slaves who had by then established themselves in the mountainous interior, helped to feed the defenders for a time. It was only in the dying years of the war that many of them defected to the enemy and precipitated the final conquest of the island by the English.

With the coming of the English, slavery took on a more evil connotation. Large gangs of African field labourers, herded, degraded, dehumanised, under the lash of their English oppressors, redefined the meaning of slavery. The slave was now chattel, an item that could be disposed of at the whim of his owner.

CHAPTER 8

Two Jamaicas emerge

Black Jamaica began to take shape during the earliest years of Spanish rule. The establishment of the African blood-line began with the small group of Africans who accompanied their masters to Jamaica in 1509, when Juan de Esquivel, the island's first governor, and a party of Spanish colonists moved from Hispaniola to New Seville, on the outskirts of St Ann's Bay, and set about building the island's first capital.

English-speaking white Jamaica began to take shape after the English took Jamaica from the Spaniards in 1655. By that time there were about 1,500 persons of African descent in the island, some of whom were free. At that time the population was of the order of a medium-sized village of about 6,000 people, one-quarter of whom were black. The island was poverty-stricken. The economy was based on hides and lard and the black labour force was small, but even so there are reports of fugitive slaves setting up *palenques* on their own. Edward Long reports in his history: "There had been a Spanish village at Paretty . . . From one or two Negroes they learned that the Blacks had entirely detached themselves from the Spaniards and were resolved to maintain their footing in the island so long as cattle remained for them to kill." (Long: 1774)

On the morning of 10 May 1655, two fishermen searching for turtles off Port Morant saw a large fleet of 38 ships moving toward them from the east. This was no pirate's raid. So large a fleet meant war. The fishermen made for land as quickly as they could and gave the news. Messengers on horseback hurried west along the coast, giving the alarm as they went, until at last they reached the capital city of Villa de la Vega. From vantage points on the Hellshire Hills African eyes kept watch while the fleet dropped anchor off Passage Fort and began to disembark a force of soldiers. There were 8,000-9,000 men aboard, more than the total population of Jamaica.

The Africans and Spaniards who watched the slow landing of men and of cannon knew that this meant conquest and settlement. What could an ailing old governor with five or six cannons and a few hundred, ill-equipped men do against so large a force?

But the fleet had no business being off Passage Fort. It should have been in Santo Domingo, with its commanders, Admiral William Penn and General Robert Venables, in the governor's residence and the army in charge of Hispaniola. Those were the instructions the commanders had been given.

English policy in the 1650s aimed at the creation of a colonial trading system based on mercantilist theory, which was the economic face of imperialism. It was based on the theory of "beggar my neighbour", one nation's loss being another nation's gain. An inflow of gold and silver meant victory, and an unfavourable balance of trade signified defeat. The doctrine decreed with Mosaic zeal and authority that each metropolitan power and its colonies should be firmly cemented into an economic unit, with the colony producing raw materials and the mother-country processing and marketing the product and achieving a favourable balance of trade by tariffs, bounties, monopolies (such as the West Indian sugar monopoly of the eighteenth century) and the use of force.

The English Navigation Ordinance or Act of 1651, for example, prohibited the import of colonial products into England except in English ships and confined the import of European goods into English colonies to English ships or ships of the country where the goods originated. Protestant Holland, the greatest trading nation of that period, protested. Their negotiators were reminded that they (the Dutch) had always forbidden English traders from doing business with the United Provinces. The Navigation Act stated a policy "from which we think it not fit to recede", said the English negotiators.

For 200 years mercantilism set Europeans to the task of killing each other with cold-hearted zest. The memorial tablets on the walls of St Peter's Church in Port Royal and the battlements and cemeteries at English Harbour in Antigua and Brimstone Hill in St Kitts reveal the cost of this theory of empire.

The English-Dutch War of 1652, and Oliver Cromwell's Great Western Design, which was planned in 1653-54, were products of these imperial policies. The Western Design revived the Elizabethan strategy of using sea-power to break the flow of Mexican and Peruvian silver that kept the Spanish armies in the field and to strengthen English trade by cutting the links that held together Spain's overstretched empire.

Francis Drake had been the incarnation of Queen Elizabeth the First's policy and its most brilliant exponent. He was "a driven man dedicated practically from adolescence to wreaking personal havoc on Philip's empire. 'El Draque' became virtually the devil incarnate to Spaniards who plied the seas, intercepting plate ship after plate ship and even further disrupting the staggering Iberian economy. By 1580 not a single bar of Peruvian or Mexican silver safely crossed the Atlantic". (O'Connell: 1989) With plunder of this size Queen Elizabeth could wage war on the cheap.

Drake's slashing raids had been based on local knowledge. His men were efficient and well-disciplined. Cromwell's project was based on inaccurate and prejudiced intelligence. Neither Admiral Penn nor General Venables was of the stature of Drake, as the attack on Hispaniola showed.

The fleet set sail from England at the end of 1654. On board were 2,500 men, more than half of whom were conscripts from the slums of London. It reached Barbados in January 1655 and took on 3,000-4,000 persons of similar status. At St Kitts, Nevis and Montserrat it enlisted another 1,200 men. These West Indian conscripts were mostly indentured labourers and time-expired individuals, who were landless, or debtors trying to escape from their creditors.

The following contemporary account gives a fair description of the recruits: "Certainly these Islanders must be the very scum of scums, mere dregs of corruption, and such upon whose endeavors it was impossible to expect a blessing." (Bridenbaugh: 1972)

On 14 April the fleet arrived off the coast about 30 miles from Santo Domingo, the capital of Hispaniola. The ships were too small to carry adequate supplies of food and water for long periods and by the time the vessels reached the Caribbean the 2,500 enlisted men from Europe had consumed most of the provisions. Supplies of corn and cassava for the army of 7,000 men who were on their way to Santo Domingo were difficult to obtain. The men suffered from thirst, dysentery, fever and hunger. They bore no resemblance to a fighting force.

The landing in Hispaniola was a disastrous failure. "All that saves it from our utter contempt is the nearly inspired element of farce that informed every moment of it . . . In Hispaniola, attacked by a detachment of Spanish Lancers, General Venables hides behind a tree, emerging after the fight to accuse his troops of cowardice." (Hearne: 1965)

Jamaica was the consolation prize. Afraid to face Cromwell's displeasure, the commanders turned their attention to that poorly defended island.

It was well-known that the governor, Don Juan Ramírez de Arellano, was old and ill. The islanders were weary of defending themselves against intruders. The Maestro de Campo, Don Francisco de Proenza, had only five iron cannons and 180 poorly armed men to defend the port and the town of Villa de la Vega and the surrounding countryside. The capital fell within a day or two. The only spoils the English found were cured cowhides which the slaves used to cover the earthen floors of their houses. These were later sold in New England.

According to the terms of capitulation which Governor Ramírez de Arellano signed, the Spaniards were to leave the island by 23 May. Although greatly outnumbered they had no intention of complying. Some moved their families and their belongings west to Pereda (Pedro Plains), while others made their way up the Rio Minho Valley to a stronghold at Los Virmejales (Veramahollis) where their African allies kept them supplied with meat and ground provisions. Realising that they had been tricked, the English intensified their attack and some of the Spaniards capitulated. On 1 July 1655 seventy of them, including women and children, carrying only their personal belongings, sailed from Caguaya for Campeche on the *Spanish Main*. In the weeks following, others who had taken refuge at Los Virmejales also made their way to the north coast and thence to Cuba.

Spanish resistance continued, however. For five years, with assistance from some African bands, the Spanish leader Arnaldo Isasi held out. A brave man, he was virtually abandoned by Spain and by his nearest neighbours, Cuba and Mexico. The aid that was sent was too little and too late. He was forced to capitulate in 1660. Our major concern is not with departing Isasi and his bedraggled companions but with the three bands of maroons that remained in Jamaica and with the early years of English settlement. The African guerrillas were divided into three bands. One was stationed in the hills above Guanaboa Vale with Juan de Bolas (Lubolo) as their leader. A second band was stationed in the Clarendon hills at Los Virmejales under Juan de Sierras and the third band was probably stationed near Porus. They kept the Spanish defenders supplied with food from extensive provision grounds hidden in deep inaccessible valleys in the St Catherine and Clarendon hills and they frequently descended to the plains in search of meat and weapons.

Not all the Africans chose to assist Isasi. Some acted on their own. It is very likely that those who allied themselves with Isasi served under their own leaders.

The English soon learned to respect the Africans, whether they were acting on their own or not. Two English commanders, Admiral Goodson and Major General Robert Sedgwick, reported on 24 January 1656: "The Negroes . . . live by themselves in several parties, and near our quarters, and do very often, as our men go into the woods to seek provisions, destroy and kill them with their lances. We now and then find one or two of our men killed, stripped and naked, and these rogues begin to be bold, our English rarely, or seldom killing any of them."

In March Sedgwick reported: "The Spaniard is not considerable, but of the Blacks there are many, who are like to prove as thorns and pricks in our side." Some months later he wrote that "in two days more than forty of our soldiers were cut off by the Negroes".

After the English defeated the reinforcements who came from Cuba and Mexico, it became clear that Isasi and his men were heading for defeat. Juan de Bolas went over to the English with about 150 followers who were based in the Clarendon mountains. This signalled the end. Some months later, after being defeated in a surprise attack led by Juan de Bolas, Isasi surrendered.

Two months after the surrender, Isasi and his men left for Cuba in two boats they had built. The party consisted of 68 Spaniards and eight Africans. There are two versions of why 36 persons were left in Jamaica. One version claims that after the boats were completed it was found that there was not sufficient room for all. The other version states that 36 Jewish traders chose to continue as residents in Jamaica under English rule.

In 1661 Edward D'Oyley, who had been military governor of Jamaica and had transformed the survivors of the mob that landed in 1655 into a fighting force, and who was serving for some months as civil governor, was instructed "to give such encouragement as securely you may wish to such negroes and others as shall submit to live peaceably under his majesty's obedience and in due submission to the government of the island". Governor, Sir Charles Lyttleton, who had been Lord Windsor's deputy, who assumed duties in 1663, was instructed to carry out the following orders: "that Juan Luyola and the rest of the negroes of his Palenque, on account of their submission and services to the English, shall have grants of land and enjoy all the liberties and privileges of Englishmen . . . that Luyola be colonel of the black regiment of militia, and he and others appointed magistrates over the negroes to decide all cases except those of life and death". A grant of 30 acres was made to each of the men. The majority of the free blacks did not approve of the alliance with the English and some of his companions cut Juan de Bolas to pieces. The *palenque* south of Cave Valley, on the Virmejales, rejected offers of permanent peace. In 1670 rewards were offered for the heads of Juan de Sierras and his men. As Hart points out, this may have been linked with the deaths of a number of white men in Clarendon.

The Africans of Spanish Jamaica had established the resistance pattern of fugitive slaves based on *palenques*, their strongholds of freedom. The English conquest of Jamaica did not mean the conquest of these free Africans nor the destruction of their *palenques*. Long's statement makes it clear that the last of the Spaniards to withdraw from Jamaica left about 30 of their Negro slaves behind, who secreted themselves in the mountains and afterwards entered into alliance with the other "unsubdued banditti". It is a tribute to the Africans that Long, the planter-historian, saw them as unsubdued banditti. To us these unsubdued banditti were following the tradition set by maroons in Brazil, Mexico and Colombia. Their *palenques*

FORT RUPERT

Bridewell Prison?

School

Palisadoes

Society of the
Artillery of
Jamaica

Court House?

St. Paul's Church

White's Line

Marshallsea Prison?

FORT CARLISLE

King's House

Herb & Fruit Market (High St.)

Wherry Bridge

Fish Market

Cope's alley

Water Lane

Waterman's wharf

Bird's alley

Smith's alley

State Storehouses

N

Sea Lane and
Common landing place

King's Wharf and
Storehouses

Catt an

E 60400

N 37800

THE STORY OF THE JAMAICAN PEOPLE

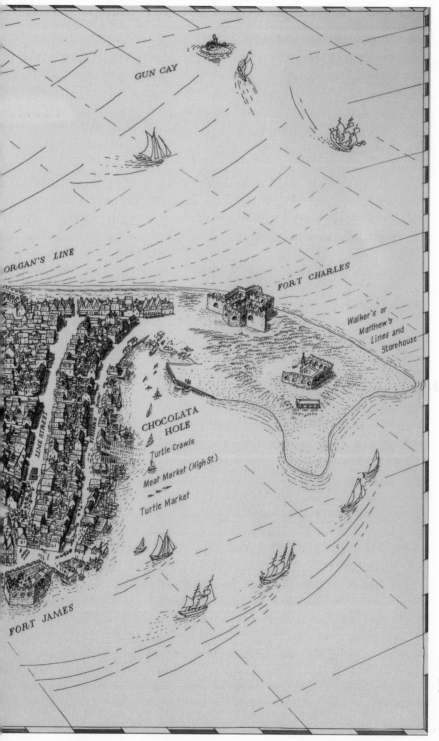

GUN CAY

ORGAN'S LINE

FORT CHARLES

Walker's or
Matthew's
Lines and
Storehouse

LINE STREET

CHOCOLATA
HOLE
Turtle Crawls

Meat Market (High St.)

Turtle Market

FORT JAMES

Courtesy of Oliver Cox

symbolise the implanting by Africans of the concepts of freedom and racial equality in plantation America.

With the establishment of civil government in 1663, English Jamaica set itself to the tasks of attracting settlers and strengthening its defences. A Spanish diplomat put into vivid words the threat that English Jamaica posed to Spain: it was "a dagger pointed at Spain's soft underbelly". Cromwell recognised that a very important strategic position had been gained. He went to war with Spain rather than give it up. At first, settlement was slow. Officers and men of the conquering army received grants of land to plant and settle, chiefly in the fertile well-watered Rio Minho Valley, but many died and few succeeded. Admiral Blake, by destroying the Spanish navy off the Canary Islands in 1657, had greatly weakened Spain's ability to mount a counter-attack, but even so the English knew that there was no time to be lost in making Jamaica secure against attack.

Edward D'Oyley, soldier that he was, hit on the quickest solution. He tried to attach the buccaneer stronghold of Tortuga to his government, but the French element there was too strong. The English buccaneers, outnumbered in Tortuga, began to make their headquarters in Port Royal. To do this on any scale, and openly, needed a governor who at the very least would close an eye to what was happening. At first King Charles II sought to secure trade with Spain by agreement and appointed Thomas Modyford, a seasoned Barbadian sugar planter, to be governor of Jamaica, in the hope that he would be able to persuade Spain to agree to trade. The Spaniards, however, doubted whether Modyford could suppress the buccaneers. In 1665 the English government, facing the possibility of war with Holland and possibly France, desperately needed fighting men in the Caribbean. The only striking force available consisted of the buccaneers. Modyford was authorised to grant commissions of "reprisal" to buccaneer captains, it being understood that the plunder they secured would be their pay for services rendered. Once again the old battle-cry was sounded, "No peace beyond the Line". The buccaneers would be a striking force at sea and would cost embattled England, fully engaged with the Dutch and French, no money.

The flaw in the plan was that the buccaneers would only fight where there was chance of booty, and rich booty at that. They proved unreliable against the Dutch and French forces in the eastern Caribbean, where Antigua and Montserrat fell to the French, but they were brilliantly, brutally successful against the Spanish, with whom England was normally at peace.

The buccaneers made their first big raid under a Dutchman, Edward Mansfield or Mansvelt. They attacked and sacked Grenada in Central America and returned with a great store of booty. They then raided Cuba.

Following on this, Henry Morgan became their leader. In 1668 he sacked the town of Puerto Bello. He returned to Port Royal with 250,000 pieces-of-eight, goods and munitions.

There followed a catalogue of successes, including the capture of three Spanish treasure ships off Maracaibo, and Morgan's crowning exploit, a march across the Isthmus of Panama and the sacking of the city. Ten bloodthirsty years of rapine were brought to an end in 1670, when, by the Treaty of Madrid, England and Spain agreed to abstain from pillage and revoke all letters of reprisal. By this treaty Spain for the first time agreed: "the most serene King of Great Britain – shall have and shall hold – all the lands and regions – situated in the West Indies or in any part of America which the said King of Great Britain and his subjects happen to have and hold at the moment." (Article 7 of the Treaty of Madrid) (Padron)

It took time to put a check to piracy and buccaneering, but by 1685 public opinion, even in Jamaica, had swung against both. The West Indian interest in England and merchants in the West Indies were determined to force a trade. As if to mark the end of an age, Henry Morgan, and General George Monk, first Duke of Albemarle, the last governor who countenanced the old ruffian, died in 1688. Four years later old Port Royal, in its time the wickedest city in the world, the Babylon of the West, was plunged beneath the waves by the great earthquake of 1692. "A punishment for their sins," the pious said.

With Morgan and the buccaneers as shield and sword, Jamaica had come safely through the early years of settlement, but at first few settlers came despite the government's generous offers of land. Some of the early settlers were officers who had served with the army of occupation. These included Colonels Samuel Barry, Philip Ward and Henry Archbould, Major Richard Hope and Major Thomas Ballard. The three names Hope, Barry and Ballard are preserved as Jamaican place-names.

Many of the earliest settlers found early graves, not fortunes. The first 1,600 to take up the offer of land came from Nevis in 1656, with Governor Luke Stokes as their leader. Within a year they were followed by some 250 others, mostly women, from Bermuda. They were given lands at St Thomas-in-the-East, some of which had been Spanish farms, but within a few months of their arrival two-thirds of the Nevis settlers had been wiped out by yellow fever and dysentery.

On 25 March 1656, a proclamation read in New England offered settlers "sufficient proportion of land to them and their slaves for ever, near some good harbour in the said land; Protection (by God's blessing) from all enemies; a share of all the Horses, cattle and other beaves, wild and tame upon the place freely, together with other privileges and Immunities". Persons born in the island of English parentage were deemed "to be free denizens of England" and would henceforth enjoy all the benefits, privileges and advantages of Englishmen born in England.

Settlers also came from Suriname. They were English exiles to Barbados who had migrated there. When the war broke out between the English and the Dutch they moved to Jamaica. They settled at Suriname Quarters (Ackendown) then in the parish of St Elizabeth, but now a part of the parish of Westmoreland. They brought with them the knowledge of sugar manufacture, and some became successful sugar producers.

The critical questions were the status of the settler, the most profitable crop and the availability of labour. The status of settlers was defined in a proclamation issued by Lord Windsor, who succeeded D'Oyley as governor in December 1661. This conferred privileges on free-born subjects of England born out of wedlock in Jamaica. The proclamation was publicised in Barbados even before Lord Windsor reached Jamaica, to allow persons from the other islands to benefit from the new law and from the generous land grants available there. African-Jamaican children born out of wedlock to Englishmen were excluded and the bastardy law ensured that their right to inheritance was severely limited. It remained in force until the twentieth century when it was removed from the statute books. Only then could African-Jamaican children born out of wedlock enjoy the same rights as children born to married couples in Jamaica.

Lord Windsor was also authorised "to grant 30 acres for every servant transported thither and at the end of indenture of four years, 30 acres for each servant". This assured every bond servant of property at the end of his period of indenture. Windsor was encouraged to establish trade with foreigners and was also authorised to ratify former land grants to planters. He used his authority to enrich himself and his associates, amongst them Thomas Lynch, Richard Hope, Henry Archbould and William Beeston. They received huge land grants, totalling somewhere about one-half the size of the parish of St Andrew, including large parts of the Liguanea Plains and extending north to Hope Bay.

The island was administered by the governor and a council of 12 men; a House of Assembly with 30 or more elected representatives; and a local council of justices and vestry in each parish. All representatives were selected from among local white freeholders and paid officials.

The council of 12 was nominated by the Colonial Office in England on the recommendation of the governor. It was both an advisory and an executive body, dealing with matters such as the jurisdiction of civil courts, law and order and the framing of acts and ordinances in keeping with English law. In time it became the Upper House of the Legislature.

The first elected Assembly met on 20 January, 1664 at St Jago de la Vega, the representatives having been "fairly chosen in the several quarters of the island". Its size was flexible and could change according to the council's determination. In the 1670s it had 30 members and in the mid-nineteenth century there were as many as 47. Seats were allocated to a parish depending on its prosperity and on the influence of certain residents. Elections were sometimes rigged to enable individuals to obtain seats.

Jamaica had representative government on a tightly limited franchise. It had the power to pass laws but these had to be approved by the Crown within two years of the date of enactment. At times the Assembly pushed its powers to the limit and there were occasions when the English government wished to restrict its authority. Finally, in 1677, on the advice of the Lords of Trade and Plantations, the Crown decided to cancel the Assembly's power to pass laws. Henceforward laws were to be passed in England and then sent to Jamaica for ratification. As in Ireland, they could be debated but not changed. The English colonists strongly objected to being degraded to the level of Irishmen.

The Earl of Carlisle brought the first of these laws to the island in 1678. The Assembly rejected them all, claiming their rights as Englishmen. The members declared: "Nothing invites people more to settle and remove their families and stock into this remote part of the world, than the assurance they have had of being governed in such manner as that none of their rights would be lost so long as they were within the dominions of the kingdom of England." (Journals of the Assembly of Jamaica) Carlisle tried repeatedly to reach an agreement with the Assembly but failed. The members insisted on keeping the rights to which as Englishmen they were entitled. After months of arguing, the leaders of the resistance, Chief Justice Samuel Long and Colonel William Beeston, were arrested on charges of treason and sent to England for trial. Long's persuasive argument before the King in council, defending the rights and privileges of members of the Assembly as Englishmen, led the council to cancel the instructions. The Jamaica Assembly continued to frame its own laws until it surrendered that power to the Crown in 1865.

The authority delegated to the Assembly in the seventeenth century gave it the power of life and death over the people of African origin. In time, it gave rise to the passing of some of the most stringent slave laws in human history. By law, the African slave was defined as a chattel, a piece of property, with few basic rights.

The term representative government applied only to male white Jamaicans with clearly defined property qualifications. All others were excluded: women, Jews, free brown and black Jamaicans and all the slaves. As far as the Africans were concerned, white representative government meant tyranny.

CHAPTER 9

Profits versus human rights

The decade of the 1680s is a convenient vantage point from which to observe unregulated capitalism at work. We watch the triumph of a small group of large landholders, who began the transformation of Jamaica into a sugar-and-slave plantation manned by enslaved Africans.

In the early years of English settlement cocoa was the favoured crop, not sugar cane. Some colonists had established cocoa walks because they required only a small labour force and modest holdings of land which yielded a profit. In 1672, Richard Blome, in his *Description of the Island of Jamaica*, based on the notes of Governor Sir Thomas Lynch, spoke of cocoa as:

> The principal and most beneficial commodity of the isle by reason of the aptness of the ground to produce and bear it above other places, here being at present above 60 cocoa-walks besides abundance of young walks which are growing up and still more aplanting, so that in time it will become the only noted place for the commodity in the world, which is so much made use of by us and other Nations but in far greater measure by the Spaniards who alone are enough to take the product of the isle, so that there is no fear that it will become a drug and lye upon the hands of the Planter.

There were other products such as indigo and tobacco, as well as hides in great quantity, dye woods, salt, tortoise shell from the "great store of Tortoises" that were taken along the coast, ginger, "better in this isle than in many of the Caribee Islands", and pimento "very Aromatical and of a curious gusto, having the mixed taste of diverse spices", growing in great quantity wild in the mountains. The Spaniards, noted Blome, esteemed it highly and exported it as a choice crop.

In the period from 1675 the settlers turned from cocoa and other crops that could be handled with modest resources to sugar, which demanded capital and a large labour force.

The changeover from smallholdings manned by white indentured servants and a relatively small number of African slaves to large sugar estates manned by gangs of enslaved African labour was revolutionary. It led to the development of the New World plantation, "a combination of African labour, European technology and management, Asiatic and American plants, European animal husbandry and American soil and climate". (Sheridan: 1970) Success had followed the establishment by the Portuguese of the first plantations in Madeira, then in the islands of Principe and São Tome in 1470 and 1472, and finally in North-East Brazil.

But Portugal had gained too many victories. Her enemies attacked her, among them the Dutch, the most relentless of all. With great enthusiasm they set about stripping the Portuguese of their conquests in the Far East, off the western coast of Africa and in Brazil. The four corners of the world shook with the noise of their cannon and their notes of credit. A small country, Holland was described by an observer in 1738 as a land floating in water, a field that is flooded for three parts of the year.

> But, proceeding with great skill, the Dutch built up a fleet the equivalent of all other European fleets put together, and pursuing a policy of toleration, welcomed international financiers and banking houses, the Jews foremost among them. They dominated the trade of Europe and built ships cheaper than anyone else at the famous shipyards at Saardam near Amsterdam, which, provided they were given two months notice, could turn out a warship ready for rigging every week for the rest of the year. Add to this the fact that in Holland, whatever the branch of activity, credit was abundant, easy to come by and cheap . . . The country became the major European market for second hand ships, and since manpower was scarce, foreign seamen volunteered or were pressed into service. (Braudel: 1982)

It was in character, then, that when Barbadian settlers faced disaster in 1635-36 because they had lost the tobacco market to Virginia, the Dutch, traders to the world, were at hand with advice and credit. It was they who pioneered the establishment of a sugar industry in the Caribbean. The Portuguese might have done so, had they not been busy evicting the Dutch from Brazil; in any case they were not anxious to sell their trade secrets to the British. It suited the Dutch, on the other hand, to encourage the production of any West Indian crop that could be sold in Europe; so, when the Barbadians lost their market for tobacco in England,

> Some of the most industrious men, having gotten plants (of sugar cane) from Fernambock, a place in Brazil, and made tryall of them at the Barbados, and finding them to grow, they planted more and more so . . . they were worth the while to set up a very small ingenio

. . . They did not know how to place the plants, the right placing of their furnaces, the true way of covering their rollers with plates . . . But about the time I left the Island, which was in 1650, they were much better'd. (Ligon: 1657)

The imperatives of sugar soon became clear. Ligon listed them as:

> 500 acres of land with a faire dwelling house and Ingenio in a room 400 feet square, a boyling house, filling house, cisterns and still-house, with a curing house 100 feet long and 40 feet broad, with stables and smith's forge and room to lay provisions of corns and Bonavist beans. Houses for Negroes and Indian slaves, with 96 Negroes and 3 Indian women with their children, 28 Christians, 45 cattle for work, 8 milch cows, a dozen horses and mares and 11 Asinigoes (asses). In this plantation of 500 acres, there was employed for sugar something more than 200 acres, about 80 acres for pasture, 120 for wood, about 20 for Cotton Wool, 70 acres for provisions, viz. Corns, Potatoes, Plantains, Cassava and Bonavist; some few acres of which were for fruit, Viz. Pines, Plantains, Millions, Bananas, Goaves, Water Millions, Orange and Lemons. Thomas Modyford, who later became Governor of Jamaica, paid £7,000 for his half-share of the plantation. Eight years earlier the whole estate was worth only £400. (Ligon: 1657)

In the 1630s there had been 11,000 white smallholders in Barbados, all planting crops on a scale suited to a farmer with a short pocket. Many of them had come from England, where they sold themselves for five years as bondservants, in the hope of a grant of land. Now no land was available.

> Whereas divers People have been transported from England to my island of Barbados in America, and have there remained a long time as servants, in great labour for the profits of other persons, upon whose account they were first consigned thither, expecting that their faithful service according to the covenants agreed upon at their first entrance there to make some advantages to themselves by settling of plantations for their own use; but . . . the land is now so taken up as there is not any to be had but at great rates, too high for the purchase of poor servants. (Earl of Carlisle)

The rich bought out the poor. About 750 large estates squeezed out the 11,000 smallholdings. Thousands of displaced settlers made their way to Jamaica and the Carolinas. The green tide of sugar cane and the black tide of Africans swept all before them. A visitor reported:

If you go to Barbados, you shall see a flourishing island, and many able men. I believe they have bought this year no less than a thousand Negroes, and the more they buy, the better able they are to buy, for in a year and half they will earn (with God's blessing) as much as they cost . . . A man that will settle there must look to procure servants, which if you could get out of England, for 6 or 8, or 9 years time, only paying their passages, or at the most but some small above, it would do very well, for so thereby you shall be able to do something upon a plantation, and in short time be able, with good husbandry, to procure Negroes (the life of this place) out of the increase of your own plantation. (Downing: 1645)

The writer echoed what Spanish colonists had reported earlier; that it was certain the Indies could not be maintained without negroes, because the lack of Indians had made it necessary to supplement them with negroes, as it was impossible to obtain Spaniards or creoles who were willing to do that kind of work.

Those who, like Colonel James Drax, had money to invest in land, livestock, factory and a labour force, made fortunes: "His beginning was founded upon a stock not exceeding £333 Sterling and has raised his fortune to such a height that he would not look towards England till he were able to purchase an estate of ten thousand pound land yearly." As for Colonel Modyford, "he had taken a resolution to himself not to set his face for England till he made his voyage and employment there worth him a hundred thousand pounds sterling; and all by this sugar plant." (Ligon: 1657)

Colonel Modyford had seen the plantation transform Barbados into a wealth-creating island. By 1666 it had increased its wealth sevenfold. African slaves had increased in number from 6,000 in 1643 to 20,000 in

Drax Hall Estate

1655, to 40,000 in 1668 and to 64,000 in 1672. By the end of the century, in 1698, there were 18 black slaves to every white man.

Modyford recognised that lack of land had put a limit to the prosperity of Barbados. Jamaica had more fertile land and fewer people; in 1677 there were only 9,000 whites and just over 9,000 blacks. In 1672, probably at Modyford's urging, the Assembly passed an act which allowed the earliest settlers to take out patents for as much land as they could plant in five years; but, lamented Governor Beeston, "Few people come."

In Jamaica the sugar plantation began its swift conquest in two belts along the south coast, one running west from Holland Point, Hordley and Bath through Lyssons to eastern areas of the Liguanea Plain where the Hope River provided water and power; the other on the fertile plains of South Clarendon. Describing land-use patterns in this period, Higman refers also to "smaller pockets along the Black River, the interior lowlands of St Catherine (St John's Precinct) and coastal St Mary in the north. Maps of Jamaica published in the first half of the eighteenth century suggest that this pattern was maintained throughout the period". (Higman: 1976)

Increased production seemed to do no more than whet the European appetite for sugar. Between 1740 and 1790 the plantations marched along the north coast, through Llandovery, Rose Hall and Tryall, and southward on to the Westmorland Plain by way of Friendship and the Roaring River and Williamsfield Estates. Soon heavy wagons drawn by cattle were moving from the estates to sugar ports, to Rio Bueno, Falmouth, Lucea and Savanna-la-Mar. "The number of sugar mills operating in the island increased from 57 in 1670 to 419 in 1739 and 1,061 in 1786. In the northern parish of St James, however, the number increased from 20 to 115 between 1745 and 1774. Between 1792 and 1799 some 84 new sugar estates were established, more than half of them in St Ann, Trelawny and St James." (Higman: 1976)

Today's landscape and the skin colour of most Jamaicans testify to the plantation's radical transforming power throughout the region. A traveller flying down the archipelago sees yesterday's change drawn out on the landscape, a spreading checker-board of sea-green fields and of brown stubble, the characteristic combination of field and factory dramatising the fact that sugar cane is a crop and that sugar is an industrial product, and occasional fields of ground provisions huddled on marginal hillsides. When he lands at Basseterre, St Johns, Bridgetown, Kingston or Montego Bay, he finds himself in the presence of Africa, and recognises that the landscape tells but a part of the story.

The shift from smallholdings to estate, from white serfs to black slaves, was brought about by the implanting of "an absolutely unprecedented

social, economic and political institution and by no means simply an inno-
vation in the organisation of agriculture". (Mintz: 1974) The Brazilian
scholar, Gilberto Freyre, pointed out that to travel through the Deep
South of the United States, the Guyanas and North-East Brazil, is to pass
through a region in which the social configuration was moulded by the
sugar-and-slave plantation, the characteristic features being racial inter-
mingling, monoculture and large landholdings.

As the estates spread, so the African presence grew. Philip Curtin's
census of the Atlantic Slave Trade shows the link between the plantation,
an instrument or unit of production, and the African, the agent of production, the worker whose muscle power, stamina and intelligence enriched
Europe; and the inflow of Africans was on so large a scale and lasted for so
long that it transformed the older English colonies of Barbados, St Kitts,
Antigua and Jamaica into predominantly black colonies.

In Jamaica in 1739 there were 99,000 Africans and 10,000 whites. The
net import of Africans into Jamaica between 1655 and 1807 was 747,506.
George Roberts lists the white population of the island in 1787 as 25,000
and the slave population as 210,894, a continuing ratio of around one
white to ten blacks.

The annual import of Africans saved the African-Jamaicans from extinction because of the high mortality rate due to overwork. The chilling fact was
bluntly stated by Richard Sheridan, that the Africans were brought to the
West Indies to form new plantations, to increase the labour force of existing
plantations and to replace workers who died or became superannuated.

> It is evident that few plantations could remain productive for long
> without imports for replacement. It is paradoxical that high profits
> were not necessarily incompatible with high mortality; not a few
> contemporaries pointed out, as did Lord Brougham, that so long as a
> slave market exists, men find their profit in working out a certain
> number of their slaves, and supplying the blacks by purchase, rather
> than by breeding. Slavery, as a profitable institution, thus depended
> on the constant recruitment of cheap labour by importation from
> Africa. (Sheridan: 1970)

Cuba in this period had a flourishing industry based on tobacco planters
with small holdings. As a result the demographic history of Cuba differed
markedly from that of the plantation islands. Early in the eighteenth
century, when the sugar plantation was absorbing the cocoa-walks in
Jamaica, tobacco was introduced into Cuba. Smallholdings of tobacco
flourished alongside the sugar industry which had been introduced
between 1590 and 1600, but which had been handicapped by lack of
markets and difficulties in importing equipment and slaves. It suffered

from the economic strait-jacket into which the laws of the Indies had forced Cuba, which "cut Cuba off completely from foreign trade and limited its traffic with Spain to the single port of Seville, to which the Spanish colonies of the New World were limited by only one expedition a year". (Guerra y Sanchez: 1964) This rigid control held back the expansion of the sugar industry for two centuries and "guaranteed that Cuban society would have a gradual internal growth based on a white population that owned and tilled its native soil." So limited a sugar industry could not threaten the infant tobacco industry. Indeed, as Guerra y Sanchez indicates, tobacco, being of excellent quality, flourished and the tobacco smallholdings contributed to the break-up of the vast cattle ranches.

In the very century in which the number of Cuban tobacco smallholdings was increasing and a white Cuban yeomanry was becoming significantly important in standing and numbers, control of large areas of Jamaica was passing into the hands of a relatively small number of owners. Barry Higman, in *Jamaica Surveyed*, points out that in 1670, just before the rise of the plantations, 724 proprietors held an average of 261 acres of patented land in the settled areas. Only seven per cent of them owned 1,000 acres or more. About three-quarters of a century later the average holding stood at 1,045 acres; 29 per cent owned 1,000 acres and four per cent held over 5,000 acres. Schemes for increasing the number of small landholders came to little and "the system of great estates employing large gangs of slaves under the supervision of small numbers of whites spread to engulf the entire island by the late eighteenth century". Cuba's turn came in the nineteenth century. We will return to her in the period of the emergence of a black yeomanry in Jamaica.

White Jamaica became from this period an absentee society that "drained the island of the very people it needed for leadership in all aspects of life". (Patterson: 1969) In consequence we watch the growth of a society that was utterly immoral, inefficient and lacking in any sense of social responsibility. In 1720 the rector of Kingston reported to the bishop of London that there were not six families in the island which could be described as gentlemen: "They have no maxims of Church or State but what are absolutely anarchic."

This was the society into which the African was pitchforked. The shock was traumatic not only because he was now the property of another human being but because of the nature of white Jamaican society. From whatever nation or tribe he came, he had been nurtured in a deeply religious society with a well-understood code of ethics and system of justice and of community obligations.

We seek guidance in this subject from one of Africa's leading theologians and philosophers, John Mbiti:

Because traditional religions permeate all the departments of life, there is no formal distinction between the sacred and the secular, between the religious and non-religious, between the spiritual and the material areas of life. Wherever the African is, there is the religion: he carries it to the fields where he is sowing seeds or harvesting a new crop he takes it with him to the beer party or to attend a funeral ceremony; and if he is educated, he takes religion with him to the examination room at school or in the University; if he is a politican he takes it to parliament.

Traditional religions are not primarily for the individual, but for his community of which he is part. Chapters of African religions are written everwhere in the the life of the community, and in traditional society there are no irreligious people. To be human is to belong to the whole community, and to do so involves participating in the beliefs, ceremonies, rituals and festivals of that community. A person cannot detach himself from the religion of his group, for to do so is to be severed from his roots, his foundation, his context of security, his kinship and the entire group of those who make him aware of his own existence. To be without one of these corporate elements of life is to be out of the whole picture. Therefore, to be without religion amounts to a self-excommunication from the entire society, and African peoples do not know how to exist without religion. (Mbiti: 1970)

We point to the African background because Europeans justified the slave trade as saving the African from savagery and moving him nearer to civilisation. The historic fact is that the European record of the conquest and settlement of the Americas is one of savagery, of the legalisation of injustice, of the most barbarous punishments and, in the English-speaking Caribbean, gross immorality.

In Jamaican society:

For the non-white and particularly the non-free, the legal system was a grim travesty. Traditional British law either completely neglected or, in the few cases where it obliquely touched on the topic, very clumsily handled the problem of slavery or other forms of unfreedom. The local masters preferred it that way. They made little attempt at formulating a slave code until the last quarter of the eighteenth century and when they did it was largely as an anti-abolitionist propaganda tactic . . . .

For the nine-tenths of Jamaicans who made up the slave population, the master was the law. In him rested the power of life and death. Occassionlly a white person might have had to pay a fine for murdering his slave, but in the majority of such cases no legal action could be taken even to inflict the mildest penalty since a negro could not give evidence against any white person. (Patterson: 1969)

The Africans were not Christians but their gods and ethical values were a very precious part of daily life, as Mbiti emphasises. Many traditional African societies thought of God as omniscient (knowing all things), almighty and present everywhere. He is the watcher of everything, the great eye, the sun, the all-powerful.

The Zulu, a warlike people, think of him as "he who bends down . . . even majesties". The Gikuyu see him as always having been in existence, as one who never dies.

No father nor mother nor wife nor children;
He is all alone.
He is neither a child nor an old man
He is the same today as he was yesterday.

A traditional pygmy hymn describes him as spirit.

In the beginning was God,
Today is God
Tommorrow will be God
Who can make an image of God?
He has no body,
He is a word which comes out of your mouth
That word, it is no more,
It is past, and still it lives.
So is God.

God governs the universe and the life of mankind. His will is immutable and man generally has to invoke it or accept it . Some, such as the Nuer people, believe that God is always right, that "God evens things out." The Akan give him the title of creator, originator, inventor; rain is the most widely acknowledged token of God's providence. He is known as the rain giver or water giver.

These examples indicate that the African could not conceive of an utterly irreligious society, nor of one so unjust as plantation society. To them justice was one of the attributes of God, who was ruler and master: "The notion of God as Judge also strengthens traditional ethical sanctions which in turn uphold community solidarity. When praying during a crisis the Azande declare to God that they have not stolen nor coveted other people's goods and they address him as the one who "settles the differences between us who are men." The Nuer believe that God is the Guardian of the traditions. (Mbiti: 1970)

Furthermore, the physical and the spiritual were seen as two dimensions of one and the same universe, and the African experienced this religious universe through acts of worship, sacrifices and offerings, prayers, innovations, blessings and salutations. Also, and this prevails throughout black America, music, singing and dancing run deep into the innermost parts of African peoples and many things come to the surface under musical inspiration which otherwise may not be readily revealed.

John Mbiti notes that in Africa he found the collection and study of religious songs very scanty, and yet this is another rich area where one expects to find repositories of traditional beliefs; ideas, wisdom, feeling. The Negro spirituals of the deep south and the Jamaica spirituals that Olive Lewin collected, shepherdesses and preachers from Moses Baker and George Lisle through Daddy Sharpe and Paul Bogle to Bedward represent a remarkable continuity of a powerful religious tradition.

We close with some African prayers that convey a sense of the reality and presence of God and of direct and easy access to him.

Thus, on becoming pregnant a Bachwa woman cooks food and takes portions of it to the forest, where she offers them to God, saying "God, from whom I have received this child, take Thou and eat."

The Bambuti pygmies in the event of a thunderstorm, pray "Grandfather, Great Father, let matters go well with me, for I am going into the forest." If they are already in the forest they pray, saying "Father, Thy children are afraid; and behold, we shall die."

The Nuer people "like to pray at any time because they like to speak to God when they are happy". A typical prayer runs:

> Our Father, it is Thy universe, it is
> Thy will, let us be at peace, let the
> Soul of thy people be cool; Thou art
> Our Father, remove all evil from our path.

The concept of God as father and judge and the images revealed in the prayers are, as Carl Jung pointed out, "always related to the primordial images of the collective unconscious. These images are really balancing or compensating factors which correspond with the problems life presents in actuality. This is not to be marvelled at since these images are deposits representing the accumulated experience of thousands of years of struggle for adaptation and existence".

The West African people belonged to different language groups, communities and tribes, but they shared certain basic cultural similarities, such as a strong sense of community, a powerful attachment to the land, a concern for children as the "buds of expectation and hope" as well as for the ancestors, for personal dignity and a respect for the tribal leaders and for the freedom enjoyed within the boundaries of tribal obligations. These are all a part of the rich religious heritage of the West African people and they explain the immediate, widespread and long-sustained struggle of the dispersed African-Amercian people for freedom.

CHAPTER 10

The beginning of the African diaspora

The African's deep longing for his country and his anger at the injustices he suffered find expression in one of the oldest Jamaican folk songs:

> If me want for to go in a Ebo
> Me can't go there!
> Since dem tief me from a Guinea
> Me can't go there.
>
> If me wan't for go in a Congo
> Me can't go there!
> Since dem tief me from my tatta
> Me can't go there!

Other work-songs run:

> Guinea corn I long to turn you,
> Guinea corn I long to eat you.
>
> Two man a road, Cromanty boy
> Two man a road, fight for you lady.

The names Iboland, Guinea, Congo, Cromanty (Coromanti) lead us back to West Africa, whence came the ancestors of most African-Jamaicans and to Kormantine, the port on the Gold Coast (Ghana) from which many of them were shipped.

The words that we use everyday confirm the origins of the folk songs, especially the names of plants, foods, utensils, spirits; afu (yam) yampee, bissy (kola nut), ackra (cakes) fufu (yam cooked and pounded), susumba, ockra, duckunu, gingy (fly), senseh (fowl), bankra (basket), abeng, nyam (eat), bufu-bufu (clumsy) and tata (father). Some forms of expression have parallels in West Africa. The Twi language, for example, has only three parts of speech, nouns, pronouns and verbs, which often do duty as adjectives, prepositions, and the like. We have parallel forms in, for instance, "duck picney"; and the prepositions "here" and "there" sometimes become "dis end" or "dat end", in "ah nebba walk dat end".

As Cassidy points out, the English part of the vocabulary of Jamaica talk is overwhelmingly the largest, but of non-British influences the African is the largest and most profound; it appears not only in the vocabulary but also in pronunciation and grammar. More than half of the Africanisms identified appear to be from the Twi language which is spoken by the Ashanti, Akwapim, Fante and Akyem. It was along the stretch of coast from Takorida to Lagos, formerly the Gold Coast, that "the Europeans built the greatest concentration of fortifications anywhere on the African coast – drawn by the gold trade to the interior and the existence of a series of rocky points with moderately safe landing beaches on the lee side or by an occasional lagoon or river mouth where lighters could load and unload in security." (Curtin: 1969)

The map shows the chief trading areas on the West African coast. Starting from the north they were modern Senegambia (Senegal and Gambia); modern Sierra Leone, which included the coastal region of Guinea-Conakry, Guinea-Bissau and a small part of Liberia; the Windward Coast which included the modern Ivory Coast and Liberia; the Gold Coast, or present-day Ghana; the Bight of Benin including today's

States of
West Africa

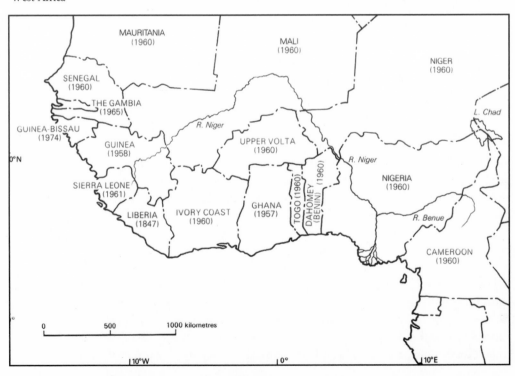

The Story of the Jamaican People

Togo and Benin; the Bight of Biafra which included the Niger Delta and the mouths of the Cross and Duala Rivers, bounded by the Benin River on the west and Cape Lopez, and from Cape Lopez south to the Orange River, the area known as Angola (Central Africa). On the Indian Ocean side the trading areas ran from the Cape of Good Hope to Cape Delgado, including the island of Madagascar.

So large is the region, and so many were the trading areas, that African-Americans can claim many and different ancestral homelands. African-Brazilians have their closest ties with Angola, African-Americans of South Carolina with Angola and the Bight of Benin and African-Americans of Virginia with Senegambia and the Bight of Biafra.

Jamaica's closest ties are with Ghana and the Akan-Ashanti people, with the Yoruba, Ibo and Ibibio of Nigeria and the Niger Delta, and with some tribes of Central Africa. Between 1751 and 1790 while only about a quarter of the total English slaves delivered in the New World went to Jamaica, about 80 per cent of these came from the Gold Coast. (Curtin: 1969)

If we were to travel north from Takorida or Accra, we would pass through three distinct vegetation zones before coming to Timbuctu or Gao on the southern borders of the Sahara. First there is a green belt of tropical rain forest some 200 miles wide; then the forest gives way to savanna grassland, but not cropped grass as in the pastures of St Ann, Trelawny, Manchester; but, giant grass that stands from 6-10 feet tall and reaches 50 feet on the savanna of Guinea. Finally we come to the Sahel, "the shore of the desert", arid country inhabited by the pastoral nomad Fulani. North of the Sudan lies the world's largest desert, the Sahara, which is traversed by ancient camel routes that linked powerful trading cities such as Timbuctu, Gao and Jenne with Tangiers, Algiers, Tunis and Tripoli on the coast of the Mediterranean.

Imagine that we are at Takorida, a seaport of Ghana. We are about to set out on a journey through Ghana and Nigeria, the ancestral homelands of African-Jamaicans and of most West African people, among them the Ashanti, Ewe, Fon, Egba Oyo, Ibo and Ibibio and Yoruba. It is a journey through a landscape, but more importantly, it is a journey back across four centuries, to the early days of the arrival of the Portugese and the beginning of the Atlantic Slave Trade.

It is a painful journey to make, one full of suffering and agony, but it is a journey that all African-Americans should make in their minds if they wish to understand the magnitude of the African-Americans' achievement, if they seek to discover the significance of the African heritage, and if they wish to liberate themselves fully from the self-doubts and ambiguities engendered by enslavement, colonialism and racial discrimination.

At the heart of the story of the African-Jamaican and the African-American is the fact that deep within him, nurtured by his experience and culture, there was "an irreducible core of free, creative, spontaneous human nature, of some elementary sense of identity, dignity and worth" (Hausheer: 1982) that empowered him to resist, and eventually to defeat, those who sought to transform him, a person, into a useful tool, a slave. The African-Jamaican and African-American liberation wars are an inspiring part of the rejection of that attempt at dominance, but not the whole of it. It is a mark of Marcus Garvey's greatness that he saw that total liberation involved recognising the centrality of Africa and the significance of the African heritage.

Our imaginary journey becomes, then, a search for roots, for that sense of historical continuity which in turn nurtures a sense of identity and of worth. In our journey we will bear in mind that human beings are "defined precisely by their possession of an inner life, of purposes and ideals, and of a vision or conception, however hazy or implicitly, of who they are, where they came from, and what they are at. Indeed, it is just their possession of an inner life in this sense that distinguishes them from animals and natural objects". (Hausheer: 1982)

Our guides and companions are two West Indians who lived and worked in West Africa: the historian Walter Rodney and the poet-historian Edward Kamau Brathwaite.

Walter Rodney, for a time professor of history at the University of Dar-es-Salaam in Tanzania, opens our eyes to the impact of the Atlantic Slave Trade on African social and political life and helps us to understand how it came about that Africans captured and sold Africans to the slave-traders.

> Europeans obtained slaves in Africa, on the one hand, by stimulating a demand for the manufactured goods they had to offer, and, on the other hand, by exploiting the tribal and religious divisions and the incipient class contradictions within African society . . . In general, however, it seems clear that the prospects of profit from the slave trade became so attractive that old rivalries were either revived or smoothed over, according to which was the most profitable.
>
> It is equally important to assess the manner in which slave-raiding affected people of different social levels within the hierarchical society of West Africa. For the vast majority it brought insecurity and fear, whether or not they were lucky enough to escape sale into slavery, because the slave trade meant violence in the form of skirmishes, ambushes and kidnapping – often carried out by professional man-hunters under the supervision of the ruling elites.

Walter Rodney draws our attention also to the fact that many members of the ruling class, who traditionally were responsible for maintaining stability and guaranteeing order, went into "partnerships of exploitation" with the Europeans. As time passed, for one reason or another the old ruling classes were replaced by a new class of men, sometimes drawn from within local society as in the Niger Delta, sometimes from the ranks of professional slave traders of part European origin: African-Portuguese, African-English, African-Brazilian. What mattered was "the skill and devotion with which they served the capitalist system".

The Atlantic Slave Trade corrupted many of the ruling classes of West Africa and corrupted West African society at the lower levels by increasing the number of servile societies. "Fulas of the Futa-Djalon and the Nike of Eastern Nigeria still kept a large labour force in conditions of bondage."

With Walter Rodney's analysis in mind, we turn to Edward Kamau Brathwaite, who in his trilogy *Rights of Passage*, *Masks* and *Islands* travels from the Americas to West Africa, claims his heritage and then returns. In *Masks* the poet tells of his journey from Takorida, one of the seaports of Ghana, to his birthplace. Knowing how deeply religious the African is, the poet begins with prayers to the ancestors, Nana Firimpong, and to the Akan goddess of the earth, Asase Yaa.

> Nana Firimpong
> once you were here,
> hoed the earth
> and left it for me
> green rich ready
> with yam shoots, the
> tuberous smooth of cassava
> Asase Yaa,
> You, Mother of Earth
> on whose soil
> I have placed my tools
> on whose soil
> I will hope
> I will hope

After the prayers we come to the Akan ritual, the making of the drum, with the two curved sticks of the drummer, the gourds and the rattles; and throughout the poem Akan rites and rhythms transport us out of the culture of Europe into that of the Akan people. The beat of the talking drums

> Kon kon kon kon
> Kun kun kun kun

is followed by the great orchestral burst of a mmenson, an orchestra of seven elephant tusk horns used on state occasions to relate history.

> Summon now the Kings of the forest
> horn of the elephant,
> mournful call of the elephant,
> Summon the emirs, Kings of the desert,
> horses caparisoned, beaten gold bent;
> archers and cries, porcupine
> arrows, bows bent;
> recount now the gains the losses,
> Agades, Sokota, El Hassen dead in his tent,
> the silks and the brasses

To the steady haunting beat of the talking drums Africa appears before us and we witness the long desert migrations from the western Sudan to the Volta, and:

> the mouth of great rivers
> that smile, of forests
> where farms may be broken;
> deep lakes in those forests
> and plains where our cattle
> may graze

In a dramatic transition from this richly tapestried background the poet, today's African-American, seeks his birthplace and his kinsmen. He lands at Takorida where, first as in St Ann and Manchester, the green struggles through the red earth.

> Mammies crowded with cloths,
> flowered and laughed;
> white teeth
> smooth voices like pebbles
> moved by the sea of their language.
> Akwaaba they smiled
> meaning welcome . . .
> You who have come
> back a stranger
> after three hundred years

The mammies give him a stool on which to sit, water to wash his hands, food to eat:

> Here is plantain
> here palm oil
> red, staining the fingers,

good for the heat
for the sweat,
and they ask "Do you remember?"

He searches in vain for his kinsfolk:

tossed my net
but the net caught
no fish
I dipped a wish
but the well
was dry

Nightmare memories buried deep in the mind begin to stir. Korabra,
the signal drum often played at funerals, beats out its message "go and
come back" and

Back
through Elmina,
white granite stone
stalking the sun
light, the dungeon unbars
the whips of the slavers
see the tears
of my daughters . . .
My scattered
clan, young
-est kinsmen,
fever's dirge
in their wounds,
rested here;
Then limped on
down to their dungeon.

What flaws in the ancestors, what flaws in himself, brought about this
enslavement? Osei Tutu, founder of the Ashanti nation, enters to shouts of
praise, Osee Yei, Osee Yei. He asks:

When the worm's knife cuts
the throat of a tree, what will happen?
It will die
When a cancer has eaten the guts
of a man, what will surely happen?
He will die
My people, that is the condition of our
country today

it is sick at heart, to its bitter clay
we cannot heal it or hold it together
from curses
because we do not believe in it

In that moment of self-discovery, from the compound where his mother
buried his birth cord under gravel, the poet asks:

why did the god's
stool you gave us,
Anokye,
not save us from pride,
foreign tribes' bibles,
the Christian god's hunger
eating the good of our tree

With self-discovery, with the claiming of the African birthright, comes
a sense of identity. The self-doubts engendered by enslavement fall away.
Revitalised by his renewed identification with Africa, the poet sings of the
coming of dawn and the symbol of life:

As the cock
now cries in the early dawn
so slowly slowly
ever so slowly
I will rise
and stand on my feet
akoko bob opa
(the cock crows in the early dawn)
akoko tua bon
(the cock rises and crows)
I am learning
Let me succeed.

Making our African pilgrimage, we need to look more closely at our
African kinsfolk and ancestors. We begin with the three ancient empires of
Ghana, Mali and Songhai. "There can be no doubt that throughout the
period under discussion (the tenth century to the time of the Moroccan
invasion of 1591) the dominating political, economic and cultural initia-
tives and influences stemmed from these three great empires. There seems
no question in fact that the empires of Ghana, Mali and Songhai rank
among the highest achievements of Negro Africans in history." (Fage:
1969)

Ancient Ghana, a kingdom of the early Sudan (from which the Gold
Coast took its name after independence in 1957) had its beginnings

among the Soninke people, hunters and food-gatherers from a period a thousand years or more BC. "Somewhat about 300 B.C. an increasing population, the demands of food-production and attacks by Libyco-Berbers led the Soninke to elect their first King." (Wallace and Hinds) The Soninke were fighting people, so they were able to gain control of the trans-Saharan trade, from which they gained a substantial revenue. Furthermore, technologically they were a jump ahead of their neighbours, for in their wars they used iron technology, spears and arrows tipped with iron. In addition, they deployed the horse, as cavalry, as well as foot-soldiers in their army. Nor was their revenue limited to their share of the trans-Saharan trade, for to the south, within easy reach, were the agricultural and gold-bearing lands of the Upper Niger and the Senegal rivers. By the tenth century AD the empire of Ghana had expanded and was widely known and respected in other parts of Africa and in the Middle East. This was a century or more before William the Norman conquered the English and possibly two centuries before Tainos began their migration from the basin of the Orinoco to the Caribbean archipelago. Two of the trades that brought Ancient Ghana glory, slaves and gold, belong to an even earlier period when Carthaginians, Greeks and Romans were engaged in commerce along the North African coast. A Greek merchant from Alexandria, Cosmas, who became a monk, wrote in AD 525 a vivid description of the "silent trade", the gold trade. His account, one of the classics of African history, engenders in us a sense of the mystery and antiquity of the African people and links us with the Queen of Sheba who brought to Solomon bars of ebony, spices and gold.

Every other year the king of Axum on the Red Sea sent agents south across the desert to bargain for gold.

> They take along with them to the mining district oxen, lumps of salt and iron, stop at a certain spot, make an encampment which they protect with a hedge of thorns, slaughter the oxen, cut the meat in pieces and lay the meat, lumps of salt and the iron on the hedge. Then come natives bringing gold in nuggets like peas, and lay one or two or more of these upon what pleases them . . . and then they retire to some distance off. Then the owner of the meat approaches, and if he is satisfied he takes the gold away and upon seeing that, the owner comes and takes the flesh or the salt or the iron. If however he is not satisfied he leaves the gold, when the native, seeing that he has not taken it, comes and either puts down more gold or takes up what he had laid down and goes away . . . The space of six months is taken up with this trading expedition . . . In going they march very slowly, chiefly because of the cattle, but in returning they quicken their pace lest on the way they should be overtaken by winter and its rains.

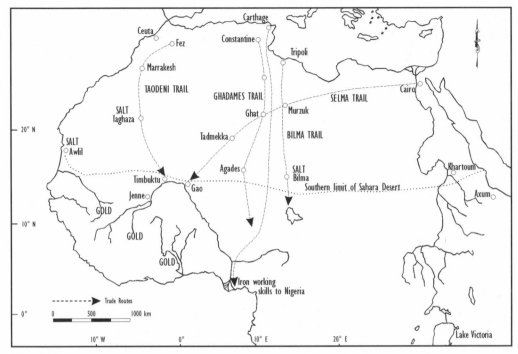

Trans-Saharan trading routes, tenth to eighteenth centuries

Another legend tells how Arab traders with goods and salt met the ancient Ghanian people, who guided them to special trading spots, signalled the opening of the market by beating large drums and then followed the procedure described by Cosmas.

The trade in gold and in slaves brought wealth and power to the Ghana, but in 1076 the empire was overrun by the Almoravids, a Berber Muslim dynasty that ruled Morocco and Muslim Spain and founded Marrakesh as the capital of their powerful empire. They dominated the caravan routes in the Sahara and, after a period of steady decline, the empire of Ghana fell apart.

The empire of Mali, which took over control of the area from Ghana, held sway over the important Niger-Timbuctu trade route, which also cut across trade routes that ran northwards from Ghana, where the Mande opened new gold mines about the middle of the fourteenth century. The Mali empire added to its wealth by levying tribute from other clans and their villages.

Although Mali had conquered the Songhai people, whose kingdom was on the banks of the Niger, between Gao and Dendi, the latter never accepted defeat. Their opportunity for revenge came when succession disputes destroyed the unity of the empire of Mali. Between 1494 and 1528 two Songhai rulers, Sonni Ali and Askia Muhammed, established an empire as extensive as Mali's had been, with a powerful army and with full access to the profitable trans-Saharan trade. But after Askia Muhammed's death in 1528 Songhai, like Mali, was torn apart by succession disputes. In 1591 invaders from Morocco regained control of the salt mines of the Sahara and severely disrupted the trading system on which the Mali empire depended. Broken by internal disputes, it was unable to beat back an expeditionary force from Morocco which captured its three principal cities, Gao, Jenne and Timbuctu in 1591. These, and other royal pilgrimages to Mecca,

> might suggest that their purpose was primarily to further political and economic relations with North Africa. They certainly had this effect. They led, for instance to the transmission of regular embassies across the Sahara; to the establishment of hostels for Sudanese students in Cairo; to the coming of the Sudanic courts of men like, Es-Saheli (who is said to have built mosques and palaces at Timbuctu and Gao) and of other less well remembered advisers, technicians, clerics, jurists and simple adventurers: and they certainly led to an increase in trans-Saharan trade, particularly with Egypt. (Fage: 1969)

But these empires were not Islamic creations; although there was a degree of Islamization in all three empires. Whether we look at Ghana, Mali or Songhai, "these empires were in origin pagan creations which, once they had become established found a degree of Islamization convenient for reasons of State . . . But in its origin, the empire building process would seem to have been fundamentally a pagan reaction to the development of North African trade". (Fage: 1969)

The wealth and splendour of these three empires echo across the centuries in the accounts of Arab scholars and explorers. Most dazzling of all were the glittering pilgrimages to Mecca of the Mansa Musa of Mali in 1324 and of Askia Muhammed of Songhai in 1495-97.

Powerful empires emerged also in other parts of Africa. In 1484, when Portugese explorers reached a point south of the estuary of the Congo (Zaire) River they found the impressive empire of the Congo. South of the Congo there were several Bantu-speaking states and to the east well-organised kingdoms based on modern Zimbabwe; and in the region to the south-east of Salisbury (now Harare), was the famous empire of Mwenemutapa.

This widespread emergence of great kingdoms and empires called for a range of administrative skills and for sophisticated procedures by which a system of checks and balances put limits on the power of the supreme ruler. It called also for sensitivity and creativity in managing extensive commercial undertakings and training large armies that included cavalry.

In the Sudan, where the Muslims were dominant, systems of education and religious centres were established. Timbuctu, Jenne and Gao, for example, were internationally recognised centres of culture as well as powerful commercial cities.

Famous though they were, the ancient empires of Ghana, Mali and Songhai do not stir our emotions as deeply as do the names of the people who lived in the forest belt and the savanna south of the Niger, the Akan-Ashanti people, the Yoruba, the Ibo, as well as the names of kingdoms such as Oyo and Benin, homes of the glorious terracottas and bronzes of Ibo and Benin that are supreme examples of human artistic creativity.

Akan-Ashanti people moved into the forest belt in the region north of Accra in the eleventh and twelfth centuries AD and established small scattered communities and trades with the savanna kingdoms of the north. To the south of them, along the coast, lived small clans and states that owed allegiance to the forest dwellers. It was with these small clans that the Europeans first traded.

Toward the end of the seventeenth century, in the years when Jamaica was turning from cocoa-walks to sugar plantations, the Ashanti came under pressure from the Denkyira people, who were supplying the Europeans with slaves. Two remarkable leaders, the warrior-statesman Osei Tutu, and a priest, Okampo Anokye, saw that the only hope for the Ashanti lay in unity. First, Osei Tutu led the united Ashanti to victory over their neighbours. Then Anokye provided them with a powerful symbol of national unity, the golden stool. He took three cuttings of the kumnini tree and planted one each at Kwaman, Juaben and Kumawa. Those at Juaben and Kumawa grew. This was taken as a sign that Osei Tutu was the leader chosen by the gods, and from that day Kwaman became Kumasi, the name meaning "under the Kumnini tree".

Soon after this a great gathering was held at Kumasi. There Anokye brought down from the sky, with darkness and thunder, a wooden stool adorned with gold, which floated to the earth and alighted gently on Osei Tutu's knees. The stool, declared Anokye, contained the spirit of the whole Ashanti nation. In this way Anokye impressed on the divided Ashanti clans the fact that they were a nation, united by a religious bond of which the golden stool was the symbol. This was the origin of the Sika Agua Kofi (Friday's golden stool) of the Ashanti.

The rulers of the Ashanti showed great skill in fostering the sentiment of national unity among the various Akan-speaking groups. They forbade them to promote their individual loyalties while the king, Osei Tutu, the Asantahene or king, took care to build up an army in which the recruits, who were drawn from the various groups, were trained together. The Asantahene, or king, governed with the help of a well-run bureaucracy

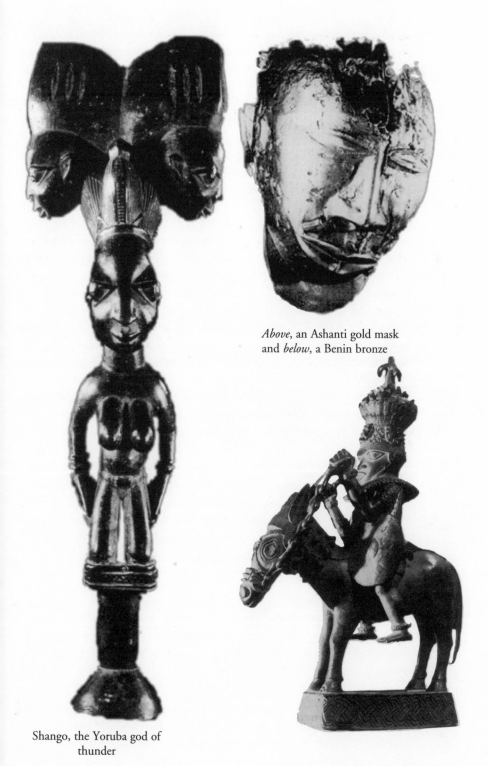

Above, an Ashanti gold mask and *below*, a Benin bronze

Shango, the Yoruba god of thunder

headed by a confederacy council. He derived his authority from the golden stool, and the office was hereditary, but he did not have absolute authority. The chief decision-making body within the government was an executive council or inner cabinet.

The Yoruba also developed a highly centralised political system in this period. The process began with the emergence, in the middle of the seventeenth century, of Oyo as the dominant power of Yorubaland. It drew much of its strength from the fact that it commanded the caravan routes which linked the Guinea Coast with the trans-Saharan trade routes and so was able to impose fees on caravans and merchants passing through. It also became a slave-dealing state. The revenue it obtained from these sources enabled Oyo to build a powerful army that included cavalry and that was in part equipped with guns bought from the Europeans. By the year 1700 the empire of Oyo dominated most of Nigeria west of the Niger as well as part of Benin.

Like the Ashanti, the office of *alafin* (king) was hereditary but a system of checks and balances put limits on to his authority. He was assisted by the *oyo mesi*, a council of notables, which was headed by a prime minister who was also the high priest and controlled all the religious groups in Yorubaland except Sango and Ita. The army was controlled by the *oyo mesi*, not the *alafin*.

The Yoruba, who today number some 12 million people and form one of the largest African societies, are not a single tribe but groups of diverse people who are bound together by cultural and political ties.

> We have in the Yoruba an ancient people moving southward from the savanna into the forest. Immigrant groups and conquerors from without and inter-kingdom wars from within have all contributed to produce a kaleidoscopic pattern of cultures and structure that seem to defy classification into three or four basic types . . . yet there is a cultural uniformity among the various Yoruba groups that clearly differentiates them from their neighbours. Common language, dress, symbolism in chieftaincy and ritual unite them. (Lloyd: 1965)

The Yoruba are history-focussed people. At major festivals the achievements of the past are recited, so that generation after generation draws strength and cohesion from their knowledge of their history, as well as from the unifying influence of their towns. The Yoruba have always lived in towns, and they look down on those people who are without towns or kings. However, the towns are not industrial centres; they grow out of the countryside.

> A typical Yoruba town has 70% of its adult men engaged in farming and 10% each as craftsmen and traders. The smaller subordinate

towns of a kingdom usually have a slightly lower proportion of crafts-men and traders than has the metropolitan town. The farmlands of Ibadan extend for twenty miles from the town; those of a smaller town say of 20,000 inhabitants, probably four or five miles. When the farm is so far from the town compound, a small hamlet is built at the farm . . . The farm population commutes between town and farm. (Lloyd: 1965)

But with over 50 different kingdoms in Yorubaland what is true of Ibadan and Abeokuta may not apply to other towns, such as Ijebu Ode and Ondo.

In contrast with Jamaica, Yorubaland is almost wholly given up to peasant farming. There are no large-scale economic units. About three out of every four adult men are farmers, the others become traders, black-smiths, woodcarvers, and the like.

For women the traditional crafts are pottery, spinning, dyeing and weaving on a vertical loom. Unlike most African societies, the women do no farm work. They trade in foodstuffs and in cloth, the men in meat-buying and in buying export crops such as cocoa and palm-oil kernels.

The markets are a joy and a perpetual surprise because of their size; sometimes there are as many as a thousand sellers, most of them women, for most of the marketing is in their hands and it may be a full-time occupation from which they may become independently wealthy.

East of Yorubaland, in eastern Nigeria, lies Iboland, a large region that extends from Lokoju, where the Benue River branches eastwards from the Niger, to the Cross River which empties into the Atlantic at Old Calabar, and from the swamp lands where the first yams are harvested and the crop is reaped by the end of August, the time of the New Yam Festival. The period of waiting from mid-May to August is the season of famine. The season between the end of August and mid-October is rain-time. The yam harvest continues up to mid-October, and in this period most of the women's small crops are harvested. From mid-October to February is the season of ceremonials and rest from farm work. During this period the bush on land that has been rested is cut and burned in preparation for cultivation, or heap-time.

Like the Yoruba, the Ibo are not a single people, but are made up of 200 or more groups that total more that 7 million people; but they differ markedly in many respects. The Yoruba religion has an elaborate hierarchy of gods, with Olorun (the owner of the sky) as the supreme god, with Shango the god of thunder and Ogun, the god of iron and war among them. The Ibo recognise forces or powers at work, but have no supreme god or hierarchies of gods; instead, there is a multitude of good and evil spirits, the most powerful of which have special shrines (orishas). The contrast extends to the ways in which political unity is secured. The Yoruba have a complex centralised kingdom and the Ibo have a close-knit kinship system that recognises descent from the mother as well as from the father and a network of associations that consult and take decisions together. Furthermore, whereas the Yoruba people are town-dwellers, the various Ibo societies live in dispersed village communities.

In order to understand the values that underlie Ibo society and the goals the Ibo people set themselves, let us look at an Ibo writer's revealing portrait of himself and his people.

> Once a young man has attained the age of reason, his parents become strict with him. He is taught the value of a busy life. Every youth, even the son of the richest man of his community, must acquire the lifelong taste of manual work. You very rarely find an Ibo man or woman begging for alms. An Ibo prefers to die than to be idle. Even the lame and crippled work for their existence. The blind find themselves work in their communities. This pride enhances the prestige of an Ibo wherever he goes . . .
>
> The Ibo looks proud because he is bred in a free atmosphere where everyone is another's equal. He hates to depend on anyone for his life needs. He does not mind if others look proud. He has much to be proud of in his land. Nature has provided for him. He is strong and able to work or fight. He is well formed. He is generally happy in his society where no ruler overrides his conscience. He likes to advance and he is quick to learn. He likes to give rather than take. (Udeagu: 1960)

From these West African nations came the men and women who left us a priceless heritage of courage and achievement. Their West African background of self-respect and self-confidence equipped the women for leadership. Many West African countries "held and still hold a high opinion of women and especially of the mother. Among such nations the most vital event of a woman's life is bearing a child . . . For without the great gift of children, the family, the tribe, the nation will die. The mother and the child are both precious". (Mathurin-Mair:1986)

The West African woman was leader as well as mother. Many of these societies have a matrilineal form of inheritance, by which property is passed on through the female members. The tribal history of the ancient kingdom of Kongo or of the Ashanti tells of women who were leaders of their nation, such as the old mother of the tribe, Mpemba Nzinga, who founded the kingdom of Kongo, and the queen mother of the Ashanti whose stool was for long superior to the king's, or the women of the royal household of Dahomey who exercised enormous influence because they were in charge of the nation's taxes. As Mathurin points out, when African men and women entered the Caribbean "they were already educated and steeped in their national culture. The culture contained among much else a tradition of warrior nations and a history of proud and respected women. This sort of heritage produced rebels and ensured that there would always be women among the rebels".

CHAPTER 11

The Atlantic Slave Trade

Slavery, or trading in persons, is as old as man. It was not limited to one race or one class of people. It was not for blacks only. Slavery recognised no colour bar. In the view of the ancients it was a law of nature to which all human beings were subject. Europe, Asia and Africa all contained slave-taking and slaveholding societies. There were internal and external slave markets centuries before an Atlantic Slave Trade came into existence. The slaves – men, women and children – were of many races and colours. Celts, Nubians, Africans, Numidians and Gauls were all to be found in the slave markets of the Old World, throughout the Mediterranean, the Black Sea region, the Middle East, India and the Far East.

Originally the term "Slav" denoted a member of the largest linguistic and ethnic European group, which included Slovaks, Serbs, Croats, Bulgars, Ukrainians, Russians and Byelorussians. In the twelfth century the Germans drove the Slavs east of the River Elbe, destroying many and enslaving others. The word "slave", which is identical with the racial name, means one who is the property of, and entirely subject to another person, whether by capture, purchase or birth. Slavery, which existed amongst both primitive and advanced peoples, is the most extreme form of lack of freedom, other forms being subjection, servanthood and serfdom.

An African scholar, Mbaye Gueye, has pointed out, as have others, that the slave trade was a very ancient practice in Africa, but that before foreign intervention it was carried out on a fairly small scale. It was chiefly a means of reintegrating into society individuals who had been cut off from their families following a war or some other catastrophe.

> The African ideal is that of a community existence based on power-ful family ties with a view to a well-ordered, secure life . . . In these conditions a man on his own formerly had no chance of survival. Enslaving people whom natural or other disasters had cast adrift was a useful means of providing them with a social framework . . . Those

who purchased them gave them a new identity. The slave would give up his own patronym for that of the new master.

It was the steadily increasing demand for slaves as a result of foreign intervention in the affairs of the continent which brought about a fairly substantial increase in the volume of the trade. (Gueye: 1986)

Such intervention led to the dispersal of African people through the Middle East and parts of Asia, some by way of the Indian Ocean, others by trans-Saharan routes to North Africa. African slaves were to be found as far afield as the valley of the Ganges, in the eleventh and twelfth centuries after the Muslim conquest of that region. Ethiopian slaves, in particular, were in wide demand as soldiers; indeed, from 1486 to 1493 two soldiers of African origin ruled over Bengal.

Africans were to be found working on plantations in Persia, in Basra and the coastlands, in the pearl-fishing industry in Bahrain and elsewhere in the Persian Gulf, as soldiers in Arabia, as dock workers and among the crews of boats in the Arab-controlled Indian Ocean, as labourers and household servants in Muslim communities throughout Asia. None was engaged in producing large-scale commodities, save, for a time, in the salt mines of the Sahara and, in the ninth century, in the salt works of Persia.

African slaves played varied roles in the economy and even in politics and culture. They made a notable contribution to the success of the Muslim armies in North Africa. In Ibrahim Kake's words,

> Black troops recruited in Egypt and Nubia were the backbone of the army which invaded North Africa. This force provided the sovereigns of Spain and the Maghreb with the disciplined, loyal and brave element which their armies lacked. In the eighth century . . . the

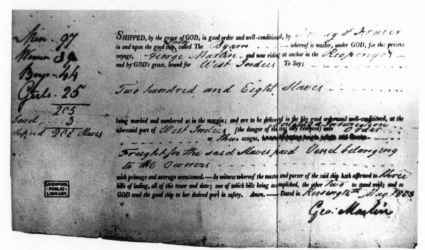

Nineteenth-century slave ship bill of sale

founder of the Caliphate of Spain rescued the Spanish peninsula from anarchy with their help and the sovereigns of this dynasty also had many blacks brought from the interior of Africa and shaped them into a formidable cavalry corps.

These old African slave trades differed in several important ways from the later Atlantic Slave Trade. The African was placed in long-established communities from which escape was difficult. The alternative to escape was acculturation, a process which was made easier for the African because generally he endured household slavery, not plantation slavery. He was a second- or third-class citizen, but regardless of colour or race he was integrated into the social life of the community in which he worked; and he was inferior because of his status as a slave, not because of his colour.

In contrast, the Atlantic Slave Trade scattered the enslaved Africans through plantation America, with its large estates and pioneering communities. It was a world in which blackness was a badge of inferiority and colour determined status.

In this chapter some essential features of the Atlantic Slave Trade are described, its genesis and the nature of its impact on West Africa, the volume and methods of the trade and the chief host areas in the Americas.

The Atlantic Slave Trade began in 1415, when the Portuguese conquered Ceuta, opposite Gilbraltar. Thrusting south from Ceuta on the Western Mediterranean, they soon came into contact with Africans. Being devout Catholics, it was a religious duty to take Muslim prisoners. A Portuguese historian, François da Veiga Pinta, tells us that the negroes to be captured were taken by men convinced that they were doing a great feat and also a virtuous deed, since every one of the "wretches" baptised meant a soul won for God . . . surprise attacks were made on isolated nomad camps and the captives brought back to Portugal with "the holy purpose of saving lost souls". But the lost souls were also a source of profit. It was Nuño Tristao who in 1441 brought back the first negroes direct from the coast of Africa south of Cape Bojador. Later, in 1443, the island of Arguin was discovered and on 8 August 1444, the first public sale of slaves was held at Lagos. (da Veiga Pinta: 1979)

In this way Portugal pioneered European slave trading on the West African coast. Using African slaves, Prince Henry the navigator introduced sugar cultivation into the recently discovered islands of Madeira and the Azores. The demand for sugar grew rapidly. The plantation economy encouraged the trade in slaves, the slaves made possible the expansion of the plantation and an Atlantic sugar-and-slave trade was born. Before long, the Portuguese changed the method of slave-trading by giving up the kidnapping of Africans and engaging in barter.

Once the Portuguese realised that they could acquire slaves by a peaceful exchange of goods which the chiefs . . . were avid for, a regular trade began to operate. There was, after all, a meeting of supply and demand: for slavery formed part of the social system of Senegambia and Guinea and it was normal to sell one's own kind if they were prisoners of war or were under sentence for adultery, or felonies or magical reasons. (da Veiga Pinta: 1979)

In this early period the long-established trans-Saharan trade in slave and gold was in contact with the infant Atlantic trade. Some of the gold and slaves taken in raids by the Islamized people of the Sahel were sent by caravans to Arguin for sale to the Portuguese.

By 1455 Portugal was importing 700-800 African slaves a year; between 1450 and 1500 about 150,000 slaves were imported. The crown wished to control the increasing trade and to make a profit from it, but not to manage it, so in order to reduce the risk it farmed out the business.

In 1469 the king of Portugal granted a five-year contract to Fernao Gomes for an annual lump sum payment and an obligation to discover a hundred leagues of the West African coast every year. (In a similar way Spain later adopted the contract system or *asiento* in an attempt to control the slave trade).

The pace of sugar production and of exploration quickened after the colonisation of São Tome in 1483 by a strange assortment of deported Portuguese Jewish children, called "new Christians", who were married off to slaves brought in from Guinea and the Congo. The Sâo Tome people, most of them of mixed race, later became slave-dealers.

Portugal soon became one of the great powers of Europe. Its seamen had rounded the Cape of Good Hope in 1486 and opened up trade with the Far East, bringing back silks and spices to Lisbon, while others brought in supplies of gold and Africans from the Guinea Coast. The country was entering its golden age. These are global events: the dawning of the age of Europe, the establishment of world financial capitals following on the dethronement of Mediterranean Venice and the rise of Antwerp and the promotion of a modern sugar industry by the Florentines and Genoese.

This conquest of Africa and the Atlantic Islands was essentially achieved by the Florentines, the Genoese and even, in the case of the Azores by the Flemish. It was after all the Genoese who had first promoted the spread of sugar plantations from the Eastern Mediterranean to Sicily, southern Spain, Morocca, the Portuguese Algarve and eventually to Madeira and the Cape Verde Islands. (Braudel: 1982)

Genoese bankers gained control of the wholesale business of Lisbon and of Portugal's retail trade. In this period Portugal created a coherent economic zone based on West Africa and the Atlantic islands, expanded it by adding the vast reserve of manpower in the Congo and Angola and then tied it to Brazil on the western side of the Atlantic. World trade routes were dramatically altered and the Atlantic trade system was established, at the base of which stood the African, without whose labour neither money nor technology would have availed.

When the Portuguese reached the mouth of the Zaire (Congo) River, they were astonished to come upon the well-organised, powerful kingdom of the Kongo. The touch of Europe carried death with it to the Kongo and its ruler as it had done to Montezuma and the Kingdom of the Aztecs and to Atahualpa and the Incas. A Portuguese historian, sensitive to the tragedy of the Kongo, tells how a special relationship developed between the Portuguese monarchy and the African monarch, Dom Afonso, who wished to modernise his country while preserving its independence.

> Several members of the Royal House went to Lisbon and Catholicism became the state religion. Nevertheless the real interests of the Portuguese crown in the early sixteenth century were elsewhere and, although the King of Portugal kept up a correspondence with the Manikongo and sent him missionaries and craftsmen, Dom Afonso's hopes were disappointed and his country fell inescapably into a decline . . . the Manikongo's hopes of giving his people access to white skills and so bringing his people out of their isolation were cruelly betrayed. Moreover the Kingdom of Kongo had no other goods to offer except slaves; and once it engaged in this trade it was bound, sooner or later, to be at the mercy of the law of supply and of demand and of various competing interests, both abroad in the shape of slave traders and at home in the shape of neighbouring peoples also involved in the trade. (da Veiga Pinta: 1979)

Dom Afonso ruled until 1543. He curbed the slave trade within his kingdom and repudiated it in letters to the Portuguese, but the São Tome settlers established themselves as slave traders along the Congo River and in the kingdom, and after the king's death the Kongo kingdom fell apart under attacks from neighbours seeking to take prisoners-of-war to exchange for European goods. Many traders also went to Angola, which was more densely populated.

Portugal held the monopoly of the trade and a powerful bond developed between it, Angola and Brazil. Thus this triangular trade expanded: Africa was the source of manpower; the Caribbean and Brazil were producers of the plantation commodities; and Europe was the market for commodities and the source of manufactured goods. Later, by smuggling, piracy and war, the Dutch, English, French and also other European powers chiselled away at the Portuguese and Spanish trade and possessions. At the beginning of the seventeenth century the Dutch-Portuguese war broke Portugal's monopoly of the Atlantic Slave Trade. It kept an important part of it, however, through the many linkages the Portuguese and Brazilians had built up with the African centres of supply.

Many fierce conflicts arose between the European powers in their attempts to control the slave trade and to grab each other's sugar colonies. They include Holland's capture of Portugal's empire in the Far East, in Angola and North-East Brazil between 1630 and 1641; the entry of the Manikongo Garcia of the Congo on the side of Holland, with whom he established diplomatic contact; the extraordinary Queen Nzinga in Angola who rallied allies to her side and established her power; the uprising of Portuguese settlers in Brazil who drove out the Dutch and sent three expeditions across the Atlantic to reoccupy the main trading centres in Angola and the mouth of the Congo. Then, in 1713 at the Treaty of Utrecht, England gained the Spanish *asiento* (contract) for supplying slaves to the Spanish Indies.

The methods of capture or sale varied from region to region. In Senegambia, for example, the Lalinke (Mandingo), who were dominant, used the following methods: general pillage, which was executed by order of the king, when slaving vessels were on the coast; robbery by individuals; and strategies of deceit on the part of both kings and individuals.

Records from the Gold Coast show that some of the local people, the Fante, were sold because they were in debt, or were charged – rightly or wrongly – with thefts, adultery or witchcraft; but the majority offered for sale were from tribes in the interior whose countries bordered on the Fante or on people nearer the coast.

The slaves were kept in barracoons at trading centres. At Sierra Leone, for example:

> The slaves when brought here have chains put on three or four linked together, under the care of Negro Servants, till opportunity for sale, and then go at about 15 Pounds a good slave, allowing the buyer 40 or 50 percent advance on his goods . . . As the slaves are placed under Lodges near the Owner's House, for Air, cleanliness and customers better viewing them, I had every day the curiosity of observing their behaviour, which with most of them was very dejected. (Atkins: 1986)

Kings, chiefs and ordinary traders were involved. The captain of a slave ship gave this account of a visit to Calabar in 1735 and of dealing with the king.

At two o'clock we fetched the King from shore, attended by all his caboceiros and officers, in three large canoes; and entering the ship, was saluted with seven guns. The King had on an old-fashioned scarlet coat, laced with gold and silver, very rusty, and a fine hat on his head, but bare-footed; all his attendants showing great respect to him and, since our coming hither, none of the natives have dared to come aboard of us, or sell the least thing, till the King had adjusted trade with us.

The price of provisions and wood was also regulated. Sixty King's yams, one bar; one hundred and sixty slaves's yams, one bar; for fifty thousands yam to be delivered to us. A butt of water, two rings. For the length of wood, seven bars, which is dear; but they were to deliver it ready cut into our boat. For a goat, one bar. A cow, ten or eight bars, according to its bigness. A Hog, one bar. A calf, eight bars. A jar of palm oil one bar and a quarter. (Hart: 1980)

Along the Guinea coast cotton cloth served as money. Slave traders used the term "piece of India" to mean the amount of cotton goods that was equal to the price of a man; then it came to be applied to a male slave, physically fit, who was between 15- and 40-years-old. English merchants worked out a tariff in the early years of the eighteenth century that fixed the price of a captive "piece of India" at 4 ounces of gold, 30 piasters of silver, ¾ lb of coral, or seven pieces of Scottish cloth.

Physical suffering, anguish of spirit and unbearable cruelty were the lot of the slave from the time of his capture. Even at this distance in time it is difficult to read the chronicles and reports of the violence involved in the capture and treatment of the slaves in the depots and barracoons on the

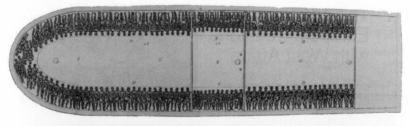

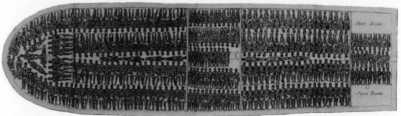

Plan of a slave ship indicating how densely packed the slaves were

West African coast and aboard the slave ships, called by the Portuguese "floating tombs."

The mortality rate on the Middle Voyage from Africa to the West Indies was high. "The recent literature on the slave trade tends to put the mortality rate at sea somewhere between 13 per cent and 33 per cent . . . mortality rates varied greatly according to the route, the length of the voyage, the original disease environment of the slaves themselves, the care they received and the chance recurrence of epidemics." (Curtin: 1969) Mortality rate amongst crew members was also high, possibly as high as 20 per cent.

Africans on a slave ship

And the living cargo, the slaves who survived? One of the best-known accounts was written by an African, Olaudah Equiano, who was born in the interior of Nigeria. He was kidnapped while still a boy, taken to Benin and there sold into slavery. Years later he obtained his freedom and wrote an account of his capture, of the Atlantic crossing and of his sale in Barbados. We keep company with Equiano on his Atlantic crossing.

> The first object which saluted my eyes when I arrived on the coast was the sea and a slave ship which was then riding at anchor and waiting for its cargo. These filled me with astonishment which was soon converted into terror when I was carried on board. I was immediately handled and tossed up to see if I were sound by some of the crew, and I was now persuaded that I had got into a world of bad spirits, and that they were going to kill me. Their complexions too, differing so much from ours, their long hair and the language they spoke . . . united to confirm me in this belief . . . When I looked around the ship and saw a large furnace or copper boiling and a multitude of people of every description chained together, every one of their countenances expressing dejection and sorrow, I no longer doubted my fate, and quite overpowered with horror and anguish, I fell motionless on the deck and fainted. When I recovered a little I found some black people about me, who I believed were some of those who had brought me on board and had been receiving their pay . . . I was soon put down under the decks and there I received such a salutation in my nostrils as I had never experienced in my life . . . I became so sick and low that I was not able to eat, nor had I the least desire to taste anything . . . but soon to my grief two of the white men offered me eatables and on my refusing to eat one of them held me by the hand . . . and laid me across, I think the windlass, and tied my feet while the other flogged me severely.

One day, when we had a smooth sea and moderate wind, two of my wearied countrymen who were chained together (I was near them at the time), preferring death to such a life of misery, somewhat made through the nettings and jumped into the sea: immediately another quite dejected fellow, who on account of his illness was suffered to be out of irons, also followed their example. Those of us that were the most active were in a moment put down under the deck, and there was such a noise and confusion amongst the people of the ship as I never heard before, to stop her and get the boat out to go after the slaves. However two of the wretches were drowned, but they got the other and afterwards flogged him unmercifully for thus attempting to prefer death to slavery. In this manner we continued to undergo more hardships than I can now relate. (Gordon: 1986)

Between 1500 and 1880 ten to eleven million Africans were moved by force. The flow began in the early years of European expansion and continued through the first period of global integration which saw a worldwide diffusion of animals, plants, technology and diseases as well as of races. Our focus is on the movement of the Africans.

The years 1701-1810 formed the peak period and between 1741 and 1810 annual delivery rates were just over 60,000. A permanent drop to less than 40,000 a year came after the 1840s. About 60 per cent of all slaves delivered to the New World were transported during the century 1721-1820. Of the total, 80 per cent were landed between 1701 and 1850.

It is appropriate here to consider the division of functions, analysed by Joseph Inikori in *The Slave Trade and the Atlantic Economies.*

Slave branding irons

Western Europe overwhelmingly dominated trade, finance, transportation and manufacturing. Portuguese and Spanish America also did some trading and transportation . . . But their main function in the Atlantic system was the mining of precious metals and export staple in agriculture plantations. The middle and north-eastern states of North America . . . concentrated on commercial foodstuff production for export to the slave plantations of the West Indian islands, export and import trade, shipping, finance, ship-building, lumber production, fishing and later manufacturing. The southern states specialized in plantation agriculture, firstly tobacco but later mainly cotton. The special function of all the West Indian islands was plantation agriculture . . . Africa did not perform any real production function in the Atlantic system. Its function was limited to the acquisition and sale of slave labour . . . of all the territories under review only the north-eastern states of North America performed economic functions closely resembling those performed by Western Europe in the Atlantic system.

Further, as Inikori emphasises, the countries engaged mostly in plantation agriculture were also those in which "foreign factors of production were most largely employed." As a result, "The positive developmental effects of the Atlantic system were largely concentrated in Western Europe and North America". Indeed, the schooling of Africa and the West Indies in the Atlantic system was a preparation for colonialism, not for independence. What Inikori says about Africa can justly be said about Jamaica and her sister West Indian countries: "Institutions and habits inimical to economic development, which developed and became hardened during over 400 years of slave trade, became in later years great obstacles to economic transformation." (Inikori: 1979)

But a greater gulf than the Atlantic lay between the African in his homeland, sustained by the structures of everyday life, close to the ancestors and ancestral shrines, and the Africans stacked aboard the floating tombs, stripped and defenceless, bound for a strange land and doomed to serve a strange owner of another race for life. Equiano's story strikes at the heart.

> At last we came in sight of the island of Barbados, at which the whites on board gave a great shout and made many signs of joy to us. We did not know what to think to this, but as the vessel drew nearer we plainly saw the harbour and other ships of different kinds and sizes, and we soon anchored amongst them off Bridgetown. Many merchants and planters now came on board, though it was in the evening. They put us in separate parcels and examined us attentively.

They also made us jump, and pointed to the land, signifying we were to go there. We thought by this we should be eaten by these ugly men, as they appeared to us; . . . We were not many days in the merchant's custody before we were sold after their usual manner, which is this: On a signal given, (at the beat of a drum) the buyers rush at once into the yard where the slaves are confined, and make choice of that parcel they like best. In this manner, without scruple, are relations and friends separated, most of them never to see each other again. (Gordon: 1986)

Equiano must have had his sister in mind when he wrote that last sentence. She was playing with him when they were both kidnapped and then separated.

Equiano's account of his capture and sale brings home to us the severing of those forms of human relationship that were most precious to the African: the ties with family, kinsfolk, tribe, relationships that governed the behaviour, thinking and life of each individual African. So many were involved, and so surgical was the severance that historians often point to discontinuity as one of the chief features of West Indian history.

But the term "discontinuity" suggests too complete a break with Africa. It suggests a mechanical process, whereas the African diaspora was fundamentally a biological process of human adaptation that revealed the extraordinary capacity of the African people to respond to the challenge of radical change, of total uprooting, of life-threatening penalisations. Deep within the African there was an obstinate refusal to be subdued. From his mind, from his biological heritage came reactions, attitudes and a creativity that spoke of Africa. The African diaspora resulted in a profoundly significant Africanising of the Americas.

In order to see the extent and depth of Africa's impact through the Atlantic Slave Trade and in order to understand also the heroic quality of the African-Americans, the enslaved Africans in the British North American colonies should be compared with the white indentured servants. Indenture was a form of servitude that was most common in Maryland, in the eighteenth century. In Pennsylvania and Virginia in 1683, one-sixth of the population was made up of white serfs. In the colonies south of New England more than one-half of all persons who migrated were indentured servants. Their servitude was limited, whereas African slaves were forced into perpetual servitude. Unlike the indentured servant, they were completely at the mercy of the master. They had neither legal nor property rights. They were drawn from every stratum of African society and not from a lower class of humble origin. They also formed a sizeable minority: in 1765 some 400,000 blacks compared with 1,450,000 whites in the northern colonies. "All but a tiny fraction were chattel slaves, fully seven-eighths of them living in the five southernmost colonies. In South Carolina they outnumbered the white population by two to one. And even in the North, especially in New York, Rhode Island and Connecticut, they were counted in thousands. Slavery existed in law and fact in each of the thirteen colonies." (Rossiter: 1956)

Rossiter pointed to two features of slavery in America that characterised the sugar-and-slave plantation. The first was that until the very days of the Revolution few whites, "even the most sincere friends of liberty, thought it anything but natural that such a condition should exist . . . most speculation about natural rights and equality simply ignored the Negro". The second feature was that slavery, even where it brought economic benefits, encouraged wasteful agriculture, "created a miasma of fear in areas where Negroes were plentiful, hardened class lines, stunted the growth of the Southern middle class, cheapened respect for labour, and dehumanized man's sympathy for man in an age already inhuman enough". (Rossiter: 1956)

CHAPTER 12

The African-American liberation wars, 1660-1739

Among the great ennobling themes in human history none is more compelling, none grander, none more universal in its appeal than the love of freedom. It speaks all languages, animates people of all races. It inspired the revolts in the slave barracoons on the West African coast, the mutinies and suicides aboard the slave ships, and the series of risings that accompanied the dispersion of Africans throughout plantation America, from the Deep South of the United States to Brazil.

In the period of the English conquest of Jamaica (1655-65) this love of freedom inspired African-Jamaicans to deal with the invaders as free men and to demand the recognition of their freedom. Nearly two hundred years later it inspired Sam Sharpe to declare to his friend, the missionary Henry Bleby, that he "would rather die than be a slave". It is this central theme of the African-Jamaican's passion for freedom and justice that gives continuity and a sense of moral purpose to Jamaican history. It links African-Jamaicans with African-Americans in a kinship that derives from a shared historical experience, which defines for Jamaicans that bright constellation of principles of which Thomas Jefferson spoke: "equal and exact justice to all men, freedom of the press and freedom of person . . . They should be the creed of our political faith, the text of civil instruction, the touchstone by which we try the services of those we trust".

The struggle for freedom and justice took three forms: flight from the plantations and the establishment of free, strongly guarded strongholds, known in various parts of Hispanic America as *quilombos, mocambos, cumbes, palenques*; sabotage on the estates, the use of poison, arson, go-slows, destruction of property or damage to it and wilful misunderstanding of instructions; and insurrection. Some examples of peak achievements in marronage reveal the epic qualities of a widespread and long-continuing liberation movement.

The first example is from Brazil, where maroon settlements, called *quilombos*, date back to about 1575. There, as the estates multiplied and the mining of gold and precious stones increased, so the maroon settlements spread. The *quilombos* in the Minas region of Brazil, famous for its gold and gem mines, were well-organised, with a population of about 20,000 blacks drawn from every part of Brazil, each with its king, officers and ministers.

The largest and most famous of all the maroon settlements in Brazil was the Negro Republic of Palmares, whose history spans the eighteenth century. It was a collection of settlements spread across mountainous country, which made up an African political system whose inhabitants were the subjects of a king called Ganga-Zumba, great lord: "He is treated with all respect due to a Monarch and all the honours due a lord . . . He lives in the royal enclave called Macoco, the capital of Palmares."

Palmares resisted attack after attack but in its last 20 or so years, from 1672 to 1695, the pressure on it increased. The Portuguese began sending expeditions against the republic about every 15 months. In 1694 the capital held out for 42 days against a Portuguese expedition of 6,000 before it was finally taken and destroyed in 1695.

The Palmares republic stands out as a remarkable example of the ability of the African to create a centralised kingdom with an elected ruler out of a large number of people of various ethnic groups from Africa and from various cultural groups in Brazil. At the other end of the scale there were a large number of other *quilombos* and *mocambos*, which were small settlements of fugitive slaves, established in Bahia, Minas and other regions of Brazil.

Colombia, Panama and Mexico provide other examples. Domingo Benkos established a kingdom in Colombia at San Basilio, near Barquisimeto. Bayano in Darien, who was regarded with the reverence due to a king, extracted from the Spanish viceroy a peace treaty which stipulated that any black who was mistreated by his master would be allowed to buy his freedom for the same price that his master had paid for him, and that the maroons would be free men but would be bound by the Laws of the Indies. The treaty with Bayano was similar to that to which the Spanish provincial governor in Colombia agreed in 1717 with King Benkos: a general pardon and the conferring of freedom, providing the maroons refused to let new runaway slaves live among them.

The story was repeated in Mexico in the treaty with the redoubtable black leader Yanga, of whom it is said that if they had not captured him he would have been king in his own land. He had been the first slave to flee from his master. For 30 years he had gone free in the mountains and had united others called Yanguicos, who obeyed him as chief. There were about 60 huts in the settlements (*palengues*). These maroon colonies had been in existence for only nine months, yet the residents had already planted many seedlings and crop plants, cotton, sweet potatoes, chile, tobacco, squash, corn, beans, sugar cane and vegetables. The settlement was a war camp oriented to the needs of self-defence and retaliation, with a constant guard. The command of the men was in the hands of a black from Angola. Yanga kept civil administration in his own hands.

Yanga and his people fought off a Spanish expeditionary force from Vera Cruz. The conflict finally ended with a truce. Yanga agreed to stop raiding Spanish settlements and in return the Spanish leader Herrera agreed to return all of Yanga's people who had fled before September of the previous year (1608); his settlements were given the status of free towns with their own *cabildos* or councils and with Spanish laymen as magistrates. Yanga was appointed governor. The Franciscans were to minister to Yanga's people. The Crown was to finance the decoration of the church. Yanga's people undertook to help the Spanish authorities to capture fugitive slaves – for a fee.

Yanga's maroon movement was a notable incident in the history of the blacks in Mexico. It is "the only known example of a fully successful attempt by slaves to secure their freedom en masse by revolt and negotiation and to have it sanctioned and guaranteed in law. This experience demonstrates that under capable leadership, slaves could maintain an active guerrilla campaign, negotiate truce and win recognition of their freedom". (Davidson: 1973)

Yanga and the Yanguicos are no more, like those who bore the title of Ganga-Zumba. However, many of the maroon communities have merged with national groupings. The bush negroes of Suriname, some 60,000 or more in number, survive as vigorous communities and flourish in the forests that border on the Marrowine, Suriname and Saramacca Rivers. Most numerous are the Djuka and Saramacca tribes. The Matawai, Aluku and Paramaca are smaller. The various communities live in villages whose affairs are run by headmen and assistant headmen who are responsible to the chief of their tribe.

The ancestors of the largest tribes escaped in the late seventeenth and early eighteenth centuries from the plantations along the coast, sought freedom and security in the forests and through 50 years of guerrilla warfare fought off the government troops. Two early accounts, one by a bush negro, Johannes King, another by an English army captain, T. G. Stedman, enable us to understand more fully the maroon struggle. King describes days spent on the run, provision grounds destroyed by the bakras, the fierce excitement of a night raid on a bakra plantation, the killing of those slaves who would not go with them, the capture of men, women and children and of all the supplies they could carry; the nature of the relationship between the maroons and the plantation which was their enemy and which they raided from time to time for their supplies of iron pots, guns, machetes, gunpowder, bullets and women. It becomes clear why years spent in guerrilla warfare made peace and a settled way of life all the more precious, and why, when the Dutch government put out feelers about a treaty, the Djukas agreed. King's account reads:

> The bakras said they would not go shoot the negroes or fight with them anymore. But they too must cease their fighting with the bakras and must no longer raid plantations or take more of the bakras' slaves back to the bush. And whenever a plantation slave ran off to join them they must not harbour him; they must bring him back to the bakras. And if a slave from the city ran off to them, they must return him to the bakras and the bakras would pay them for that. The government's forests were all open to them, and the Bush Negroes along the upper courses of the rivers could do whatever they wanted. In other words they were free to clear the underbrush, cut lumber, fell trees, make horticultural camps, clear gardens, and plant crops. They could do any work they were able to do and bring things to sell in the city . . . But the government did not give the Bush Negroes permission to do as they liked along the lower courses of the rivers, where the tide was still visible and where the bakras themselves worked . . .
>
> The Bush Negroes were satisfied with the agreement and the bakras were satisfied too. It was good for them all. The bakras took a knife and cut their hands, drawing a little blood. They wiped it onto the inside of a glass. And then the blacks took a little blood the same way and put it in the glass. The bakras then swore upon the blood of the blacks, and the blacks swore upon the blood of the bakras. Then they mixed a little wine with blood and 'drank the oath'.
>
> When the forefathers got back safely to their villages they fired many salutes for the people who had waited at home. These people came to the bank of the river singing, to escort them to shore. They played drums, danced, blew African trumpets and sang, danced until nightime and the whole night until morning. (Stedman: 1973)

So pleased was the government that it distributed among the Djukas salt, cloth, guns, powder, shot, pots, knives, axes, cutlasses, adzes, grindstones, shovels, scissors, mirrors, large griddles for making cassava cakes and pans for cooking fish, cloth for hammocks, hammers, barrels of salt meat, barrels of salt cod, flintstones, nails, and the like.

A passage in Stedman's narrative reveals the desperate measures to which lack of supplies drove the bush negroes. He tells how, at dawn, after a skirmish, when the rebels dispersed, and the surgeons began to attend to the wounded, the reason why the casualties were so few was soon explained. The surgeons extracted very few leaden bullets but many pebbles, coat buttons and pieces of silver coin which had penetrated scarcely more than skin deep.

Stedman's estimate of maroon skills in guerrilla warfare brings to an end our account of the bush negroes.

> On the morning of the 22nd our commander ordered a detachment to cross the bridge and go on discovery on all hazards. Of this party I led the van. We now took the pass without opposition . . . We found ourselves in a large field of cassavas and yams, in which were about thirty houses, now deserted . . . In this field we separated into three divisions . . . And here, to our astonishment, we discovered the reason for the rebels shouting, singing and firing on the night of the 20th, was not only to cover the retreat of their friends by cutting off the pass, but by their unremitting noise to prevent us from discovering that they were employed, men, women and children, in preparing warimboes or hampers filled with the finest rice, yams and cassavas, for subsistence during their escape . . .
>
> This was certainly such a masterly trait of generalship in a savage people, whom we affected to despise, as would have done honour to any European commander, and has perhaps been seldom equalled by more civilised nations. (Stedman: 1973)

These examples show that the African liberation movement was not limited to any one African tribe but involved slaves of all categories and of diverse cultures. The maroon wars of Jamaica have an honoured place in that remarkable resistance movement. Alongside them stand the uprisings and rebellions of the plantation slaves, their demoralising use of sabotage, all a part of "an heroic challenge to white authority and the living proof of the existence of a slave consciousness that refused to be limited to the white's concept or manipulation of it". (Price: 1973)

CHAPTER 13

The African-Jamaican
liberation wars, 1650-1800

We move now to the harsh cockpit country of Jamaica, to the Land of Look Behind, Accompong, Maroon Town, to the forested slopes of the Blue Mountains, to Nanny Town, Kill Dead and Watch Hill, lonely places soon to become places of refuge for maroon bands.

The struggle of the African-Jamaicans for freedom began with the first groups of maroons in Spanish Jamaica, with Juan de Bolas, Juan de Serras and the Virmejales (Veremahollis Savanna) maroons. This phase extends to the 1660s, when the English granted de Bolas and his band full civil rights and 30 acres of land each.

The second phase began in the 1670s, when large numbers of Africans began to be imported to man the expanding sugar plantations. The population figures reflect the rising demand for labour. In 1658 there were about 1,400 black slaves in the island. The number rose to 8,000 in 1664 and levelled off, reaching 9,500 in 1673. Then the sugar-and-slave plantation swept in, lifting the number of blacks to 45,000 in 1703 compared with 8,000 whites. In the next 100 years, between 1701 and 1810, Jamaica alone imported 662,000 African slaves. In consequence, the second phase of marronage began in a period when the number of slaves greatly outnumbered the white owners.

Many of the imported Africans came from the region of modern Ghana, Nigeria and Benin which between 1660 and 1775 was the scene of large-scale tribal warfare. For a brief period the Akwamu were in control but by 1775 the young Ashanti nation overcame them and became the supreme military power among the Akan-speaking people of the Gold Coast and the Ivory Coast. This meant that they controlled the slave trade. "Ashanti thus deliberately became a slave dealing state. Many slaves were bought in the markets of the north, but many were obtained by raiding and warfare, and the great slave-market at Hanso, near Cape Coast, was largely kept supplied from the captives of the Ashanti Wars." (Ward: 1958)

Of all the African names that ring around the Caribbean none sound more clearly than Ashanti and Coromanti, who were known as the most turbulent and desperate people on the coast of Guinea. They were, declared a West Indian planter, Codrington, accustomed to war from infancy, energetic of mind, hard and robust, "but bringing with them into slavery lofty ideas of independence, they are dangerous inmates of a West Indian plantation". Speaking of the people of various tribes who were shipped from the port of Coromantin, he said, "not only the best and more faithful of our slaves but are really all born heroes . . . There never was a rascal or coward of that nation". From the Akan-speaking people, the Fon people of then Dahomey, the Yoruba from the forested region of the Niger, the Ibo from the eastern region of modern Nigeria, the Ibibio and Efik-speaking people from the delta of the Niger and the Calabar river came the men and women who shaped Jamaican history in the eighteenth century. From them came those who led the series of uprisings which heralded the first maroon war.

Early in the 1670s night skies angry with the red glow of cane fires signalled the beginning of the second phase of the African-Jamaicans' rejection of slavery. In William Beckford's words, "A cane-piece fire is a most tremendous object; no flame is more alarming, none more rigid, none more rapid, and the fury and the velocity with which it burns and communicates cannot possibly be described."

The catalogue of insurrections and uprisings gives the impression of a land shaken by a series of disasters. In 1673 some 200 slaves, most of them referred to as Coromantis, on Major Selby's estate in St Ann, killed their master and 13 whites, plundered the estate and the surrounding neighbourhood and retreated to secure positions in the mountains on the borders of Clarendon, St Ann and St Elizabeth. These groups developed into the Leeward band of maroons of which Cudjoe was to become the leader.

Five years later, in 1678, the slaves on Captain Duck's estate, only four miles from Jamaica's capital city of St Jago de la Vega, rebelled, killed some whites, and made for the mountains with such supplies as they could carry. Some were captured and executed but some escaped.

In 1685 about 150 slaves on Mrs Gray's estate at Guanaboa and from four neighbouring estates took to the mountains. This may have been the uprising which was led by Cofi, who was killed in 1686.

Gradually various bands of rebel slaves moved eastwards to the parish of St George's, where they settled in three villages. There they were joined by the followers of Cofi. From their bases they raided the plantations along the coast with such success that the governor reported that the poorer settlers were threatening to desert their settlements.

In July 1690 a large party of 400 slaves on Sutton's plantation in North Clarendon, most of them from the Gold Coast, rose in rebellion, plundered the neighbouring estate, beat back an attack by the troops who had been called out and joined the Leeward maroons in the mountains. The governor lamented that it was very dangerous to the mountain plantations, all the more so because they had good arms and plenty of ammunition. In 1696 another uprising occurred on the estate of Captain Herring. Most of the rebels also joined the Leeward band.

These were uprisings organised by plantation slaves. They were the prelude to a more sustained campaign known as the first maroon war. Up to this point, the surviving maroons from the Spanish period had remained aloof. Understandably, they were not prepared to risk the freedom they had won or to put in danger the settlements they had, including a township of about 300 people and 100 acres of land planted out in provisions. Now, induced by the successes of the "new maroons" and driven by a shortage of supplies, they threw in their lot with the rebel bands nearest to them. For the next 20 years the combined maroons waged war against the English.

Jamaica entered the 1720s with anxiety and foreboding. More than 50 years had passed since the slaves had sacked Major Selby's St Ann plantation. In that time Port Royal had been destroyed by earthquake (1692) and by fire (1703), Kingston had been founded and had become the island's chief port and commercial centre and under William Beeston's leadership the island had defeated a French invading force led by Jean Baptiste Du Casse. By the Treaty of Utrecht (1713) Spain had granted to England a contract, or *asiento*, for supplying Spanish America with slaves. Jamaica had become the distribution centre for this trade and cargoes of Africans were shipped in locally manned sloops made in Jamaica to the mainland.

Kingston and the smugglers were busy. Ships and slave-carrying sloops carried lawful – and ostensibly lawful – cargoes to Latin American ports; other ships came crowding in to Kingston with plantation supplies and provisions from England, North America and the other islands. Out of sight on the horizon Spanish coastguards watched and waited, for Spain still claimed and exercised the right to stop and search foreign ships anywhere in the western hemisphere. Over the years a long list of financial claims and a mounting wave of national indignation accumulated in England against Spain. Another imperial war was in the making. That could wait, as far as the Jamaican planters and merchants were concerned. They already had a war on their hands. Peter Beckford, lieutenant-governor in 1703, warned that the former runaway slaves were targeting isolated plantations.

By this time the maroons of the 1680s and 1690s had grown into two formidable bands, the Leeward maroons who were based on the central mountains and the Windward maroons in the north-eastern mountains. New leaders had emerged. Somewhere about 1720 a Madagascan slave had built up a strong band of followers in nearby Deans Valley, but, in the power struggle that followed, the Madagascan was killed and his party was merged into the Leeward group. The Leeward maroons elected Cudjoe as their chief, a short, powerfully built man with a humpback, who brooked no rivals. Soon the Leeward maroons "began to pursue a more regular and connected system of warfare and in their frequent skirmishes with the troops sent against them, acquired an art of attack and defense which, in the difficult and hardly accessible fastness of the interior of the island, has since so often failed the best exertions of disciplined bravery". (Dallas: 1803)

Cudjoe appointed captains from amongst his ablest followers, each with very clearly defined responsibilities. They included Accompong and Johnny, both Cudjoe's brothers, Cuffee and Quao. Each was put in charge of as many men as Cudjoe thought he could manage. Their responsibilities included providing the community with food and organising hunting parties to track down wild hogs. They also directed the women in planting provisions and managing domestic affairs.

The Windward maroons were also well-organised. Nanny Town was under the command of the guerrilla leader, Cuffee. With him were Quao and Kishee, able commanders who repeatedly outmanoeuvred the whites. Not even Cudjoe's name carried with it a greater sense of power and of

Maroon settlements in Jamaica

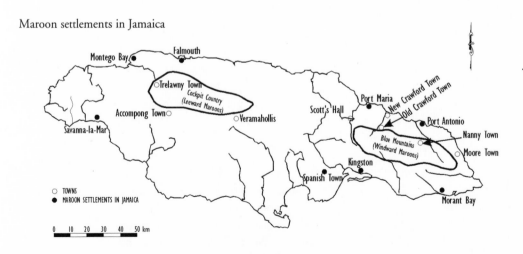

THE STORY OF THE JAMAICAN PEOPLE

authority than did that of Nanny, rebel leader and tactician, who by sheer force of personality and her powerful oaths of loyalty breathed courage and confidence into her followers. The dread her name inspired among the whites can be judged by the joy with which they greeted the news of her supposed death in 1733. A slave called Cuffee claimed to have killed her and was given a reward. The claim was false for Nanny was very much alive; she survived the end of the first maroon war in 1740 and received from the government of Jamaica 500 acres of land for herself and her people. (Mair: 1974)

Old and young, women and warriors worked together as units, each skilled in his or her own duties. Together they were committed to a free, independent way of life, subject to their own customs and laws and accepting also the harsh insecurities and privations of guerrilla warfare.

The maroon priorities were food gardens and capturing plantation slaves. To their carefully hidden food gardens of eddoes, plantains and yams they added other concealed gardens in remote parts of the countryside, for use as reserves. Some of the bands also had sexually segregated patterns of settlement which ensured the protection of their womenfolk and children from the savagery of the whites. They developed a sophisticated intelligence system that involved slaves on the plantations, who were able to send them word about the plans and movements of the whites. (Patterson: 1969)

The Leeward and Windward bands maintained contact with each other in this way. The system worked so well that in 1733 a committee of the House of Assembly complained that the rebels were as well-informed about their plans as they themselves were. "Cudjoe was always apprized in time of the parties that were fitted out, and knowing the route they must

Document showing land granted to Nanny and the Maroons

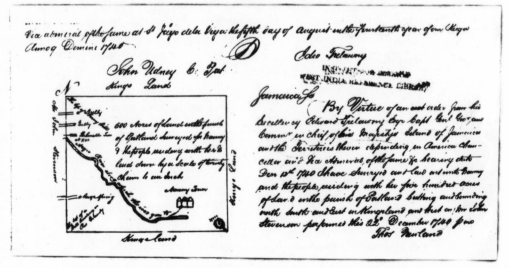

take, prepared some ambushes accordingly. As he frequently defeated his assailants his success was one of the means by which he supplied his men with arms and ammunition." (Dallas: 1968)

The 1720s saw a steady build-up of frustration amongst the whites. In 1720-22 the government turned in desperation to a strange ally, Jeremy, king of the Mosquito Indians on the Honduras coast. At their request he agreed to supply 50 expert trackers to help in the pursuit of the rebellious and runaway slaves. This was thought to be a better and cheaper expedient than sending out parties to suppress them. Nothing came of this attempt. Nor did the parties sent out by the governor in 1725 have greater success.

Towards the end of the decade the government moved from a policy of containment to one of harassment. Although Jamaica had been battered by three powerful hurricanes and two droughts during this period, the trends pointed to more prosperous times. Sugar production was expanding. Jamaica had become an important trading centre with Spanish America. However, there were fears that Spain might attempt an invasion from Cuba, and would offer freedom to all slaves who rebelled against the English. The new strategy called for more settlements around Port Antonio to make the north side more secure, and for an all-out effort to defeat the Trelawny Town and Windward maroon bands and destroy their towns. The increase in the number of blacks added urgency to the task. The population figures for 1730 reveal the cause for anxiety; the total population was 83,038, made up of 7,644 white persons and 74,525 slaves. The maroons understood what was being planned. They were especially concerned about the spread of new settlements on the north side, around Port Antonio, for these would deny them contact with the coast.

Disaster attended the government's first attempt to clear the maroons out of the mountains overlooking Port Antonio. A force of "ninety-five shot and twenty-two baggage negroes, chiefly volunteers and detached men from the militia" was held up by rains and then was routed by the rebels. While these things were happening a party of maroons had fallen upon a settlement to the windward of Port Antonio and burnt it. A settler reported that by this defeat the rebels also acquired 32 guns and had since become so insolent as to come down to the very town at Port Antonio, notwithstanding they saw the king's ships riding there.

There were reports also of fighting in the Leeward parts, where the militia destroyed one or two small settlements but had no success against the main body of the maroons.

England now took a hand, despatching two regiments from Gibraltar, which proved ineffective. A year later one of the English officers reported on his return home that the regiments were dispersed over the island and that though they might be of use against the rebels in the valleys they could not follow them into the mountains. The governor spoke bluntly to the House of Assembly on 4 January 1732. "Your slaves in rebellion, animated by their success, and others . . . ready to join them on the first favourable opportunity, your militia very insignificant, the daily decrease of the numbers of your white people and increase of the rebel slaves: these circumstances must convince you of the necessity of entering upon more solid measures." He even referred to a suggestion that a peace treaty be negotiated with the maroons but this was disregarded.

The "more solid measures" took the form of two expeditionary forces, one of four columns of soldiers, 93 armed blacks with five white overseers and 28 baggage blacks who moved west against the Leeward band. They destroyed Wiles Town, a maroon base in Trelawny, and planned to set up a permanent post there. The other band of 86 whites, 131 armed blacks and 61 baggage blacks operated from Port Antonio. They succeeded in taking Nanny Town but heavy rains, the high desertion rate of black baggage carriers and the incompetence of the white leaders prevented the force from following up its initial success. The Windward band took refuge in Guys Town or scattered in the Cotterwoods. Early in 1733 Kishee, one of the commanders of the Windward maroons, retook Nanny Town, driving back the whites who held it. On 3 July 1733 the governor reported to the Assembly: "On Sunday last about noon I received advice . . . that the parties were beat, or frightened out of that place [Nanny Town] by the slaves, without any loss . . . except it be of arms and ammunition, and had fled back to the breast-work." (Hart: 1985)

The governor organised a strong force to retake Nanny Town. It included 100 trained soldiers, 200 seamen and 100 whites. They were split into two groups and the local whites were being directed to occupy Carrion Crow Hill, above Nanny Town, so as to cut off the Maroons from the rear. They were ambushed and fled back to Port Antonio. The rest of the force was to advance against Nanny Town, with the seamen in the vanguard, a position with which they were most unhappy. After several skirmishes the black guides refused to show the way through the woods. The seamen moved to the rear and plundered their provisions, thus making a sustained attack impossible, and the whole force returned to Port Antonio in confusion. It is little wonder that a planter in a letter from Jamaica that December wrote, "We are in terrible circumstances in respect to the rebellious Negroes, they got the better of all our party, our men quite dispirited and dare not look them in the face in the open ground or in equal numbers." (Hart: 1985) That was not all. News came of groups of slaves in rebellion in Hanover, where it was least expected.

The year 1734 saw an increase in the number of slaves deserting the plantations and joining the rebels, who "openly appear in Arms and are daily increasing . . . they had already taken possession of three plantations within eight miles of Port Antonio . . . They have also attacked a place called the Breast Work where several Men armed were lodged to cover the workmen." (Hart: 1985)

But the Windward maroons were spread thin and were feeling the strain of continuous campaigning. In April 1734 two large parties of whites attacked and took Nanny Town after five days of heavy fighting. Governor Hunter had died that March. His successor, Governor Ayscough, warned that the capture of Nanny Town did not mean the end of the war. He complained bitterly to the House of Assembly that "the country had been at the expense of one hundred thousand pounds within these five years and no Benefit received or relief had".

The Windward maroons, driven from their beloved Nanny Town, split into two bands. One retreated deeper into the Blue Mountains. The other, made up of 300 men, women and children, made a 100-mile march through trackless, mountainous country to join Cudjoe and the Trelawny maroons in the cockpit region. Their march greatly disturbed the whites who feared that they were settling in a strong fastness and that, once settled, they would renew their ravages.

Cudjoe did not welcome the refugees. There were now 300 more people to feed. Also, his tactics were defensive rather than aggressive. Reports say that he blamed them for great indiscretion in their dealings with the parties sent against them. It is probable that he did not wish to include in his group independent bands loyal to other commanders. The refugees were granted temporary accommodation. In May 1737 they set out on the return journey and during 1738 they began to make their presence felt once more in the north-east. During 1736 and 1737 more and more of the whites began to accept Governor Gregory's view that a treaty was the best way of settling the maroon problem, guerrilla warfare having proved costly and ineffective.

Cudjoe and
Dr Russell
exchange hats

In February 1739 Colonel Guthrie, a planter-commander who had long advocated negotiations, was told to contact Cudjoe and start peace talks. A month later, on 1 March, a 15-point peace treaty, called Cudjoe's Treaty, was signed between the Leeward maroons and the whites. The treaty ensured the liberty and freedom of Cudjoe and his followers and their right of ownership of all lands in the vicinity of their towns, up to 1,500 acres. The maroons agreed to remain in the area occupied by them, but they were free to hunt wild hogs wherever they wished, except within three miles of any white settlement. Runaway slaves who had joined Cudjoe within the past two years were given the choice of returning to their masters with full pardon and indemnity or of remaining with the maroons.

Further, the maroons were allowed to sell their provisions in the markets of neighbouring towns as long as licences were obtained. These were to clean-cut and keep open roads from Trelawny Town to Westmoreland and St James and if possible to St Elizabeth. Two white men, appointed by the governor, were to reside among them constantly.

By the treaty it was agreed: "Captain Cudjoe and his successors would use their best endeavours to take, kill, suppress or destroy, either by themselves or jointly with any other number of men commanded on that service by his excellency the Governor or commander-in-chief for the time being, all rebels wheresoever they be throughout the island, unless they submit to the same terms granted to Captain Cudjoe and his successors." (Cudjoe's Treaty Sec. 6) It was further agreed: "if any negroes shall hereafter runaway from their masters or owners and fall into captain Cudjoe's hands they shall immediately be sent back to the chief magistrate of the next parish where they were taken; and those that bring them in are to be satisfied for their trouble, as the legislature shall appoint".

The treaty signed by Quao of the Windward maroons on 23 June was similar in terms to that signed by Cudjoe save that the Windward maroons were to return to their former owners those who had joined them within three years; also, they were on demand required "to suppress and destroy all other . . . rebellious negroes that now are or shall from time to time gather together or settle in any part of the island".

Many of the plantation slaves were disturbed at the agreements reached with the maroons. They complained that freedom had been granted to those who had rebelled but had been withheld from those who had remained loyal. Mutinous and angry groups who gathered in Spanish Town were dispersed by a troop of horse sent against them and some of the leaders were executed or transported. In 1742, in Trelawny, a conspiracy between Coromanti blacks of Colonel Foster's and adjoining plantations with other Coromantis in the woods was crushed in the early stages, when "Captain Cudjoe discovered that some of his chief men, who were dissatisfied with the treaty . . . had entered into private caballs with the negroes in the neighbouring plantations and incited them to revolt." Cudjoe had two of the leaders hanged, and sent the other two to the governor, who transported them. (Hart: 1985)

So it came about that these maroons, after a long and courageous struggle, having achieved their objectives of freedom, and the right to manage their own affairs, gave up their revolutionary role, became the allies of the government and closed the route to freedom by means of flight from the estates. Moved by a passion for freedom and justice, these African men and women, virtually weaponless, relying on their own skills, their own courage, their own will, their own capacity for leadership and organisation, waged war against England for more than 60 years and secured recognition of their freedom and independence.

We can relive the closing days of that long campaign in the company of Alan Eyre, geographer, who visited Pette River Bottom, where the British and maroons had bases.

> Pette River Bottom is a quiet and beautiful glade, inhabited only by cattle and abundant wildlife, accessible only by a barely perceptible foot track through banana groves. The British Army's Tramping Ground, a large parade ground carefully levelled by slaves, is now a community sports centre. The military cemetery is an overgrown pasture with a few tombstones of grey limestone visible in the rough grass. The soldier's Bathing Place, a natural spring at the bottom of a steep cockpit, is still used for the same purpose by descendants of the Maroons. For the geographer, perhaps the most interesting survivals of this protracted, bitter and inconclusive conflict are the place names. Land of Look Behind, Quick Step, Me no Sen You no Come, First Breakfast Hill, Flagstaff, Horse Guards, Don't Come Back, Cum See and many more – peasant farming districts today – tell us where long forgotten British soldiers once passed and left their mark.

The maroons won an important victory, but the peace treaties with the English were a severe setback for the plantation slaves because they put an end to marronage. No longer did flight to the mountains open up an escape route to freedom. The maroons were no longer allies and kinsfolk, their gardens no longer sources of food. The treaties taught that rebellion was the only road to freedom and that the plantation was the final battlefield.

Calm prevailed for 20 years. The annual inflow of 3,000 or 4,000 Africans from amongst the most warlike people of West Africa, reinforced African morale. These people had neither knowledge of, nor connections with the maroons. Resolute and determined, they renewed the liberation struggles in the 1760s making this the decade of the Coromanti. The two areas of greatest turbulence were St Mary and Westmoreland.

The uprising began in April 1760 in St Mary's parish, on the estates of Ballard Beckford and Zackary Bayley due to whose wisdom, activity and courage it was that the rebellion was not as general nor as destructive as that which then raged in St Domingue.

> On these plantations were upward of one hundred Gold Coast negroes newly imported and I do not believe that an individual

amongst them had received the least shadow of ill-treatment from the time of their arrival there. Concerning those on Trinity Estate. I can pronounce of my own knowledge, they were under the government of an overseer of singular tenderness and humanity. His name was Abraham Fletcher and let it be remembered in justice even to the rebels, and as a lesson to other overseers that his life was spared from respect for his virtues. The insurgents had heard of his character from the other negroes, and suffered him to pass through them unmolested. (Edwards: 1793)

But even as cultivated a man as Bryan Edwards failed to understand that the blacks were fighting for freedom, not for kindness from their masters.

In 1760 a Coromanti slave, Tacky, who had been a slave in West Africa, at the head of a small band of slaves captured Fort Haldane at Pt Maria, set fire to the works at Heywood Hall Plantation, destroyed buildings at Esher Estate, then doubled back to Ballards Valley. A number of slaves joined them but there was no general uprising. Many of the private men in the militia had the insolence to tell their officers that they would not appear under arms and were ready to pay the fine of ten shillings. Thereupon the governor imposed martial law. In addition he summoned to his aid the maroons at Crawford Town, Nanny Town and Scotts Hall.

The blacks fought bravely. At Bagnolds they drew the troops into an ambush, displayed no little skill in retreating to a narrow pass where they obtained a decided advantage; they staged successful night attacks on the troops sent against them; in one of these at Down's Cove, the maroons who had joined the troops "behaved most shamefully at this attack, lying the whole time on their faces". (Long: 1774) Probably their hearts were not in the business. Gradually, however, the tide turned against the freedom-fighters. By June the insurrection had been put down. But in that month another brief insurrection broke out in St Thomas-in-the-East and at about the same time uprisings were reported from several plantations in Westmoreland.

At one of these plantations, the freedom fighters showed the same chivalrous spirit that Tacky's followers had shown to Abraham Fletcher at Trinity Estate:

A gentleman . . . remarkable for his humanity and kind treatment of his slaves, upon the first alarm, put arms in the hands of about twenty; of whose faithful attachment to him, he had the utmost confidence; these were all of them Coromantins who no sooner had got possession of arms . . . having ranged themselves before his house, they assured him they would do him no harm but that they must go and join their countrymen, and then saluting him with their hats they every one marched off. (Long: 1774)

The freedom fighters, benefiting from surprise, defeated a party of the militia.

The unrest was not limited to Westmoreland. Discontent in Hanover and St James was ruthlessly repressed; the ringleaders were executed. Finally, after some months, the freedom fighters were defeated; but not after sporadic outbreaks in many parts of the island, including Kingston, where a female slave called Cubah, "Queen of Kingston", was transported to Cuba, but somehow succeeded in returning to Jamaica, landed in Hanover, was captured and executed. (Hart: 1985) The women stood shoulder to shoulder with the men, for freedom was not a male prerogative.

The 1760s was turbulent, with the Coromanti in the lead, plotting, conspiring from one end of the island to another. Thus, in 1765, "there was a private meeting . . . of several Coromanti headmen, who entered into a conspiracy for a fresh insurrection to take place immediately after the Christmas holidays".

The Coromanti on 17 estates were involved. Some of them acted before the appointed day. "On the night of 29 November (1765) the works and trash houses at Whitehall plantation were set on fire." The plan was "to decoy the overseer and other white persons there from their beds to extinguish it and then cut off their retreat and secure the arms lodged there without fear of resistance". (Long: 1774) This premature uprising, the work of a leader called Quamin, led to the defeat of the conspirators. But in the following year the Coromanti in Westmoreland were yet again in rebellion. At 4 o'clock in the Afternoon at Cross Path and Cornwall in Westmoreland 45 Negroes Coromanties rose in rebellion and in one night killed four whites and eleven Negroes. This uprising also was put down.

A committee set up by the Assembly to enquire into the 1760 rebellions proposed "that a bill should be brought in for laying an additional higher duty upon all Fantin, Akim and Ashantee Negroes and all others commonly called Coromantins, that should after a certain time be imported and sold in the island". The reprisals were savage beyond words. After the rebellions of 1760 in St Mary and Westmoreland 400 slaves were executed and 600 transported to slavery in the Bay of Honduras. "Teach the blacks a lesson", was the formula. The blacks never learned the lesson of submission. They chose to fight for freedom against the Jamaica militia and English regimental forces; chose to attack the plantation, bastion of white power; chose in Claude McKay's words, to nobly die.

The decade of the Coromanti marks a middle point in the long series of liberation wars which began with Lubolo (Juan de Bolas) and Juan de Serras in the 1660s, extended through the plantation battlefields of the 1670s and 1680s, the maroon war of the 1730s, the Coromanti Western Rebellion of the early 1830s and the Bogle-Gordon struggle for justice in

1865. Human history records few liberation struggles that spanned so long a period and that, in the end, achieved both emancipation and the fall of a planter oligarchy.

The second maroon war broke out in 1795. For 56 years the relationship between the various maroon communities and the government had been good. They hunted wild hogs, cultivated their land, brought in fugitive slaves, helped to suppress slave insurrection and observed the terms of the treaty. Then war broke out between the Trelawny Town maroons and the government. It was not part of the liberation struggle. They were already free. Not all the maroons were involved, only the Trelawny Town people who fought because they considered the government had breached the treaty of 1739.

Early in July, two Trelawny Town maroons who were accused of killing some tame hogs were taken before magistrates in Montego Bay, convicted and sentenced to be publicly flogged. The sentence was carried out in a common work-house by a slave.

The maroons were incensed at this indignity. They were not concerned about the two men, who were not in good standing with them, but with their own right to try and punish them. It is probable that they saw in this incident an opportunity also to press other claims, such as the need for more land and their dissatisfaction with the white superintendent, Captain Thomas Craskell, whom they felt was not qualified to discharge the necessary duties of the office. They wanted Captain John James, their former superintendent, to be reappointed.

The dispute could have been settled but for the recently appointed governor, the Earl of Balcarres, who saw an opportunity to make a name as conqueror of the hitherto invincible maroons and as defender of a British colony against the French Jacobins, members of a French political club established in Paris in 1789 to maintain and propagate the principles of extreme democracy and absolute equality.

The magistrates and property owners of St James and Trelawny met the maroons and then advised the governor that their demands be granted: that the law be altered in respect of the punishment of public whipping; that Captain Craskell who had been recently appointed by the Earl of Balcarres be removed; that the former superintendent Captain James be reinstated; and that an additional 300 acres of land be given to the maroons, since the fertility of the original allocation had been exhausted. The chief magistrate of Trelawny urged a conciliatory course on the governor, who misrepresented the situation to the Secretary of State for War and informed him that Trelawny Town maroons had rebelled and reported that he had marched troops against them. The troops were under the orders of the magistrates in Montego Bay.

To General Maitland commanding the British forces in St Domingue, Balcarres expressed his fear that French revolutionaries were behind the unrest in Trelawny Town. "If my hands had not been fettered," he wrote on 30 July 1795, "I could have put an end to this disturbance last week. It may be in my power next week – and a fortnight hence, instead of the action of a soldier, we may hear of the Rights of Man." In order to build up tension he proclaimed martial law, convened a council of war in August, and declared: "I am of opinion that the minds of the Trelawny Maroons have been corrupted by incendiaries from the enemy . . . Whether this rebellion has proceeded from internal grievances or from the machinations of an external foe, it does not alter the fact that they have been in rebellion."

On 3 August Balcarres took command of the main body of troops, planning "to strike at the source of the rebellion . . . I have rung the alarm. It is long since it existed in my mind". He had at his command 1,200 or more regular troops in addition to the local militia. The Trelawny maroons numbered about 300. The governor addressed a hysterical proclamation to them in their two settlements of New Town and Old Town, announcing that martial law had been proclaimed and that every part of their town had been occupied.

> You are surrounded by thousands. I have issued a Proclamation offering a Reward for Your Heads. That terrible edict will not be put in force before Thursday the Thirteenth Day of August.
>
> To avoid these terrible proceedings I . . . command every Maroon of Trelawny Town capable of bearing arms, to appear before me at Montego Bay on the 12th Day of August . . . and then submit themselves to his Majesty's Mercy.

Colonel Montague James and 37 of his best marksmen, at their old chief's urging, surrendered on 11 August. With their hands bound behind them they were marched under guard to Montego Bay and imprisoned in irons aboard a warship.

The maroons in Trelawny Town now made ready for war. They persuaded two of their captains, Johnson and Smith, who had settled on their own holdings in Westmoreland to rejoin them and to take command of two companies. At about the same time two other leaders, Palmer and Parkinson, who had been taken to Montego Bay, were released and sent back to Trelawny Town to persuade the remaining maroons to surrender. Instead they persuaded their kinsmen to resist, and remained with them. On 12 August fighting began. Balcarres, in command of the government forces, launched an attack. After an initial repulse, the two maroon settlements of New Town and Old Town were occupied. Balcarres reported

A maroon settlement at Trelawny Town

that victory was within grasp, the maroons, "having been reduced by surrender, capture and death upwards of one third . . . they may escape in small numbers and give disturbances as a band of robbers but never are to be considered as an enemy capable of endangering the security of the island". By the end of August he was beginning to sing another tune, for "the seasons are now against me". (Hart: 1985) He handed over the field operations to Colonel Fitch and returned to Montego Bay. Fitch wrote to Governor Balcarres that the maroons desired peace but would not treat with him till two or three of their people appeared from Montego Bay. They were apprehensive that they had been destroyed. As a result two maroons were allowed to visit those who were being held in Montego Bay and Colonel Montague was allowed to return with these two to the rebels. Having heard their report, the maroon bands decided not to surrender but to fight to the end. Engagements followed and Colonel Fitch was killed. Major-General Walpole succeeded him as field commander.

By mid-October the resistance of the maroons, the losses they had inflicted on the troops, the extent of damage done to plantations, the desertion of a number of slaves to the maroons, the approach of the dry season when the rebels would set fire to the cane-pieces and the nature of the terrain, led Balcarres to explore the possibility of coming to terms with them. The most influential members of the assembly were in favour of this, and Balcarres thereupon instructed General Walpole to negotiate with the maroons. He reported that contact had been made with them. So, "on 21 December 1795, nearly 57 years after the solemnization of Cudjoe's Treaty another undefeated body of maroons received an offer of a treaty of peace. On this occasion, however, the tribute to their courage and tenacity implicit in the offer was so much the greater, for the Trelawny Town maroons had been isolated for attack and none of the other maroons in the island are known to have come to their assistance". The terms were that the maroons would beg His Majesty's pardon, go to Old Town, Montego Bay or any other place to settle on whatever land might be allotted to them, and return all runaways. Walpole reported to Balcarres that he had been obliged to promise, on oath, that they should not be sent off the island. Colonel Montague alone, having experienced what dealing with Balcarres meant, objected to making peace. It was known that the government planned to bring in Cuban chasseurs with hunting dogs for use against the maroons, but General Walpole's opinion was that the dogs would be of little value in the waterless cockpit country.

On 24 December, at a meeting held by Balcarres with members of the Council and Assembly, it was resolved that if the Trelawny maroons delivered the runaways who had joined them and if they laid down their arms, (which arms were to be taken away from them), General Walpole's promise not to send them off the island would be ratified; but that they were to remain in Jamaica, subject to such regulations as the governor, council and Assembly thought proper to enact.

Balcarres appointed "Friday morning the first day of January next at ten o'clock for the Trelawny maroons to come in a body to Castle Wemyss to perform the treaty." He deliberately gave the maroons too little time for reporting to him. They were dispersed in the forests. However, at General Walpole's urging, by the end of March practically all the maroons had surrendered. During that period he had resisted the governor's wish that "nothing will prevent the dogs from going out tomorrow".

Walpole became greatly disturbed in early March that the terms of the treaty would not be kept. "My Lord," he wrote to Balcarres, "to be plain with you, it was through my means alone that the maroons were induced to surrender, from a reliance which they had on my word . . . from conviction impressed upon them by me that the white people would never break their faith".

But Balcarres persuaded a joint committee of the Council and Assembly to break faith with the maroons and to transport them, to the great distress of General Walpole, who resigned his commission in protest. Many white residents were also very unhappy.

The Trelawny maroons were transported to Nova Scotia (of all places). There a number perished in the longest and coldest winter the colonists could remember. In August 1800 a transport ship, the *Asia*, took most of the 550 survivors to Sierra Leone where they settled.

General Walpole rejected the Assembly's offer of 500 guineas to purchase a sword: "As the House has thought fit not to accede to the agreement entered into between me and the Trelawny maroons, and as their opinion of that treaty stands on their minutes very different to my conception of it, I am compelled to decline the offer."

Angry at having been made an instrument to dupe and entrap the maroons, Walpole atttempted to have the matter reviewed in England. He obtained a seat in parliament and there moved a resolution seeking for an examination of the treaty negotiations, but he failed to win sufficient support.

The Earl of Balcarres had no hesitation about accepting the Assembly's offer of 700 guineas to purchase a ceremonial sword.

CHAPTER 14

The sugar estate: Bastion of white power

Contemplating a ruined great house, Derek Walcott, West Indian Nobel Prize laureate, painted in vivid language the beauty of the setting, "green lawn, broken by low walls of stone dipped to the rivulet", and against that tranquillity he placed the brutality and transience of imperial power.

> I thought next
> Of men like Hawkins, Walter Raleigh,
> Drake
> Ancestral murderers and poets;
>
> The names spoke of great victories and of Africans whose lives
>   paid for those victories,
>
> Ablaze with rage I thought
> Some slave is rotting in that
> manorial lake . . .

Throughout his poems and plays Walcott interprets and illuminates the West Indian historical experience and reveals that his own search for a sense of complete creative selfhood reflects every West Indian's need to claim his roots and his heritage. Kamau Braithwate (on whose work we drew heavily in the chapter on the West African Homeland), opens the eyes of West Indians to the centrality of Africa as mother and as an indispensable resource of spirituality.

Throughout this book we call on the creative artists of Jamaica and of the West Indies. We affirm that the story of the people of Jamaica cannot be told without their participation. They are our griots, bards, minstrels, storytellers, interpreters, historians, prophets. Their artifacts are found in the historical experience of the Jamaican and West Indian people, in the culture and way of life of the folk, in the necessities of the shanty towns and country homes, in deep-buried memories of their roots, of colonialism and of social change. Through their gift for entering into the inner world of West Indians, of understanding their purposes, ideals, sense of personal dignity and creativity, they add precious insights to our understanding of ourselves. We will find that the creative artists, especially the poets, including those who write in the vernacular, and the novelists, add insight, depth and texture to our story.

Today the sugar estate is one of the great mainstays of the Jamaican economy, a provider of commodities for export and of public service to the nation. Many of the great houses that survive are of elegance and charm, with high-quality joinery and woodwork; they settle into the landscape with an air of distinction. They are among Jamaica's historical treasures. The modern plantation systems in the islands and in many parts of plantation America are efficient units of production and their earnings contribute to national development. The labour force is protected by labour unions and industrial relations in line with developed countries. Worthy Park, Frome, Innswood, New Yarmouth and other sugar estates contribute to Jamaica's economic and social well-being. In many cases the estates serve smaller cane farmers as well as the large suppliers and they also receive substantial investments from overseas.

The plantation we are considering was very different. Its labour force was made up of slaves brought in from Africa under conditions of great cruelty. Each slave was required to remain within the boundaries of the estate to which he was assigned. Political representation and religious instruction were closed to him. He was almost wholly at the mercy of the master or his representative. His skin colour, black, branded him as inferior. He was the victim in a detestable system of apartheid. Every aspect of the plantation represented conflict: black slave and white master, slave quarters and great house, provision ground and plantation, outlawed religions, cults and established church, justice for whites and legally instituted injustice for blacks, chattel status for blacks and civil rights for whites, restricted movement for blacks and freedom of movement for whites, pickney gangs for blacks and schools for whites, the "bongo image" against the "busha image", yard-talk and English, slave and freeman. Conflict was the characteristic feature.

The sugar estates spread along the north coast from Agualta Vale in St Mary, west to Tryall in Hanover and south to the plains of Westmoreland. They prospered, but drought often plagued the southern belt. As Charles Leslie, a visitor to the island in 1740 wrote, "Liguanea is quite dry and fine sugar-works that used to produce many hundred hogsheads of sugar are now turned into cattle penns. This likewise is the fate of the parishes of St Catherine's, St Dorothy's and Vere which once were the choicest and richest spots in the whole Island but are now good for little but to raise cattle." (Leslie: 1739)

Even in these high-technology days King Sugar is an imperious ruler. He was much more so when the only sources of power were wind, water and animals. The requirements for making good sugar were good soil, level land for the crop, ease of access, convenience of distance from the shipping place and a stream running through the premises. Layout was important. The principal objectives were a central location for the works and an overall symmetry in the ordering of buildings and crops. An important component of the industry was that the cost of transporting the cane to the mill, especially when the load of cane was moved by ox-carts or asses, should be kept to the minimum. Another critical question was the source of power. Animal power was slow and costly; watermills called for aqueducts and a reliable source of supply, windmills had to be on hilltops or exposed sites. In the late eighteenth century steam power, most efficient of all, became available, but called for new roads and buildings.

Barry Higman in his book, *Jamaica Surveyed*, has brought together a valuable collection of surveyor's drawings of a number of Jamaican sugar estates, pens and coffee plantations, with clear, historical and descriptive case studies that identify important characteristics. He notes:

> Within tropical America, the dominance of the large slave plantation was nowhere greater than in Jamaica. Around 1830, for example, 36 per cent of Jamaican slaves lived in units of more than 200, compared to 5 per cent in the sugar-producing regions of Louisiana and a mere 1 per cent in Bahia. Roughly 60 per cent of slaves in Louisiana and Bahia belonged to holdings of less than 50, whereas only 25 per cent of Jamaica's slaves were in such units. Within the British Caribbean only Tobago, St Vincent and Antigua matched the concentration of slaves in very large plantations found in Jamaica. The French and Spanish colonies always possessed a relatively substantial small holder class and even St Domingue and Cuba in their short-lived climax periods as slave societies failed to approach the Jamaica pattern.
>
> Further, in spite of the much larger slave population of the United States, there were only 312 plantations of 200 or more slaves in 1860 compared with 393 in Jamaica in 1832. Although the large plantation typified the relations of production in the slave societies of Brazil and the United States, the plantation itself remained something of a myth, most slaves living outside its physical context. In Jamaica myth and reality converged.

The figures for plantation expansion are impressive. Periodic droughts notwithstanding, the number of sugar-works or mills increased rapidly in

the period 1670-1800. Between 1670 and 1739 the number increased from 57 to 419, and stood at 1,061 in 1786. The north coast expansion was spectacular. There were only 20 mills in St James in 1745, but 30 years later, in 1774, there were 115. In the seven years between 1792 and 1799 some 84 new estates were established in the island, more than one-half of them being in St Ann, Trelawny and St James. By 1804 the north coast had as many mills as the south coast.

Hope, Papine and Mona Estates were three estates of more than 1,000 acres each, which had three different owners and date back to the early years of English rule. Major Roger Hope, who served under General Venables, founded Hope Estate in the 1660s. The estate passed to the Elletson family by Hope's daughter's marriage to Chief Justice Elletson. Lady Nugent, wife of the governor of Jamaica, visited the Papine and Hope estates in October 1801. She described the Papine estate as being beautiful, with a fine walk of bamboo supported by a coconut tree at every 12 feet; breadfruit trees in great perfection; jackfruit trees with fruit like huge pumpkins hanging from the trunks, being too heavy for the limbs. The situation of the house was bad, for it was shut out from the seabreeze by the Long Mountain. The owner, Mr Hutchinson, who served an enormous breakfast of all sorts of meats and fruits, "was a quiet, awkward Scotchman and so overcome by the honour we have done him that it is quite distressing to see the poor man".

Lady Nugent went on to the Hope Estate:

> Driving through a cane-piece as it is called, a negro man running before us to open the gates . . . It is said to be an old estate . . . As you enter the gates, there is a long range of negro houses, like thatched cottages, and a row of coconut trees and clumps of cotton-trees. The sugar-house and all the buildings are thought to be more than usually good. The overseer, a civil, vulgar [common] Scotch officer on half-pay did the honours to us. I went to the overseer's house [and] talked to the black women who told me all their histories. The overseer's chere'amie, [sweetheart] and no man here is without one, is a tall black woman, polished and shining, well-made. She showed me her three yellow children and said with some ostentation she should soon have another . . . [Lady Nugent described the husband as] a Scotch Sultan, who is about fifty, clumsy, ill-made and dirty. He had a dingy, sallow brown complexion, and only two yellow discoloured tusks, by way of teeth. However, they say he is a good overseer, . . . almost all the agents, attorneys, merchants and shopkeepers are of that country [Scotland] and really do deserve to thrive in this, they are so industrious . . . I should mention there is an excellent hospital on this estate which is called a hot-house where the blackies appear perfectly comfortable.

The three estate owners, beset by drought, wisely joined together to meet the cost of supplying water from the Hope River. At first, they used cattle to turn the mills but that was slow and unproductive. They built water works, starting "from a dam near the northern boundary of Hope estate. The water passed through a series of ground-level masonry gutters, solid and arched brickwork aqueducts and underground channels for a distance of 2 miles, turning the mill wheels on Hope, Papine and Mona in its course". (Higman: 1988)

The reservoir was at the northern boundary of Papine Estate. From this, Higman records that Papine supplied water to Up Park Camp under contract to the value of £630 in the early 1850s and to the Lord Bishop of Jamaica at £27. The water from the Papine reservoir (passed) through the cane fields and provision grounds of that estate, rising to 12 feet in an aqueduct at Papine works, then underground . . . to emerge at the flood gate and rise again into another aqueduct before reaching Mona works. Hope Estate abandoned sugar cultivation in the 1840s, selling its water rights to the Kingston and Liguanea Water Company. (Higman: 1976) Papine continued to make sugar until the 1880s and Mona until 1914 when it was the only estate in St Andrew. Sections of the aqueduct remain in the Hope Gardens and on the grounds of the University of the West Indies.

From these struggling estates we move to Drax Hall in St Ann, founded in 1669 by William Drax, an English planter from Barbados.

Whereas Mona, Papine and Hope experienced water shortages, Drax Hall was concerned with milling efficiency and making the best use of the typical north coast topography of a ribbon of plain and sharply rising hills. Travellers who take the coastal main road today from St Ann's Bay to Ocho Rios will find that it forms the dividing line between the flat land where 40 or more cane-pieces once flourished and the steeply sloping hills where pimento trees still grow.

In 1715 Charles Drax sold 1,000 acres of the estate to Peter Beckford, probably the richest Jamaican planter of the time. At his death he owned nine sugar plantations and was part-owner of seven others, nine cattle pens and a mansion in Spanish Town. His second son, William, inherited a large part of his father's estate and by 1754 owned more than 22,000 acres. In 1762 he bought the remainder of Drax Hall in a manner, reported some, "that excited the indignation of every honest man who became acquainted with the transaction". William found Jamaica too small for his energies and wealth. He became an absentee proprietor, starting off as a London merchant, shipowner and alderman. He was elected Lord Mayor of London twice. The estate was sold to John H. Pink in 1821. The calamitous fall in sugar prices notwithstanding, William Sewell, who purchased Drax Hall after its listing as an encumbered estate in 1863, produced sugar through the 1880s, then changed over to bananas and cattle and finally to copra and limes.

The Negro village is of special interest because of data found there when nine of the house sites were excavated. The houses were made of locally available materials, marl, rough limestone cobbles, bricks. "Three distinct rooms were identified, one with limestone block flooring, the middle room with marl cobble flooring, and the third with soil only." The data supports the view that West African housing patterns and construction practices contributed to the techniques employed in African-Jamaican building. Perhaps the most significant of all was the house-yard layout, with yard space provided within a garden area, where decisions were made, family quarrels took place as in a play, friends entertained and all the family conversed together. (Higman: 1988)

One of the exciting discoveries was a small bent piece of sheet metal. It was being cleaned when it was identified as an oil lamp similar to those which are still in use in Ghana. It was bent at each of the four corners, with one corner folded over itself. A wick was placed in the metal fold. The lamp could provide illumination for hours.

In the kitchen area found behind each house at Drax Hall, the archaeologists discovered many utensils found in food preparation: grinding stones, pieces of iron cooking pots, yabba fragments and a fireplace or hearth demarcated by several stones which, as in West African practice, were put around the fire to support the round bottom earthenware yabbas. (Armstrong: 1990)

Part of the yard area served as a garden plot. A survey of remnant vegetation growing at the site yielded 124 identifiable species. Over half (64) had known ethno-botanical uses in Jamaica, such as goatweed and susumba for colds and flu, ackee, guava, soursop. Ackee trees were found not only at Drax Hall but at all six sites in the preliminary survey. Perhaps clusters of ackee trees provide indications of the sites of slave villages.

Those conducting the survey at Drax Hall concluded that the archaeological data confirmed the presence of house-yard living areas which "provided a clear picture of an emerging culture within the slave settlement. This local expression of the emerging African-Jamaican culture system incorporates both continuity and change . . . It was created by the slaves in spite of the oppressive economic and political institution of slavery".

There were about 300 African slaves on the Drax Hall estate in the 1750s, with a small number of whites, ranging from manager and supervisors to skilled artisans. There were no Jamaicans. They were all exiles: the whites were homesick and often quarrelsome, surrounded by much larger groups of resentful slaves given to mocking the master or the slave driver, singing:

> It's time for man go home
> It's time for man an' it's time for beas'
>
> Time for man go home
> Da bird in de bush bawl qua qua
> Time for man go home
> Buckra bring ol' iron to break a man down,
> time for man go home,
> De monkey a bush bawl qua, qua, qua
> Time for man go home.

No one belonged or wished to belong. The name "Jamaica" was no more than a label. The impression of a place without homes and settlements was deepened by the fact that, as John Dennes wrote to the Earl of Wilmington (1718):

> The island may be divided into eight parts, four of which is good arable land, two other pasturage (or what is call savanna) which is uninhabitable, but the four parts that is good land tis not because people will not or do not care to go and settle there, but because the land is engrost by a few rich men there and in England, who have run

out vast tracts & obtained patents for them, but having so much are not able to settle them.

An example was the Modyford family. Sir Thomas Modyford, at one time lieutenant governor of the island, his two sons and his brother owned among them 21,218 acres in eight parishes. Governor Lynch also noted in 1683 that 3,000 patents had been issued for 1,080,000 acres. One hundred years later, when much of this land still lay undeveloped the local Assembly resisted attempts by the Colonial Office to withhold the patents because according to them "it would strike at the very existence of property". In 1739 Leslie claimed that two-thirds of the island was still uninhabited. Some 30 years later the situation had not changed.

This much we have learned from our visits, that the West Indian sugar-and-slave plantation brought into existence a special kind of society "created for sugar; Jamaican customs and culture were fashioned by sugar; sugar, for two hundred years, was the only reason behind Jamaica's existence as a centre for human habitation". (Hearne: 1965)

During those two centuries two other types of holdings were developed, the pens and the provision grounds. The sugar estate, pen and coffee mountain and the provision ground each marched to its own music, its

Crop Time
by Albert Huie

The sugar estate: Bastion of white power

own lifestyle fashioned by the purpose that brought it into being, a technology and methods that sustained it, a changing rhythm of its own dictated by the seasons for breeding, weeding, nurturing, harvesting. The influence of the leader of the supervisors and labour force, the seasons bringing rain or drought, the changing mood of the landscape all stamped their impress on each place, yet held them inescapably within general confines of their own.

William Beckford captured the surge of energy on a sugar estate at crop time. He described how every object about the plantation, but especially around the buildings, appears at this time of year to be alive; and "the beating of the coppers, the clanking of the iron, the drivings of the logs, the wedging of the gudgeons, the repetition of the hammers, and the hooping of the puncheons are the cheerful precursors of the approaching crop".

The driving purpose was to produce sugar for export to Britain. African slaves, British managers, overseers, bookkeepers and the creditors advancing money in London and Liverpool all marched to the beat of sugar. The tempo rose to a fury of activity in crop-time. Unlike Beckford, Lady Nugent was overcome by the demonic energy and the supremacy of the machine:

> At each cauldron in the boiling-house was a man with a large skimmer upon a long pole, calling constantly to those below, attending the fire, to throw on more trash, for if the heat relaxes in the least all the sugar in the cauldron is spoiled. Then there were several negroes employed in putting the sugar into the hogsheads. I asked the overseer how often his people were removed. He said every twelve hours; but how dreadful to think of their standing twelve hours over a boiling cauldron and doing the same thing, and he owned to me that sometimes they did fall asleep, and get their poor fingers into the mill, and with a hatchet nearby always ready to sever the whole limb, as the only means of saving the poor sufferer's life I would not have a sugar estate for the world.

An estate boiling house

Beckford and Maria Nugent pictured more than a system of production process. They pictured a totally servile society. John Hearne's description is of compelling force: "There was nothing in West Indian plantation slavery, granted the fortuitous differences of colour, to distinguish it, say, from the pitiless exploitation of slaves in the Athenian silver mines or on the Roman estates. Expect for one factor: its total nature. Society in the ancient world, as in the American South, had always enough free citizens to think the thoughts, establish the customs, generate the moral climate that only flourish in liberty." (Hearne: 1965) But within a few years of Henry Morgan, who was no source of redemption, Jamaica was a slave society in which the slaves heavily outnumbered the free. Personal advantage, not the public good, was what counted; the exploitation of woman, man, land, not responsible conduct; profits, not morality; a society totally corrupted by its perception of nine-tenths of the total population as property, as an inferior form of human being.

The result was a society from which those whites who could afford to do so, fled. Higman notes that by 1775 about 30 per cent of the island's sugar estates were in the hands of absentees, many of whom were descendants of early settlers who returned to Britain after establishing their fortunes. The number of absentees rose after the decline in the plantation economy forced many to surrender their mortgaged properties to metropolitan merchants and bankers, beginning a trend to corporate ownership. By the time of emancipation 80 percent of the sugar estates were owned by absentees. (Higman: 1988) White planter society was steadily deteriorating to the point where it reached moral bankruptcy in 1865.

Free blacks and coloureds resided mostly in towns where many worked as shop assistants, servants, porters, and women worked as milliners and small shopkeepers selling preserves and provisions. A few even owned one or two slaves who took the goods for sale into the estates. Some, by dint of hard work, acquired wealth but they still could not gain acceptance from the whites. If, for instance, whites and non-whites attended a theatrical performance the two groups entered through separate doors and sat in different seats. Sometimes different performances were put on for the two groups. The same discrimination existed in churches where pews were reserved for whites while coloureds and blacks sat in the gallery.

They were barred from the legislature, from serving on the jury and from giving evidence against whites. Most of the offenders against blacks and coloureds were white, and the blacks and coloureds could not expect justice in the courts.

Nor was whiteness a bond between rich white, with big house, coach and horses, fine saddles and riding horse and a "walking bakra". No disgrace was considered so great "as that of a white man being seen walking on foot when away from his home; only such as have forfeited their character and were destitute would have been found in such a situation, so 'walking bakra' a name synonymous to beggar, coupled with that of vagabond." (Marly: 1828)

The plantocracy and all white owners of property, being heavily outnumbered by the blacks, kept legislative power in their hands and erected a protective wall of legislation around themselves. White landowners dominated both houses of the Legislature and the Vestry. At all times the disparity between the numbers of blacks and whites was great. In 1778 there were 18,420 whites to 205,000 blacks. At about this time coloureds, outnumbered whites by three to one. The whites felt their position threatened and to ensure that the free blacks and coloureds would not be socially or financially independent, made it a criminal offence in 1711 for them to hold public office, to work as supervisors on estates, or to engage in any activity that allowed them a measure of independence. In the following year, they were debarred from acting as navigators or from driving carriages for hire. However, by the mid seventeenth century the shortage of headmen was such that managers ignored this law, and when charged gladly paid the fines and continued to use the blacks and coloureds.

At one time, persons who had been freed or who had purchased their freedom but did not own land and at least 10 slaves were required to wear a badge with a blue cross on the right shoulder. This law was however not rigorously enforced and by 1790 it had been allowed to lapse.

All free persons were compelled to register in a parish and had to appear before a magistrate in order to obtain their certificate of freedom. Every conceivable stumbling block was put in their way to deprive them of their dignity. In 1733, legislation allowed a brown man and his family the same rights as a white man born of English ancestors but it usually required the brown man to marry a white person if his children were to inherit this status.

Even more oppressive was the plantocracy's deliberate use of the law to pervert justice and to leave the slave defenceless. One of the most shocking instances dates back to the year 1748 when the Jamaica Assembly rejected a bill that would have prohibited the mutilation or dismembering of slaves by their owners without the consent of a magistrate. Slavery was both cruel and arbitrary, and even humane owners were not likely to sacrifice an iota of authority over a slave since this would mean reducing authority over his property.

We have looked at the plantation in its physical setting, sometimes of tender, charming beauty, and we have considered briefly the purposes and ethos of the plantation, seeking in vain for signs of some civilizing influences.

The resident planter-attorneys were the real rulers of island society; they filled the public bodies – not only the nominated councils, but also the elected oligarchic assemblies. In the British colonies, planters also filled, in effect, most of the public offices, for though the more important officials were appointed by letters-patent in England, the actual work was commonly done by deputies in the islands who were remunerated by fees and who paid a rent to the principals. Office, like land, was thus a form of property, often owned by absentees. (Parry and Sherlock: 1958)

Each estate appeared to be a world in itself, self-sufficient with its own labour force in residence from skilled artisans to field gang, its own hospital, water-supply, its warehouse, cattle, mules, horses, its own drays and source of fuel. In reality, however, each slave plantation was a wealth-creating machine serving the rich, tied to finance houses and banks in London, Bristol, Liverpool; and linked through them with the Atlantic Trade System within which both the Plantation Trade – whether it be tobacco, sugar or cotton – and the Slave Trade operated. Just as the French colonies were a part of France so, as Edmund Burke declared, "the whole of the import and export trade revolved and circulated in the United Kingdom and was, so far as it affected profit, in the nature of a home trade as if the several countries of America and Ireland were all pieced on to Cornwall". Burke failed to see that Britain itself and Western Europe were functioning parts of an Atlantic trading system in which as Joseph Inikori, points out, the buying and selling of slaves to the Americas benefitted Europe by stimulating considerable mercantile skills, expert financing, improved shipbuilding, the production of new types of goods, an expand-ing market in the slave-producing regions of tropical Africa. "The creative responses of the economies of Atlantic Europe to the requirements of this function (the slave trade) formed an important part of the development in those economies." Inikori points to studies of the British economy for the period 1750-1807 when Britain dominated the buying and selling of slaves to the Americas and the demand for insurance cover led to the develop-ment of marine insurance in Britain as well to the expansion of credit facil-ities and banking. Further, it increased shipbuilding to meet the demand for ships; "between 1791 and 1807 about 15 per cent of all tonnage built in Britain was destined for the Guinea trade, about 95 per cent of which went into the shipping of slaves". Manufacturing also benefitted and expanded.

As we point to ways in which the West Indian sugar trade and African labour produced the wealth that financed the Industrial Revolution, it is appropriate to acknowledge the pioneering work of two West Indian scholars. C. L. R. James and Eric Williams. Williams "points repeatedly to the causal links between the slavery, near slavery, serfdom, quasi wage-earning in the New World and the rise of capitalism in Old Europe. The essence of mercantilism, he concludes, was slavery". Inikori shows how Britain, through its activities in the slave trade, benefitted not only from a growth of world trade in this period but in this most important aspect, that "the critical developments and the technological developments of the period were all called forth and made economic by the practical problems of production for an extended world market"; (Inikori: 1979) or, as a British economist points out, "Colonial trade introduced to English industry the quite new possibility of exporting in great quantities other than woollen goods to markets where there was no question of the exchange of manufactures for other manufactures. The process of industrialization in England from the second quarter of the eighteenth century was to an important extent a response to colonial demands for rails, axes, buckets, coaches, clocks saddles . . . and a thousand other things."

The pens and "coffee mountains" diversified Jamaica's system of large holdings without weakening the power of the plantocracy or the structure of slavery. They enshrined slavery. In contrast, the "Negro grounds", "Negro houses", and slowly growing "Negro marketing system" based on a chain of Sunday markets symbolise the cradle of freedom.

CHAPTER 15

Pens, provision grounds and higglers

The word "pen" derives from the Old English "penn", the name for to a small enclosure for sheep and other animals. In Middle English, "pennen" meant "to shut in", "pen in", "bolt in", with the Old English variants, "penn" meaning a "pin" or "peg", and the verbs "to pin", "to pin in", "to unpin". Early English colonists of the period 1660-90, finding Jamaica stocked with wild cattle, often spoke of "penning" those they caught.

In Jamaica the word was used early on to denote an enclosure for animals and also a farm or gentleman's estate. A law passed by the Jamaican legislature in 1695 decreed: "All owners of Neat cattle cows shall keep one white man at each Pen, and two white men at every Pen where-unto belongs above 200 Head of Cattle." We read also of "breeding pens" and "lowland pens". In 1801 Lady Nugent wrote of driving to "Lord B's Penn". By then "pen" meant a cattle farm or enclosure and also any country estate or gentleman's estate. For example, "at these pens or country houses, and on the land adjoining, they breed plenty of hogs, sheep, goats and poultry" (Marsden: 1788); or "his pen produces a super-abundance of maize and guinea corn". Others write of "these beautiful parklike estates called pens". (Cassidy, LePage: 1967) The English writer Anthony Trollope, who visited Jamaica in 1860, said: "Hardly any Europeans, or even white creoles, live in the town. They have country seats, pens as they call them, at some little distance." There was even a "penn punch", which consisted mainly of brandy and cherry brandy.

The names of the few surviving pens, such as Bamboo Pen, should be preserved and not forgotten as Admiral's Pen, Liguanea Pen, Rollington Pen have been. How wise and pleasing it would have been to have preserved two or three of the "little grass penns with good houses on them" that were dispersed about Half Way Tree, "and a small grass penn stocked with sheep and goats".

Another word taken from the farmers and peasants of England into Jamaica talk is "ground", with its Jamaican equivalent "grung". The word "ground" was commonly used in the dialects of South-West England and in parts of southern Scotland to mean "a field or piece of cultivated land". In Jamaica "grung" denotes a smallholding cultivated by the owner, as in "mi a go mi grung now", or as in the folktale, "Bredda Puss was a tie up him food fe leff him grung goh home." (Cassidy, LePage: 1967) On every slave plantation there was a portion of land called "Negro grounds", out of which each slave was allotted a portion to cultivate. In Jamaica-talk a cultivator today often speaks with affection and pride of "going grung", which he may describe with a smile as "mi piece of rockstone", for the "grung" may indeed consist very largely of saucers of red earth in between razor-edged rocks. Sometimes the word "mountain" was used for "grung" as well as in connection with crops, as in "coffee mountain". Lord Adam Gordon, in *Travels in America and the West Indies (1764-65)*, told how he "attended him also to his farm (Pen) and to his Mountain which is cool and pleasant".

A record of a conversation in St Ann in 1957 ran:

> "Where is Uncle Charles now?"
> "Ah mounten".
> "Doing what?"
> "Gone dig food".
> "What does he do with the food?"
> "Cook a mounten" (Cassidy, Le Page: 1967)

The pens and coffee mountains greatly expanded and diversified Jamaica's system of agriculture based on large holdings and committed to using African slaves and to protecting white power. We will visit Goshen, one of the largest pens, Union in St Ann, Montrose in St Mary, which was owned by Simon Taylor, Jamaica's wealthiest planter and largest slave holder, Salt Pond Hut and finally Vineyard, where we will observe the seasoning of the overseer Thomas Thistlewood. We will find that in Jamaica a pen was not always a small enclosure but was often a fairly large property.

The sugar plantation produced for export whereas the pen supplied the demands of the local market. Their programmes were not dictated by a monoculture, but moved to different rhythms, meeting the needs of a variety of animals, planning the care of pastures, picking the purple pimento berries at the proper time, sending cattle to distant markets, dispatching logwood chips to the port of shipment, selling grass and cordage to an urban market, buying worn-out cattle from an estate to fatten and butcher for local consumption.

Goshen Pen, at the foot of the Don Figueroa Mountains, situated between Horse Savanna and Bull Savanna, was famous for its livestock. In the days of carriages, buggies, kittareens and horse riding, customers often bought their ponies and mares from Goshen Pen.

In 1780 Goshen comprised 3,917 acres, including 12 pieces in guinea grass and 12 pieces in common grass. South of the pastures were a number of buildings, a dwelling house and garden circled by stables, a coach house, store houses, offices, a well, a sheep pen and further to the south slave houses, shown as 36 squares set out in regular lines. Scattered through the pastures were several wells and natural wells. The chance introduction of guinea grass in 1744 had greatly enriched Goshen and other pens through-out the island. A bag of the seeds had been given to George Ellis, twice chief Justice of Jamaica, as feed for some rare West African birds by the captain of a slave ship. The birds died shortly after and the seeds were thrown away in a field where they flourished. It was soon noticed that the cattle enjoyed the strange grass and, in the process of time, many penkeepers planted it.

"Fifty years later, at the time of emancipation, Goshen and Long Hill Pen had a combined population of 420 slaves. The total number of taxable livestock on the pens in 1832 was 1744, making the enterprise a very extensive one." (Higman: 1988)

Union Pen was in St Ann, about five miles inland from the north coast and near the border with St Mary. At the time of its survey in around 1825 it covered 1,130 acres, including 803 acres in guinea grass and 204 acres in wood and "Negro grounds". The pimento was concentrated close to the dwelling house and its barbecues, which were on a central hilltop that overlooked the slave houses. The proprietor was a coloured man, Benjamin Scott Moncrieffe, who belonged to a wealthy, educated family which had applied for special rights under slavery and had been welcomed in white society before abolition. His son Peter became a barrister and sat in the Assembly in the 1840s. Benjamin Moncrieffe also owned neighbouring Friendship and acquired Eltham and Benham Spring Estates. Union sold working cattle and fat cattle as well as pimento. Moncrieffe also tried to make money at the races at the popular courses of the day at Drax Hall, Montego Bay, Spanish Town and Kingston. His personal accounts show that he took with him some slaves as grooms, domestic servants and occasionally as jockeys. He paid his jockeys when they won and gave his "boys" allowances to cover living expenses and sometimes money to place bets. His total race meeting expenses in 1828 came to £110.14.3. He was lucky, for he won "the Free Prize by St Ann's beating Watt's Eclipse and Davis' Superior £100", and "£133.6.8 by St Ann's beating Watt's Eclipse, Davis Superior and Doctor Roper's Vanity over the Montego Bay course". In 1829, in Clarendon "Romp fell while running well".

Montrose in St Mary was a pen developed by a wealthy planter, Simon Taylor, to supply one of his sugar estates, Llanrumney, also in St Mary. Burrowfield Pen in St Thomas served his two sugar estates in that parish, Lyssons and Holland. He also owned Haughton Court in Hanover and Prospect, now Vale Royal. Montrose and Burrowfield Pens were not tied to trading only with the Taylor estates but were free to trade with others also.

Simon Taylor (1740-1813), was, we are told,

> in the habit of accumulating money, so as to make his nephew and heir . . . one of the most wealthy subjects of His Majesty. In strong opposition to Government at present and violent in his language against the King's Ministers for their conduct toward Jamaica. He has most extraordinary manners and lives principally with overseers of estates and masters of merchant vessels; but he has had an excellent education [he went to Eton], is well-informed and is a warm friend to those he takes by the hand. He is also very hospitable but is said to be most inveterate in his dislikes. (Nugent: 1939)

It was said that Taylor exercised greater influence in Jamaica, and for a longer period, than any other individual.

Lady Nugent, who charmed him into a measure of civility, wrote

> I cannot here avoid mentioning that Mr. Taylor is an old bachelor and detests the society of women . . . A little mulatto girl was sent into the drawing room to amuse me. She was a sickly delicate child, with straight light-brown hair, and very black eyes. Mr. T appeared very

anxious for me to dismiss her, and in the evening the house keeper told me she was his own daughter and that he had a numerous family, some almost on every one of his estates. (Nugent: 1939)

On 20 August 1802, the Lt Governor, George Nugent, had reported to the Colonial Office that Taylor,

a rich proprietor in Jamaica, who by a misrepresentation to the members of the House of Assembly, was the principal cause of their refusing to grant any further supplies to His Majesty for the Maintenance of the Military Establishment, (having stated to them that it was in contemplation in England to lay an additional Tax of 20's [20 shillings] on sugars and which he attempted to prove that the Planters cannot support any additional Burthens. (Nugent: 1939)

The real author of that report was supposed to be the West India merchant George Hibbert.

Salt Pond Hut was at the other end of the social scale from the gracious pens of the merchant-planters of Kingston, such as Prospect, with its long avenue of yokewood trees, 120 sheep and lambs to crop the grass and charm the guests, a few cows to supply milk, five mules and some horses for riding and for drawing a variety of chaises. Salt Pond Hut made money. The plan showed a property of 1,413 acres, a section of it running from Spanish Town to Passage Fort and Dawkins, Salt Pond Hut and another section along the Rio Cobre to where it met the Salt River. It contained 162 acres of Scots grass, a rough variety that grew on brackish land, and 78 acres of mangroves suitable for planting Scots grass.

Every day bundles of Scots grass were sent into Kingston, usually by sea, along with cordwood, corn and a few cattle, mules, horses and asses. The income from the sales for 1811 was £14,342, which was more than the historian Edward Long estimated that a typical sugar estate earned. The plan, drawn by John Fullarton in 1808, noted: "The place marked near Passage Fort shows the situation of several huts made by free negroes being a trespass on the property."

Vineyard Pen in Westmoreland, between Black River and Lacovia, was where Florentius Vassall appointed Thomas Thistlewood overseer in1750. They fell out in the course of the year, and in 1751 Thistlewood went to Egypt Pen beyond Savanna-la-Mar where he remained until 1767, when he bought a small property of 160 acres between Egypt and Kirkpatrick Pen and established himself as the leading horticulturist in western Jamaica. He died in 1786.

Before coming to Jamaica Thistlewood had travelled to India, Brazil and western Europe. He kept a diary throughout his adult life. He knew nothing about managing slaves or a pen, or about Jamaican planter society, and as Douglas Hall observes in his edition of *Diary of a Westmoreland Planter*, these papers "are unique and provide a veritable treasure house of information on life and labour in slave-day Westmoreland . . . Thistlewood recorded events as they occurred but very seldom did he attempt to interpret or explain his or any other's actions." The diaries enable us to watch the encounter between a white stranger, totally inexperienced as an overseer, and a group of African slaves who became his teachers and companions, for he had little opportunity to mingle with other whites or to learn from other white overseers.

Vineyard Pen was over 1,000 acres but much of it was in swamp, through which a track led to the Vineyard barcadier or jetty, where supplies were loaded on to canoes or larger craft to save heavy carriage on the deeply rutted roadways.

Vineyard carried some cattle, horses, mules, asses, sheep, goats, pigs, ducks, turkeys and fowls; it produced timber, mostly mahogany and logwood, and a variety of trees and crops in the garden, as well as in the slaves provision grounds. Thistlewood lost no time in making some improvements: "the fattening pasture is about 23 acres, the plantain walk about 11½ or 12 . . . .The Negroes new cleared ground about 8 acres. The common road leading from my house to the stile into the corn ground is about 1,568 yards". He increased the cultivation of foodstuffs and the corn walk became a plantain walk which in January 1751 carried about 1,800 plantain trees. The slaves possibly had about 1,800 plantain trees also.

The housing for the penkeeper and slaves was modest. Thistlewood had cracks in the walls of his house mended. "When mud walls are sufficiently dry and very much cracked in this country, they mix water, soft cow dung and wood ashes with a small quantity of fire mould, till it be as scarce to run out of the hand. With this they rub the walls once or twice over, and it will fill and cover all the cracks."(Hall: 1989)

It is probable that the slaves lived in houses like the one Thistlewood built for his mistress Marina before he left Vineyard. It was of wattle and plaster, thatched, with two connecting rooms, one 9 feet by 7 feet, the other 6½ feet by 7 feet. The larger had a single door leading out.

From the time of his arrival Thistlewood became involved in chronicling the seasons:

> In St Elizabeth (above us) the rain, or season, that comes in July, August, September is called the great spring, and the corn that is gathered about Christmas, the year corn. The rain that comes in March, April, May, the crab rain from the great density of land crabs which then run at night – and the crop of corn which is gathered in July, the parrakeet corn, because they then abound.

As Hall points out,

> The emphasis on land for food production reflected the hard condi-
> tions of cultivation in south St Elizabeth and the small possibility of
> finding supplementary supplies for neighbouring properties. Here
> provision grounds apparently provided no marketable surpluses
> moving from neighbouring estates to Vineyard or vice-versa, and
> there is, remarkably, no mention whatever of the existence in the area
> of a slave-supplies Sunday Market. (Hall: 1959)

Thistlewood had to learn to eat what the slaves ate; not the 26 capons,
one young roast cock, 20 laying hens, three maiden pullets, 16 young
fowls, one laying duck, two squabs, one musk melon, 19 sweetsops, that
he sent by road on 12 December to the Vassalls.

> He made intriguing discoveries: "On 10 July 1750 have boiled goats
> milk (which is very rich) every morning to breakfast; eat some
> Docono, made of plantain, very good (17 July 1750); at dinner had
> pepper pot of callaloo and prickly pear with some ochro. Had for
> supper hominy, it eats like cracked oatmeal pretty much, made of
> Indian corn beat and cracked; had some Cayya boiled for dinner to
> my beef.

This may refer to a condiment made of "Cayan pepper", or, less likely,
to a preparation of a healing weed now called "strong back" or to a type of
root crop similar to eddo which is called taya.

There were 42 slaves when Thistlewood took up his duties as overseer
in July 1750. The diaries show that 13 of them were "new", that is,
recently acquired. They included Accubah, a Coromanti, a field slave who
had been given a new hoe. About two months earlier she had been
whipped, with Mary and Mr Banton's Will, for having helped the boy to
escape custody on the night of Wednesday 10 October; Betty or
Accramah, a new Negro, a Coromanti . . . Christie or Gesse, a new negro
field worker, a Congo; Cynthia or Naccuma, a Bambarah Negro, "what
the Coromantees call Crappah or Temme donko being brought into this
country young; Deborah or Binda, new, a Congo who at first worked in
the field; Jenny or Cragua, a new negro; Marina or Worree, new, a
Congo," Thistlewood's mistress up to the end of his year at Vineyard. He
asked Dick to build a house for her. Mary or Adomah, new, a Congo who
had been housed with Charles, but in May 1751 her provision ground was
separated from his "as they can't agree and he uses her very ill".(Hall:
1988)

Attention was given to the provision grounds. In addition to the old and
new grounds Thistlewood developed the Negro cleaned ground, bushed

and cleaned by the slaves, each of whom received at least 100 square feet. It was tough going, but, as a slave informed Thistlewood, "There were tricks in the trade for if the hands blister by hard work, piss upon them and it will harden them."

They worked at these tasks and received their separate allocations. Thoughts of the homeland must have come to the new slaves; memories of the men going about the traditional African tasks of clearing the fields that had lain fallow with bush and making yam heaps, with women and boys helping; men planting the yams and after sprouting tying the vines to the poles to keep them off the soil; the women hoeing and weeding the fields of yams and, after the men had harvested them, carrying them to the yam barn with high wooden racks built on the edge of the village. This background of tradition, the inherited skills of generations of West African farmers and the accustomed crops, the corn, yams, plantains, beans, peas, made the provision grounds a part of Africa, the only places in Jamaica where Africans were free to make their own decisions, reap their own crops and enter into the money economy by selling the livestock and vegetables they produced.

> The word "higgler" came from England to Jamaica; it is rarely used there, whereas it is in common use in Jamaica to denote a seller of any kind of small produce or goods; formerly an itinerant peddler, now also one who brings produce into a market to sell. (Cassidy, LePage: 1967) The word "higgler" is related to the English "to hack" and "to haggle", to argue with a vendor. "Haggle" has the variant "higgle". A higgler forms the link between the isolated small farmers and the market, usually a woman of the neighbourhood or a nearby area, who walks and buys produce to take to the market. Some country higglers spread their goods in the market and sell directly to house buyers, and others sell to town higglers, town residents who rent stalls in the markets where they buy at wholesale and sell at retail. (Katzin: 1959)

The expert higgler at Vineyard Pen was Phibbah. Other slaves, Joan a washerwoman for example, kept and sold pigs and poultry as well as produce. Phibbah, however, deserves special mention. A woman of great reliability and dignity and not afraid to speak her mind, she seems to have engaged in business and to have accumulated property of her own. On 6 August 1750 she bought a sow from Simon for 3 cobbs and a boar piggy for a crown. She paid for them with a pistole (then equal to one pound, three shillings and nine pence Jamaica currency). She was a trader in the tradition of the West African women. Sometimes, usually once a month, she, with Scipio as escort, went out on the road. They went out, for instance, on Wednesday 17 April 1751 and returned to Vineyard on Monday 22 April. Financed by the pen, Phibbah had sold 58 yards of "garlix" and 9 yards of "across bar" cloth at 7 beads a yard and 44 yards of "check" at 5 beads a yard. She brought home 689 beads or twenty-one pounds ten shillings and sevenpence half-penny in Jamaica currency. After a later trip on which she apparently had had some difficulty, Thistlewood gave her a note: "Gave Phibbah, a ticket that she may not be molested, thus Vineyard Pen. June 5, 1751. The Bearers hereof, (a Negro man and woman named Scipio and Phibbah in company) belong to the Vineyard Penn and are the property of Florentius Vassall Esquire by whose orders they go out with cloth to sell, which is certified by me, Thomas Thistlewood." (Hall: 1989)

The Sunday market was the selling place for produce from the provision ground and for stock reared by the slaves, a good fat farrow for example of small pigs, milch goats, kids, capons, pullets, bananas, sweet potatoes, peas, corns, avocado pears, yams and twisted tobacco.

For the plantation the provision ground was a necessity. Feeding the growing army of slaves was a priority. No provision ground, no salted fish, meant no sugarcane fields, no sugar trade. Bryan Edwards argued that it was better to export sugar and import food because one acre of his canefield would buy more Indian corn than could be raised on five times that area of land and pay the freight as well. Ground provision had to be grown, and in quantity. Hungry belly walked the land and thousands died when war or hurricane disrupted the food supply.

The English Government enlarged the local supplies by importing food plants. Taro a root brought to the Americas by the Portuguese proved to be a valuable supplement. So, in Jamaica especially, was the ackee, brought in from West Africa in 1776 to be combined with salted codfish. The mango, an Asiatic tree, added flavour and invaluable vitamins to a heavy diet of starch. The breadfruit entered in the 1790s but was fed only to pigs for its first 50 years. Then Jamaicans discovered what they had been missing in the "yellow heart". Other life-savers included the "red afu" (a dark yellow yam) and the "white afu" (a pale yellow), the mozella, "Madam sit-down" (a Portland yam with a big round bottom) and the St Vincent yam, called "come here fe help we" because it gives an early crop and stays in the earth for a long time without going bad. With these were various versions of the taro or coco known as hog-taya, or eddo. Sir Hans Sloane wrote in 1725: "Tayas or Eddos are eaten in Jamaica, and cause a heat in the throat, called commonly there scratching the throat, and this when well-boiled." Among other varieties are the purple coco and the delicious commander coco. Its other names are "leff man" and "leff back" because it does not disintegrate in the pot.

These names illustrate how the provision ground and the yard gave rise to folk names rich in laughter and sparkle, such as: "scissors tail" for a variety of sweet potato with split leaves; "full pot" for another variety that swells and fills the pot; "tie-leaf" and "blue-drawers" for the ducknu, wrapped in plantation or banana leaf and boiled or baked. In the process the leaf turns bluish green.

The male and female cultivators through the provision grounds and the rural and urban higglers through the chain of Sunday markets on which an internal marketing system was based, worked without access to education and risk-financing and established a system of smallholder agriculture complementary to the large plantations. The system was West African in origin, as this account shows:

> The Yoruba enjoy trading and huge markets with over a thousand sellers are a common sight. Yoruba traders are conspicuous as far afield as Accra and Abidjan, Bamako and Duagadogou. The nineteenth century travellers reported meeting large caravans of traders passing from one region of Nigeria to another; today the collection of export crop and the distribution of goods imported by sea are both important. There is also an extensive trade in local foodstuffs.
>
> The marketing process is complex. One woman visits a farmer on his land and buys a headload of yams; she sells these to a second woman in a small rural market. Then at a larger rural market – held every four days – the latter sells to a woman wholesaler from the town, who later resells to women who will sit in the town's night market (among the Oyo) and sell to the consumers. In a similar manner, imported goods travel from the warehouse of the expatriate firm to the rural consumer. Most four or eight day markets are held in cycles, the women visiting each in turn. (Lloyd: 1965)

In Jamaican towns there was a sharper sexual division of work than in the country parts where both women and men were cultivators. In the ports the men were artisans, seamen, coopers, butchers, fishermen, droghers and the like. Some of the women were in domestic service as cooks, nannies and washerwomen, but they dominated marketing and they became a powerful force, as we can see by looking at early nineteenth-century Kingston, where in 1817 there were 17,798 slaves, 9,865 of them females. Of a total slave-holding population of 3,499 slave holders, 1,957 were female. Female slaveholders owned a total of 5,900 female slaves.

The picture was similar in other urban centres in Jamaica. For 26 towns in Jamaica for the years 1829-32 there was a ratio of 83.29 males to 100 females. The closest to that of Kingston in favour of females was 90.2: 100 for the parish of Vere. There were also more Africans than creoles in the urban slave population, the figures for 1817 (ten years after the abolition of the slave trade), being 9,147 compared with 8,651 creoles. It is estimated that 66 per cent of all urban slaves worked as domestics in Kingston, and that many female slaves were involved almost exclusively in higglering and hawking goods about the streets, generally for the profit of the mistress.

Whatever they marketed, the urban slaves generally enjoyed a fairly independent existence and were always responsible for dealings in cash or kind. "The seller was involved in a series of commercial transactions which could not be directly controlled by the owner and which provided experience of a way of life separate from the slave condition." (Higman: 1988)

The world of the higgler was a hard one, for the authorities disliked their marketing activities. Street vendors were frequently apprehended and fined. Newspapers carried regular reports on penalties imposed: "two negroes . . . fined in the mitigated penalty on ten shillings, five pence each for hawking and peddling goods through the street".

As marketing activities increased, the authorities were constantly engaged in regulating public markets and providing new facilities. In 1817 the Kingston Common Council proposed "suppressing the irregular

Slave higglers

marketplace on the parade for provisions and goods coming in from the country for sale". (Simmonds: 1987)

Slaves travelled over land and by sea to markets and estates to sell their goods. The authorities in Spanish Town complained bitterly in 1822 about the streets being greatly infested by a set of hawkers and peddlers from Kingston to "the great injury of the trading part of the community and in the very eye of the police". Kingston Harbour had its market canoes, which were not always safe. In March 1819 several women and children drowned when a market canoe going from Passage Fort to Port Royal upset. Four slaves travelling by market canoe from Port Henderson were more fortunate. When their market canoe overturned in a sudden squall, sailors from the Sapphire man-of-war rescued them. Their provisions went to the bottom.

Phibbah, Scipio and Dick of Vineyard Pen and throughout the generations, other higglers, peddlars and itinerant traders prepared the economic foundations for a society of free smallholders. Today's higglers and peddlars keep us alive with the islandwide food distribution system that the early higglers established, and enrich our lives with their concept of a market as a "gathering place for kinsfolk, district folk, the whole community; around market, school and church the life of the whole district revolved".

Higglering calls for a range of skills. Along with the counting and change-making, they must develop what they call profit-making techniques.

> This involves the ability to acquire steady customers, buy high quality produce, to barter, stand ground, to judge one type of customer from the next. The higgler must also learn to keep track of her money, to distinguish between money which is overhead and that which is profit. She must acquire the skill of offering a little extra in order to attract and maintain a steady customer, yet at the same time not give away all her profit. She must acquire the skill to maintain a delicate balance in this area. (Durant-Gonzales: 1976)

The first task in the markets is to establish one's own spot: "Once space is acquired, each higgler maintains her spot week in and week out. It becomes her business address, the place with which she is identified and at which she is easily located by customers and friends. Miss Addy is a street higgler who sells from the sidewalk and says that her location is always reserved for her. Over an eight-month period, I observed her and 50 other street higglers selling from the same sidewalk location.

I was told by higglers that market space is maintained through a system of mutual recognition which is based on the higgler establishing the fact that she is there each week. If her space is occupied upon her arrival, says Miss Addy, "The women just 'small up' [make room]." In the event that a woman is coming to market for the first time, the policy is that the other higglers 'small up' and make room for the additional person. One veteran of 25 years in the higglering business explained: "We all have to sell, and all the women know and understand and accept this. For each of us must make a living." (Durant-Gonzales: 1976)

An urgent priority is to establish staunch customers, which is based on unspoken loyalties between higgler and customer. In her study Durant-Gonzales describes the relationship as defined by Miss Addy, who told how "A customer would come together well". In the words of another higgler, "If my staunch customers buy yams from me each week, I must have yams for these customers. Even if I am not selling yams, I will buy them from another higgler just so that my staunch customers get them." (Durant-Gonzales: 1976)

During slavery while higglers and male peddlars were building an economic foundation that was bonded together by common loyalties, they were building stable family units in response to the plantation system of moral degradation. In these various ways the African-Jamaicans of the plantation grounds, the male and female traders, the higglers laying claim to market space through their efforts to better themselves, chiselled away at the base of plantation slavery and modified the whole system by establishing rights through custom and usage.

They added an even more significant achievement by their response to the destruction of the traditional African codes governing family relationships and the kinship system. The functions of the natural father as protector, provider, counsellor and model were usurped by the slaveholder who sexually exploited the women, using them as breeders of slaves. The Africans, barred from the religous rites of the church and denied Christian marriage, responded by establishing basic family units through common-law unions. Through this response to the marginalisation of the natural father and the degradation of motherhood they maintained a form of social structure that reflected moral and ethical principles and satisfied fundamental human needs. For this the white slave-holding society with brazen hypocrisy branded them as immoral, but our poets, George Campbell among them, remind us of the significance of what they achieved.

> No degradation resented by our fathers
> That is not glory unto us.
> No suffering of our ancestors
> That is not part of our Emancipation.

CHAPTER 16

Into a new age

The liberation struggles of the 18th century did not weaken the sugar-and-slave plantation. They did not diminish the trade in African labour. The great house appeared as formidable a symbol of white power as it ever had been. The slave ships sailed into Kingston harbour as frequently as they had always done. Sugar was doing well. In the 25 years from 1751 to 1775 Jamaica imported 172,500 Africans compared with 128,000 in the preceding quarter of a century. In spite of the fact that they were known as leaders of rebellions, 39 per cent came from the Gold Coast.

For the Jamaican sugar planter the skies were clear. The mills would continue grinding, the slaves continue working, the money continue flowing. It appeared that nothing would weaken the basic principles that slavery was a necessity and that one human being had the right to buy another. No one in his senses would have predicted that in 1776 the North American colonies would declare their independence from England, that the French Revolution would break out in 1788, that the Napoleonic wars would tear Europe apart between 1795 and 1815, and that steam power, industrialisation, science and technology would begin to displace the humanities as the foundation of civilisation in the 1780s.

The slaves watched and registered change in their minds. They were illiterate, but illiteracy is not a synonym for stupidity. The planters and overseers often made the mistake of underestimating the intelligence of the slave, his capacity for understanding, his skill in behaving as if he were indeed a "bungo" or simpleton.

The white planters and merchants, like the ancient Romans, who usually called their slaves, "little one" or "boy", and considered themselves infinitely superior to these "overgrown children", looked with contempt on the private lives of the blacks and on their intellectual ability. It was safe to discuss the rights of man in their presence for they certainly were unable to understand. The planters should have remembered that during the 1730s plantation slaves had established efficient information networks with the maroons.

Often the informers of the slaves were the great house people themselves. Baron de Wimpffen, who visited St Domingue in 1790, at a time when the rights of man and liberty were fashionable table talk, expressed alarm at the behaviour of the whites. "Surrounded by mulattoes and negroes, they indulge themselves in the most imprudent discussions on liberty etc. To discuss the 'Rights of Man' before such people, what is it but to teach them that power dwells with strength, and strength with numbers."

We turn at this point from the Jamaica sugar plantations to Europe and search the decade of the 1760s for the signs of radical change, some at that time no larger than the outline of a man's hand against a distant sky, some no more than the publication of a book, the announcement of an invention. Nothing seemed powerful enough to fracture the structure of mercantilism, the rigidities of a feudal class structure based on the rights of the propertied and the obligations of labouring classes and serfs.

The signs were to be found in the preaching of an obscure Anglican priest, John Wesley, in the ideas and reasoning of two philosophers, François-Marie Voltaire and Jean-Jacques Rousseau, in the reflections of Adam Smith, a Scottish professor of philosophy at Cambridge, in his *Wealth of Nations*, in the experiments of a Scottish engineer, James Watts, about ways of harnessing steam power, and in James Hargreaves' use of technology to produce the spinning jenny, all reminders that ideas are more powerful than an army with banners.

We will also consider ways in which the Evangelical Movement and the Enlightenment touched and changed the world of the African-Jamaican on his remote plantation, destroyed slavery and the West India sugar monopoly in England, and established white-black alliances based on religious conviction and the acceptance of the principle of human rights. We will refer also to the scientific and technological advances of the age, the emergence of an English working class and their involvement in the passing of the Act of Emancipation.

The Evangelical Movement was a response to the preaching of John Wesley. In May 1738 Wesley "felt his heart grow strangely warm within him" at a meeting with Moravian Brethren in London, and in that moment of conversion received from God an assurance of salvation through faith in Christ alone. Up to the time of his death in 1791 John Wesley, with his brother Charles, and for years with the help also of his friend George Whitfield, delivered this message of personal salvation to the people of England, usually at crowded open-air meetings.

John Wesley's passionate message and the hymns written by Charles, such as "Hark, hark my Soul", "Jesu, lover of my Soul" and any of the 6,000 hymns he wrote, brought England to its knees in prayer. His message reached the poor, the outcast.

> Outcasts of men to you I call,
> Harlots and publicans and thieves.
> He spreads His arms to embrace you all,
> Sinners alone His grace receives.
> No need for him the righteous have,
> He came the lost to seek and save.

So widespread and so fervent was the religious revival that by the 1790s the old dissenting churches, such as the Baptists, were having their own religious revival. The Baptists founded a missionary society in 1792. The London Missionary Society was founded in 1795 and the British and Foreign Bible Society in 1803.

The revival also inspired a reform movement within the Church of England, which up to then had been somnolent and complacent. Among the reformists was William Wilberforce. But slavery had not yet become a moral issue. Granville Sharp, a terrier of a little man who never let go, made it so. Sharp took up the case of a slave, James Somersett, whose master lived in England. Somersett fell ill and was turned adrift by his master. With Sharp's help he recovered. On his recovery his master claimed him. Sharp resisted the claim. The case finally went before Lord Mansfield, Chief Justice of England, who on 22 July 1772 decided: "The

Early Moravian church and mission school

THE STORY OF THE JAMAICAN PEOPLE

state of slavery is of such a nature that it is incapable of being introduced on any reasons, moral or political, but only by positive law . . . It's so odious that nothing can be suffered to support it, but positive law. Whatever inconveniences, therefore, may follow from a decision, I cannot say this case is approved by the law of England and therefore the black must be discharged."

As a result of this ruling all 10,000 of the slaves held in England at the time gained their freedom. Encouraged by the ruling, the abolitionists intensified their efforts. The Quakers formed an anti-slavery society and were joined, among others, by Granville Sharp, Thomas Clarkson and James Ramsay, a clergyman who had been in the West Indies for 19 years and spoke with great feeling about the cruelty of slavery. In 1784, Wilberforce was converted and became a member of the Saints, the name given to a group of god-fearing English abolitionists. Having read Clarkson's book attacking the slave trade, Wilberforce decided to devote his life to destroying the system.

Wilberforce, Clarkson and Sharp made a gifted team. Clarkson was a brilliant publicist and mobiliser of public opinion, Sharpe was known for his bristling tenacity, Wilberforce for his charm, eloquence, gifts of leadership, popularity and dedication. Of course they had limitations. William Hazlitt, the English essayist, pointed to the lack of a coherent philosophy of benevolence in one who protected property and saw poverty as due to laziness, and he mocked at "the gentry, Mr. Wilberforce and the Prince Regent and all those who governed . . . by no other principle than truth and no other wish than the good of mankind! This puff will not take with us! We are old birds and not to be caught with chaff."

The fact is that Wilberforce committed his talents, time and strength to persuading parliament to abolish the slave trade. Napoleon got in the way but Wilberforce pressed on, and for the first time in their history the African-Jamaicans discovered that they had allies and friends in the world of white power.

Among the first were the Moravian missionaries who started work in Jamaica in 1754 at the invitation of two absentee proprietors, William Foster and Joseph Barham. They gave 300 acres of land at Bogue in St Elizabeth for a mission station. They accepted the system of slavery and kept slaves but they showed kindness to the slaves. Malaria, yellow fever and dysentery struck down the missionaries. Jamaicans remember these Moravian missionaries, and those who followed them and founded Bethlehem College at a later date.

In 1787 members of the Clapham Sect used their political influence to found the first English colony in Africa by organising and financing a company to establish Sierra Leone as a home for freed slaves. Then, in 1788, one of the abolitionists, Bolben, horrified at the conditions he had seen on a slave ship in the Thames, introduced a bill in parliament to limit the number of slaves that ships might carry in proportion to their tonnage.

Public interest was mounting. Anti-slavery pamphlets maintained the pressure. So did the celebrated potter, Josiah Wedgwood, whose cameo of a negro pleading for freedom, the chains hanging from his wrists and fettered legs, caught public attention. Anti-slavery groups were organised. Hundreds of petitions were sent to the House of Commons, the first time that this form of large-scale public pressure had been tried. A motion was passed in the House for the abolition of the slave trade in four years. The four years became 14. In that period, when the Napoleonic wars demanded the full attention of the government and the planters staged counter-attack after counter-attack, Wilberforce stuck to his task. Year after year he grimly moved his resolution for the abolition of the slave trade. In 1805 the Commons passed the bill but the Lords deferred it. At last in 1807 the bill was passed and on 1 January 1808 the Act for the Abolition of the Slave Trade came into force.

This victory told the West Indian planters that the forces of change were working against them despite a declaration by the Legislature of the Leeward Islands "that no power shall endeavour to deprive us of obtaining slaves from Africa". No mouse ever roared more loudly.

The Evangelical Movement exerted a powerful influence in Jamaica through two black preachers, George Isle and Moses Baker. Towards the end of the War of Independence in 1782, a number of loyalist families moved from the United States with their slaves to Canada, the Bahamas and Jamaica. Among those who came to Jamaica were two black ex-slaves, George Lisle and Moses Baker, who founded there the native Baptist Church. George Lisle's preaching attracted large numbers of people, and the government prosecuted him for uttering seditious words. The charge failed but he was thrown into prison on a trumped-up charge of debt. Moses Baker, and Lisle after his release, continued their ministry and built up a large following.

Lisle and Baker hold a place of honour in the story of the Jamaican people. They did two things that neither the Moravians nor the English Baptist and Methodist missionaries who came after them, could have done. They planted the seed of an indigenous evangelical movement amongst the people, blending the Christian message with traditional African modes of worship, including spirit possession dancing, the clapping of hands and swaying of the body. Like Africans, African-Jamaicans are deeply religious. No aspect of their story is more important than their religion, folk beliefs, native churches. It cries out for closer and fuller study by our own and other scholars, especially African theologians and philosophers. The work of George Simpson and of other recent writers on religious movements indicate how much more needs to be undertaken, and urgently. Such efforts are beyond the scope of this book but we would be at fault if we did not indicate the importance of the missionary work done by these two black Baptist preachers, through whom the Evangelical Movement first touched African-Jamaicans. The Moravians had set an example of religious brotherhood, but Lisle and Baker established a religious movement through itinerant preachers, "daddys" or deacons, and warners, men and women who felt called "to go through the villages and fields for to warn them".

This use of assistant preachers was in itself a significant development. It was a "ranking" of the slaves by blacks and not by white owners, masters, overseers; an appointment of slaves by the preachers to guide, counsel and convert, not to act as drivers whose symbol of authority was the whip. Their symbol was a sacred book that contained messages of brotherhood and love. Through their preaching George Lisle and Moses Baker defined the mission of the Christian church in Jamaica and gave it a system of organisation based on small chapels and deacons. They brought within the reach of the people two books that soon became the treasured library of the African-Jamaican people, the Bible and a Hymn Book. Baker himself was prosecuted, early in his ministry, for quoting from this hymn in his sermon:

> Shall we go on in Sin
> Because Thy grace abounds,
> Or crucify my Lord again
> And open all His Wounds?
> We will be slaves no more
> Since Christ has made us free,
> Has nailed our tyrants to the cross
> And bought our liberty.

Driven by this vision, teams of "daddys" and preachers were active amongst the enslaved. Some who were not licensed became itinerant preachers. Adam, for example, was a creole runaway slave: "a fisherman by trade, much pitted in the face with the small pox, short and well-made, and will attempt to pass for free; being a great smatterer in religious topics, has been lately converted by Parson Lisle, and is always preaching or praying; he was seen on board a ship this morning, going to Old Habour, and no doubt will sail out with her when she is completely loaded".

Lisle and Baker were Baptists. So were most of the English missionaries, Knibb, Burchell, Phillipo and others who enter our story in the following chapter. The term "dissenters" covers many diverse groups but we use it here for two of the oldest, the Quakers and the Baptists, both of whom were committed to the principles of self-government with a great measure of local autonomy for each congregation, in contrast to the established Church of England with its principle of centralised authority. Lisle and Baker were committed to these principles of greater autonomy for the local churches so there was no basic conflict between them and the English Baptists over church organisation.

The English Baptists had no problem, for example, in appointing slaves as deacons. Indeed, they could not have carried out their work without them. The black missionaries prepared the way for the Europeans in the matter of church organisation, and by ministering directly to the African-Jamaicans, they established typical Baptist linkages between working-class people and their church. Further, Lisle and Baker, because they had experienced slavery, passed on a tradition of passionate concern for the enslaved and for the mass of the people and the tradition of a church where African-Jamaicans were at home and participated both in managing its religious affairs and also in maintaining the principles of freedom, equality, brotherhood. In maintaining this tradition William Knibb and his colleagues were indispensable, but the first steps were taken by Lisle and Baker and carried on by Baptist churches and also of the religious and revivalist churches of George William Gordon, Paul Bogle, the prophet Alexander Bedward and the Rastafarians.

Nor should we forget that the African-Jamaicans, without allies, had done a great deal to modify slavery, to lay the foundations of a free society with a substantial infrastructure for food production and internal trading. The forces of change began to touch their lives in the years when they were reaching the limits of what was possible. Without powerful allies it would have been difficult for them to achieve more than they did. The Evangelical Movement exerted a powerful influence which, strengthened by the Enlightenment, became a liberating force.

The Evangelical Movement quickened conscience whereas the Enlightenment quickened minds and drove men to storm the barricades of tyranny. Each was a transforming force, but historical forces do not operate in isolation. Each reinforces the other. We are looking at an age in which they combined to spawn revolutions and counter-revolutions, collisions between working class and propertied class, noble and serf; and, in the world of ideas, an often brutal collision between patriotism and liberty, between the natural rights of man to political representation and the power of "men of riches, men of estates, to make man a perpetual slave"; a world of conflict between "levellers" who the leveller Colonel Rainsborough declared, "the poorest he that is in England hath a life to live as the greatest he . . . every man that is to live under a government ought first by his own consent to put himself under that government . . . I should doubt whether he was an Englishman or no, that should doubt of these things" (Woodhouse: 1951) and on the other hand a vision of the mass of the English people as inferior, depraved, degraded. As the Duchess of Buckingham firmly assured the Countess of Huntington, the Methodist doctrines were "most repulsive and strongly tinctured with impertinence and disrespect toward their superiors in perpetually endeavouring to level all ranks and to do away with all distinctions. It is monstrous to be told you have a heart as sinful as the common wretches that crawl on the earth". (E. P. Thompson: 1963). The lesson for us is that the confrontation took place in the stinking courts and alleys of London and of Paris and also in the slave plantations of the Caribbean. The great moulding forces of this period, whether generated by appeals to conscience, to intellect or by technological advance, make it abundantly clear that the story of the Jamaican people is both an essential part of the story of African-Americans and in many ways has parallels with the European working class.

The Enlightenment broke into the Caribbean with hurricane force. Rousseau and Voltaire were not cloistered European philosophers remote from us. They stoked a revolution in New England in 1776, another in Paris in 1788, yet another in St Domingue, in 1792. Their teachings may even have influenced the second Maroon War in St James in 1795. It is time to turn to them.

The Enlightenment emerged as a major trend, a widespread intellectual awakening, in the decade of the 1760s. The most prominent leaders were Voltaire and Rousseau. In his *Social Contract* published in 1762, Rousseau argued that, by an implied contract, the State is bound to guarantee the rights and liberties of the subject. He maintained that "natural man" was essentially good but was corrupted by the introduction of property, science and culture. His views on the rights of man strongly influenced leaders of the American War of Independence, such as Thomas Jefferson and Benjamin Franklin; leaders of the French Revolution, including Robespierre; leaders of the Romantic Movement in Europe and German philosophers such as Kant and Goethe. In 1763 Voltaire's play *Saul* attacked sections of the Old Testament and then, in 1764, his *Pocket Philosophical Dictionary*, denounced oppression, untruth and dogma.

The words of these two philosophers sounded throughout Western Europe and the American colonies. Voltaire's words were trumpet calls: "Faith consists in believing when it is beyond the power of reason to believe. It is not enough for a thing to be possible for it to be believed", or again, "I disapprove of what you say but I will defend to the death your right to say it," (attributed to Voltaire) and "If God did not exist it would be necessary to invent him." So did Rousseau's powerful "Man was born free and everywhere he is in chains," and his warning that "The strongest is never strong enough to be always the master, unless he transforms his strength into rights, and obedience into duty" and "Nature never deceives us, it is always we who deceive ourselves."

Freedom, the rights of man, equality and brotherhood became realities. Thomas Jefferson, in drafting the American Declaration of Independence wrote: "We hold these truths to be self-evident, that all men are created equal, that they are endowed by their creator with inherent and inalienable rights, that among these are life, liberty and the pursuit of happiness." The Enlightenment fashioned the battle cries for the French Revolution with the words "Liberty, fraternity, equality".

The first great explosion took place in Paris on 14 July 1789 when a Paris mob stormed and took the Bastille, a prison fortress and symbol of royal tyranny in the centre of the city. Simon Schama in his work on the French Revolution describes the explosion. "The bringing together of political patriotism and social unrest – anger with hunger – this was (to borrow the revolutionaries' favourite electrical image) like the meeting of two live wires. At their touch a brilliant incandescence of light and heat occurred. Just what and who would be consumed in the illumination was hard to make out."

There were years of debate in western Europe – and especially in France – about the rights of man. In the French Caribbean colonies the white colonists, landowners and slave owners loudly demanded liberty, meaning the right to run the colony as they wished, as well as to deny liberty to the mulattoes and to the blacks. In Paris the Friends of the Blacks, a society recently formed on the pattern of the English anti-slavery society, campaigned on behalf of the mulattoes.

The all-white colonial assemblies in St Domingue, Martinique and Guadeloupe sent six representatives to the French National Assembly, which under intense pressure in its decree of 15 May provided that mulattoes born of free persons, if qualified in other respects, should have the right to vote for the provincial and colonial assemblies which had been established four years earlier. The St Domingue planters reacted with cries of "Secede" just as Jamaican planters were to do some 20 years later.

The white colonists refused to obey the decree. The mulattoes in St Domingue demanded their rights. Some took up arms. The ruling whites executed Oge, one of the mulatto leaders, by breaking him on the wheel. As a result, revolutionary opinion in France turned against the planters.

The white colonists were determined to keep political power in their hands. They were adamant that they would not share it with the mulattoes, for, as one of their leaders declared, "The mulattoes themselves are but pawns in a larger game. For once our slaves suspect that there is a power other than their masters . . . if once they see that the mulattoes have successfully invoked this power and by its aid have become our equals – then France must renounce all hope of preserving her colonies."

While the white colonists tried to bar the gate and the mulattoes struggled to break though, the slaves were active with nocturnal rituals and oath-taking. In August 1791, drums, discreet but insistent, dominated the night, speaking from secret places in the dark forest to the Africans on the plantations of the great northern plain.

Desperate, determined Africans gathered in the forest in a circle around their leader, a Jamaican called Boukman, while the throbbing of the drums increased, keeping time with their quickening heartbeats. They drank a blood oath, swearing to be loyal to each other, and then Boukman invoked the ancestors:

> The god who created the sun which gives us light, who rouses the waves and rules the storm, though hidden in the clouds, he watches us. He sees all that the white man does. The god of the white man inspires him with crime, but our god calls upon us to do good works. Our god who is good to us orders us to revenge our wrongs. He will direct our arms and aid us. Throw away the symbol of the god of the whites who has so often caused us to weep, and listen to the voice of liberty, which speaks in the hearts of us all. (Gordon: 1983)

Following on this period of preparation, they rose in arms. Within a few weeks the Great Houses were smoking ruins, the cane fields smouldering stubble.

St Domingue was soon a shambles. Everywhere "big whites" and "small whites", royalists and revolutionaries, mulattoes and blacks, free men and slaves fought and plundered in shifting alliances and confusion. Not until September 1792 did a French revolutionary army reach St Domingue, charged with orders to enforce the rule of liberty, equality and fraternity. Faced with royalist resistance, the commander, Leger Felicite Sonthonax, associated himself with the blacks, who with his backing sacked the town of Cap Français. That August Sonthonax proclaimed a conditional emancipation which was confirmed in 1794 by the French National Assembly. It declared: "Negro slavery in all colonies to be abolished, consequently all men, without distinction of colour, living in the colonies are French citizens and shall enjoy the rights guaranteed by the constitution." The action taken by Sonthonax alienated the browns, many of whom were slave owners. The surviving whites in the north fled, some to the United States and others to Cuba, Puerto Rico, where the west coast town of Mayaguez retains its French characteristics to this day, Trinidad, the eastern Caribbean and to Jamaica.

The names of black leaders now emerged, among them Boukman, Henri Christophe from St Kitts, Jean Jacques Dessalines (who was African-born) and Toussaint.

In 1793 England and Spain, both of whom were at war with revolutionary France, sent expeditions to invade St Domingue. The English force under General Maitland took Port-au-Prince. They were defeated by yellow fever, force of numbers and the military skill of Pierre-Dominique Toussaint.

Jean Jacques
Dessalines

In Jamaica Lord Balcarres was convinced that the outbreak of the maroon war of 1795 was inspired by the example of the French islands and by French revolutionary agents, although this was never proved. The effect, however was that the government of Jamaica refused to send reinforcements to General Maitland. The troops which arrived from England were fresh and unseasoned, and the final outcome of the expedition to St Domingue was never in doubt.

Toussaint L'Ouverture had been a slave on a Haitian estate in the north. He took little part in the 1791 uprising but on the outbreak of war with Spain he entered the Spanish service as a royalist mercenary, and built up a very effective force of about 4,000 men. In 1795, alarmed at the progress of the English and at the prospect of the restoration of slavery that an English victory would bring about, he deserted with his troops from the Spanish army and offered his services to the battered French republican army. By 1798 he had so worn down the English that General Maitland was glad to withdraw his forces in return for an amnesty to his Haitian partisans and for a commercial treaty. In signing this agreement Toussaint acted like an independent head of state. He was so, indeed, in

Toussaint L' Ouverture

St Domingue. He, more than any other black leader, held the loyalty of the people and of his troops. Abroad, he enjoyed the respect and friendship of John Adams, the president of the United States. This had enabled him to get from the United States the ships and supplies he needed to combat the English.

After expelling the English, Toussaint subdued the mulattoes under Pierre de Rigaud in the west in 1800, a year of terrible carnage in which about 10,000 mulattoes – men, women, children – were killed. In 1801, in defiance of Napoleon's orders, he took control of Spanish Santo Domingo. Napoleon, however, had plans for rebuilding the French colonial system in America, basing it on Louisiana, with St Domingue as the outer fortress. The first step was to reduce Toussaint to obedience. He sent out a strong force under General Charles Victor Emanuel Leclerc, who succeeded, at great cost. Toussaint's chief supporters, Jean Jacques Dessalines and Henri Christophe, and their followers, joined the French. The French kidnapped Toussaint, took him to France and imprisoned him in the fortress of Joux near the Swiss border. The French regained control but yellow fever, that terrible enemy, was destroying their army.

Leclerc's prestige with Dessalines, Christophe, Maurepas and other rebel leaders was high. Then news came from Guadeloupe that Napoleon's General Antoine Richepanse, who had regained control of the island, had reintroduced slavery. Thousands of Haitians sprang to arms once more. They felt certain that Leclerc had orders from Napoleon to reintroduce slavery in Haiti. Some recalled Toussaint's warning to Napoleon when the government of France was changed to a Directorate in 1795, that if the French tried to reimpose slavery they would expose themselves to total ruin and the colony to inevitable destruction. "Do they think", he had asked indignantly, "that the men who have been able to enjoy the blessing of liberty will calmly see it snatched away?"

Toussaint was dead, but Dessalines, Christophe, Maurepas and the other Haitian leaders knew that under Napoleon the French were a foreign enemy. The Haitians knew that Leclerc's army had been greatly weakened. It was no longer the formidable force it had been. All their supplies had to be bought at high prices and brought in. Leclerc had reported to Napoleon that he was: "master of the North but almost all of it had been burnt and I can expect no resources from it. The rebels were still masters of a part of the West and they had burnt the positions they no longer held; for the present he could expect no supplies from there". At this critical time in November 1802 yellow fever claimed Leclerc.

In Europe, Napoleon broke the Treaty of Amiens in 1803, resumed the war, gave up his plans for an American empire and abandoned his forces in St Domingue. Leclerc's successor surrendered to the English in 1803, and Dessalines started a campaign of extermination against all surviving whites in Haiti. Just before the treaty was signed in 1800 in which France abandoned its claim to St Domingue, Dessalines and Christophe declared: "Restored to our former dignity, we have won back our rights and we swear never to let them be destroyed by any power on earth."

The old Taino name, Haiti, land of mountains, was restored to what had been the colony of St Domingue, and in 1804 Dessalines was declared Emperor of Haiti. On his assassination in 1806 he was succeeded by Christophe.

Thinking over the events we have described, and the impact of the two forces of change that we have identified, these differences become clear: the Evangelical Movement, largely rooted in the Protestant world, contributed significantly to social change in Jamaica but not in Haiti; the people of colour in Haiti suffered the same civil disabilities as those in Jamaica, but their political and social aspirations were opposed by a much larger body of resident whites, both rich and middle class, than in Jamaica, where the mulattoes were essentially conservative. They shared the "terrified consciousness" of the whites for the blacks.

The Enlightenment reinforced the anti-slavery movement in England, but it did not provide Jamaican browns with a battle cry. The Evangelical Movement was concerned with religious principles and man's conversion. The Enlightenment dealt with the principles of government and the rights of man. Each movement exercised a powerful influence in the Caribbean, one through the work of Lisle and Baker in Jamaica, the other through the Friends of the Blacks and the Black Jacobins in Haiti. We turn now to African-Jamaicans in this period: to their capacity for response to change and the impact of science, technology and the Industrial Revolution on them.

In the decade of the 1760s, when Voltaire and Rousseau were challenging tyranny and generating revolution, a few obscure scientists and technicians were taking the first steps towards mankind's first global revolution. In 1765 James Watt invented a separate condenser, then moved on to make the first steam engine, which put steam power at the service of mankind, made possible the mechanisation of the British textile and mining industries and transformed transport by land and sea. Four years later, in France, an artillery officer, Nicolas Cugnet, road-tested his steam-driven gun carriage, regarded as the first mechanically propelled vehicle. By 1770 the first steps in mechanising the cotton industry were pioneered by James Hargreaves with his spinning jenny.

Edmund Cartwright followed in 1785 with a power loom and a few years later two American inventors introduced power-driven cotton spinning. Eli Whitney's cotton-gin of 1793 marked a decisive step towards a massive increase in English cotton production. Land and water transport soon felt the impact of steam power: Robert Fulton with the first steamboat, *Clermont*, on the Hudson River (1807), Henry Bell's *Comet* on the Clyde (1812) and George Stevenson's *Rocket* (1829), the first successful steam locomotive.

When we look at these inventions and the mechanisation of English industry over the period 1790-1830, we are also witnessing the formation of the English working class. It is appropriate to bear in mind the judgement of an English historian: "the changing productive relations and working conditions of the Industrial Revolution were imposed not upon raw material but upon the free-born Englishman . . . The factory hand or stockinger was also the inheritor of Bunyan, of remembered village rights, of notions of equality before the law, of craft traditions". Nor was slavery imposed upon raw material, but upon the freeborn African who had been nurtured in communities with ethical codes and well-developed forms of social organisation that respected the human being. They also inherited notions of individual rights, justice and liberty. These were a part of the African birthright, to be fought for and defended to the death.

CHAPTER 17

Challenge and response, 1760-1830

Liberating forces from Europe swept across the flourishing sugar islands of the Caribbean, spreading dismay and panic through white Jamaica, ravaging St Domingue with invading armies, with rebellious bands of African slaves bent on freedom, desperate mulattoes and white planters broken and in flight from a land that was yesterday's pride. The foundations and structures of French imperial power crumbled before the assaults of Toussaint and Dessalines. Meanwhile, Bryan Edwards, the historian of the Jamaican plantocracy, lamented that the devouring forces of subversion were abroad and the horizons were red with the flames of revolution.

In Jamaica the slaves were establishing hillside chapels under the leadership of their own black deacons. The field-workers in their songs mocked the white managers and overseers.

> One, two, three
> All de same
> Black, white, brown
> All de same,
> All de same.
> One, two three

We ask ourselves how it was that planter society in Jamaica was so resistant to change, so monumentally stolid, and how was it that enslaved blacks were able to respond to change, even though the 1780s and 1790s were decades of hardship and disaster.

Five hurricanes devastated Jamaica between 1780 and 1786, and the American War of Independence sharply reduced the flow of food and plantation supplies from the North American colonies to the West Indies. During the years 1780-81 Barbados was on the point of starvation. Malnutrition and physical hardships cut her slave population from 68,500 in 1773 to 54,500 in 1783. Famine threatened Jamaica. Antigua lost 1,000

Challenge and response, 1760-1830   *191*

slaves in 1778, Montserrat nearly 1,200, Nevis and St Kitts 300-400 each. So severe was the shortage of food in the 1780s that the West India interest and the English Government went searching for new food plants. The Jamaica House of Assembly resolved that every encouragement should be given to cultivating yams, eddos, maize, plantains and such exotics as nutmeg, cloves, cinnamon and coffee. The exploratory voyages of Captains James Cook and Louis Antoine de Bougainville to the South-East Pacific in the eighteenth century and the later voyages of William Bligh augmented the West Indian food supply.

The import of food plants, especially breadfruit, from the newly discovered islands of the South-East Pacific began in the last three decades of the eighteenth century. Jamaican planter society still remained set in its attitudes, incapable of a positive response to the challenges of the age. One reason was that the sugar plantation remained the prime source of Jamaica's life and wealth.

> The society created by sugar was rigid, base and greedy. It consumed life, energy and thought, and manured the industrial revolution of England with the profits from its labour. (Hearne: 1965)

Sugar was tenacious. Once a mill and boiling house had been established, land bought and planted in cane, slaves acquired and trained, there was no breaking its grip. The estate had to go on producing sugar. But the cause went deeper. The paralysing factor was white racism. Racism split the population into two segments, and colour prejudice fragmented it. The mulattoes were firmly told by the House of Assembly in November 1813: "The free people of colour in this island have no right or claim whatever to political power, or to interfere in the administration of the Government as by law established in the Governor, Council and Assembly."

Throughout the British colonies, peopled largely by non-whites, the colonial ideologies were racist. As Anthony Maingot observes:

> The majority of English scholars, for instance, steadfastly held to two fundamental tenets; first, that Teutonic, and especially Anglo-Saxon, races were superior in all respects; and secondly that inferiority could only be ameliorated through tutelage to the former. The French, Dutch, Belgian, Italian, Germans all shared this racial vision.

Since there were only a few white women in Jamaica, white males mated with black women and mulattoes became an important component of the population. There are no reliable figures of the racial mixture of the population of Jamaica in the period before emancipation, but the census taken in 1844 showed a total population of 377,433, made up of 293,128 (77.7 per cent) black, 68,529 (18.1 per cent) brown and 15,776 (4.2 per cent) white.

The whites remained completely dominant, holding all political and economic power. The group was split apart by class distinctions but united by race. Their superiority was institutionalised in law as well as in social terms. Below them came the "free coloured", who often owned property, including slaves, and pressed in season and out for civil rights. They aimed at entry into the white world. The base of the pyramid was black, and consisted of three-quarters of the population of the island.

These figures demonstrate that the sociocultural history of Jamaica was the history of an attempt by Europeans to contain a people more numerous than themselves, phenotypically different, whom they feared but whose labour they wished to keep available for economic exploitation. They indicate too that it is the history of the resistance of Africans to strategies of control and the Africans' anger at the system's tenacity that brought change about.

The deep fear the whites had of the blacks, their "terrified consciousness", caused chiefly by the great difference in numbers between them and the black slaves drove them to barbaric reprisals after black uprisings; for instance, it threw Lord Balcarres and the planter class into a panic over Haiti. It explains the heavy emphasis placed on law and order by the plantocracy and the colonial governments and their quick resort to violence as a means of enforcing authority. Plantation Jamaica was a garrison society, committed to the production of one major commodity, sugar, for export to the protected market in Britain, as an integral part of the mercantile system. It was dedicated also to maintaining white superiority by a closed system of representative government and by maintaining and protecting the system of slavery and making money from sugar. It was incapable of change.

In contrast, the African-Jamaicans somehow found within themselves the obstinate strength to reject, and to continue to reject, slavery. They did so by marronage, sabotage and sporadic outbursts of violence, as well as by acquiring the language, skills and knowledge of their white "masters".

In this response, we detect a process that was deliberate and selective: rejecting the system and yet adjusting to it and using it for their own betterment. This was a finely tuned sensing of the possible, of how to use the provision ground and traditional trading skills of the African-Jamaican women to establish a domestic market in produce and livestock.

It would have been a remarkable achievement for any people anywhere. It becomes a miracle when we realise that the African-Jamaican's lifespan under slavery averaged little more than seven years. Yet the dynamics of the society had its origins in them and brought a Jamaican culture into being.

The mortality rate was extremely high among children under four-years-of-age who died of epidemic diseases and ignorance. Monk Lewis, an absentee slave-owner, in his journal of his visit to Jamaica, tells of a woman, "a tender mother who had borne ten children and now has but one alive; another, at present in the hospital, has borne seven and but one has lived to puberty. So heedless and inattentive are the best-intentioned mothers and so subject in this climate are the infants to dangerous complaints. The locked jaw (tetanus) is the common and most fateful one, so fatal indeed that the midwife (the grandee) told me the other day: "Oh massa, till nine days over, we no hope of them." Alongside these there were others who declared that "They preferred to see their own children dead rather than be obliged to witness their daily punishment."

Recently arrived slaves also had a high mortality rate. Their period of seasoning extended over two or three years. For example, at Worthy Park Estate where the records were carefully kept and health care was good, between March 1792 and late 1793, of the 181 Africans bought, one-quarter died, the majority from dysentery and yaws. Environmental diseases, smallpox, fevers, lack of the will to live soon struck them down. Add to disease the tendency of some planters to overwork the slaves during the period of seasoning and so causing their death.

Whence did our ancestors, the African-Jamaican woman, man, child in threadbare osnaburg clothing, draw the strength to lay the foundations of our nation by their insistence not only on freedom but also on justice, and to create that rich unique Jamaican seed-bed of culture, our folk lore, from which come the tunes and music, the rock-steady and reggae that carry the name of Jamaica around the world?

The poets, like the griots of the West African people, lead us to some answers. Derek Walcott does this in a poem in which he describes the absence of history, tradition, ruins. He writes, "I saw the figures of ancient almond trees in a grove past Rampanalgas on the north coast (Trinidad) in a group of dead uprooted ancestors."

Lorna Goodison reminds us that our history is both chronicle and chronology, synthesis and analysis, poetry and archaeology, art and science, compilation of data and intuition. We also have tried to see our history "not as a march of ideologies but as a human event of complicated and often tragic outcomes". We have tried to understand how the enslaved people revealed their inner selves through the mechanisms they developed, through the language they bequeathed to us, the culture they created, a culture rich in its own right. The very names that the people gave to places tell of their moods, hopes and fears.

> I love so the names of this place,
> how they spring brilliant like "roses . . .
> Stonehenge . . . Sevens, Duppy Gate, Wait a Bit,

Wild Horses, Tan and See, Time and Patience,
Unity. It is Holy here, Mount Moses
dew falls upon Mount Nebo, south of Jordan,
Mount Nebo . . .
Paradise is found here, from Pisgah
we look out
and Wait a Bit, Wild Horses, Tan and See,
Time and Patience . . .

(Sherlock)

The landscapes with their picture names remind us of the African gift for animating phrases. The names and the language disclose "a visible history". Land of Look Behind takes us into an impenetrable region of razor-edged limestone pinnacles, hidden caves, tangled withes; Starve Gut Bay confronts us with famine, the country bus becomes Gaiety or Western Pride; a fisherman's boat becomes "In God we Trust".

The African-Jamaican was not a solo performer in this process of adaptation and of fashioning a Jamaican culture and a history. The environment played its part, the soil and the climate dictating planting time, crop time and crop-over; drought and hurricane imposed their timetable; the moon defined the best times for planting. The plantation moulded the way of life and laid out the daily routine, while the sugar cane combined with the seasons to set the calendar; northers, generated in the Arctic, spread the chills and fevers that killed so many, and hurricanes spawned off the West African coast flooded the Portland valleys and drove sailing ships ashore.

The other participant was the European, the coloniser, who imposed his laws based on the overriding importance of property instead of the human being; his religion with its division of human affairs into sacred and secular, compared with the African whose religion "accompanies the individual from long before his birth to long after his physical death"; and his language, one of mankind's most powerful and flexible means of communication. It served the colonisers' primary purposes of giving instructions, doing business and indoctrinating others in European superiority and African depravity; but it also provided the African with a base for creating his own language, Jamaica talk.

They did this without the inspiration of psalmists and prophets, knowing only that they had to find ways of communicating, of fashioning a new language quickly, and they did. There was no Jamaica talk in 1700 but by 1800 the folk had "an English learned incompletely with a strong infusion of African influence", a vigorous, vivid language made up of "preservations, borrowings, new formations, transferred meanings, and special preferences, the two chief components being English of various kinds and African".

Africa contributed more than vocabulary. It provided ways of forming new words or plurals by repetition, as in "wass wass" meaning plenty of wasps, or "fool fool" for foolish, as well as our way of speaking with the whole body, of using sounds as exclamation marks or full stops.

The proverbs are sparkling nuggets of sunshine. They take us into the inner world of the ancestors, where they record in a sentence years of experience, evaluations, warnings. Their ancestors, not having mastered the art of writing, passed on their experience and wisdom in their proverbs, the wise sayings of the dark. Their eyes are Yoruba, Ibo, Ewe, Efik, Fon; but they had made the Middle Passage, worked as plantation slaves and absorbed the lessons of their new condition. The proverbs of the homeland are polite, elegantly embroidered, tactful, poetic, as in the riddle:

> We call the dead, they answer,
> We call the living, they do not answer.
> The dry leaves on the earth are dead, crackle when trodden on,
>   whereas green leaves, the living, make no sound when we step
>   on them.

The Yoruba and the West Indians delight in irony, but West Africans speak from a more stable, more secure society, in which throughout the generations the elders have spoken with authority, knowing that "When we divide the meat, the gall must get its share."

The African-Jamaican's historical experience is that some get all the gall. His proverbs are as witty, as ironic. The sense of the comic is as keen, but there are sombre moods also, an inaccessible loneliness, the menace of lightning hidden in a cloud. The plantation taught him that "Poor man never vex" because he dare not show his anger; "Man you can't beat, you have fe call him fren." Let the overseers remember that "Time longer dan rope" and "Every day you goad donkey, one day him will kick you." "Not everybody who kin dem teet [smiles] wid you is fren." Let the blacks beware of those who carry tales: "When six yeye meet, story done"; and "De dog dat carry bone come will carry bone go." Never forget that "White man yeye burn neger (Negro)" and "When black man tief, him tief half a bit (five cents), when backra tief, him tief whole estate." Above all, be tactful: "Do not be seen counting the toes of a man who has only nine." Never overestimate your power: "The river carries away an elderly person who does not know his own weight." Always be on your guard: "Not because cow don't have tongue him don't talk". Remember that "You never tek popgun kill alligator," and beware how you mock at the elders: "Little pig ask him mumma (mother) say what mek you mout"so long an' she say 'Never mind, me pickney, the same thing that mek fe mi mout long will make fe you long too.'"

The Ashanti handed down to us brilliant folktales about the trickster Anansi, the spider-man, as the hare is the chief character in the Yoruba folk tales and the tortoise in the stories of the Ibo people.

As in the West African stories Anansi is "craven" (greedy), and, being small and weak, he wins by guile, not by strength. It is Anansi "who mek wasp sting, who mek dog belly come hollow, who mek Jackass bray".

The Anansi stories belong to "evening time", the work-songs or "jamma" to sun hot time, when field work becomes tedious, as in yam time, when in Hanover "to tek out yam without Jamma" was impossible. "The song itself may not be poetical, but the charm lies in the tune, the voice of the "bomma" (the leader) and the rhythmic swing of the workers." One of the oldest of the work-songs is among several recorded in the 1790s by J. B. Moreton. "Jamma, is certainly African and must have been in use for a long time . . . Bomma is very likely African, meaning either to shout, sing out or join together – as this leading singer leads the group. When Bomma wants to end the song he shouts "Black Water" or "Bog Walk".

Songs recorded by J. B. Moreton and Monk Lewis include references to slavery, being stolen from Guinea and having to face the cruelties and restrictions of plantation slavery. "This," observes Orlando Patterson, "is in marked contrast to the American slave songs where there are surprisingly few references to servitude." Lewis records a song entitled "We very well off", sung by the blacks. The reference to the cruelty they can expect from the overseer after the owner's departure comes out in the second verse.

> Hey ho day! neger now quite eeri [hearty]
> For once me see massa – hey-ho-day
> When massa go me no care a dammee
> For how dem usy me hey-ho-day

The ring games and dancing songs tell of ways in which our African ancestors amused themselves. Some of the earliest recordings of these songs, by Sloane in his *Natural History of Jamaica* (1680), show that songs were being sung in African languages. He recorded tunes from Angola, Pawpaw and "Koromanti".

It is as if the ancestors stepped out of the eighteenth century to whisper their proverbs and songs to us, and to take us into that inner world of dreams, hopes and prayers where they gained relief from the plantation horrors. One song is about a planter who ordered that an elderly ill slave should be carried to a lonely gully on the estate, and abandoned there, but "bring back the frock and board".

> Take him to the Gully! Take him to the Gully!
> But bring back the frock and board,

"Oh massa! massa! me no deadee yet",
Take him to the Gully. Take him to the Gully
Carry him along!

We feel at home with the songs and the music, the proverbs, the stories, for deep down they are ours, and we can see how the ancestors, by fashioning them out of their African memories and their plantation experiences, prepared the way for our poets and musicians. The mood is the same here.

I was down in the valley for a very
long time
But I never get weary yet . . .
I was walking on the shore and
they took me in the ship
And they throw me overboard
And I swam right out of the belly of the whale
And I never get weary yet . . .

(Toots Hibbert)

Sun a shine but things nuh bright,
Doah pot a bwile, bickle nuh nuff,
River flood but water scarce yah,
Rain a fall but dutty tough

(Louise Bennett)

The dances and the masquerade are treasures. The juncunoo, which links "music and dance, mime and symbol" is an early traditional dance form of African descent that still survives in Jamaica.

The mask has a central place in African religions, and it may be that juncunoo, a masquerade form, and myal, a possession-healing form of religion, were closely allied in their early forms in Jamaica, as they are allied in the two powerful male secret societies of West Africa, Poro and Egungun. The juncunoo moved through three phases in Jamaica. The first was the early years of introduction and adaptation, and this was followed in the 1770s by the addition of a European feature, the set girls. The third stage came after emancipation and it was this masquerade which shows the British influence most clearly.

The capacity for response was in itself complex, for the African slaves came from different tribes, spoke different languages and worshipped different gods. Also, as Patterson reminds us, if we were to examine the slave society at any given time we would find a basic division between the communities of the African-born and the Jamaican-born slaves. The unifying forces were blackness and the passion for freedom. It remains true, however, that most of the slaves imported into Jamaica came from the same culture area, and "underlying the great regional or tribal differences . . . there is a very wide substratum of basic ideas that persists in the rituals, myths, and folk tales of West African peoples." (Forde: 1954)

This African-rooted, African-inspired body of folk culture, was the African-Jamaicans' response to uprooting and alienation during the century after emancipation, when society felt the full force of colonialism. There was no other link, no other "indigenous form of self-expression", no other source from which to nourish the sense of African identity. Neither brutality nor hardship broke their spirit. They preserved through three centuries of exploitation an unquenchable vitality and an equally remarkable ability to "tek bad someting mek laugh".

Denigrated as "ole nayga music" and "black neyga foolishness", the folk kept their tunes, their stories and masquerade until Marcus Garvey and the Rastafarians drove home the fact that "the Western black man's attitude to Africa, whether he knows it or not, is at bottom his attitude to himself". It is in the exciting vitality of today's culture that we find a demonstration of the capacity of the African-Jamaicans of the eighteenth century to respond positively to penalisation and indoctrination. The folklore is the living memorial which the people fashioned as their answer to the castles and ruins, their source of healing, recognition of each other as shipmates on the long voyage to nationhood.

CHAPTER 18

The primacy of freedom

The nineteenth century dawned to the cannonade and battle cries of the Napoleonic war (1802-15), to the flames and carnage of the Haitian revolution and, in Jamaica, to terrifying rumours that slaves brought from St Domingue by fugitive French planters were planning an uprising. More than 1,000 were transported. There followed conspiracies in Kingston in 1803, and in 1808 a mutiny of 50 African Chambas and Coromantis in the West India Regiment at Fort Augusta.

For more than 100 years African-Jamaicans had battled for survival and freedom. Towards the end of that harsh, difficult century they had felt the impact of a new age, heard of talk in England about a law to abolish the slave trade, seen Haiti become an independent black and free republic, talked secretly under cover of night about the rights of man, discussed messages from Jacobin agents. Then, in 1807, word came that William Wilberforce and his followers had at last won their long battle for the abolition of the slave trade. Many concluded that this meant the abolition of slavery.

Earlier liberation wars had centred on the maroons or on plantations in specific parishes. Now freedom for all African-Jamaicans seemed a possibility. The Jamaica born blacks were in the majority. All spoke a Jamaican dialect, shared the same creole culture, the same desire for freedom and through their folk language communicated fully with each other.

Work songs recorded in this period reflect a change of mood a more open mockery of backra, a growing distrust of him, more frequent references to freedom, an increasing restiveness. There is the steady rhythm of the provision-ground in some work songs; others mocked at backra's frailty and told of the early coming of freedom.

> New-come backra
> He get sick

He tek fever
He be die
He be die
New come backra
He be die,

Another folk song that dates back to the early 1800s speaks of freedom as if it were already here.

Talla ly li oh
Freedom ah come oh!
Talla ly li oh
Here we dig, here we hoe.
Talla ly li oh
Slavery ah gone oh,
Talla ly li oh
Here we dig, here we hoe.
King George me ah go
Here we dig, here we hoe, . . .
Me nuh work no more,
Massa, he ah go
Freedom ah come oh
Talla ly li oh
Here we dig, here we hoe.

The revolutionary songs were the Christian hymns, some of which were introduced by the black Baptist missionaries, others by the white missionaries. They met the deep need of African-West Indians for musical forms of religious expression, set a wholly new valuation on the human being and portrayed the close continuing spiritual bond with the father of all mankind. The militant mood of some hymns relieved their frustration.

We will be slaves no more
Since Christ has made us free,

The new chapels resounded to the hymns of the Evangelical Revival, such as Charles Wesley's:

Hide me, O My Saviour hide
Till the storm of life is past,
Safe into the haven guide,
O receive my soul at last
Soldiers of Christ arise
And put your armour on.

The hymns touched the imagination of the folk who (as Olive Lewin has shown us) composed songs that are rich in feeling in the mood of such

Jamaican intuitive painters of the mid-twentieth century as Kapo (Mallica Reynolds) and Everald Brown.

> Moses saw the fire burning,
> Moses saw the fire burning
> Moses saw the fire burning over there,
>
> Shining light
> Shining light
> Shining light in the wilderness
> over there, over there

Yet closer to the intuitives of Jamaica and the primitives of Haiti are early folk spirituals, such as that which tells of a synod in heaven, with God asking:

> Who will go and die for Adam?
> Who will go and die for Adam?
>> I will go
>> I will go
> When the question was asked in heaven
> There was half an hour silence
> There was half an hour silence,
> Who will go and die for Adam?
>> I will go
>> I will go.

The people in a very African way felt the closeness of the spirit world as a direct, not a mystical, experience, and spoke of immediate and personal contact with a God of dreams and visions.

The hymn book and the Bible added a new dimension to the drab agony of an osnaburg or crocus bag world, from which the vivid colours and drama of tribal Africa had been drained. We have seen how the African-Jamaicans met the challenge of alienation and deprivation by creating dance forms, songs and the drama of the masquerade. To these were now added the grand imagery of the Bible, unforgettable pictures of the armies of the oppressor swept away by the waters of the Red Sea; David with his sling-shot victorious over Goliath; Daniel in the lion's den; a bush that burned but was not consumed, a valley of dry bones resurrected in Ezekiel's vision, divine messages delivered through dreams, visions, a whirlwind and a still small voice. The impact on the African-Jamaican was profound. He found hope in the presence of the missionaries, strength and spiritual comfort in the message of salvation which they brought, in the hymns and in the Bible, both of which enriched his imagination and deepened his aesthetic experience.

As we have seen, the English missionaries came by invitation. George Lisle had been converted by a Baptist preacher in Savannah, Georgia, so it was natural that as a loyalist refugee he should turn to the recently founded Baptist Missionary Society in London for help. In 1791 he wrote to the secretary, Dr John Rippon saying: "We have purchased a piece of land at the East end of Kingston containing three acres for the sum of £146. currency and on it we have begun to build a meeting house. We have raised the brick wall eight feet high and intend to have a gallery." Lisle made his living by farming and moving goods with a wagon and team of horses, but he got into debt over the chapel and was imprisoned for three years and five months. In this difficult time the rector of the Kingston Parish Church helped him. As soon as he was free, he resumed his work. Of the slaves who were members he wrote: "Out of so small a sum (as their gifts) we cannot expect anything that can be of service from them. If we did it would soon bring scandal upon religion."

The missionary pioneer in western Jamaica was Moses Baker, who was born in New York and was a barber by trade. When the English evacuated New York in 1783 he left with his wife and child and came to Kingston as a loyalist refugee. In 1788 he was employed by Mr Winn, a planter, to instruct the slaves on his estate. His missionary work progressed and in 1813 Baker appealed to the Baptist Missionary Society in London for help. The society responded by sending out the first missionary, John Rowe, in 1814. In 1815, when other English missionaries were beginning to arrive, slave discontent broke into rebellion. Around Christmas some slaves at Lyndhurst property in St Elizabeth got together with a black from St Domingue and a brown preacher and began to plan a rebellion. They met at night and sang a freedom song which the brown preacher taught them:

> Oh me good friend Mr. Wilberforce
> make we free
> God Almighty thank ye, God
> Almighty thank ye,
> God Almighty mek we free.
> Backra in this country no mek
> we free,
> What Negro for to do? What
> Negro for to do?
> Take force by force! Take force by force!

The freedom fighters elected a "King of the Eboes" and two captains who were to serve under him. However, information was laid against them and the authorities took action. One of the captains escaped to the woods but the "King" and the other leaders were seized and executed. The governor, the Duke of Manchester, reported:

At a trial held in the Parish of St Elizabeth, it appeared in evidence that nightly meetings had been held on the property . . . That the object of their meeting was to impress the slaves generally with a belief that Mr. Wilberforce was to be their deliverer, and that if the white inhabitants did not make them free, they ought to make themselves free . . . It further appeared in the evidence that these slaves have been taught that there was no necessity of being chris-tened by the clergyman of the Parish, for that they had permission to be baptised by a Negro preacher belonging to Earl Balcarres, and the Negroes so baptised ever after paid a part of what they possessed to the head Preacher whom they call the Bishop. (Hart: 1985)

The freedom song reveals powerful forces at work among the slaves, who were skilled in reading the mind of "that trickified man", backra. They knew that Britain had abolished the slave trade. The arrival of the British missionaries was proof that they had friends in the white world. The drumbeats of revolution grew more insistent, and many took seriously the words of the king of the Eboes at his execution, that he left behind enough of his countrymen to carry out his plans and to revenge his death.

In 1816 African-West Indians underlined their demand for freedom. In that year the first of the last three great liberty uprisings in the West Indies took place in Barbados without prior consultation with slaves elsewhere. The outbreak revealed an awareness of the erosion of planter power, a belief that freedom was near at hand and a distrust of negotiation. The words of Nanny Grigg, one of the rebels, set the mood: "they were all damn fools to work, that she would not, as freedom they were sure to get . . . the Negroes were to be freed on Easter morning and the only way to get it was to fight for it, otherwise they would not get it". Nanny Grigg's message was the same as the brown priest's song: "Take force by force!" She stands amongst the leaders of the freedom-fighters, represen-tative of the African-West Indian fighting women, brief, blunt and as resolute as Nanny of Jamaica and her Nanny Town people, firm as an old mahogany tree with its roots deep in the earth.

William
Wilberforce

In 1823 in Demerara (Guyana) the largest slave rebellion in that country's history took place under the leadership of Tacky. At Le Resouvenir Estate the slaves rose, demanded immediate emancipation and very nearly seized control of the country.

The plan said Colonel Leaky, in evidence before a govern-ment inquiry into the causes of the rising, was to remain quiet on the estate and not to work. We were desirous that no injury should be done to any of the whites, so that no complaint might be made against them. The governor of Demerara, in a despatch to the Colonial Office, said that the slaves demanded unconditional emancipation.

> They declared that the Act for the amelioration of slavery by abolishing the flogging of females and carrying whips was no comfort to them. God made them of the same flesh and blood as the whites. They were tired of being slaves to them, they should be free, and they would not work any more. I assured them if by peaceful conduct they deserved His Majesty's favour they would find their lot substantially though gradually improved, but they declared they would be free.

The missionary John Smith was thrown into prison and died while awaiting execution. The words he wrote to the London Missionary Society deserve to be widely known.

> Under my persecutions and afflictions it affords me no small consolation that the Directors cherish the assurance of my entire innocence. The instructions I received from the Society I always endeavoured to act upon. I have endeavoured from the beginning to discharge my duty faithfully. In doing so I have met with the utmost unceasing opposition and reproach. But so far have these things been from shaking my confidence in the goodness of the cause in which I was engaged, that if I were at liberty, and my health restored, I would again proclaim all my days the glad tidings of Salvation amidst similar opposition, but of this I see no prospect. The Lord's hand is heavy upon me. I can still praise his name.

The Demerara freedom fighters took the line that Daddy Sharpe was to take some eight years later in Jamaica: no violence to whites and immediate freedom because there was no moral justification for slavery. In contrast, the Barbados planters in 1823 followed the example of the Demerara counterparts in their treatment of the martyr John Smith. They forced William Shrewsbury, a Methodist missionary, to leave the island, the charge being that he had urged the slaves to take their freedom by force. "The slaves are as much disregarded and neglected as if they possessed no immortal souls", he reported to his missionary society.

The year of the Demerara rebellion was marked in Jamaica by increasing tension and frequent reports of conspiracies and plots. The parish of Hanover, for example, "was thrown into a state of excitement, though treachery once more baffled the designs of the conspirators". The governor reported that those who were planning rebellion were fully impressed with the belief that they were entitled to their freedom and that one of the leaders had said that the war had only begun. He was right; and it is at this point that we turn to the only friends that African-Jamaicans had in Jamaica, the newly arrived white missionaries.

The missionaries had been instructed by their societies to adapt to the existing order, to concentrate on preaching the gospel, saving souls and inculcating moral values. In their early years they followed a cautious course, but, as Edward Brathwaite so dramatically portrayed, their presence was a challenge to slavery and an affirmation of brotherhood with the slaves:

> At once novel levels of equality appear – both here and in heaven. The evangelical missionaries not only eroded estate boundaries with their 'circuits' or 'districts', but to convert they had to get down off the horse, traditional symbol of superiority, and walk from door to door like modern-day political campaigners. For the first time, then, the slave was looking at a white man eyeball to eyeball, face to face, mouth to ear, hallelujah. And the congregations that were formed were not only exempt from (or rather, eroded) the curfew laws, but were holds in a ship bound for Zion which didn't clank with chains; though since slavery was a sin, many masters might be destined – not unhappily – for somewhere else.
>
> And there was their own religion also, transformed by the Middle Passage, it is true; but still their own. And Deacon/Daddy in his distant chapel had to call on dream and vision, had to shout out locomotion, if the people of his passion were to know him, love him, let him lead them. Mask, Myal, Memory of Mackandal. Sharpe laid 'pagan' oaths upon the Holy Bible. They could have spoken in tongues like kongo kumina; like cowhead jankonnu. The leadership of liberation of the slave was only possible when all the elements of his culture could be raised, utilized and used. (Braithwaite: 1971)

The Christian doctrines of the fatherhood of God, the brotherhood of all human beings, the call to personal salvation, the valuation of the human soul as precious beyond price in the sight of God, these were revolutionary concepts in the world of the sugar-and-slave plantation. So was learning to read and write, especially when the Bible was the book of instruction. So were the methods of religious instruction, especially the class meetings and the tradition of self-government in church affairs. These built habits of consultation and of leadership. The Baptist missionaries were bred in the political tradition of the Dissenters, of the notion of being freeborn Englishmen, "the inheritors of Bunyan, of remembered village rights, of notions of equality before the law and of the folk as the creators of political traditions". They revived in the minds of the African-Jamaicans memories of their own communal traditions, of tribal values, rights, obligations. And most explosive of all was the value placed by God on the individual human being compared with the £30 or £40 of the slave market. The missionary's behaviour said far more than he realised.

Further, and wholly unrecognised by the missionaries, yet of profound importance, was the fact that the concepts of eternity, of a future judgment, of a paradise in the future, were wholly new to the African-Jamaican. In John Mbiti's words,

> The linear concept of time in western thought, with an indefinite past, present and infinite future is practically foreign to African thinking. The future is virtually absent, because events which lie in it have not taken place, they have not been realised, and cannot, therefore, constitute time. Actual time is what is present and what is past. It moves 'backward' rather than forward and people set their minds not on future things, but chiefly on what has taken place. (Mbiti: 1970)

The memory of Africa had faded, but the plantation regime had not totally implanted the European concept of time. Mervyn Alleyne has pointed out that to this day, "the folk's concept of time is defined in terms of the events that are taking place or have taken place. It is not an imposed mathematical formula; it is a phenomenal event." This concept of time being determined by the events and by individual participation in them explains why Vic Reid, in his historical novel *New Day*, makes Joseph Campbell, the narrator of the story, say "They do not know what we have seen, for no place has been found in their English history books for the fire that burnt us in sixty-five". This recognition of the need to participate in past events explains the importance of the griots in the African tribe, leading the Africans, through their ancestors, to claim and participate in their past; it reveals the power of shrines in the lives of all people and it explains why today's Jamaican needs to claim his heritage and so make it a part of his present.

In these circumstances talk about the abolition of slavery at some vague period in the future made no sense. Neither present conditions nor the traditional concept of time gave it any validity. Freedom now was the demand.

After 1823 the missionaries became more militant than they had been, and even more so with the arrival of William Knibb in 1824. His brother had come in 1814 and had succumbed to disease a few months after his arrival. Knibb was asked by the missionary society if he would replace his brother. He consulted his sick mother, who said that he would be no son of hers if he failed to answer the call. He had not been long in the island before he confessed to a "burning hatred of slavery which was glutted with crimes against God and man". He was anxious to secure for the slaves the

William Knibb

few rights they had in law and in letters to Britain he urged greater speed and urgency to end the system of slavery.

The missionaries counted heavily on the support of the English Abolition Society, which had been inactive since securing the abolition of slavery in 1807. Joseph Sturge, Quaker and abolitionist, explained: "It was not until 1823 that Mr. Buxton submitted to the House of Commons the first resolution ever moved in that Assembly that brought in question, and then only in a very cautious form, the lawfulness of negro slavery." Thomas Fowell Buxton was one of a group of abolitionists who played an important part in getting the British Government to pass legislation to ameliorate the condition of the slaves in the West Indies and eventually to pass the abolition law. After referring to the Napoleonic war and its terrible drain on British time and energy, Sturge continued:

> Nor does it appear that the excellent men who laboured so long and so successfully to put the traffic in men under the ban of law . . . ever contemplated speedy emancipation as a thing either practicable or safe. By degrees, however, attention began to be directed more and more to the conditions of the slaves by men such as Wilberforce, Brougham, Lushington, Denman, Whitemore, William Smith, and above all [Thomas Fowell] Buxton, whose vigilance nothing escaped.

In 1823 the abolitionists formed a Society for the Gradual Abolition of Slavery, and agreed to launch a parliamentary campaign to that end. William Wilberforce wrote his appeal on behalf of the slaves, rebutting the argument of some planters who claimed that the West Indian slaves were better off than the British peasant as far as feeding, clothing and lodging were concerned. Wilberforce countered:

> Are these the only claims, are these the chief privileges of a rational and immortal being? Is the consciousness of personal independence nothing? Are self-possession and self-government nothing? Is it of no account that our persons are violated by any private authority, and that the whip is placed only in the hands of the public executioner? Are all the charities of the heart, which arise out of domestic relations, to be considered as nothing, and I may add, all their security too among men who are free agents and not vendible chattels, liable perpetually to be torn from their dearest connections and sent into a perpetual exile?

Some slaves could read. They knew of the appeal by Wilberforce and of the campaign against slavery. Certainly they learned about the Society's decision in 1830 to press for immediate emancipation. Wilberforce and Buxton had not been in favour of this decision but once it was taken they threw their full weight behind it.

Forces generated by the Industrial Revolution were strengthening the anti-slavery trends. They brought new groupings into existence, among them new industrial interests, hostile to the West India monopoly of the British sugar market. New economic thinking, stimulated by Adam Smith's *Wealth of Nations*, was raising questions about the efficiency of slave labour and of the West India sugar planters. The West India interest found itself being forced from a central position of power to the periphery.

In Britain the West India Committee of Planters and Merchants fought a bitter rearguard action. Led by Lord

Joseph Sturge

Chandos, Lord Seaford and the recently appointed agent for Jamaica, William Burge, a virulent opponent of the missionaries, the committee sought to win public support by emphasising the importance of the West Indian sugar-producing colonies to Britain and the need to protect slavery as an institution created by law. They denounced the preaching of the missionaries as subversive, especially the Baptists, who consistently and provocatively taught the equality of all men in the sight of God, and assured the slaves that the time had come for all men to be free. They declared that emancipation would strike a dangerous blow at the fundamental principle of the sanctity of property. The committee warned that to set the blacks free would be, as a correspondent to the *Times* put it, "to let loose so many wild beasts. Immediate emancipation would destroy not only their masters but the slaves themselves".

The planters, both absentees and locals, saw themselves as patriotic Englishmen who had rejected suggestions from the North American colonists to join them in their war of independence. With the abolition of the slave trade, which they had strongly opposed, they realised that they were losing ground.

Hurt and angry, the whites in Jamaica grew desperate. The House of Assembly rejected the British parliament's proposals for purging slavery of its cruellest features, and in February 1831 reduced from three to two the number of days' holiday the slaves were entitled at Christmas. The planters angrily denounced the British Government around their dining tables and in their newspapers. At public meetings in many parishes they abused the British Government for planning to deprive them of their property, for delivering them "over to the enemies of our country", for throwing them "as a prey before misguided savages". The hurricane signals were out.

When we put these two decades of mounting African-West Indian discontent alongside developments in Britain, we observe an unexpected concordance of events and extraordinary linkages between the African-West Indian enslaved workers and the emerging British working class, themselves virtually enslaved factory hands and coal mine-workers; for the African slave trade and African-West Indian slaves produced much of the wealth that financed the Industrial Revolution.

The calendar is revealing. In the West Indies there were slave uprisings in Westmoreland and St Elizabeth in 1815, a rebellion in Barbados in 1816, another in Demerara in 1823, yet another in Jamaica in 1832. In Britain there was the Luddite crisis in 1811-13, when mobs rampaged through Lancashire smashing machines in a protest against industrialisation; in 1817 the Pentridge rising of miners; in 1819 the Peterloo massacre, when armed militia men charged a mob of working folk; the Ten-Hour Movement and trade union activities of the 1820s, and in 1831-32 a revolutionary crisis over the reform bill. (Thompson: 1963)

The inventors, technologists and scientists towards the end of the eighteenth century put steam power at the service of mankind, pioneered the mechanisation of British industry, spread William Blake's "dark satanic mills" and factories through Lancashire and Yorkshire. This led to unregulated industrial growth and the emergence of an English working class. Their condition in this period throws light on the conditions of African-West Indians. English social reformers, such as Richard Oastler recognised this, when they attacked the mill-owners for their savage exploitation of the workers. "You are more Tyranical, more Hypocritical than the slave drivers of the West Indies." The "big gang" and "pickney gang" had counterparts in:

> The little infants and their parents taken from their beds in all kinds of weather . . . the miserable pittance of food chiefly composed of water gruel and oatcake broken into it, together with a few potatoes and a bit of bacon or fat for dinner, and if late a few minutes a quarter of a day is stopped in wages. The negro slave in the West Indies has probably a little breeze of air to fan him. The English spinner slave locked up in factories eight stories high, has no relaxation till the ponderous engine stops. (Thompson: 1963)

Few accounts of child labour in this period are more affecting than the account, quoted by E. P. Thompson, of a boy whom the minister of religion had recently interred who had been found standing asleep with his arms full of wool and had been beaten awake. This day he had worked seventeen hours; he was carried home by his father, was unable to eat his supper, awoke at 4. a.m. the next morning and asked his brothers if they could see the lights of the mill as he was afraid of being late, and then died. No wonder that Thompson considering the "pickeny gangs" of the British industrial revolution, commented:

> The exploitation of little children on this scale and with this intensity, was one of the most shameful events in our history: at the centre of our story stands the human being. The enslaved African, the English mill-workers and coal-miners of the period of unregulated industrialization the indentured East Indian Labourer. The basic relationship had to do with economics, with the owner or employer who had access to capital and the worker whose capital lay in his strength and intelligence. Market forces have no special sanctity.
>
> The differences between the emerging English working class and the African-Jamaicans are as revealing as are parallels. In the Caribbean the basic conflict was between white-owner black-labour; in Britain of the 1800-1830's, white-master white-labour. The determining factor is economic, not racial: capitalist-labour; money-hands. In the Caribbean the shortage of labour led to forced labour, the sequence being American Indian, white indentured servant, African forced labour. In Britain there was no shortage of rural poor. Where the relationship between capitalist and worker was not regulated it became one of conflict and bitter hostility. In 1832 it was defined by Sam Sharpe: 'had rather die than be a slave'. In Britain it was defined in 1834 by sanctioning the transportation of Dorchester labourers for forming a trade union, and in the same year by a Leeds stuff-weaver, William Rider: 'The war-cry of the masters has not only been sounded, but the havoc of war; war against freedom; war against opinion; war against justice; and war without justifying cause.' (Thompson: 1963)

The white factory worker of this period was also "a hand", a tool, and in consequence his major disputes were about wages and working conditions, by the potters against the truck system, by the building workers for direct cooperative action and by all groups of workers for the right to form trade unions. The African-West Indian's priority was freedom. The exploited white hands, through their experience in the mines and factories, through study of Tom Paine's *Rights of Man*, and their advocacy of the infant Chartist Movement, understood the nature of the support the abolitionists needed.

CHAPTER 19

Rebellion and emancipation

The Western Liberation Uprising of 1832, which marks the climax of the African-Jamaicans' struggle against slavery, and the British parliament's Act of Emancipation of 1833, belong together. The uprising was not an isolated event. The works of leading scholars of slave resistance in the West Indies enable us to identify its four basic stages. The series of liberation movements began with escapes and struggles during the period of forced recruitment in Africa and the Middle Passage, moved through the rooting of the slave plantation in the Americas (1500-1700) to the 50 years (1750-1800) of total dependence on slave labour, to a final period of crisis in the plantation economy and of the general growth in Britain of anti-slavery sentiment (1800-34).

This long conflict was an African response affirming the right of man to freedom in which, finally, the African prevailed. In this final phase, although the Western Liberation Uprising failed in its immediate objective, it succeeded in achieving its primary goal of emancipation.

Who would have imagined that the rebel leaders swinging from the gallows in Montego Bay during that agonising May of 1832 were to become the honoured dead of a predominantly African-Jamaican people or that their leader, Sam Sharpe, would be revered as one of the heroes and creators of the nation?

The Western Liberation Uprising differed from earlier uprisings, such as that of Tacky's Coromantis recently arrived from Africa and that of the King of the Eboes with his small band of plantation slaves, in that more than 20,000 African-Jamaicans were involved. The call was to slaves everywhere, not a call to arms but a call to withdraw their labour, and it was issued to people who were determined to win their freedom.

Kamau Brathwaite emphasises that "western Jamaica was, by the early years of the 19th century, psycho-culturally prepared for revolution against the plantation system". (Brathwaite: 1971) From the late 1820s Sam Sharpe had been talking of strike: of locking down all plantations.

There was also man-and woman-power. In the western part of the island (St James, Trelawny, St Elizabeth, Hanover, Westmoreland) some 30 per cent of all the colony's slaves were concentrated, that is 106,000 out of more than 310,000. Of this 106,000 between 18,000 and 40,000 were involved in the revolt; among them were urban blacks and coloureds, and free black women, two of whom were executed for their part in the rebellion. (Brathwaite: 1971)

The leaders formed the élite of the labour force, men who had exercised as much authority as a slave could exercise, some of them deacons of the Baptist Church, literate, aware of events in Britain, and especially of the work of the abolitionists.

Sam Sharpe planned and led the rebellion. He was born in Montego Bay, worked there as a domestic slave, and was a deacon of Thomas Burchell's church. He also built up a following of his own among the Native Baptists.

Of medium height, with a fine sinewy frame and a broad, high forehead, Samuel, or Daddy Sharpe was an outstanding leader who impressed all whom he met with his sincerity, intellectual grasp, oratorical power and personal magnetism. His eyes were unforgettable, with a brilliance that was almost dazzling. The Methodist missionary Henry Bleby, who visited him while he was in prison, spoke of his power as a speaker and leader.

> I heard him two or three times deliver a brief extemporaneous address to his fellow prisoners on religious topics . . . and I was amazed at the power and freedom with which he spoke and at the effect which was produced upon his auditory. He appeared to have the feelings and passions of his hearers completely at his command and when I listened to him once, I ceased to be surprised at what Gardner had told me, that when Sharpe spoke to him and others on the subject of slavery, he Gardner was wrought up almost to a state of madness. (Bleby: 1868)

The blacks believed all that Daddy Sharpe told them because he had been born and brought up in Montego Bay, could read and was a trusted leader of Thomas Burchell's church, "and the negroes considered that what Sharpe told them when he came to the mountains must be true, as it came from the church".

One of Daddy Sharpe's followers was Edward Hylton who told how, while at Mountain Spring, he received a message from Sharpe asking him to come to a meeting at Johnson's house on Retrieve Estate in St James.

The gathering at Retrieve took the form of a prayer meeting but Sharpe, William Johnson, who became one of the leaders in the rebellion, Hylton and a few others stayed on. After a while Sharpe spoke to them in a low, soft tone so that his voice would not be heard outside. According to Hylton, he kept them spellbound while he spoke of the evils and injustice of slavery, "asserted the right of all human beings to freedom and declared, on the authority of the Bible, that the white man had no more right to hold the blacks in bondage than the blacks had to enslave the whites". (Bleby: 1868)

Then came these vital words.

> Because the King had made them free, or was resolved upon doing it, the whites and Grignon [of the militia] were holding secret meetings with the doors shut at the house of Mr. Watt of Montego Bay, and had determined to kill all the black men, and save all the women and children, and keep them in slavery; and if the black men did not stand up for themselves and take their freedom, the whites would then put them out at the muzzle of their guns and shoot them like pigeons. (Bleby: 1868)

The meeting continued far into the night. Sharpe outlined the plan of operation. They bound themselves by oath not to work after Christmas as slaves but to assert their claim to freedom and to be faithful to each other. If backra would pay them, they would work as before. If any attempt was made to force them to work as slaves, they would fight for their freedom. They took the oath and kissed the Bible.

Sharpe campaigned actively. "We must all agree to set down after Christmas. We must not trouble anybody and raise no rebellion. We did not swear to burn anywhere or to fight." But realist as well as visionary, he knew that the planters, so intransigent, so angry, might not be willing to negotiate. He knew that they might use force. If they did, the slaves would use force. His "set down" movement was like Gandhi's *satyagraha* (holding to the truth) campaign of civil disobedience through non-violent resistance to unjust laws, but, said Sharpe, if need be, force would be met with force. The first act was to be "the sitting down, the laying down of tools, not swords, on Tuesday after Christmas, and the negotiation thereafter of a wage". (Brathwaite: 1971) William Knibb stressed that point in his testimony to parliament. "There was no design of leaving the property, but they intended what would be called in England a turn-out, till they were promised remuneration for their labour, and the price they had fixed was 2/6 a day." Bleby stated that he had the opportunity of ascertaining the fact beyond doubt, that the destruction of property formed no part of the plan of the original conspirators; and that life was not to be sacrificed, except in self-defence.

Sam Sharpe

There were contingency plans: "the burning plan, the land a flaming telegraph; trash houses, wood roofs, plantation flooring, stairways, jalousies and shutters and the long waiting miles of sugar-cane, conjoint with the paramilitary operation of Gardner and Dove: Black regiment, drill, rank, uniform, chains of command, redoubts, rendezvous, flash-points, fortifications, escape routes." (Brathwaite: 1971)

Robert Gardner, Thomas Dove and Sharpe's other "officers" were untrained men, but a British officer who fought against them said it was astonishing what sagacity had been displayed by them in the selection of their positions. They invariably availed themselves of such as commanded a full view of the hostile approaches and a secure but concealed retreat for themselves, with a supply of water and ground-provisions, always constructing impediments to each entrance. In addition to being on a hill, the headquarters was within gunshot of the roads to Montego Bay, to Black River, Barnyside. "And in the last resort, scattered riots, retreat into the forests and mountains, maroon tactics." (Brathwaite: 1971)

The date set for the withdrawal of labour was Tuesday, 28 December. On that day the Christmas holidays would come to an end, the slaves would not resume work and negotiations would begin. Incidents at Salt Spring Estate on 15 December led the Montego Bay magistrates on 19 December to order the commanding officer of the militia to send a company of the 22nd Regiment to the bay. The authorities were on the alert.

Crisp, clear mornings, night skies brilliant with stars, the Pleiades, Sirius, Orion and Venus near the moon, make this a season of magical beauty. An army officer, Bernard Martin Senior, who served with the British in putting down the revolt, remarked:

> At this period of the year the scenery cannot be surpassed, being so diversified by the various hues of the different crops. The bright yellow of the ripened sugar cane, forming a fine contrast with the deep green of the Indian corn, just beginning to spear, which tint is again carried by an occasional luxuriant pasture of Guinea grass. Now and then an occasional avenue of coconut trees . . . a noble pile of buildings, surrounded at some trifling distance with innumerable neat-looking houses, inhabited by the negroes.

Tension was high. The missionaries urged patience. On 27 December William Knibb, visiting Moses Baker's chapel at Crooked Spring, now Salter's Hill, tried to persuade the slaves that rumours about freedom having been granted were untrue, but his words were received with evident dissatisfaction by many of the slaves present, several of whom left the chapel offended. Others remarked: "The man . . . must be mad to tell them such things." (Bleby: 1868)

That same evening the Presbyterian missionary Hope Waddell bade his congregation "Be patient". He was at one with them in desiring their freedom but it could come only in a peaceful way, by the efforts of their friends in Britain. But "time longer than rope and time run out", was what the people thought.

On the evening of 28 December, Hope Waddell, returning to his station at Cornwall, near Montego Bay, found the congregation dispersing in fright. The only answer that could be got was

> "Palmyra on fire." It was not an ordinary estate fire. It was the pre-concerted signal that . . . the struggle for freedom had begun. It was the response to "Kensington on fire" . . . the one hoisted the flaming flag of liberty and the other saluted it, calling on all between and around to follow their example . . . Scarcely had night closed in, when the sky toward the interior was illuminated by unwanted glares as fires rose here and there in rapid succession. (Waddell: 1970).

The editor of the *Cornwall Courier* wrote at 11 o'clock that night from his office in Falmouth: "The whole sky in the South West is illuminated. From our office we at the moment perceive five distinct fires."

Waddell and Samuel Barrett, owner of Cornwall, took their message from Cornwall to Spots Valley which belonged to an absentee proprietor. There the case was different.

> They listened to Mr. Barrett reading the proclamation issued by Sir Willoughby Cotton till it spoke of their returning to work, when they all lifted up their voices and overwhelmed him with clamour. 'We have worked enough already, and will work no more. The life we live is too bad; it is the life of a dog. We don't be slaves no more; we flog no more. We free now . . . no more slaves again.' (Waddell: 1970)

"In the space of five minutes after the pre-concerted signal was made, fifteen enormous fires were seen in different directions around this once charming scene; and then it was but too plain that the work of devastation had commenced in its most horrific form. The conch shell was heard to blow in every quarter, accompanied by huzzas and shouts of exultation from the infatuated slaves." (Senior: 1978)

The voices of the exultant slaves echo across the generations through the shouts of a lonely slave, a black Paul Revere, with a blazing torch, racing through the night shouting, "No watchman now! no watchman now! nigger man . . . burn the house, burn backra house! Brimstone come . . . bring fire, and burn massa house!"

Whispered across the years, we hear Joseph Williams, a former slave of Mr Tharpe of Hampton Estate in St James, who told his granddaughter,

Beatrice Williams, about slavery and about the night at Mr Tharpe's great house, when

> De white people dem a play dem . . . ah hear say dem have a billiard table deh . . . and when dem a bun down di house . . . black people knock fire pon dem house. Mi hear seh wen Missa Tharpe come him say him doan mind di house wa burn, like the billiard table . . . for it was class. Kensington . . . an dem lick fire pan backra house again (laugh) . . . Is big fire a night you know . . . but dem no have no wisdom . . . because the man wha deh afar, him can see ina di light . . . When backra see dem im fire gun afta dem . . . bow! Shoot afta dem! Dem run, bwoy. (Brodber: 1983)

Exaltation echoes through the voices, exaltation, a sense of freedom, a feeling or release, of liberation.

On 29 December 1831 Montego Bay was in a panic with rumours that the rebel slaves were going to set the town ablaze every night. Pandemonium reigned. The townspeople took comfort from the arrival on New Year's Day of a party of marines from Port Royal on the *HMS Sparrowhawk* and General Sir Willoughby Cotton, commander of British forces in Jamaica. The commodore of the fleet stationed at Port Royal disembarked from the *HMS Blanche* a day later with 300 soldiers and 16 artillery men with two field-pieces and rockets. The general reported that he "had relieved apprehension and quieted the feeling of alarm" in the bay, "but the eastern part of Hanover and the whole of the northern portion of St James are in open revolt and almost the whole of the estates destroyed, and the negroes gone boldly away".

In Trelawny, Custos James McDonald reported to the governor that many of the slaves in the parish were at that moment in a state of rebellion and that nine-tenths of the slave population had that morning refused to turn out to work.

Westmoreland and St Elizabeth were involved. The editor of the *Cornwall Courier* reported that the parishes of Westmoreland and St James had for some days been in a state of considerable excitement, with rumours of intended insurrection among the slave population. The Westmoreland Regiment had been on duty since Monday morning. In this western third of Jamaica there were about 106,000 slaves, most of them attached to the sugar estates and cattle pens, but there were a number of slaves in the urban areas also, in elegant Falmouth with its Georgian buildings and sugar-loading wharves; in Montego Bay, in the busy sugar port of Lucea, in Savanna-la-Mar and Black River. The harbours were busy with sloops and schooners trading with Spanish America.

Jamaica's long central watershed begins at Holland Point in the east and continues westwards across the full length of the island to Dolphin Head and Negril. The watershed defines the course of the rivers, sending the Jones and Y. S. Rivers south through Lacovia to join the Black River, while the Great River Valley runs north to empty its waters into the sea just west of Montego Bay. Along its course are those names which figure in the Western Liberation Uprising of 1831-32: Marchmont, Lapland, Catadupa, Retrieve, Cambridge, Greenwich, Hazelymph, Seven Rivers, Montpelier, Copse and Lethe. This watershed and the two river systems dictated the shape and fate of the enterprise.

The first round went to two bands made up of about 500 badly armed, inadequately trained men, who challenged the St James militia under Colonel W. S. Grignon, planter and plantation attorney (known as "Little Breeches"). The colonel reported that the company of the St James Regiment most positively refused to remain at the post. He retreated the whole body to Montego Bay, thus enabling the freedom fighters to cut the road from Montego Bay to Savanna-la-Mar, but they lost their two leaders, Johnson and Alexander Campbell. Johnson was killed "so near the white people that they could not carry him away", and Campbell "died in the morning – we made a rough coffin and buried him. Gardner read the funeral service over him".

For a brief period the freedom fighters held the initiative, and there were reports of activity along the Great River into St Elizabeth. In early January the tide began to turn under pressure from the St Elizabeth and Westmoreland militia regiments and the British soldiers. General Cotton was steadily augmenting his forces with marines and 100 additional soldiers from Kingston, but he also made sure that a large force was held ready in Kingston to deal with any discontent there or elsewhere; and he called on the Accompong maroons to cover the Great River area from Chesterfield to Duckett Spring.

The African-Jamaicans were not skilled in guerrilla warfare. Only a small number of them had firearms or were trained to use them. Most were armed with cutlasses, sharpened sticks and wooden clubs. With these they fought bravely, attacking armed militia men and soldiers. The torch was their most effective weapon. Breaking up into small groups, they established bases in the forests and moved frequently

Attack on Montpelier Estate during the "Baptist War"

Rebellion and emancipation

from place-to-place. In late February the governor, Somerset Lowry, Earl of Belmore, reported to his council-of-war in Spanish Town that the rebels had been driven into the fastness of the country and that their forces were greatly diminished; but they remained a threat, and he was forced to continue martial law for another 30 days. In the words of the *Royal Gazette*, 21-28 January 1832:

> We had hoped that by the early arrival of the Commander of the forces in St James, with the overwhelming disposable force of Regulars and Militia under his command, the Rebels, would long ere this have been captured or killed. Such we lament to say is not the case. The Rebels have had breathing space allowed them; of this they have availed themselves most amply, and they are now much better organized than they could possibly have been at the commencement of the insurrection.

This assessment was inaccurate. The end was in sight, notwithstanding the courage of the freedom fighters. General Cotton's forces bottled them up in the Great River Valley, closing the northern exit at Roundhill and the mouth of the Great River, taking control of Montpelier and the Great River Barracks and pushing the Black Regiment on to Belvedere and Greenwich. By 26 January the freedom fighters had been forced to break up into small bands and take refuge in the forests. At the end of March Sam Sharpe gave himself up, joining Robert Gardner, Linton, Thomas Dove, Dehaney and other leaders in prison in Montego Bay.

But the spirit of the slaves was not broken. The Anglican rector in Westmoreland, who spoke to some of those taken prisoner, was convinced that the rebellion would break out again, not only from the causes which had occasioned the late one, but also because the blacks believed the king had given them freedom. Even more telling is this passage from a letter written by J. B. Suicke, a white resident, on 23 May, the day of Sam Sharpe's execution: "The question will not be left to the arbitrament of a long angry discussion between the government and the planter. The slave himself has been taught that there is a third party and that party himself. He knows his strength and will assert his claim to freedom. Even at this moment, unawed by the late failure, he discusses the question with a fixed determination." (Suicke: 1832)

The freedom fighters had demonstrated also, by means of the torch, how vulnerable the sugar plantation was. Through the five western parishes and far away in eastern Portland, where discontent had erupted, burnt-out sugar works, estate buildings and ravaged cane-pieces testified that "the rebels, though defeated, had destroyed an appreciable part of the material basis of their enslavement. They had succeeded in making slavery an insupportably expensive system to maintain." (Hart: 1985)

The people had responded to Sam Sharpe's call in large numbers. Between 25,000 and 40,000 withdrew their labour from the estates. These freedom fighters, and they were numerous, by so massive a response and by sacrifice made emancipation an act of necessity, not of philanthropy.

Joseph Williams speaks of white reprisals against the backs. He tells how "dem haffi live a . . . tek long thatch an mek house . . . ena bush". He refers to the suffering, "Di black people meet it. If me even come an' see dem a do a white man anyting me nah talk, no man, I don't business wid it, I couldn't business wid it. The ole generation pay for it . . . Lawd, them meet it! Dem meet it."

Some liberal whites were outraged at the reprisals on the slaves and the attacks on the missionaries. Joseph Williams tells of Mr Tharpe, owner of several properties in Trelawny:

> im always work wid dem slave dem . . . and him kinda have sympathy wid dem . . . One day when him [a fugitive] came out of the bush to find something – You know you have you pickney dem – you haffi go look something gie dem . . . him come out, dem ketch him an anoder man a go along . . . an dem shoot di first one so, Bam . . . There was Missa Tharpe . . . drive up same time and seh 'What? I wont have that, No, loose him down, loose him. Shoot none of my slaves.' Granpa seh dem loose him an' him live a hundred years. (Brodber: 1983)

Mr Tharpe's reference to "old slaves" suggests that the incident which took place in the hard time after the 1832 rebellion had been crushed. The freedom fighters engaged in a widespread destruction of property in protest against a barbaric system of forced labour, but they did not go on a crusade against white people. The records of the parishes that were involved show that 14 whites and three of their brown allies were killed, and that at least three of the whites were soldiers. As a Presbyterian missionary wrote, "Had the masters, when they got the upper hand, been as forbearing, as tender of their slaves' lives as their slaves had been of theirs, it would have been to their lasting honour and to the permanent advantage of the colony." Through their courts martial and their civil courts the plantocracy and the military instituted a reign of terror, with summary trials, savage floggings and hangings. About 750 slaves and 14 free persons were convicted for alleged participation in the rebellion and of that number 580 were executed. Fouteen whites and three browns were killed and 12 whites and three browns wounded. The occupations of those convicted provide an illustration of how widely based the uprising was. The field slaves were in the majority but a high percentage of the participants possessed mechanical and other skills. Most significant of all was the involvement of a large number of drivers.

A white backlash followed. The old formula, "Teach them a lesson" was the cry of those who had seen their property destroyed, their labour force broken up. Mingled with anger was fear of the black majority. Resentment took several forms: floggings and executions under a show of legality, personal attacks on missionaries, an organised campaign to expel them from Jamaica. A few liberal Jamaicans were outraged by these excesses. Mr Roby, Collector of Customs in Montego Bay, and Samuel Barrett, Speaker of the House of Assembly, wrote to William Knibb expressing deep disgust at the way in which he and Thomas Burchell had been treated. These were in the minority.

The white backlash took the form of an uprising organised by the Colonial Church Union which was formed by estate owners and Anglican ministers of religion at a meeting in the Anglican rectory at St Ann's Bay, on 26 January 1832. The rector, the Rev. William Bridges, was present. The union resolved "to present a general petition to the Legislature for the expulsion of all sectarian missionaries, and to prevent the dissemination of any religious doctrines at variance with those of the English and Scottish Churches". Members then set about destroying nonconformist chapels. Rev. Henry Bleby's chapel in Falmouth was destroyed. He was tarred and feathered. Some Moravians were affected, but the Baptists bore the brunt of the attack. Before the governor could take steps to stop this unlawful action, 11 Baptist churches had been destroyed, including those at Salters Hill, Falmouth, Montego Bay, Rio Bueno, Brown's Town, Lucea and St Ann's Bay.

The Baptist missionaries took up the challenge. At a meeting in Spanish Town they decided to send William Knibb to Britain to tell the British people what had happened and to affirm that the Jamaican slaves had a right to religious instruction and to worship God.

News of the Western Liberation Uprising reached the British government on 19 February 1832. The despatch from Lord Belmore, governor of Jamaica, was published in full in the *London Extraordinary Gazette* on 22 February and the struggle for West Indian freedom moved from the cane-fields and towns of Jamaica to Britain, to the British parliament and people.

This took place during a period of great crisis in Britain over the reform of parliament and the extension of the franchise to a much larger number of people. Reform was the top priority. The Whigs had been given a handsome majority over the Tories in the 1831 general election so that they might extend the franchise. The Tories, however, had a majority in the House of Lords and they were holding up the Reform Bill.

By blocking the bill the Lords ignited popular discontent. A mob sacked Nottingham Castle. Extensive riots devastated Derby and Bristol. The military was called out to prevent the colliers from burning aristocratic properties. On Guy Fawkes night (5 November, 1831) the Bishops who had voted against the Reform Bill were burnt in effigy, coal pits were set on fire and gas pipes cut. The industrialists, fearing that the sabotage would spread, pressed the government to resolve the deadlock. Working men organised political unions and started military drilling. The underlying threat of civil war receded when the political process recommenced in December; but the Reform Bill had yet to be carried.

In 1830 the Abolitionist Society decided to press for immediate emancipation. There was little chance that the emancipation of African slaves in remote West Indian islands would receive priority at a time when popular discontent over wider political representation for the British people was strong and deep. The Whigs were committed to the principle of protecting property rights. How at such a time could they give priority to setting free the West Indian labour force, the property of English owners? By following the calendar of events and bearing in mind a picture of Britain itself torn apart by dissensions and riots, we come to recognise Thomas Fowell Buxton's superb qualities of leadership. We see also how by its size and by the extent of the destruction Sam Sharpe's demand for immediate emancipation put the Jamaican issue on the front burner alongside parliamentary reform. The Colonial Church Union, by its fanatical behaviour, destroyed the case of the West Indian planters while the victims of their attack, the missionaries, helped the Abolitionists to transform their case into a national cause, a cause that had to do with freedom of conscience, and not only with property. Freedom of conscience was an issue which England itself had settled during the Reformation.

Thomas Fowell Buxton

As soon as news of the rebellion was received, the West India interests immediately strengthened their propaganda campaign, denounced the "incendiary preachers", emphasised the importance of the sugar colonies to Britain, highlighted the savagery of the slaves and inveighed against the lunacy of "letting loose so many wild beasts". These statements improved their public standing. Buxton counter attacked on 7 March when he declared in the House of Commons: "If the question respecting the West Indies was not speedily settled it would settle itself in an alarming way (i.e., by further rebellions) and the only way it could be settled was by extinction of slavery."

On 23 March William Burge returned to the attack. In a debate in the House of Commons, he charged that disturbances in the West Indies were always a result of discussions about reform and amelioration in the House of Commons. Buxton rebutted the charge, declared that the planters were responsible for the rebellion and pointed to the white insurrection in which the planters had publicly advertised their intention of seceding to the United States.

Two weeks after the debate, on 1 April, Lord Belmore's report on the white insurrection was published in Britain. It described in detail the attacks on chapels and on the missionaries. The burnt-out cane fields had signalled an attack on property while the burnt-out nonconformist chapels signalled an attack on the right of dissent and freedom of conscience. The talk about secession and open defiance of the law by the Colonial Church Union shocked many who had been wavering in their support of the anti-slavery campaign. The tide of public opinion began to turn against the planters.

On 12 May, in the midst of the crisis, the Abolitionists held their annual meeting and called on their supporters for even greater effort. Pointing to massive national support, Buxton urged immediate action. The committee passed a resolution calling on the government to emancipate the slaves without delay. Heartened by the growing swell of public support, Buxton lifted the meeting to a moment of greatness with the closing passage of his address:

> When we look at the career of affliction of our brother man . . .
> When we view him entering this life by the desert track of bondage
> . . . and see him consigned to a premature and unregarded grave,
> having died in slavery . . . there can be but one feeling in my heart,
> one expression on my lips: 'Great God, how long is this inequity to
> continue?' (Buxton: 1832)

The political crisis came to a head in the middle of May 1832. On 12 May the king refused the request of the Whigs that he appoint a number of peers so as to give them the necessary majority in the House of Lords which would allow them to outvote the opposition. The Whigs resigned. The King recalled Wellington. For ten days Britain was on the brink of revolution. The popular slogan was "Stop the Duke – Go for Gold." The Whigs returned to power on 19 May, the Lords accepted the Reform Bill and the king signed it on 7 June.

While these things were happening, public support for the abolition of slavery was growing. During May missionaries from Jamaica arrived, amongst them the formidable William Knibb, who told the committee of the Baptist Missionary Society: "But if it be necessary I will take them [my wife and children] by the hand and walk barefoot through the Kingdom, but I will make known to the Christians of England what their brethren in Jamaica are suffering." Some members hesitated at making slavery the central issue but finally all who heard him decided to give their support. He began his campaign at the annual missionary meeting at Spitalfield's Chapel in London, where he declared, "Whatever the consequence I will speak. I will not rest day or night until I see slavery destroyed root and branch," and he pointed to the story of the anti-slavery campaign as "a wonderful evidence of the force and influence of the truth when brought home to the heart and conscience of a Christian nation".

Never before had the case against slavery been presented so forcibly to the British people by white men who had spent some years in Jamaica, ministering to African-Jamaicans, observing the plantation system from within, acquainting themselves with the slave laws and learning how great were the powers of the owner.

Buxton lost no time. Public opinion was behind him. His instinct told him to act now. Against the advice of his closest advisers, Dr Stephen Lushington among them, in the interval between the return of the Whigs to power and the king's signing of the Reform Bill, Buxton proposed a Motion in the House of Commons for a Commons Commission of Enquiry into Slavery to counterbalance the pro-slavery Lords Committee. He framed the resolution in such a way as to commit the Whigs to immediate emancipation. They could hardly refuse, but they actively tried to avoid the commitment Buxton sought.

Ministers of government and members of the Whig Party pressured Buxton to withdraw the motion. "It was like a continual tooth-drawing the whole evening," he said. But he stood firm. In his speech to the Commons he declared that "a war against people struggling for their rights would be the falsest position in which it was possible for England to be placed".

Buxton's motion was defeated by 136 to 90, but the size of his minority impressed the government and heartened the society for a nationwide drive. It made good use of the evidence of persecution which the white insurrection provided. The evidence was fully documented by the governor of Jamaica's May despatch as well as by the missionaries.

The British parliament passed the Act of Emancipation on 28 August 1833. It came into effect on 1 August 1834. Brathwaite's analysis of the voting on the bill reveals how effective the campaigning had been. It demonstrated that 70 per cent of the minority votes came from English and Welsh boroughs with large dissenting congregations, just the constituency the abolitionists had been aiming at.

Throughout the islands jubilation prevailed at the news of freedom. On 31 July 1834, at a great gathering at Knibb's church in Falmouth, at midnight the cry went up, "The monster is dead, the monster is dying", and some of the hated symbols of slavery were buried.

The old slave Joseph Williams tells of the celebrations and the burial of the hated whip and chain in his account to his granddaughter.

> (Female): Him say ef you ever hear bout slavery? Yes, dem tell me about slavery, tell me about Parson Knibb and Parson Burgess [Burchell]. Parson Knibb and Parson Burgess? Yes. A Him go to h'England ask fi freedom fi Jamaica. A so freedom come yah. Mi fader did tell me about dat dem parson. . . . Sorry fi de people dem, dem go to England and ask di Queen – di King or di Queen – fi gie dem freedom in Jamaica.(Brodber: 1983)

For nearly 130 years, from 1834 to 1962, the official version of the emancipation struggle was in substance the story of the old slave, Joseph Williams. The Western Liberation Uprising was defeat and disaster, to be forgotten, rubbed out as though it had never been. Sam Sharpe, Linton, Robert Gardner, the others who were executed, mouldered in their shallow unmarked graves. Year after year, throughout Jamaica, on 1 August, Jamaicans – and children particularly – celebrated the British gift of freedom and sang: "Rule Britannia, Britannia rule the waves/Britons never, never, never shall be slaves." This was also the story as seen through the eyes of British officials and educators.

These are not the facts. Through the uprising of 1831-32 Sam Sharpe and the other freedom fighters reset the timetable for freedom. It is a story of missionaries who struggled for emancipation and then spent themselves in developing a system of education. It is a story of British abolitionists, Buxton and William Wilberforce pre-eminent among them; and it is the story of British dissenters, Christian working folk whose support was vital in making abolition a national movement.

Samuel Sharpe, Thomas Dove, Linton, Dehaney and the rest claimed freedom and the right to rebel against a system that denied them freedom. They saw themselves as free men. This is the message Sam Sharpe burnt into the minds of his followers, that he "had rather die than be a slave". This is what Patrick Ellis meant when on 6 February 1832 finding himself surrounded by soldiers, he stepped forward, uncovered his breast and cried out, "I am ready, give me your volley. Fire, for I will never again be a slave." This is what the hundreds of freedom fighters meant by the way they faced death.

They paid the price. In justice to them the price exacted should be known. Trial was a summary affair. By far the greater number were executed "In many instances, . . . criminals were condemned during the morning and executed between two and four o'clock". (Senior: 1969) Of

106 slaves tried in St James, 99 were convicted, six executed, one pardoned and two dismissed. Of the 99 convicted, 84 were sentenced to death. In Hanover, 96 of the 138 convicted were sentenced to death; in Westmoreland, 33 of the 64 convicted were sentenced to death. Other punishments in St James included one sentence of 500 lashes, one of 300 lashes with life imprisonment, one of 200 lashes with six months' imprisonment, and so the dreadful story of barbarity went. (Hart: 1985)

It was a searing picture of a society in which property was put before the human being and violence was the first resort in maintaining authority.

Sam Sharpe learned of the executions while in prison. He himself was tried at Montego Bay on 19 April. He was publicly hanged there on 23 May 1832. At no time did his courage, his nobility of spirit shine more brightly than on the day of his execution. Henry Bleby reports that he seemed to be unmoved by the near approach of death. He addressed the assembled crowd in a clear, unfaltering voice, admitted that he had broken the laws of the country and declared that he depended for salvation upon the Redeemer who shed his blood for sinners upon Calvary. Sharpe's reference to the crucifixion of Jesus by the Roman authorities was significant. Relating the event to his own execution could not have escaped his audience. (Hart: 1985) Sharpe declared that the missionaries had nothing whatever to do with the uprising. This meant that he took full responsibility. Then in Bleby's words, in a few moments "the executioner had done his work and the noble-minded originator of this unhappy revolt had ceased to exist".

But he did not die in vain. Bleby's judgement was:

> The revolt failed of accomplishing the immediate purpose of its author, yet by it, a further wound was dealt to slavery which accelerated its destruction for it demonstrated to the imperial legislature that among the Negroes themselves, the spirit of freedom had been so widely diffused as to render it most perilous to postpone the settlement of the most important question of emancipation to a later period. (Bleby: 1868)

Daddy Sharpe was the leader, strong yet modest, deeply religious and compassionate, heroic in character and in life's daily testings. In the following poem he speaks of his encounter to the Jamaican people.

> I love the strong and fighting things,
> and I do miss the belly laugh at evening time,
> and talk and singing with my brothers them
> at night time on the mountain top.
> And now the darkness fall upon them all
> on Thomas Dove, and Gardner and on William James

from Ducketts; and on Johnson from Retrieve,
and on Dehaney who did tell them straight
he know they have determined he must hang
so hang him then and he will take with him
whatever things he knows,
and will not sign confession.
Them all have gone. How I to stay?
Them all be dead. How I to live?

Sherlock

CHAPTER 20

A home of their own

The Act of Emancipation (1833) set in motion forces of radical social change that confronted Jamaica's white governing class – the plantocracy – and her newly-freed African-Jamaicans with challenges that could not be ignored.

The critical question was the same for the governing class and the African-Jamaican labour force – could either or both find a way of laying the foundations of a free and just society?

The answers lie in the history of the period 1838, when full freedom came into effect, and 1865. We begin with the year 1831 when the Jamaica House of Assembly removed the civil disabilities under which some free Jamaicans had laboured for these reflect the racist and vicious character of white plantation society.

In 1831, three years before Emancipation a law was passed which conferred on black and coloured people "of free condition" the right to vote provided they met the necessary property qualifications. They were entitled to "have and enjoy all the rights, privileges, immunities, etc." as if they were "descended from white ancestors". The power of the ballot was a privilege until then exercised only by the white minority. The free people moved from being faceless exiles to becoming citizens, albeit of limited status.

The 1831 Act declared that "whereas it is expedient to grant additional privileges to coloured and black persons of free condition . . . it is hereby enacted and ordained . . . that all such persons of free condition, whether lawfully manumised or being the free-born subjects of His Majesty shall from the first day of August next be permitted to vote at any election for any person to serve in the assemblies of the island provided he possesses an estate to freehold or a house . . . of the annual value of one hundred pounds . . . or shall possess an estate of freehold in land and premises . . .

in such parish where such election shall be held, of the actual annual value of fifty pounds." (*Laws of Jamaica* 1831)

In claiming his rights under the law, George William Gordon declared in the House of Assembly in November 1863, "I stand here tonight as one of the sons of free Jamaica. I claim all the ancient privileges and rights granted to us by Magna Carta and the Bill of Rights."

Slavery, racism and the plantation had up to that time shaped the social and economic structure of West Indian societies, with the exception of British Honduras whose economy had been sustained by logging rather than by the sugar-and-slave plantation.

The Act of Emancipation set in motion the most significant and far-reaching social and economic revolution in the history of Jamaica and of the other countries of the Commonwealth Caribbean. It mandated that in the first instance large numbers of individuals were no longer slaves but neither were they free citizens. They were "apprenticed labourers". Full freedom was granted in 1838 but full and free citizenship was still a long way off.

The decisive section of the Act decreed that "whereas divers persons are held in slavery within divers of His Majesty's colonies and it is just and expedient that all such persons should be manumitted and set free and that all reasonable compensation should be made to the persons hitherto entitled to the services of such slaves for the loss which they will incur . . . be it therefore enacted that from the first day of August, one thousand eight hundred and thirty four, all persons who have been duly registered as slaves shall by force and virtue of this act . . . become and be apprenticed labourers . . ." (Abolition of Slavery Act 1833)

Slave owners in Jamaica received compensation from the British Government amounting to £6,616,927 for the inconvenience and loss they were expected to suffer when they no longer controlled the forced labour which had been the mainstay of their opulent lifestyles. The emancipated people, ten times in number to the plantation owners and the other white employees, received no compensation, no guidance, no training to enable them to rearrange their lives independent of the oppressive slave-plantation system.

For the duration of the apprenticeship period the employers (the former masters) were required to supply this new labour force "with such food, clothing, lodging, medicine, medical attendance . . . as by any law now in force in the colony". The governor was required to appoint Justices of the Peace and Special Magistrates to maintain law and order and to protect the interests of the apprentices but they generally sided with the planters. This led to many abuses and as a result the apprenticeship period was terminated in 1838, two years before it was due to end.

Emancipation struck at the heart of the system of slavery by introducing the payment of wages to labourers. Under slavery, planters had operated with little working capital. They did not pay wages except to overseers and their kind, and they cut the outlay on food to a minimum by letting the workers grow much of what they required. They sold their sugar through agents in Britain who in turn purchased supplies required on the plantation and advanced working capital in lean years.

These arrangements suited the agents admirably because they could collect interest on the moneys loaned by insisting that all the debtors' sugar should pass through their hands. The price of Jamaica sugar was therefore fixed after taking all these factors into consideration.

Jamaica planters faced strong competition from European beet sugar, and from Mauritius, Brazil, Puerto Rico, Fiji and Cuba, countries continuing to rely on slave labour. They either had to improve efficiency through controlled expenditure and use new, improved equipment: ploughs, harrows, steam engines to turn the mills, or go bankrupt. Now wages for the workers had to be paid in reasonable time and this created cash flow problems. The planters required more working capital than formerly, and many were still in debt to their London agents although much of the compensation money had gone to repay debts, mortgages and sub-mortgages.

While all of this was taking place the price of sugar continued to decline, mainly because of inefficient management practices. The price had risen for a while when the Haitian revolution put Jamaica's chief competitor, St Domingue, out of business but cheap sugar from Cuba was rapidly becoming a threat.

Emancipation scene, Spanish Town

Planters blamed emancipation for their economic woes although the slide in production had started many years earlier. By 1775 about 30 per cent of estates in the island were already in the hands of absentee owners. In most instances the overseers and attorneys in charge were more interested in feathering their own nests than in seeing to the economic welfare of their employers. A further decline in the economy after 1790 forced many planters to surrender their mortgaged properties to metropolitan merchants and bankers thereby beginning a trend towards corporate ownership. (Higman: 1976)

Between 1805 and 1850 the market price of sugar fell repeatedly: by 25 per cent between 1805 and 1825, by another 25 per cent between 1825 and 1835, and again by another 25 per cent between 1835 and 1850. (Sewell: 1968) At the time of emancipation, 80 per cent of the sugar estates were owned by absentees while approximately 75 per cent of coffee plantations and roughly 85 per cent of pens continued to be operated by proprietors resident in the island.

The final blow came between 1846 and 1854 when, in order to meet the demand for cheap food to feed her rapidly increasing population, Britain removed the preferential tariff on West Indian sugar and opened

News of emancipation being read

the market to international competition. Once 24,895 tons of foreign sugar entered Britain in 1846 at a lower tariff rating than had been set previously, British and West Indian financial houses collapsed. Merchant houses, which in the past had financed the planting of sugar crops also lost their investments on failed wheat and potato crops in Britain and on over-speculation in other industrial ventures. In 1847 13 West India houses which had been founded to meet the urgent need for capital in the islands went into bankruptcy. These included the Planters Bank in Jamaica and the West India Bank in Barbados.

The Jamaica sugar industry was almost wiped out. Planters were forced to sell their crops on the open market, often at a loss. Production fell by more than 50 per cent from 71,000 tons in 1832 to 25,000 tons in 1852. The inbond price of sugar in Britain which had been £49 per ton in 1840, dropped to £23 in 1846. Many of the already struggling sugar and coffee plantations were partly or wholly abandoned and the price of property plummeted. On some estates the wage bill was cut by as much as a half or two-thirds, to the detriment of the labourers.

Added to this, natural disasters struck. Between 1850 and 1851 the island was ravaged by cholera, smallpox and drought. About 32,000 persons died leaving the already dwindling labour force sadly depleted. One Scottish doctor in the island took advantage of the depressed conditions to purchase 50 plantations, and later became exceedingly wealthy from banana and coconuts.

Planter society had never been free. It had always been in bondage to the sugar-and-slave plantation. Just as the slave carried on his body the marks of servitude, whites – resident owners, managers, overseers – carried in their minds the tensions and anxieties generated by living in a garrison society dominated by fear and also by feelings of betrayal and abandonment by Britain.

The hysteria that gripped whites in Montego Bay at the outbreak of the Western Liberation Uprising, the viciousness and scale of white reprisals against blacks and against white missionaries which followed in 1832, the enactment of punitive laws to enforce subjugation which remained in place up to the time of the Morant Bay Uprising in 1865 – these all signalled the decline and fall of the planter oligarchy.

From this withering plantation society we turn to the African-Jamaicans who, in the face of planter hostility following emancipation, were laying the foundations of the Jamaican nation. In these early years are to be found the source of empowerment and ennoblement that came from the defeat of the planter's attempt at coercion, refusal to be bound to the estates at less than subsistence wage, efforts to make emancipation meaningful and to triumph over what appeared to be insuperable obstacles. Few whites understood the implications of the changes taking place and therefore the need to reorganise their operations and ease the transition process.

First, we will give an account of planter coercion and exploitation in the apprenticeship period and the creation of an African-Jamaican yeomanry. In the chapter that follows we will describe in some detail the people's rejection of planter domination by means of political monopoly and by coercive legislation.

Many former slaves turned peasants, built their own homes, formed new communities and determined, however humble their circumstance and no matter how difficult the struggle, to remain outside of the inflexible plantation system.

The only Jamaican planter to grant full freedom to his field hands in 1834, thereby attempting to save them from further victimisation, was the Marquis of Sligo. He was possibly influenced by his Antiguan colleagues who declared full freedom in 1834, knowing that the only source of employment on that island was on the plantations and that the emancipated people would therefore still be under their control.

In Jamaica, however, "Many masters in their bitterness of heart, vented their wrath upon their unfortunate labourers . . . within a period of two years 60,000 apprentices received a total of a quarter of a million lashes and 50,000 other punishments by tread-mill, chain-gang work, or some other device . . ." (D. F. Walker: 1930)

The following account demonstrates the useless waste of human energy, loss of valuable time, and numerous atrocities meted out to some unfortunate apprentices. The narrator, an apprentice from Penshurst Estate, knowing that he was to be brought before the visiting magistrate the following day, hid from work. Finally after about seven weeks he was caught and taken by the Captain of Police at St Ann's.

> I met him on the road; he took me and put me in dungeon at Carlton; was kept there from Wednesday until Friday morning, then policeman came and took me to Brown's Town, and put me in Cage till next day; then Mr Rawlinson [the magistrate] had me handcuffed and sent me to Penshurst, and put me in dungeon for ten days before he try me . . . Then he sentenced me to St Ann's Bay Workhouse, for nine days, to get fifteen lashes in going in; to dance the treadmill morning and evening, and work in the penal gang; and after I come back from punishment, I must lock up every night in dungeon till he visit the property again, and I have to pay fifty days out of my own time for the time I been runaway.

At the workhouse he was given fifteen lashes with the cat-o-nine tails and chained by the neck to another man. Next morning he was put on the treadmill along with others. The treadmill ground the cornmeal which fed the prisoners. He was not flogged because he quickly learned how "to catch the step by next day but they flog all the rest that could not step the mill, flogged them most dreadful." (Lalla & D'Costa: 1990)

The apprentice, Williams, also described in detail the brutality of the punishments meted out to other unfortunate victims. From the viewpoint of today it should be noted that the orders of the magistrates were carried out by fellow blacks in the name of justice.

Full freedom in 1838 left the former slaves destitute. All they thought they owned or were accustomed to having, even their English names, belonged to someone else. The Emancipation Act had provided that they should continue to live on the estates and receive the same food, clothing, medicine and medical attention for the duration of their apprenticeship. They were then to be allowed three months grace to continue living in their huts and to come to some arrangement with their former masters. There was some confusion over the interpretation of the specific clause that permitted them to continue to live in their huts but the Jamaica Attorney General ruled in favour of the planters. If they remained on the plantation they should pay rent for their dwellings. Immediately almost every planter began issuing notices to their former slaves requiring them to pay about one-third of their weekly wages in rent or quit the premises. The average wage was about three shillings a week. Those who failed to pay could be evicted on one week's notice, and if they failed to leave at the end of the time they could be arrested and imprisoned. The former slaves and their families found themselves destitute, without food or shelter or means of livelihood, "turned adrift and exposed to great misery and distress".

Emancipation gave them the right to free movement; the right to choose where and when they wished to work, but without a basic education and training many were compelled to remain on the plantation as field hands and tenants-at-will under conditions determined by the landlord, and for wages set by him. It was not sufficient to be legally free from slavery; they had to be free from unjust bonds, free to lead normal, healthy lives of their own choosing.

The rent they paid in a year could have purchased at least an acre of land and turned them into smallholders with some limited degree of independence. The planters believed that because the labourers could earn more by weekly work on the estates, they would prefer to stay. They also believed that, in keeping with African tradition, the labourers would be reluctant to move away from the houses in which they were born, their provision grounds and the graves of their ancestors which served as shrines. Above all there was nowhere for them to go. But they underestimated the will of the majority who went to great lengths to preserve their newly gained freedom.

The labour force decreased considerably but the planters thought that this was only temporary.

They squatted on Crown lands in the mountains or on abandoned estates, rented or leased marginal lands from individuals strapped for cash, and in some instances managed to purchase small plots on which they built modest cottages, from which they could not be evicted on the whim of an individual. Only the most destitute without any option became tenants on the estates.

When the planters realised that the labourers did not wish to work for them, they resorted to legislation which maintained their white monopoly and made life intolerable for the African-Jamaicans. For instance, anyone found carrying produce without a written permit could be arrested on the assumption that the goods had been stolen. The Trespass Act permitted the shooting of small stock: goats, sheep, pigs, which were generally owned by smallholders, but horses and cows from the plantations were exempt. To aggravate the situation further, when these animals destroyed the peasants' provision grounds there was no compensation.

In the Grange Hill area of Westmoreland at about this time, the Rev. Henry Clarke expressed his distress at the spite and vindictiveness of landlords who constantly relocated workers' cottages to prevent them from taking advantage of permanent crops such as breadfruit and coconuts which they had planted. "Every village of the estates in this district, of five thousand inhabitants, has been moved within the last ten years; and as the people have to pull down and rebuild their cottages at their own expense, they have got into the way of erecting miserable little huts, in which the poor things are compelled to live, like pigs in a sty." The tenants refused to maintain these flimsy huts because of the uncertainty of their conditions of tenure.

The average wage was sixpence a day with the use of cottage and provision grounds and some missionaries, especially William Knibb, urged the people not to accept such extortionist arrangements. Some misguided ones took this as a signal not to work and began wandering about the countryside fully believing that Queen Victoria had freed them from labour of every kind, and would supply them with food and provisions from England for the rest of their lives. Rumours spread rapidly that they had also been granted free lands and that the planters had bribed some authorities and missionaries to rob them of their rights. They therefore refused to pay rent and by so doing placed themselves at the mercy of landlords only too anxious to evict them from their cottages and provision grounds.

The only real assistance the former slaves received came from some missionaries who obtained loans from their English friends, and then used the money to purchase small acreages which they then subdivided into

small lots for sale to their church congregations. They frequently had to use friends to carry out such transactions as the lands would not have been made available otherwise. Pride of ownership gave the people the self-confidence they badly needed, but the extremely small lots could not support the purchasers and their families by the only method they knew, which was agriculture.

Sligoville, the first free village, founded by the Rev. James Phillippo, below

In 1835 through the efforts of the Rev. James Phillippo the first free village was established at Sligoville in the hills above Spanish Town. He sub-divided 25 acres into one- and two-acre lots and sold them. They were quickly taken up and in June 1838, two months before full freedom was declared the first lot was fully paid for by Henry Lunan, a headman and former slave from an adjoining property.

In one of his letters to a friend asking for a loan, the Rev. Knibb emphasised,

> Should any of our members, as I know they will, be the victims of treachers, scorn or trickery, they may have a home . . . While the land owners have all the land they can, and they will, and they do daily oppress the people by demanding abominable high rents for their houses. In many cases though the house is no better than a hog-sty. I have seen demands of eight shillings and fourpence per week rent at the same time only one shilling and eightpence per day for wages, so that a man must work five days to pay for his house and grounds.

Knibb noted that the people were not asking for charity, they were paying back their loans and would continue to do so.

Some estates charged rentals as high as eight shillings and fourpence per week, and some out of spite refused employment to these tenants. The emancipated people who entered into financial transactions without the help of the missionaries often fell victim to unscrupulous landlords and attorneys who cheated them openly. Some were issued false documents; others received valid receipts but discovered later that these were not sufficient proof of ownership and so lost their investment. Few held proper deeds.

Petty tradesmen and artisans such as carpenters, masons, shoemakers and fishermen began migrating to the towns, especially to Kingston and Spanish Town, where they soon found that life was more difficult than on the plantation. They found that it was not easy to obtain employment. They lived in squalid conditions often as many as nine and ten to a room. They were among the first victims of epidemics.

At emancipation owners had been directed to make reasonable time and opportunity for labourers to be given religious and educational instruction. Missionaries in the field were also advised to engage themselves actively in this exercise.

Government's policy of restricting the amount of Crown lands available to the former slaves and of keeping vast tracts in the hands of a few, ensured that agriculture could not become a viable option for the masses. But the peasants tried to find ways of circumventing these restrictions. In some instances, they obtained grazing rights or the right to gather wood for fuel or to plant their provision grounds. The landowner in return received a share of the smallholder's profits. In addition he sometimes transported and marketed the produce for a fee which was not always in the best interest of the small farmer.

When planters stopped ejecting the people and began paying fairer wages production improved. Those who charged excessive rents, including charging rent for each member of the family and demanding payment in cash or working it out in days on the estate, found that they were short of labour. Some deliberately offered irregular employment believing that by increasing the hardships the labourers would be forced to work harder and the planter would benefit. But this only alienated the labour force further.

The authorities disapproved of the efforts of the missionaries to assist the peasants to establish communities and to educate themselves. They felt there was no need for the former slaves to aspire to become more than field hands. Nevertheless, in spite of strong resistance from both the planters and the authorities, the settlements of the smallholders in time grew into organised communities with the assistance of the missionaries.

Knibb possibly did more than anyone else to develop the free villages. He raised about £10,000 and with this he acquired at least three estates, including Birmingham and Kettering not far from Falmouth, divided them into small lots and resold them to the former slaves. Joseph Sturge, the English Quaker, who with another Quaker, Harvey, had been sent by the Anti-Slavery Society to report on the workings of the apprenticeship system, in one instance loaned £400 to purchase part of Mt Ablyla (also called Standfast) Estate. One hundred families were settled there. He also bought the freedom of James Williams, the apprentice from Penshurst, (whose story appears above), and took him to England.

The missionaries designed the layout of the ideal village but because of the steepness of the terrain and the lack of access roads the original plan could not always be implemented. Most villages could be reached only by narrow bridle paths; water had to be fetched from springs and gullies some distance away, and proper sanitary facilities were often unheard of. The following is a description of what the typical village was expected to be like:

> The villages are laid out in regular order, being divided into lots more or less intersected by roads or streets. The plots are usually in the form of an oblong square. The cottage is situated at an equal distance from each side of the allotment, and at about eight or ten feet, more or less, from the public thoroughfare. The piece of ground in the front is, in some instances, cultivated in the style of a European garden: displaying rose bushes, and other flowering shrubs among the choicer vegetables and fruits of the country, heterogeneously inter-mixed. (Phillippo: 1843)

Retreat Pen near Manchioneal is one of those villages laid out using the plan. It had 41 half-acre lots, more or less.

In contrast to the dilapidated plantation huts they once lived in, the peasants constructed modest dwellings often of Spanish wall or board which they cut from forest trees; roofs were shingled with wood or thatched with palm leaves. Some had wooden floors. A typical cottage consisted of two or three rooms – one or two bedrooms and a living room or hall which was sometimes converted into sleeping quarters as the family outgrew the bedroom space.

A few concerned persons of influence on the island called upon the government to assist with the development of the villages but their appeals fell on deaf ears. Lyndon H. Evelyn, Deputy Receiver General and Public Treasurer at Savanna-la-Mar recommended that the villages should be modeled on the English Agricultural Village plan, having a chapel and minister, "as religion held great attraction for the masses". He also called for schools, "as education was wholesome training for the young and held happy memories". He recommended that there should be houses and provision grounds for the elderly and that merchants and skilled workers should involve themselves in village activities. Smallholders were to be encouraged to grow export crops such as ginger, arrowroot, pimento, coffee and sugar cane, and so improve their living standard.

The Custos of St Elizabeth suggested that in addition to a church and school there should be a marketplace where African-type entertainment could be encouraged. But this only elicited a negative response from the planters and those in authority. They thought that if the labourers paid exorbitant rents and taxes they would be forced to work harder, production would increase and the planters would benefit.

Where it was possible, the people built a chapel and sometimes a schoolhouse usually under the guidance of a missionary. Walter Dendy, the Baptist missionary, architect, builder and philanthropist who arrived in Jamaica twelve days after the Western Liberation Uprising, was one of them. In time, the government provided teachers and on occasion when they proved unsuccessful the villagers sometimes employed their own teachers. The wives of missionaries taught Bible classes, sewing, fancy work, cookery, music and general reading.

More ambitious adults learnt from their children attending day school, especially as they wanted to learn to read the Bible for themselves. The result was evidenced by a high level of literacy in some villages. Education became the means by which upward mobility was usually achieved. "The spelling book was a powerful factor of Christian enlightenment, and through the schools thousands were daily brought under the direct influence of the Gospel. All the churches took part in this great work of education." (Walker: 1930)

Mico College, which opened in 1836

As the need for more teachers grew missionaries selected young men of promise from among their congregations and instructed them. The training of these adults as class leaders and lay preachers opened opportunities for some of them to become "confidential servants in business houses, subordinate estate managers, governesses and school teachers".

In 1836, through the bequest of Lady Mico, the Mico Institution (Mico College), had been established "for the benefit of African slaves made free and engaged in the work [of teaching]". The educational level of the students was at first low, but the level of performance improved.

Knibb was the first to express the need for the training of local men for the ministry and in 1842, along with James Phillippo and Thomas Burchell, he approached the Baptist Missionary Society in England. A year later, in 1843, Calabar College was opened at Rio Bueno in Trelawny with ten students. They were all older men, very dedicated but mostly illiterate. However, three eventually graduated as ministers and seven as teachers. Under the tutelage of the Rev. Joshua Tinson, they acquired skills in reading, composition and pronunciation as well as some Hebrew and Greek, and "took the gospel of love to their brethren in the villages of the interior". In 1868 Calabar was transferred from Trelawny to Kingston.

Church and school were the centre of village life following the English tradition. "The church choir was a training ground for vocalists; the school provided recitations, the schoolroom was the natural venue for any entertainment except for organ recitals and concerts of sacred music, which were held in the church." (Jacobs: 1973)

Overall, about 19 unprofitable sugar estates were turned into free villages as well as some abandoned coffee plantations in the parishes of St Andrew, St John, Manchester and Metcalfe. Ewart, one of the special stipendiary magistrates assigned to the parish of St Thomas, to administer justice and prevent social and economic disturbance, reported from Morant Bay in October 1840 that three extensive villages had been established on former sugar plantations in the interior of that parish. He observed that the lots ranged in size from one to ten acres and that there were already in place about 300 cottages, "neat and comfortable and surrounded by gardens and provision grounds".

In November of that same year, Richard Chamberlaine, another stipendiary magistrate from the parish, who had been away for two years, remarked on the number of settlements and cottages that had sprung up "right and left" where before had been "bush and jungle". He was pleasantly surprised at the expansion of existing villages, the number of new shops, improved construction methods and the more spacious houses being built. Chamberlaine was a coloured man who later became custos of the parish.

Ten years after emancipation, Knibb reported that there were 23 villages in Trelawny with 1,790 houses; in St Thomas-in-the-Vale, 10 villages with 1,780 houses and in St James 10 villages with 1,000 houses all completed. In several areas, for example in Manchester, in upper Clarendon and St Catherine, among the foothills of the Blue Mountains in Portland and St George, in the Port Royal Mountains of St Andrew, villages developed in spite of the lack of government support.

They were also to be found in other remote areas across the island. Fifteen were at one time located in St Mary, 15 in the Dry Harbour

Mountains of St Ann where the village of Dumbarton consisted of 60 quarter-acre lots. There were also villages at Harmony Hall and Trysee not far from Brown's Town. The Methodists established the village of Epworth, also in St Ann, and well into the twentieth century it remained a "dry" village where alcohol could not be sold. Not many settlements were located near to large estates and small towns. Usually lands in these more advantageous areas were denied the aspiring smallholders.

Eventually about 2,000 such villages were established, allowing many thousands of freed people to become proud owners of homes of their own. Those who could not afford to purchase lands sometimes rented or leased plots and house spots. The house spots were at times so small they could hardly hold the tiny cottages, but their owners wanted homes of their own.

The most spectacular growth of smallholdings occurred immediately after the apprenticeship period. In 1840, two years after full freedom, only about 883 persons owned holdings of under ten acres; five years later, the number had increased to 20,724 and by 1865, at the time of the Morant Bay Uprising, the number stood at about 60,000. The planters were suffering as a result of the movement of workers away from the plantations, since only about one-third of the labourers available at the time of emancipation were then willing to work on the plantations.

Although the Jamaican peasantry could now become involved in the island's administrative affairs the requirements were stringent. They could register to vote if they owned real property worth £6 or paid £30 in rent or paid £3 in direct taxes. By the middle of the century some 20,000 could have met these requirements but under 3,000 registered to vote. The Baptist missionaries began a concerted effort to get small settlers to register and by 1863 in one or two parishes they made up as much as 63 per cent of the voters list. They could not however exert much influence through the electoral process as the property clause required a member of the Assembly to have an annual income of £300, and unencumbered property worth £3,000. Without sympathetic representation there could be no meaningful change.

Although planters and officials thought otherwise, the smallholders were generally industrious people. In 1850, John Candler, an English Quaker, observed that on the whole they performed as much work on the estates as in the days of slavery. He said that no one who had seen them at work in the cane fields, or hoeing coffee on the steep hillsides, or who had travelled among their provision grounds in the mountains, could call them idle. "I have seen them again and again, hundreds and thousands of them, men, women and children, loaded with provisions and fruits, which they carry on their heads, pouring down from the hills to market carrying weights which no European would encounter, and sweating under the heavy toil, yet all labouring cheerfully because they are free." (Olivier: 1933) The redistribution of the population across the interior of the island had a positive impact on the internal economy as trade followed settlement into the interior.

Sewell noted that planters blamed their economic ruin, not on their own inefficiency but on the shortage of labour and the refusal of the labourers to work an eight-hour day. As a stranger he could not answer these charges, but the people whom he had encountered were eager to work, to carry his luggage, to run errands and to offer their assistance for a paltry remuneration. He had never seen so many servants and attendants as in Jamaica. A government clerk had as many servants as a foreign ambassador. "Servants must have under-servants, and agents, sub- agents . . . He sees labour everywhere – on the roads, the streets, the wharves, and it is only upon the plantations that he hears any complaint. Yet even there he detects none of the labor-saving machinery that he has been accustomed to see at home, where labor is really scarce and dear . . ." (Sewell: 1968) The master-slave mentality was still very strong.

The Chief Commissioner of Roads told Sewell that he had 3,000 men in constant employment who worked diligently for five days a week, and marketed and cultivated their grounds on the sixth. They were never idle although stone breaking was harder than plantation work.

The Superintendent of the Rio Grande Copper Mines also told him that for eight years he had never experienced any labour shortage even though the men worked eight hours a day, six days a week. When the mines eventually closed, one sugar estate near Annotto Bay recruited 36 of the miners at thirty-six cents a day. It was three months before they were paid, and then they received only half the amount agreed upon. No wonder the labourers preferred to keep far away from the estates.

The rapid expansion of free villages in the interior enabled some strategically located older villages to grow into prosperous market towns. One observer noted that before emancipation Old Harbour consisted of two taverns, one or two houses, a post office, a pound, a blacksmith's shop operated by a slave, and a jail. Within two years it had become a thriving town through the flourishing marketing activities of the villagers from the interior. There was now a new court-house, many good houses and buildings, ten to twelve small shops, three blacksmith's shops, a tinsmith's shop and police station, in addition to the pound and two taverns from earlier days. It was the scene of a flourishing Saturday Market where all sorts of ground provisions, baked products, meat, poultry as well as items of haberdashery were sold.

Porus, another of these villages, owed its existence to a land speculator, Andrew Drummond, who had purchased 700 acres for £500, divided it into 15- to 25-acre lots and sold the whole at a profit of £1,500. Several individuals either grouped together to purchase a lot, or the lots were subdivided again immediately after purchase. In 1839, not long after the transaction had taken place, another writer noted that some 1,500 residents were located there on half-acre to two-acre lots. The village was ideally situated, within easy reach of plantations in both Clarendon and Manchester but the writer observed that not one villager had gone out to seek employment. They engaged in shared labour, "day for a day", which allowed poor families to complete their projects, whether it be land preparation for planting or house building, without having to pay in cash. The person receiving the assistance would give back the day or days to those who had assisted him and this would continue until the projects were completed.

Another observer mentions the irreproachable conduct and industry of the Porus residents, and the fact that they were little troubled that the land was not particularly productive. (In the twentieth century it was analysed as having a high bauxite content.) Their main goal had been accomplished, they owned a home of their own. After that they could choose where they wished to work.

The composition of the village of Maldon in the hills of St Elizabeth gives some idea of the activities of many villagers. Of the 52 smallholders in the village, one was a teacher, another was a servant, 27 were jobbers: carpenters, masons and some who did task work. Twelve grew provisions for sale, split shingles and engaged in other activities such as cleaning pastures.

This display of self-reliance was not to the planters' liking. At a meeting of landowners and attorneys held in Trelawny in 1858, the planters, frustrated by the fact that they could no longer exploit the labourers as before declared, "The people will never be brought to a stage of continuous labour while they are allowed to possess the large tracts of land now cultivated by them for provision." To subvert their efforts the government had by then begun to import cheap labour from China and India to fill the gap created by the refusal of smallholders to work on the estates. The story of the East Indians and Chinese and how they fared is told in chapter twenty-five.

Education was not encouraged by the authorities who felt that it would give the field-hands political and social ambitions and this would make them unfit for labour. But the more enterprising smallholders wished their children to take advantage of the educational opportunities they had missed. They wanted them to become lawyers, doctors, teachers and rich businessmen even when the basic educational preparation was obviously inadequate. The majority settled for apprenticing the children to tradesmen especially in the towns. Agriculture as a means of earning a livelihood was frowned upon. The elders hoped to spare their children the experiences and drudgery they had endured as plantation labourers but not everyone was so motivated. To some individuals, school was a waste of time. They considered that the children could be more profitably employed working in the fields, doing domestic chores or taking care of their younger siblings. With these ingrained attitudes illiteracy remained a major problem condemning many intelligent young Jamaicans to frustration and poverty.

The industry of the average free village accounts for the rapid development of the internal economy of the island. By 1879, the island was self-sufficient in basic food items. Lucea yam from Hanover was sold in other parishes across the island; yam from Portland was exported to Central America where many Jamaicans had found employment. Almost every village had its own small animal-powered sugar mill and boiling house. About 50 per cent of sugar consumed in the island during this period was produced by these small farmers and sold in the form of "wet" sugar. Village shopkeepers became produce dealers, purchasing exportable crops in small quantities or exchanging them for basic food items. They in turn resold the goods in bulk to exporters in Kingston and other parish towns.

Twenty-five years is a short time in the life of a people. Some African-Jamaicans who had been young at the time of the Sam Sharpe and Western Liberation Uprising were middle-aged at the time of Gordon, Bogle and the Morant Bay Uprising, Yet in that relatively short period of time the African-Jamaicans with help only from the missionaries, and out of their own limited resources, had settled large areas of inland Jamaica and had founded a landed yeomanry with homes of their own.

CHAPTER 21

Towards political liberty

The heroes of a nation embody its cherished values, express its highest purposes, inspire its noblest achievements. They speak to those who will listen and to minds that will understand. They sacrifice their lives even to death to win freedom, justice and political independence for the majority.

Just as Sam Sharpe set African-Jamaicans on the road to freedom, in 1832 George William Gordon and Paul Bogle in 1865 moved them towards political liberty by championing resistance to white minority oppression that divorced morality from the exercise of power.

Gordon and Bogle did not initiate the struggle. That began with the first African slaves to come to the Americas and was continued through the centuries by others who resisted planter coercion and oppression by means of parliamentary control. But by articulating an ideology, Gordon and Bogle (and earlier, Sam Sharpe), transformed a wide-ranging series of protests into a campaign for civil liberty. By giving this campaign moral force as well as ethical sanction they gave it purpose and continuity. They identified the basic concepts of good government for the newly emancipated peasant folk who chose to assert their rights to political liberty and justice guided by religious principles.

The Greeks in the age of Pericles had recognised that in a democracy the administration's function was to favour the many instead of the few. So did the Saxon kings Edgar and Alfred the Great. In Edgar's words, "This is what I will – that Every Man be worthy of folk-right, poor and rich alike, and that righteous dooms be judged to them." In the same spirit Alfred decreed that English history should be truly set down in an English book, "Thus, law by law, record by record the prescriptive right of the folk to safe conduct in their life and work, and to justice at the hands of their rulers and governors, is asserted and re-asserted." (Rhys: 1921)

Governor Eyre and Jamaica's nineteenth-century planter oligarchy disregarded the fact that they, being of English descent, were the inheritors of a long and proud tradition of struggle for political liberty for which their forefathers had died. These were the very rights that the African-Jamaican people were claiming.

The concept of justice as an attribute of God was familiar to the peoples of Africa. Many saw God as king, lord and maker. As ruler and maker he was judge: the one who settled the differences between us who are men. (Mbiti: 1970) The African-Jamaicans inherited West African attitudes and beliefs and expected authority and political justice to be exercised with regard to God's teaching.

Gordon and Bogle became the icons of the great mass of the Jamaican people in the same way that Sam Sharpe had incarnated their consuming desire for freedom. The mission of the two heroes and their martyrdom make Bogle's Stony Gut chapel and the Morant Bay court-house shrines that commemorate the memory of those who chose to enlarge the freedom they had gained, by continuing the struggle of their African ancestors for equality such as they had known in their homelands.

These two leaders, one brown, one black, along with thousands of simple folk, understood no less clearly than the founders of the English nation that the rights of the many had to be protected against the power of the few. Preacher Gordon appealed to the Higher Judge when he accused Governor Eyre of oppression: it was the Lord who would soon pluck his hand out of his bosom and so confound the whole band of oppressors. In St Thomas-in-the-East, where magisterial oppression was worse than in other parishes, Gordon wrote to his friend and estate manager at Rhine: "The Governor is an evil doer: the Lord will plenteously reward him."

A bulletin published for the capture of Bogle at the time of the Morant Bay Uprising described him as: "very black, shiney of skin, heavy marks of smallpox on face, especially on nose, good teeth – large mouth, red thick lips; about five feet eight inches tall, broad shoulders; carries himself indolently, with no whiskers". He was an independent small farmer in the village of Stony Gut where he owned a large piece of land on which he had built his own Native Baptist church.

Bogle's church blended Christian and African beliefs and values with strong religious militancy. "Central to its functioning was a remarkable relationship between Bogle and George William Gordon . . . part political and religious alliance, part friendship, their relationship was founded in resistance." (Holt: 1992)

In their last three or four years, the two men defined the central themes of justice and concern for the "many", which widened into a struggle against the monopoly of political power that was taken up by Robert Love, Sandy Cox and Bain Alves with their trade unions, Marcus Garvey, Norman Manley in his campaign for universal adult suffrage and

Alexander Bustamante in his formation of the labour movement, and led to political independence in 1962.

Gordon was born a slave. The baptismal register at Spanish Town records his birth in December 1815 as the son of a quadroon slave at Cherry Garden Estate, and notes that it had taken place three months earlier. His father was Joseph Gordon, an attorney who had come to Jamaica to manage a number of sugar estates for absentee owners, and had become a property owner himself. The boy was intelligent and industrious and by the age of ten could "read, write and keep accounts". He was manumitted by his father and sent to live with his godfather, James Daley, a businessman of Black River. At age 16 Gordon launched out into the business world by opening a produce-dealer's store in Kingston. It is said that he was assisted by his father and a white woman who loaned him £1,000.

George William Gordon's baptismal entry

Gordon prospered and in time set up his counting-house on Port Royal Street. In 1843 he was reportedly worth £10,000 and could afford to send his three sisters to Europe to be educated. He was engaged in several business ventures and became a large landed proprietor owning estates and other property in several parishes, including two or three estates in St Thomas-in-the-East and Cherry Garden in St Andrew, which he purchased when his father ran into financial difficulty.

Gordon's disquiet at the appallingly poor social conditions then obtaining caused him to draw public attention to a number of issues that needed to be addressed: lack of medical attention for the poor and infirm, the insanitary conditions in prisons and the treatment of prisoners, especially in St Thomas.

In 1844 at age 29 he was elected representative for the parish of St Andrew and continued his battles in the Assembly for one term. He codemned the victimisation of poor blacks and criticised fraud and corruption in high places – forgery, burglary, cattle stealing – and other crimes which went unpunished while the peasants were penalised for petty crimes. As was to be expected, these attacks on the establishment brought him into open conflict with some of his brown colleagues and with other members of the Assembly and the vestries. He failed to gain another seat until 1863 when he was elected to represent the parish of St Thomas-in-the-East.

Gordon's business deals extended to several parishes and this enabled him to serve as justice of the peace in several of them. Because of his unrelenting criticism of the political administration and the social conditions in St Thomas, the custos refused to let him take his seat in the vestry, using the excuse that he was not a practising member of the Church of England. When Gordon would not leave the meeting, the custos had him physically removed. Bogle and other St Thomas small settlers then voted him in as "the people's church warden", but the governor withdrew his commission as justice of the peace and he once again was denied a seat. Gordon took the rector and custos to court and won.

Although he was an untiring political advocate, contrary to popular belief Gordon was not a member of the Town Party, which was then comprised mostly of coloured professionals and businessmen residing mainly in Spanish Town and Kingston. (Robotham: 1981)

In addition to his political activities, Gordon was a man of deep religious conviction. He was christened an Anglican but converted to the Baptist faith and was baptised by the Rev. James Phillippo. He was always on the move, travelling from one church to another, preaching, offering counsel, starting new missions or serving in whatever way he could. In 1860-61 a great religious revival swept the island, and at Christmas 1860 Gordon transferred his allegiance to the Native Baptists and established his own independent Baptist chapels at Bath, at Spring Gardens near Stony Gut and in Kingston. At the same time he continued his association with the Presbyterians and Baptists and other religious organisations.

Paul Bogle, a younger charismatic leader, was also converted at about this time. Gordon ordained Bogle as a deacon in his tabernacle in Kingston in March 1865, after the latter had built his own chapel at Stony Gut in December 1864.

Bogle's letters to his pastor, "elder brother" and friend, Gordon, concerned urgent matters to be addressed: an ethical base for justice, votes to be registered and bakras to be defeated. In one letter he wrote, "We want to see you at our village . . . for we have plans [to] arrange with you. Come up, we beseech you as quick as possible so that we may arrange how the baptism is to go at Spring." A second letter written later that day followed.

> At a meeting held at the Liberal School Society Meeting House at the above named place [Stony Gut] to take into consideration what plans we might adopt to recover your place that is lost in the political world but in the religious one we are assured your progress is great; may God grant it so. Among other plans we resolve to have a hundred tax payers put on [the electoral roll], independent of freeholders, and those who will or can without borrowing from us. (Holt: 1992)

Eric Williams, political leader and historian, sums up the nature of the system that Gordon and Bogle were attempting to reform.

George William
Gordon

Massa had a monopoly of political power in the West
Indies which he used shamelessly for his private ends
. . . He used this power ruthlessly . . . [Massa] developed the necessary philosophical rationalization of this
barbarous system. It was that the workers both African
and Indian, were inferior beings, unfit for self-government, permanently destined to a status of perpetual
subordination, unable ever to achieve equality with
Massa. It was there in all the laws which governed the
West Indies for generations, – the laws which denied
equality on the grounds of colour . . . the laws which
equated political power and the vote with ownership of
land, the laws which . . . attempted to ensure that the
non-European would never be anything but a worker
in the social scale, the improvement of whose standard
of living depended, as a British Secretary of State once
told the workers in Jamaica in 1865, on their working
on Massa's plantation for wages. (Williams: 1981)

The response of Gordon and Bogle and other African-Jamaicans was
the rejection of the dominance of a minority of property owners whose
attitudes were rooted in the monopoly of political power and racism.
Their struggle which culminated in the Morant Bay Uprising marks an
important phase in the demand for justice but it did not end there. As in
the pre-emancipation period, so in the century that followed, the
dynamics of change came from the African-Jamaican people. With sacrifice and determination they finally, in 1945, achieved full political representation through universal adult suffrage and the secret ballot.

In order to appreciate more fully why Gordon and Bogle and countless
others worked unremittingly to change the system, we must remind ourselves that the oppressive social and economic conditions had not changed,
and look briefly at some of the laws implemented during the period which
adversely affected the lives of the masses.

The Master and Servant's Act, which came into force following
emancipation, and remained in force after 1842 allowed the planter to
reduce wages and provide employment irregularly to the detriment of the
labour force. Those dependent on plantation employment never knew
when they would be laid off, or when they would be paid. They could be
fined for trivial offences, so that sometimes they lost almost all their
wages and had nothing left to take home to their families.

The Jamaican peasant was denied cultivable land for rent. He was
prevented from utilising abandoned estates. Access to Crown lands was

restricted by prices fixed so high "as may place them out of reach of persons without capital". (House of Commons, 14. 600-699) European, Indian and Chinese indentured labour was recruited to deprive Jamaicans of a means of livelihood. "A Jamaican man" writing in the *Liverpool Standard* of 1833 about the European immigration noted that "This would benefit the planters without injury to the negroes: to the former it would give a greater quantity of labourers, consequently a greater competition in the market . . . to the latter it would make the necessity of working greater, consequently, less fear of their relapsing into barbarism."

Paul Bogle

The Assembly used the ballot to retain its hold on power, and introduced legislation to ensure that the situation would not change. The 1840 Franchise Act which was based on proof of ownership of property was amended to include an hereditaments (inheritance) tax which put the poor small settler at a further disadvantage. In 1851 a literacy clause proposed in the Assembly was defeated by a slim margin of 13 to 11. It would be introduced again some ten years later. Eight coloured representatives voted against the bill. The hereditaments tax no doubt affected the number of voters, as between 1840 and 1852 voter registration declined from 1,800 to 753 in a country with a population of over 400,000. Epidemics of cholera, influenza and smallpox in 1850 and 1851 devastated the population and may also have contributed to the decline. It was now obvious that the voters' roll had to be increased.

Proposed new legislation in 1854, ostensibly to rectify the inadequacies of the earlier election law, also had an underlying motive, to add to the financial burden of the peasant. It was defeated by a narrow margin.

The hereditaments tax which had imposed a charge of twelve shillings, six pence on voters met with so much opposition that it was withdrawn in 1858, but was replaced in the following year by a ten shillings poll tax. In the debates which followed in the Assembly the governor admitted that although there was no great change in the amount taxpayers were being called upon to pay, it would in practice be "a great discouragement of the exercise of the Franchise, by the more numerous and humbler Class of Freeholders, and that it was advocated in Assembly for no other reason". (Holt: 1992) A compromise was reached and a stamp duty of ten shillings was introduced only for those wishing to exercise the franchise. According to Holt, the impact on the £6 freeholders, the peasant voters, was especially crippling. They were now forced to pay an additional sum of money in order to exercise the ballot. Previously this group had made up one-third of the voters' list. By 1860 it was one-sixth of the list, and by 1863, one-eighth. This meant that their ability to choose a representative to their liking was greatly reduced.

Political equality for the masses could only be achieved through their ability to exercise the vote and to this end the Baptists had been campaigning since 1840 to increase their numbers on the electoral roll. They were joined by the Methodists and a number of activists across the island, among them Gordon and Bogle and their Stony Gut associates.

Bogle was influential throughout the St Thomas area and was respected as a political and a religious leader. Along with his brother Moses and an associate James Maclaren, he had worked zealously to get the St Thomas small settlers to meet the requirements that would enable them to register and to vote. Both he and Gordon were in the habit of advancing the tax moneys for financially hard-pressed freeholders. In other parishes other committed individuals were doing the same thing. In a few instances they made dramatic strides, but much more needed to be done. Only 1,903 names appeared on the electoral roll in 1863 out of a population of 450,000, and of that number only 1,457 cast their ballots in 1864. They voted in 47 representatives from 23 constituencies, an average of 31 voters per representative. In such circumstances the voice of the masses was not being heard.

Taxation was also used as a weapon. Plantation owners paid considerably lower duties on imported goods than did the poor. Food and clothing attracted duties sometimes twelve times higher than previously. Andrew H. Lewis, protesting against the state of affairs in the Assembly in 1861 said, "They were taxed on their bread, their salt, their lucifers, their clothes, and everything else they use." The tax on donkeys was more than that on horses. Peasant carts which previously went untaxed were now charged eighteen shillings per year while plantation carts continued to go untaxed. The revenues collected provided services for the benefit of the planters while the needs of the peasants were ignored.

As social conditions deteriorated, financial burdens piled up, living expenses increased and sporadic outbursts of anger and discontent erupted across the island. Some persons, homeless and without employment, resorted to stealing foodstuffs and to picking wild fruit in pastures. They were punished with flogging and imprisonment. Gordon continued to organise public protests.

Toll gates were placed at strategic locations on roads leading to the town of Savanna-la-Mar, which poor people frequently used. For three nights in February 1859 the protestors tore down the toll gates and when they were brought to trial, tensions ran so high that according to one reporter, "The peasantry of the parish assembled in such large numbers, and were in so excited a state, that it was deemed advisable to adjourn [the trial]." Resentment against the system was widespread and the legislation was withdrawn in 1863.

Protests against unfair property laws sometimes united whole communities. This happened at Florence Hall in Trelawny where the villagers kept vigil every night for three months to prevent Theodore Buie from being ejected from the property of which he was part owner. The resistance led to arrests, to a march on the police station at Falmouth, and to burning the wharf in the town. In the end some persons lost their lives and over 120 were punished.

Squatters and legitimate tenants objected to being turned off the lands they were occupying when they refused to pay rents additional to the legally required quitrents they had already paid. Sometimes they obstructed attorneys and surveyors in the course of their duties and threatened them with bodily harm.

Having to provide proof of ownership was another common method used to defraud inexperienced land purchasers who could not produce proper deeds. Gordon urged resistance against some of these oppressive measures. He helped many peasants to acquire lands for free villages, loaned small farmers money to plant economic crops, such as coffee, and then sold the crops for them. It is claimed that he also gave cattle to his supporters so that they could become taxpayers and meet the voting requirements. In the Assembly he urged the extension of the franchise to a wider cross-section of the population and in 1865, when he could make no headway with the local administrators, he took his complaints to the Colonial Office. He was seeking fair representation which meant that the majority, not the few, would have the power to pass laws.

Governor Eyre came under his attack for mismanagement and lack of integrity. He said,

> But when everyday we witness the maladministration of the law by the Lieutenant-Governor, we must speak out. You are endeavouring to suppress public opinion, to pen up the expression of public indignation; but I tell you it will soon burst forth like a flood, and sweep everything before it. There must be a limit to everything: a limit to oppression – a limit to transgression – a limit to illegality. (Gordon)

When challenged and asked if he was speaking of insurrection he replied, "Ay! that will be the result."

News of growing discontent among the masses and the unwillingness of the white minority to compromise reached Britain, and the London secretary of the Baptist Missionary Society, Dr Edward Underhill, undertook to visit the region to obtain first-hand information. His findings, which were published in 1862, confirmed the reports of the harsh social and economic conditions the peasants had been protesting about for a long time.

After two years, nothing having been done to improve the situation, Underhill brought the matter to the attention of his friend Edward Cardwell, acting Secretary-of-State for the Colonies. The letter outlined many irregularities, acts of oppression, unjust tribunals, denial of political rights, declining social conditions and the indifference of the island's administrators to the worsening conditions and the high level of unemployment. Underhill wrote:

> Crime has fearfully increased. The number of prisoners . . . is considerably more than double the average, and nearly all for one crime, larceny. Summonses for petty debts disclose an amount of pecuniary difficulty which has never before been experienced; and applications for parochial and private relief prove that multitudes are suffering from want, little removed from starvation.

He described the nakedness of the poor, which he attributed to the increase in duties and the high cost of cotton cloth. Unemployment was also a major contributing factor.

The Colonial Office forwarded Underhill's letter to Governor Eyre for his comments. In his reply of 2 March, 1865 Eyre claimed that the accusations were exaggerated and distorted; that the problem of poverty was to be blamed on the low moral character of the people and on their willingness to squander money on such things as fancy church clothes. Several members of the legislature supported his claims that the peasants had brought these privations upon themselves by "sheer idleness, a growing dislike to steady industry, and a consequent preference to a dishonest mode of living".

Eyre admitted that social and economic conditions were bad and growing worse, but maintained that laziness was the major problem of the blacks. Eyre had Underhill's letter printed and circulated widely, along with comments from himself.

The island had been affected in 1864 by severe floods, followed by drought, which had destroyed coffee crops and provision grounds and had added to the worsening conditions. The whole island was suffering but the situation in St Thomas appeared to be particularly bad. Poor and inadequate medical facilities, poor housing for the sick and infirm, lack of medical attention for persons awaiting trial, led Gordon to protest to the governor. When he attempted to bring witnesses to confirm his accusations, especially concerning the insanitary conditions at the jail, the local justices refused to hear them because they claimed that their testimony was irrelevant. By then the jail had already been cleaned.

Intolerance and bias in the judicial system also caused Bogle and his associates to organise their own unofficial court system at Manchioneal, Serge Island and other places in the parishes of St Thomas, St David and St Andrew. They selected their own judges, clerks of the peace and police force, issued summonses, tried cases and levied fines. The courts may have been linked to the local churches, so that disobeying the court's authority could mean expulsion from the church. The membership fee was one shilling. (Holt: 1992)

Bogle began training his followers in military drills and apparently contemplated the use of force if necessary to bring down the oppressive system. Underhill's letter became the rallying point for concerned persons both black and white wishing to change the system. The meetings became known as Underhill meetings. Gordon presided over one in Kingston on 3 May, the Spanish Town meeting of 16 May was called by the Honourable Richard Hill, a respected member of the Assembly and a special magistrate and was presided over by "H. Lewis, Esquire", a member of the Assembly for St Catherine.

There was an orchestrated campaign to document the conditions and the reports were sent to the governor to be transmitted to the Colonial Office. The organisers were determined to have their cause heard and were prepared if necessary to send a delegation to Britain. George Price, Custos of St Catherine, actually went to Britain to lay the matter before the Secretary-of-State for the Colonies. On 5 September, on the eve of his departure from the island he was handed a petition signed by 40 persons from St Thomas who complained of short payment of wages and other hardships they were suffering.

At least three parishes also prepared petitions. There was a much publicised one from the people of St Ann, one from the people of St Elizabeth and another from free Africans employed as indentured labourers at Vere in Clarendon. Excerpts from the St Ann petition of April 1865 are quoted below because they set out most vividly the hardships the people faced and their appeal for help.

> We the undersigned of this island beg with submission to inform our Queen that we are in great want at this moment from the bad state of our island. Soon after we became free subjects We could get plenty of work, and well paid, then all the estates was in a flourishing state, but at this moment the most of the estates are thrown up . . . Some of us, after we became free subjects, purchased a little land, some of us a lot, half acre, one acre, and so on, at the rate of £10. and £12. per acre merely as a home.

We have to leave our homes every day when we can get employment, so that we may have means to go to market on Saturdays, by
working on an estate or pen. Our little homes, we, having turned up
the soil so often, that it becomes useless for provision, by which
means we are compelled to rent land from the large proprietors at the
rate of two pounds eight shillings per acre for one year, and the rent
must be paid in advance. In many instances our provisions are
destroyed by cattles; and if the proprietors find the most simple fault,
three months' notice is given, and we have to destroy our provisions,
at the same time numbers of us having a large family of eleven or
twelve children depending on the provisions for subsistence . . .
Formerly we could get from one shilling and sixpence per day as
labourers, as a carpenter or other tradesmen three shillings to four
shillings per day. A job that we formerly would get two pounds for at
this moment is only twelve shillings. Three or four of us may take job
work and when it is finished in many instances we have to wait for
weeks for payment for our work . . . If our Most Gracious Sovereign
Lady will be so kind as to get a quantity of land, we will put our
hands and heart to work, and cultivate coffee, corn, canes, cotton and
tobacco, and other produce. We will also form a company for the
purpose, if our Gracious Lady Victoria our Queen will also appoint
an agent to receive such produce as we may cultivate and give us
means of subsistence while at work . . . We your humble servants will
thankfully repay our Sovereign Lady by installments of such produce
as we may cultivate. Your humble servants are willing to work so that
we may be comfortable . . . If it had not been for the breadfruit and
coconut numbers of us would have perished . . . Our difficulties are
very great. We have to pay fourpence per yard for cloth of the worst
kind. The cloth in general is so high in price that numbers of our
people is half naked. If our Gracious Sovereign will be so kind as to
grant our request in a few years time our Sovereign Lady Queen
Victoria will see the improvement of our island, and the benefit that
your humble servants will derive . . . We think that our distress is felt
throughout the island and we hope that some of our adjoining neighbours, in other parishes will also state to our Sovereign their distress
. . . We, your most humble servants, will as a duty bound ever pray,
God bless the Queen.

Of the 108 persons who signed the petition only 26 could write their
names. The others marked with an "X".

In spite of this, the government stubbornly refused to acknowledge the
seriousness of the situation and the need to redress the grievances.

Cardwell relied on Eyre's advice and his reply of 14 June 1865 showed no compassion. He said that the letter had been laid before the Queen, and that he had been commanded:

> To inform them that the prosperity of the labouring classes as well as of all other classes, depends in Jamaica and in other countries on their working for wages, not uncertainly or capriciously, but steadily and continuously, at the times when their labour is wanted, and for so long as it is wanted; that if they would use this industry, and thereby render the plantations productive. They would enable the planters to pay higher wages for the same hours of work than are received by the best field labourers in the country [Britain] and as the cost of the necessities of life is much less in Jamaica than it is here [in Britain] they would be enabled by adding prudence to industry, to lay by an ample provision for seasons of drought and dearth.

Their own industry and prudence would avail them of the means of prospering, not by any schemes which had been suggested to them by instigators. Her Majesty would regard with interest and satisfaction their advancement through their own merits and efforts.

Eyre had 50,000 copies of the "Queen's Advice" with his own preface printed and distributed throughout the island. It was read from some pulpits, but other preachers refused to comply and returned the parcels unopened. It was posted in all public places but served only to increase the discontent.

Gordon's attacks on the administration did not let up and on 24 March 1865, he drew the Assembly's attention to the reintroduction of the treadmill, an instrument of torture withdrawn after full freedom. These severities and tortures, he said, were diabolical and were intended to consign the prisoners to an early grave. His pleas fell upon deaf ears.

An Underhill meeting called for 29 July at Morant Bay was postponed because the custos refused to allow the courthouse to be used. On 12 August the custos again refused the use of the courthouse and Gordon presided over the meeting in the open air. The meeting passed resolutions denouncing the government's policy concerning the economic depression, low wages and the use of public funds which the governor had authorised for paying the law suit which Gordon had won.

The meeting resolved to send a deputation to Spanish Town to place the grievances before the governor. Paul Bogle and a group of men including James Maclaren walked more than 40 miles to Spanish Town with the letter, but Eyre refused to meet them or hear their complaints.

Frustrations were at boiling point and came to a head a few weeks later when a special magistrate whom the people trusted was dismissed. On

Saturday 7 October, while the custos, Baron von Ketelhodt, was presiding over a petty sessions court, spectators were gathered in the square and in the court because they were on the lookout for any miscarriage of justice. After the first case was heard and the fines imposed, James Geohegan, another campaigner, shouted to the defendant, a boy, to pay the fine of four shillings but not the other costs of twelve shillings, six pence, which usually went towards the salaries of the clerks. Two policemen ordered to arrest him were dragged from the steps of the courthouse and beaten. Geohegan and his accomplices escaped and the court adjourned prematurely.

On the following Monday the second case which had been put off from the Saturday before came up for hearing. The defendant, William Miller, was cited for trespassing because he had gone into a pasture to recover his horse which one James Williams had impounded. Williams was demanding that Miller pay for the grazing. The court found Miller guilty of trespass. At that point Bogle and some ten or twelve other onlookers urged him to appeal. The magistrates were irate. They later had 28 warrants prepared, all backdated to Saturday 7 October, giving the impression that the beating of the policemen and the disturbance in the court had all taken place on the same day.

On Tuesday 10 October, six policemen and two rural constables went to Stony Gut to execute the warrants. They attempted to seize Bogle but armed men lying in wait in the chapel rescued him. Then about 350 other supporters emerged from the cane fields and surrounded the police. Three of them were captured and beaten and threatened with death unless they swore upon oath to stop serving the "Bukra", and "Cleave to the Black".

The men for whom the warrants had been issued, including Bogle, agreed to present themselves at Morant Bay on the following day. In the meantime, they despatched a petition to Governor Eyre at Spanish Town, requesting his protection against the "outrageous assault" committed upon them by the policemen at Morant Bay.

News of the disturbances at Morant Bay spread rapidly throughout the eastern parishes and on 11 October sympathisers set out on foot from Manchioneal and from Stony Gut for Morant Bay. Details of what followed are confusing but it seems clear that they were prepared to support Bogle and his companions in whatever way was necessary.

Stony Gut was only about five miles from Morant Bay and some 400 demonstrators from that village reached the town first. They were in a noisy and belligerent mood. They sacked the police station before moving on to the courthouse where the vestry was sitting. The custos, Baron von Ketelhodt, feeling that the situation could have become explosive, had arranged to call out the volunteer militia from Bath. On the approach of the Stony Gut demonstrators he came out on the courthouse steps and began reading the Riot Act. The crowd began advancing towards the courthouse, whereupon the volunteers fired a volley into the crowd. About ten people died. Pandemonium broke loose. The crowd scattered, regrouped and retaliated with sticks, stones, machetes and inadequate fire-power. The custos was hit by a flying object.

They attacked the courthouse, set fire to the schoolhouse and adjoining buildings, and burst open the jail. Fifty-one prisoners escaped and it is said that they later returned to Stony Gut with Bogle and his followers where Bogle held a meeting of thanksgiving for his victory. Members of the vestry and the magistrates took refuge in the schoolhouse and in another house close by until they were driven out by fire. They were then attacked as they fled. Some were shot, others were chopped, and still others beaten to death. A few escaped injury by hiding during the night under hedges and in a latrine. Baron von Ketelhodt, was found dead next day with his head smashed and one of his fingers on his right hand cut off and his ring taken.

The marchers from Manchioneal were intercepted by a contingent of black soldiers from Port Antonio who shot about 160 persons, hanged seven in Manchioneal and shot three others travelling in the opposite direction towards Port Morant.

On 12 October, the day following the riots, Governor Eyre's reply to the petition arrived at Stony Gut. It was signed by his secretary, Edward Jordan. It noted that the governor had received unsavoury news about their activities. It continued:

> Some of you had been guilty of gross outrage and violence, and he [the Governor] warns you that such proceedings cannot be allowed to take place with impunity. His Excellency feels it to be his duty at once to inform you that you are misled by the misrepresentations of evil disposed and designing men and that unless you promptly withdraw from the unlawful attitude which you have assumed, very serious consequences must follow.

By then the situation was out of control. On 13 October martial law was declared. A week of bloody fighting ensued with reprisals on both sides. Some of the protesters, led by Bogle, captured the courthouses at Bath and Morant Bay. Bogle's appeal to the maroons at Hayfield was refused because the maroons had sworn in the 1739 peace treaty signed with the English to assist the government in capturing runaway slaves and in crushing slave revolts. But this was no slave revolt; Bogle and his supporters were free men fighting for justice. On 23 October, the maroons captured Bogle and handed him over to the authorities. The following day he was court-martialled and hanged.

Gordon was nowhere near Morant Bay while all of this was taking place. He was ill and staying at a cousin's house on North Street in Kingston. Nevertheless, some persons declared under oath that he was the chief instigator of the Stony Gut protests. A warrant was issued for his arrest. On learning of this, on 16 October Gordon went to Headquarters House where Commanding General O'Connor lived to give himself up, whereupon he was promptly arrested by Governor Eyre himself, in the presence of the custos of Kingston, Dr Bowerbank. Eyre took him by ship, *The Wolverine*, to Morant Bay, then to Port Antonio and back to Morant Bay, and on 20 October handed him over to the provost marshal, Gordon Ramsay. He was refused legal advice and spiritual consolation and witnesses willing to testify on his behalf were refused a hearing. On Saturday, 21 October he was tried for treason and found guilty; and on Monday, 23 October he was hanged.

The commission's records are filled with accounts of atrocities. Some people were given as many as 100 lashes before they were tried and hanged.

One man, a butcher, claimed that he was forced to flog 49 persons on the day after the riots. When his arm became tired he was given a glass of rum and water to refresh himself. He started flogging at 9 o'clock in the morning and did not stop until 4 o'clock in the afternoon.

In retaliation for the 29 white persons killed and 34 others seriously injured, the homes of all the would-be protesters were burned and their crops destroyed. The official records state 1,000 homes burned, 354 people executed by court martial, 50 shot without trial, 25 shot by the maroons, ten "killed otherwise" and 600 flogged. Commodore McClintock, who helped to quell the uprising, estimated that the loss of life was nearer 1,500. The first set of hangings took place at Port Morant "under the eye of Mr Eyre himself". (Robotham: 1981)

The hangings continued day by day, and so many people were packed in the graves that, as one witness told the Commission, "last night a particularly disagreeable effluvia arose from the graves . . . [and] pervaded the entire town. It was only with the greatest difficulty that one could avoid nausea". (Jamaica Royal Commission: 1866)

Despite these atrocities, Gordon's last letter to his wife displays a quality of nobility and generosity of spirit which remain an inspiration to all generations. He wrote:

> I do not deserve this sentence, for I never advised or took part in any insurrection. All I ever did was to recommend the people who complained to seek redress in a legitimate way . . . Say to all friends an affectionate farewell; and that they must not grieve for me, for I die innocently . . . Comfort your heart. I certainly little expected this. You must do the best you can, and the Lord will help you; and do

Gordon's body being taken down after hanging at Morant Bay.
Painting by Barrington Watson (Wycliffe Bennett Collection)

not be ashamed of the death your poor husband will have suffered . . . I thought his Excellency would have allowed me a fair trial, if any charge of sedition or inflammatory language was partly attributable to me; but I have no power of control. May the Lord be merciful to him . . . I have been allowed one hour, I wish more time had been allowed . . . And now may the grace of our Lord Jesus Christ be with us all. Your truly devoted and now nearly dying husband, G. W. Gordon. (Olivier: 1933)

CHAPTER 22

The people betrayed and vindicated

Sometimes, in the mist-shrouded Portland and St Thomas valleys, in the sad evenings and in the grieving time in Stony Gut with its burnt-out houses and desecrated chapel, a song born of the killings carries its message through the darkness.

> War down a Monkland
> War down a Morant Bay,
> The Queen never know,
> War oh, war oh,
> War oh, heavy war oh.

In those months Governor Eyre and his supporters in Britain were declaring: "Black insurrection could not be treated in the same way as a white one, because the negro in Jamaica . . . is pestilential . . . a dangerous savage at best." (Holt: 1992)

The debate raged in Britain, where Eyre explained that persons living at a distance, who were unacquainted with the country and with the negro character, were "unable to appreciate the value of all the little incidents or circumstances which to my mind indicated a great and imminent danger". On the basis of those "little incidents or circumstances", magnified by paranoia into a "great and imminent danger" possibly as many as 1,500 innocent people were massacred.

> Soldiers from Newcastle
> came down a Monkland
> With gun an sword
> Fe kill sinner, oh,
> War oh, war oh.

The royal commission enquiring into the Morant Bay Uprising praised Eyre for acting quickly to put down the rebellion, but condemned him for prolonging the period of martial law, for the illegality and injustice of

Gordon's trial and for the barbarous and wanton punishment inflicted upon many people. They decided that the causes of the uprising were the people's demands for land and a breakdown in the system of justice. They did not face the basic issues which Gordon and Bogle had championed and for which they died, the need for a political system that favoured the many and not the few, equality before the law and a system of justice founded on ethical principles.

In Britain, as in Jamaica, most of the upper and middle classes sided with Eyre against Gordon, Bogle and the African-Jamaican people. Most of the British working class were against Eyre. They burned him in effigy in Hyde Park. They were campaigning for the very goals for which Gordon and Bogle died, an administration in favour of the many and an extension of the franchise to reduce the political power of the few. They won their battle in 1867. Three-quarters of a century was to pass before the Jamaican people won their campaign for adult suffrage and self-government.

But Morant Bay marked the beginning, not the end, of Gordon and Bogle's work. It was the planter oligarchy that surrendered the right of self-government which, 200 years earlier, Edward Long and William Beeston had battled for and preserved.

The end of planter rule was an ignoble one. It becomes even more shameful when considered alongside the action of the Barbados House of Assembly. When it was pressured by the Colonial Office in 1876 to surrender its right to self-government and accept Crown colony rule, a coloured member of the Barbados House, Conrad Reeves, urged his colleagues to reject the proposal in these words: "We are not, like some other colonies, afflicted with absenteeism . . . The leading men in this country are persons whose ancestors for generations have lived and died here . . . all classes of the country have the utmost confidence in its institutions." Reeves spoke of his vision for his country: "Here in Barbados all our situations are framed to meet exigencies of a single community, though made up of different classes, and to fit them for the enjoyment of that self-government which is the common right of the entire colony."

In contrast, Governor Eyre, full of self-congratulation and self-righteousness, before leaving for England appealed to the House to abolish itself. He paraded before them the terrifying spectre of black Haiti, appealed to the "fears" of the white and coloured and portrayed patriotism not in terms of country but of a surrender of the democratic principles advocated by Gordon and Bogle.

> It is necessary to bring these facts before you in order to convince you how widely spread and how deeply rooted the spirit of disaffection is; how daring and determined the intention had been, and still is, to

make Jamaica a second Haiti, and how imperative it is upon you, gentlemen, to take such measures as, under God's blessing may avert such a calamity . . . I invite you, gentlemen, to make a great and generous sacrifice for the sake of your country, and in immolating on the altar of patriotism the two branches of the Legislature of which you yourselves are the constituent parts, to hand down to posterity a noble example of self-denial and heroism.

A small group of coloured members opposed Eyre, but they were defeated. Robert Osborn had urged on the governor, Charles Grey, in a debate in May 1853 that responsible government was the way to protect coloured interests: "Do away with the Assembly and the coloured people would sink into the insignificance from which they had risen." Class interests, property rights and security were the factors that counted with most of the members of the Jamaica House of Assembly.

In 1866 Jamaica was made a Crown colony. "Massa" was still there, but the Crown was now in control. The governor was clad in all the panoply of imperial power, a helmet bedecked with plumes and feathers, a ceremonial sword that symbolised armed might. A nominated legislature dramatised the fact that the people had been stripped of the right to self-government. The basic philosophy was the same as that of the planter oligarchy, however, although the imperial mission was stated in other terms: "the direct protection by the Crown of the unrepresented classes, which takes the place of representation". Governors were instructed: "Her Majesty's government has also the right to expect in those to whom such great trusts are committed that they will show themselves able to withstand the pressure of any one class, or idea, or interest, and that they will maintain that calmness and impartiality of judgement which should belong to the governor of an English colony." As for the officials: "The business of all the official members is to consider the interests of the peasantry very closely and, without making themselves exclusively the representatives of those classes, to see that their interests do not suffer."

Governors and officials set worthy examples of professional competence and integrity, and many developed an abiding affection for Jamaica and the Jamaican people. The first governor under the new constitution, Sir John Peter Grant, for example, laid the foundations for the development of an efficient, honest civil service, greatly improved the island's deplorably bad communications and transportation systems and introduced a railway service linking Kingston with Port Antonio and Montego Bay. A few, such as Lord Olivier and Sir Hugh Foot, transformed an official position of limited tenure into a mission on behalf of the Jamaican people. But all were trapped in a system that was based on the doctrine of white superiority and imperial control. The most scathing indictment of Crown colony rule is to be found in the report of the Royal Commission of 1940.

The concept was that of a shepherded dependent people. Its justification lay in the conviction, as the English historian James Anthony Froude emphasised, that blacks had not demonstrated any capacity for civilisation except "under European laws, European education, European authority . . . and the old African superstitions lie undisturbed at the bottom of their souls. Give them independence and in a few generations they will peel off such civilisation as they have learnt as easily and as willingly as their coats and trousers". (Froude: 1887) The central issues remained what they had been under planter rule: property and colour. The Colonial Office spoke in the same terms as the Jamaican plantocracy: "The planters, being the best educated class and most interested in the permanent prosperity of the c[ountry], should have great power controlling the Government and great share in the Government of the island." So administration would continue to favour the whites, for not only were the blacks regarded as being morally deficient, but also in Carlyle's words, they were "born to be servants . . . to the whites." (Olivier: 1933) To govern a country was beyond them.

The gospel of a divinely ordained trusteeship of non-white people by Europeans was soon to be preached with great urgency, for in the closing decades of the nineteenth century and the opening decade of the twentieth century (1870-1917) mankind moved into a global age. The second Industrial Revolution, the rapid rise of the United States to the rank of world power and the spread of European imperialism marked the beginning of this global age.

Forces of change generated or reinforced by these developments touched Jamaican society in significant ways. We will identify related trends which began to manifest themselves in Jamaica from about the 1870s onwards; in order to show the connections, we will turn from the local to the global perspective.

The new age began with Europe's theft of the continent of Africa, an event of the greatest importance for all African-Americans. Between 1880 and 1900, in 20 years, the European powers – Britain, France, Germany, Italy, Belgium, Portugal and Spain – carved up Africa amongst themselves. In those two decades:

> The entire continent had been seized, annexed, fought over and partitioned. Of the forty political units into which it had been divided – often with little more than a ruler and pencil wielded in London, Paris or Berlin – direct European control extended to thirty-six. Only Ethiopia, which had fought off the Italians, and Liberia, with its financial links to the United States, claimed real independence. (*Times Atlas of World History*)

Explanations were offered for this shocking use of armed force. One was that new markets had to be found for the products of the second Industrial Revolution. Another was that colonisation provided Europe with productive new outlets for its many tensions and rivalries. The true driving forces were in fact distrust of each other, greed for power, greed for riches. The whole non-white world was involved. Non-Europeans fought back against this overwhelming imperialism, which "unleashed an anti-colonial reaction throughout Africa and Asia, the extent, intensity and significance of which have rarely been fully appreciated". (*Times Atlas of World History*) Just as the African-Americans waged a liberation campaign for 150 years against enslavement, so non-whites throughout Asia and Africa fought against imperialism. Among them were: the Ethiopians, who decisively defeated the Italians at Adowa in 1896; the uprising of Arab Pasha and his followers in Egypt against the British; the fierce Ashanti wars against the British in West Africa in 1876 and 1878; the Mahdi who captured Khartoum; the Zulu and Matabele, the Herero and Maji-Maji in South West Africa and Tanganyika, who rose in 1904 and 1906 against the Germans. The remarkable feature of this resistance is summarised in words that bear directly on the liberation movement of the Jamaican people, even though the scale was so very much smaller:

> The remarkable fact is the persistence of opposition in spite of disheartening set-backs and harsh repression. None of the powers which had launched the scramble for colonies in 1884 was secure in its possessions; nowhere was the finality of European rule accepted. The tangible achievements of nationalists in this period were negligible; but by keeping the flame of resistance alive, they inaugurated the process which led, a generation later, to the emancipation of the colonial peoples. (*Times Atlas of World History*)

By 1910 the strength of the anti-colonial movement throughout the colonies and also among liberals and intellectuals in Europe itself revealed grave weaknesses in the system. The American historian Barbara Tuchman portrayed this instability in her dramatic description of the funeral procession of Edward VII of Britain in May 1910.

> Nine Kings rode in the funeral . . . the crowd, waiting in hushed and black-clad awe, could not keep back gasps of admiration. In scarlet and blue and green and purple, three by three the sovereigns rode through the palace gates, with plumed helmets, gold braid, crimson sashes, and jewelled orders flashing in the sun. After them came five heirs apparent, forty more imperial or royal highnesses, seven queens . . . Together they represented seventy nations in the greatest assembly of royalty and rank ever gathered in one place and, of its kind, the

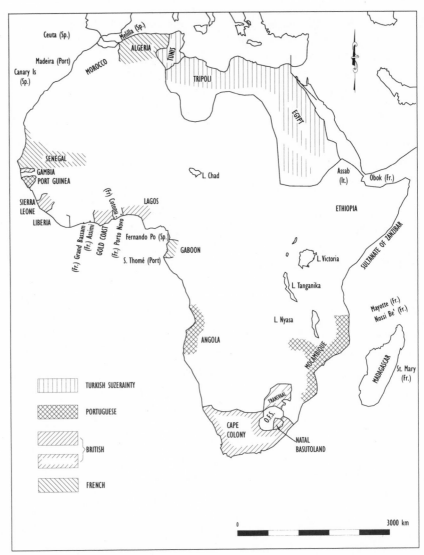

Map legend:
- TURKISH SUZERAINTY
- PORTUGUESE
- BRITISH
- FRENCH

last. The muffled tongue of Big Ben tolled nine of the clock as the
cortege left the palace, but on history's clock it was sunset, and the
sun of the old world was setting in a dying blaze of splendor never to
be seen again. (Tuchman: 1910)

With the European colonisation of Africa, the West Indian colonies
shrank overnight to proportions in keeping with the bankrupt condition
of its sugar industry in the 1880s. In the great days of sugar the islands had
been the darlings of empire. The partitioning of Africa so enlarged the
empire that the West Indian colonies, small and with limited resources,

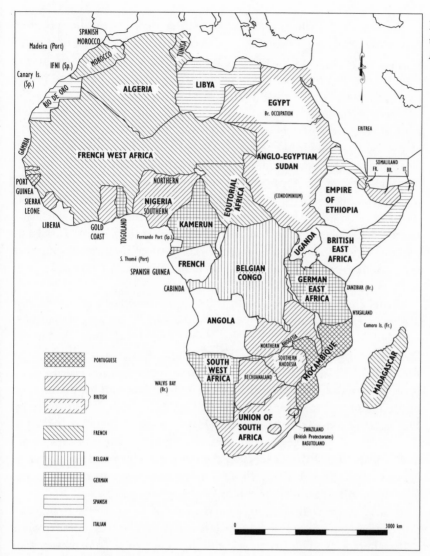

SPANISH MOROCCO

Madeira (Port)

IFNI (Sp.)

Canary Is. (Sp.)

MOROCCO

RIO DE ORO

GAMBIA

ALGERIA

TUNISIA

LIBYA

EGYPT
Br. OCCUPATION

ERITREA

FRENCH WEST AFRICA

ANGLO-EGYPTIAN SUDAN

(CONDOMINIUM)

SOMALILAND
FR. BR. IT.

PORT GUINEA

SIERRA LEONE

LIBERIA

GOLD COAST

TOGOLAND

NORTHERN

NIGERIA
SOUTHERN

KAMERUN

Fernando Port (Sp.)

EQUATORIAL AFRICA

EMPIRE OF ETHIOPIA

S. Thomé (Port)

SPANISH GUINEA

FRENCH

CABINDA

BELGIAN CONGO

UGANDA

BRITISH EAST AFRICA

GERMAN EAST AFRICA

ZANZIBAR (Br.)

NYASALAND

Comoro Is. (Fr.)

ANGOLA

NORTHERN RHODESIA

SOUTHERN RHODESIA

MOCAMBIQUE

MADAGASCAR

WALVIS BAY (Br.)

SOUTH WEST AFRICA

BECHUANALAND

UNION OF SOUTH AFRICA

SWAZILAND
(British Protectorates)
BASUTOLAND

PORTUGUESE

BRITISH

FRENCH

BELGIAN

GERMAN

SPANISH

ITALIAN

0   3000 km

were pushed from a central position to the very limits of the periphery. Their market of some 3 million people was but a fraction of the market provided by Western Nigeria alone. The West India interest, so powerful in the 1750s in the councils of the old empire, so much a part of the English nation, was gravely weakened when France captured the European market with its cheaper beet-sugar. By then it was evident that Cuba, with its vastly larger production of cane-sugar, was destined to dominate the American market. Big Massa, inefficient and over-protected for over-long, bent on cheap labour instead of the use of modern technology, no longer had the credibility he had enjoyed in the eighteenth century.

The people betrayed and vindicated

The world as a whole was characterised at the time by the spread of divisive colonial systems and white power based on the concept of trusteeship. Black Jamaicans began to take pride in their country's development; Robert Love and Marcus Garvey pioneered Jamaica's national and political development.

There were other major developments in the world at large that radically affected Jamaican society. The most important was the formation of a world economy in the period 1870-1914, the chief features being the development of a worldwide system of communications based on telegraphy, railways, steamships, greatly improved road systems and canals, notably the Suez and Panama Canals. The expansion of these communication systems made possible also the growth of world trade in which the United States played an increasingly powerful part through industrial and trading corporations that established a US sphere of influence throughout the Caribbean, with its attendant forms of imperialism and political as well as financial control.

These manifested themselves in 1898, when the sinking of the warship *Maine* in Havana harbour provided the United States with a cause for declaring war on Spain in the course of the Cuban revolution. The United States destroyed a Spanish fleet in the Philippines and invaded Puerto Rico. By the Treaty of Paris, Spain withdrew from Cuba and ceded Puerto Rico, Guam and the Philippines to the United States. This marked the beginning of the Americanisation of the Caribbean Basin. In 1901, led by President Theodore Roosevelt, the United States decided to build the Panama Canal, following this up with buying French shares in the Canal and a treaty with Panama in 1903 that gave the United States perpetual control of the Canal Zone. In such ways Europe's imperialism in the Caribbean influenced the growth of US imperialism.

It is as if we were looking at two maps of the Atlantic Basin, one portraying the physical features, the other showing the sweep of ideologies and technologies. The first represents the continental land masses with their archipelagoes and vast oceanic currents such as the southern and northern equatorial currents that stitch Africa and western Europe to Central and North America, and the Gulf Stream that ties Mexico and the Bahamas to western Europe. We can identify also the giant wind systems, the north-east trade winds that transported Columbus and his ships from the Azores to the Caribbean and the westerlies that took him back by way of the Florida channel. The picture is one of interlocking, interconnected wind systems and ocean currents that facilitated man's movement into an Atlantic Age. The second map shows the ideological and technological currents that moved mankind into the global age and underpinned European and North American dominance.

So vast a background enlarges those communities whose people prove capable of response. From the 1870s African-Jamaicans responded to the challenge of European imperialism and racial discrimination by developing a nationalist movement and by the affirmation of an African identity. They responded to engulfing poverty by grasping the opportunity to initiate an export trade in bananas and by joining the labour force that built the Panama Canal, established the banana plantations in Central America, expanded Cuban sugar production and manned the assembly lines in United States and Canadian industrialised cities.

Towards the end of the century a little black boy, Marcus Garvey who was born in the seaside town of St Ann's Bay, had his first lesson as a schoolboy in racial discrimination and discovered at the same time the world of books.

The Jamaican people, in response to local pressures and global influences, contributed through their labour to the creation of a world system of trade and transport, to the growth of national movements and they demonstrated Africa's creative power which manifested itself in the people's capacity for response to persecution and restriction.

Our first step is to look more closely at the nature and structure of Jamaican society during this period. Our focus is on the distribution of the population, the occupational status and the literacy levels. It is significant that in the nineteenth century only 10 per cent of the black population lived in Kingston and St Andrew; the rest lived in the rural parishes. In contrast, 20.6 per cent of the coloureds and 52.9 per cent of the whites lived in Kingston and St Andrew. This pattern of population distribution follows that of the plantation period and of the years in which inland Jamaica was being settled mainly by black smallholders.

The cluster of schools, churches, professional services, newspapers, government offices and commercial organisations in Kingston gave it a great advantage. St James was not far behind. The black majority who lived in the rural areas were at a disadvantage in respect of education and the health services.

The growth of the working class also throws light on changes in the society. Table 1 below shows how slow the transition was to a completely free economy, and how very small the number of professionals was, especially between 1843 and 1891. On the other hand the increase in the commercial class signifies increasing diversification of enterprises and growing urbanisation.

The literacy figures for the parishes reflect the government's neglect of public education which reached only a small proportion of the population. In mountain villages, where the majority of the people had settled, access was difficult and schools were few and far between. Adults could not afford

Table 1

Year	Professional	Domestic (personal)	Commercial	Agricultural	Industrial	Total
1891	5,900	5,300	8,100	137,600	26,500	183,400
1911	6,800	5,500	13,700	158,400	36,300	220,600
1921	7,100	7,200	13,500	160,300	36,300	224,300
1891	1,100	21,400	2,800	133,700	31,100	190,200
1911	2,400	32,500	6,000	113,100	36,200	190,300
1921	4,300	45,400	7,200	125,400	37,300	219,600

to attend day school and only the more determined attended evening classes two or four nights per week after a strenuous day's work. Most of those who wished to learn to read attended classes once a week, at Sunday schools, where their only reading text was the Bible. Education was not free. Schools collected a small weekly charge for pupils learning to read and an additional sum for those learning to write. It was generally accepted that labourers had no need for literacy.

The very small Negro Education Grant that had been made after emancipation to assist in erecting school buildings ceased after the Morant Bay Uprising. In its place two education grants were made which were based on the average school attendance and on the quality of the annual examination results. This forced teachers to ensure that more children passed the test but it did not necessarily mean improved teaching methods.

Few opportunities existed for upward mobility in society. The people were taught to be "content with that place in life to which God had called them". If their fathers were labourers or cowherds or were engaged in some other menial task, that was as far as they should expect to go. The few who managed to surmount the educational and social hurdles were not allowed to rise to positions of responsibility in the government service. Government departments were headed by white expatriates and all other senior positions were filled by whites or near-whites. It was the policy in the civil service that the few blacks and coloureds employed were not to be promoted above a certain level. In practice, the darker the complexion, the lower the category in which individuals were placed.

Improvement in literacy levels was brought about largely by the Jamaican elementary schoolteacher and the Jamaican trained parson; and it was with these, as well as with the "banana man" and the peasant cultivators, that social change began. The three decades that followed the 1865 uprising witnessed remarkable manifestations of this creative, unquenchable spirit. One manifestation was the founding in 1894 of the Jamaica Union of Teachers (JUT) and in 1895 of the Jamaica Agricultural Society (JAS). "It would indeed be difficult to over-estimate the importance of such professional associations in the pre-independence period when the Crown Colony machine, even modified as it was in 1944, meant practically unmixed official rule by expatriate departmental heads uncurbed by any form of a national will." (Lewis: 1968)

Lewis emphasised that these two organisations acted as focal points in the anti-colonial struggle by initiating the forming of a national will in a variety of ways, by campaigns in defence of teachers' rights against school management boards, the setting up of vocational schools, methods of teacher payment, forming an independent bloc of farming opinion, and formulating Jamaican points of view on a wide range of public issues, including racial discrimination and the "foreign" content of school education with its almost complete disregard for Jamaican history. These early manifestations of a national will indicate the same quality of spirit that the Portland and St Thomas banana cultivators displayed in the 1870s. The Jamaican responses had their origins in diverse groups and took different forms. Gordon and Bogle had symbolised the common interests of educated and illiterate, brown and black. The JUT and the JAS represented the identification of educated professionals with the peasant folk.

Recent studies by Holt, Satchell and other scholars throw light on the sale of private land in the three last decades of the nineteenth century. This enables us to trace the course of land purchases by peasants in the 1870s and to identify the beginnings of a black proletariat in the years that followed. We watch also the beginnings of the banana trade, the growing dominance of the United Fruit Company (UFC), and the flight of black labour from engulfing rural poverty.

In the period 1870-1900 some 2½ million acres of private property in Jamaica changed hands. The peak period for the peasants was the decade of the 1870s, when large numbers bought small parcels of land of 10 acres or less from planters in financial need. The 1880s saw sales to peasants slowing down and sales to people with capital increasing. This trend strengthened in the 1890s. "Although other actors – planters, merchants, and other élites – were coming increasingly to dominate the land market and to engross larger and larger shares of Jamaica's arable land, peasants held their own until the 1890s which, ironically, was precisely the moment that the British and Jamaican governments embraced the promotion of small proprietorships as official policy." (Holt: 1992)

Holt's reference to Jamaican government policy has to do with the reports of two royal commissions, one headed by Crossman in 1885 and the other by Norman in 1897. These reports represented a radical change in the thinking of the British government. Up to this time the sugar plantation had been regarded as the foundation of West Indian prosperity and the planters as the only acceptable advisers on political affairs. As

Arthur Lewis put it, with these two reports, little Quashie, for so long derided and despised, moved to the centre of the stage.

The Crossman Commission indicated this change in colonial policy:

> It is to the possession of provision grounds that the industrious negro turns with the greatest liking, and there now exists in Jamaica a substantial and happily numerous population of the peasant proprietor class, which easily obtains a livelihood by the growth of the minor tropical products of fruit and spices, cocoa and coffee, and so contributes materially to the general prosperity . . . Again, the negroes have found in other ways means of earning money. Public works in Jamaica, such as the construction of railways, provide them with regular pay at home.

The Panama Canal proved a great attraction: "The negro who refuses to work on estates in Jamaica will willingly labour for wages on these other undertakings even when the rate of wages is in reality not higher, but where he imagines himself to be more of a free agent."

These were the first words of vindication and endorsement from the Colonial Office; not sermons about the beauty of industry or the moral muscle developed by hard work, but a tribute to the peasant proprietor.

Ten years later, in 1897, another royal commission was even more enthusiastic about turning its back on the sugar plantation system and endorsing the further development of smallholdings. It urged that the interests of the general public should be safeguarded against those of the sugar producers:

> It must be recollected that the chief outside influences with which the governments of certain colonies have to reckon are the representative of the sugar estates, that these persons are not interested in anything but sugar, that the establishment of any other industry is often detrimental to their interests and that under such conditions it is the special duty of Your Majesty's Government to see that the welfare of the general public is not sacrificed to the interests or supposed interests of a small but influential minority which has special means of enforcing its wishes and bringing its claims to notice. (Norman Commission)

Traditionally, the government and the planters had done everything in their power to block the establishment of smallholdings. Now the Norman Commission endorsed the programme the peasants had pioneered:

> The settlement of the labourer on the land has not as a rule been viewed with favour in the past, by the persons interested in sugar estates. What suited them best was a large supply of labourers,

entirely dependent on being able to find work on the large estates and consequently subject to their control and willing to work at low rates of wages. But it seems to us that no reform offers so good a prospect for permanent welfare in the future of the West Indies as the settlement of the labouring population on the land as small peasant proprietors; and in many places this is the only means by which the population can in future be supported. (Norman Commission)

It was in this period that the trend against peasant smallholders and in favour of large proprietors began to manifest itself. In order to see the development of this trend, we focus now on the rise of the banana trade.

In 1866 a chance meeting took place between a Yankee skipper and a group of peasant cultivators at Oracabessa. The captain, George Bush, was searching for bananas for the growing US fruit market. The trade had started with the sale of some bunches of Cuban bananas in the United States early in the century and had grown to the point where, by 1830, Cuba was exporting some 15,000 stems to Boston. Sea captains went scouting for supplies in other islands. The Oracabessa cultivators supplied Bush with 500 stems and urged him to call in at Port Antonio. There he completed his purchases, returned to Boston and before long was back in Port Antonio where, in 1869, he opened an office as agent for a number of Boston fruit companies. Other shippers included Lorenzo Dow Baker, who soon became the moving spirit in forming the Boston Fruit Company, (later the United Fruit Company).

The conflict that developed involved the African-Jamaican peasant who grew bananas on a smallholding that he either owned or rented, an American corporation that aimed at complete control of the sources of production, the means of transport and distribution in the United States, and the government of Jamaica, which had been urged by two royal commissions to undertake the settlement of the labouring population on the land as peasant proprietors.

Two pioneering sociological studies, *Cuban Counterpoint* by Fernando Ortiz and *My Mother who Fathered Me* by Edith Clarke, guide us to a fuller understanding of the conflict as seen through the eyes of the Jamaican smallholder.

Ortiz illumined Cuban history by contrasting the independent tobacco farmer with his smallholding and the intensive system of sugar agriculture which demands large-scale production. Edith Clarke pointed to the contrast between the smallholders of Orange Grove, an integrated society "in which kinship plays an important part", and Sugar Town, which,

is not so much a social entity as a conglomerate of disparate sections, held together only by a common involvement with the sugar estate .

. . The town's population rose and fell with the sugar-growing seasons as migrant workers flooded in seeking work and out again once jobs grew scarce . . . If lucky enough to be employed, the father went off early to the mill, having washed down bread, or an occasional cornmeal dumpling with bush tea.

Turn to the banana and the coming of the multinational corporation, and we become witnesses to a fundamental transformation in Jamaica's social and economic life between the mid-nineteenth and twentieth centuries. The two central figures in this change were the US corporation organised by Lorenzo Dow Baker and the banana man of whom Claude McKay wrote and whom the poet Evan Jones portrayed:

> Touris, whiteman wipin his face
> Met me in Golden Grove Market place,
> He looked at me ol clothes brown
> with stain
> An soaked right through wid de
> Portlan' rain
> He cas his eye, turn up his nose,
> He says youre a beggar man I
> suppose . . .
> I said, by God an dis big
> right han
> You mus recognise a banana
> man . . .

His great treasure, his source of pride, were in his ten acres of mountain side, his Gros Mitchel and Lacatan bananas, some coconut trees, some hills of yam; and his livestock:

> . . . on dat very same lan'
> Five she-goats an a big black ram.

Bananas, yams, coconuts, goats, gave the banana man the dishes he and his family loved. Boiled green bananas went perfectly with salted fish, with salted mackerel, cod, herring; and how could "run down" be prepared without green bananas? As porridge, as dumpling or as fried ripe banana fritters or as baked ripe bananas served with coconut milk, or as ripe fruit, it kept company throughout the generations with the Jamaican people. When the smallholder looked at a cane-piece he saw "busha", but he saw in his banana walk the money to send his children to school, to clothe and feed his family, to pay his taxes.

The extent to which the banana tree and the stems of bananas were woven into his everyday life can be judged from the list of names it inspired, by its shape and colour. Cassidy listed banana bird, banana borer, banana breeze (meaning one of 40 miles an hour or more, strong enough to blow the tree down), banana chips, banana Cudjoe, banana Katy, banana quit, banana spider, banana yoky, banana fig. Folk beliefs clustered around the tree which, like yams, sweet potatoes and plantains should be planted about five days before the full moon.

Loading bananas at Port Antonio

The fruit, handled with care, was well-suited to large-scale as well as to middle- and small-scale agriculture. The black peasant pioneered the Jamaica banana trade and in so doing contributed also to the development of the Jamaica tourist industry. It was to the Jamaican peasant cultivator also that two royal commissions paid tribute for providing Jamaica with a complementary system of smallholding agriculture and for diversifying the range of export crops. Jamaican society was restructured by bringing into existence a self-supporting peasantry.

These things being so, how was it that the trustee of the people, the governor and his chief officials, heads of the departments of lands, finance, agriculture and trade, did not seek to strengthen his bargaining position with US customers who, at an early stage, showed that they aimed at control?

A part of the problem lay in the nature of Crown colony government, which separated rulers from the ruled by discouraging any form of representative government or of popular participation. This bred attitudes of superiority rooted in race, which blinded them to the relevance of the history of the English working class (in this instance of the English cooperative movement) to the needs of the peasant banana growers. The vindication of the peasantry in the 1880s and 1890s was accompanied by their betrayal.

Production in the 1870s and 1880s was in the hands of smallholders; the fruit came from 2,880 or more smallholdings in Portland. In the last 30 years of the century Port Antonio's banana trade reached one-quarter of the island's total:

> A little sleepy town of 1,305 in 1880, the port was transformed with new wharves, new roads and bridges, and a 37 per cent increase in population. The surge of depositors and savings in its government savings bank suggests both the impact of the fruit trade on the town and the role of the peasant class in the trade. The number of bank

depositors and their total savings increased from 238 with £5,000 in 1880 to 778 with £10,155 in 1889 . . . Much of that growth came from small depositors, which suggests a more prosperous peasant class. (Holt: 1992)

In these critical years the government remained blind to Lorenzo Dow Baker's control strategy and to the need of the peasantry for guidance and support. Baker (1840-1908) made his second trip to Jamaica in 1871 when he called in at Port Antonio with a cargo of saltfish, flour and pork. He sold his cargo, took on board some coconuts and 1,450 stems of bananas and returned to Boston where, after a 17-day voyage, he sold the fruit, making a profit of $2,000. Encouraged, he started to devote himself to the banana trade, competing with other shippers such as J. E. Kerr and Company in Montego Bay. Rainfall and temperature made Port Antonio a good base, so in 1880 the L. Baker Company, with Baker as resident manager, opened its doors there. Baker, a shrewd, energetic New Englander, saw the importance of controlling his sources of supply. He lost no time in buying Bog Estate of 1,850 acres, which bordered on the town, at a cost of £1 an acre. Bog, which he renamed Boundbrook, included about one-third of Port Antonio's waterfront, with good port facilities. His next step was to acquire control of a shipping line for, like his competitors J. E. Kerr and Company in Montego Bay, he saw the great advantage that steamships had over sailing ships, since bananas were perishable. Pursuing his strategy of control, and realising that efficient shipping arrangements were vital, he gradually gained control of the carrying trade. This, in turn, gave him control over production.

The other chief source of bananas was Central America. By a series of mergers Baker's company and some other fruit companies formed the Boston Fruit Company, and later merged with Minor Keith's company in Costa Rica to become the United Fruit Company.

In the meantime a British company, Elders, Dempster and Company, on the urging of the Colonial Secretary, Joseph Chamberlain, set up the Imperial Direct Line of banana steamers in 1901 and formed Elders and Fyffes as a fruit and shipping company. But the British company was no match for the experienced and now strongly based United Fruit Company which had gained virtual control of the trade. In 1902 the American company bought 45 per cent of Elders and Fyffes stock, and by 1913 had come to control all the stock. Then, by cutting its freight rates, the United Fruit Company put the Imperial Direct Line out of business.

The Jamaican smallholder was squeezed out. What had happened in the 1650s to the white smallholders of Barbados, when they were bought out by Modyford, Drax and other sugar planters, now happened to the small

Jamaican banana planters. By 1899 most of the sugar estates were going in for the "backwood's nigger business" and were finding it profitable. Between 1895 and 1897 about 2,000 acres of land in the Rio Cobre delta around Spanish Town were in bananas. Peasants found it difficult to add to their holdings and too costly to rent.

The United Fruit Company's control of the trade now enabled it to dictate the price of bananas. Whether growers had contracts or not, the price they received depended on what the buyers judged the quality to be. The small growers were no longer in a position to bargain. Their fruit could be downgraded or rejected without redress. Lord Olivier described the process: "Only those actually acquainted with the manner in which bananas are purchased can appreciate how easily the buyer can convert a contract promising attractive prices into an unprofitable arrangement for the growers by means of heavy rejections and downgrading." (Olivier: 1936)

For the first time in his history the African-Jamaican faced the reality of economic coercion from a non-British source, a US version of corporate imperialism in the form of the United Fruit Company.

Baker summed up his self-image and his methods in his statement that he saw his work in Jamaica as an evangelical mission, and his wealth as an indication from God that he was succeeding in the work to which he had been called. His instructions to his son showed that he saw the peasant suppliers only as units of production: "Tell the people that if they wish to sell their fruit they must bring it down." Also, "Never mind what people say, throw it back on their barrels, let them suffer for it if they will not mind you."

As the company grew in strength and tightened its control, and as the large landholders bought up all available land, the banana man realised that he was confronting an oppressive reincarnation of the slave owner. Banana land was slipping out of his grasp.

The peasants were shrewd, intelligent people who had for generations learned to read bakra's mind. It had not taken them long to learn that Crown colony rule meant that even if they were granted the vote their elected representatives would have no power, since the governor had the right to nominate more members at any time and so outvote them. They knew that Crown colony rule had resulted in taxes falling more heavily on the poor than on the rich. They realised that the political process now meant less to them than it had done in the days when Gordon and Bogle built them into a voting bloc. It was all a pretence, a masquerade in which Pitchy Patchy would never rise above the role of Pitchy Patchy.

While land was available, there had been hope of change, but the grass-roots people saw that under a government whose laws equated political power and the vote with ownership of land, and which attempted to ensure that the black would never be anything but a worker in the social scale, he would never have full freedom. Once again the African-Jamaican demonstrated, as he had done in the western Jamaica and Morant Bay Uprisings, that the dynamics of social change rested with the mass of the people.

That response took three forms, each a total rejection of corporate economic coercion and monopoly of land ownership. The favoured response was emigration. As George Roberts points out, the dominant feature of the period 1881-1921 was a net outward movement. This increased with each decade and attained considerable dimensions (77,000 persons) during the decade 1911-21 when the total net outward movement was nearly 146,000 or about 3,600 a year. Some 46,000 went to the United States, 45,000 to Panama, at least 20,000 to Cuba and some 43,000 to other areas, including Costa Rica. (Roberts: 1957)

Another response was the beginning, although small in the period 1881-1911, of a movement from the rural areas to Kingston, which became the capital city in 1872. The city had been enlarged in 1867, when its boundaries were extended to include Smith Village, Hannah Town and Fletcher's Land, at the time parts of St Andrew. A major movement of people to Kingston and St Andrew took place in the 1920s but the trend had become obvious already in the 1880s. An 1880 report on the island's juvenile population noted that there was a tendency for the rural population to move to Kingston in search of work. This tendency underscored the emergence of a Jamaican proletariat, which became a significant political force by the 1930s.

These responses were, in the course of time, to reinforce and enlarge the third major development, which was of primary importance, namely the growth of political consciousness and the formulation of Jamaican political objectives. This continued with Robert Love and Marcus Garvey and provided the cohesive, generative force that found expression in a national movement and in early efforts to organise trade unions.

CHAPTER 23

Robert Love points the way

We have seen how the Jamaican peasantry over the 30 years following the introduction of Crown colony government succeeded in achieving some measure of financial independence through agricultural pursuits and how, just as the colonial government was beginning to acknowledge their industry, although not their right to political equality, they were once more subjected to foreign capitalist domination and brought to a state of near economic slavery. Sugar had fallen on bad times, accounting for only 18 per cent of the island's exports in 1897, but the United Fruit Company and the banana plantations were flourishing and applying economic pressure on the workforce. The peasantry was under siege.

Some were coerced into selling their small acreages to people anxious to get into the banana trade. Others unable to pay their mortgages and meet outstanding debts lost their lands in official seizures. Many frustrated, landless, homeless and unemployed began to leave the rural countryside for the towns in search of a better life but unable to find suitable employment they ended up in overcrowded slums and expressed their disaffection by resorting to violence. Others joined the recruiting lines to Central America, and even when the news coming back from the Canal Zone was of disease, repression and frustration, the migration continued. There were also the thousands of field labourers who, after completing the reaping and replanting exercises on the banana and sugar plantations, faced the long "dead season" when there was no employment, "and starvation roamed the land".

The island continued to suffer from regressive taxation. High customs duties had been introduced after emancipation, ostensibly to make up the revenue lost by the downturn in the economy, and brought in far more than was required. Duties were levied not on manufactured goods but on consumer goods: on the basic necessities such as corn, flour, rice, salted fish and meat, which were needed mainly by the labouring class. Revenues collected for the year 1845 illustrate this. Import revenues came to 65 per cent, or £186,085; the rest was made up of £77,440 from land tax and £6,121 from stock traded. It was a pattern that remained in place for the next 60 years. Jamaicans bought their foodstuffs dear and sold their produce cheap. Taxation fell heavily on the poor.

Governor Musgrave's paper delivered to the Colonial Institute in London in 1880 noted that the great mass of consumers who furnished this revenue were not labourers on sugar estates but small settlers and peasants. C. S. Salmon, writing about the situation in *Depression in the West Indies*, 1884, concluded that a great injustice had been done to the islands; that they had been handed over, as it were, to a powerful corporation, and that the consequences of this monopoly were to be seen in underdevelopment and stagnation.

The voice of conscience raised on behalf of the faceless masses after emancipation had been suppressed in 1866 and was not to be heard again until the last decade of the century. With the introduction of Crown colony government, political control was passed to the governor. He was advised by a council of six government officials and three elected from among the local plantocracy. These appointees, all white, held office at his discretion and were reluctant to intervene on behalf of the African-Jamaican majority lest they offend their patron and forfeit their privilege.

The Jamaican upper class had willingly surrendered the island's constitution in 1866, and now found that they had also lost their political influence. It would take years of struggle on the road back to political representation, black empowerment and eventually political independence. Late in 1883, in the face of local and international pressure, the Colonial Office announced as a moderate step in advance the reintroduction of limited elected representation.

At the general elections in May 1884, nine representatives were elected and to these the governor added six officials, heads of government departments, appointed by the governor to the Legislative Council. The representatives had limited authority as the governor held in reserve four other appointments which he could utilise as he saw fit, and he also had the power of veto. If the representatives voted unanimously on an issue the governor could overrule them on grounds of paramount importance or by deploying "the official majority", that is, by simply increasing the number of ex-officio members to ten. In W. Adolphe Roberts' words, "The period was to be uneventful . . . and apathetic politically . . . . The island settled down to a version of feudalism that succeeded in being a mild copy of the old order, without its sporadic wealth, without its turmoil. Socially the Negro was 'kept in his place'." (Roberts: 1955)

This may have been the generally accepted impression, but the facts are otherwise. The petty bourgeoisie – successful smallholders, teachers, parsons, low-level civil servants and clerks – were frustrated by their exclusion from mainstream politics and began to mobilise the black electorate. They set about identifying and recruiting persons having the necessary property and educational qualifications to add their names to the electoral roll. The 1884 electoral roll showed the following registrations: 98 Indians, 1,001 Europeans, 2,578 mulattoes, 3,766 "Africans", making a total of 7,443 out of a possible 15,000 eligible to register but with active recruiting, among the African-Jamaicans, the numbers grew to 42,266 in 1889.

Whites were greatly outnumbered and this rekindled fears about the power of the natives. A literacy clause was introduced into the Franchise Act to prevent those unable to read and write from exercising the ballot. At the next elections in 1893, this effectively excluded almost half the number of voters. In the past illiterate electors had cast their ballots with the assistance of literate people. The beleaguered masses were now more frustrated than ever and desperately needed articulate leadership to challenge their exploitation and press for social reform.

Dr Robert Love, the black Bahamian anti-colonialist who had visited the island for a few weeks in 1889 while on his way to Haiti returned a year later to make Jamaica his home. Having lived in Panama and Central America, Love was only too familiar with the unfair trading practices of large companies such as the United Fruit Company. He empathised with the Jamaicans in their efforts to gain black empowerment and rid themselves of exploitation.

Robert Love

The most urgent issue was to increase black representation in the Legislative Council. In 1890 there were no blacks in the Council, although a few had managed to win seats on parochial boards. Although the successful voter registration campaign had taken place in 1889, the year before Love settled in Jamaica, he was in time to witness the panic of the whites and the introduction of the restrictive literacy clause.

The campaign to increase the black vote intensified with his participation. He and his associates compiled lists of suitably qualified black persons to counter the propaganda that black candidates were not available to run for elections. Love began to take the limelight by publicly supporting the call for greater representation in the government, for social reform and for black participation in the administrative life of the country.

He was born possibly in 1839, not far from the

town of Nassau where Africans, found aboard slave ships after the abolition of the slave trade in 1807, were liberated by the British navy and allowed to establish free communities. When he was still a small boy, his mother, sister and aunts had been abducted and brought to Jamaica as slaves. Whether or not Love ever managed to make contact with any of them later is not certain.

He grew up in the Anglican church in Nassau, received a basic education (including Greek and Latin) and became a deacon in the church. Not one to accept opinions without question, Love apparently had serious differences with the church leadership, then migrated to the United States where he completed his religious studies in the South and where, from time-to-time, he was embroiled in controversy.

Haiti, the first black country in the world to throw off the colonial yolk, was then in the midst of its liberation struggles and Love, caught up in the euphoria of race pride, offered his services. He trained as a medical doctor because he felt that in this way he could contribute meaningfully to the black liberation cause. He first went as a missionary, then accepted an appointment with the Haitian army in 1881 as a medical doctor but his stay in the republic was shortlived. Within two years he had become so involved in the politics of the country that he supported a palace coup led by the party in opposition and was exiled. From Haiti he apparently went to Panama where he lived for some time before deciding to make Jamaica his home.

Love adjusted to the Jamaican way of life without difficulty, especially as he was still a British subject. Ironically, on his arrival in the island the establishment press of the day, assuming that he was white, described him as an Englishman and practising physician. In those days no ordinary black man became a professional.

Many people were expressing progressive ideas similar to his own at the time. Some were to influence the formulation of the Fabian socialist philosophy which was "to guarantee to the dependencies the institutions of liberty, the social health and material prosperity on which their struggle depends . . . constructive reform [of] social and economic policies, civil liberty, local government, preventive medicine, nutrition, mass education, literacy, free association, co-operative organization, trade unionism, political representation". (Jones: 1945) Love and his associates campaigned for the issues set out in the Fabian socialist philosophy, which included greater black empowerment, fair employment practices, equal opportunity for blacks in the civil service and other public institutions.

Love first attracted public attention in 1893, when he delivered a lecture on Toussaint L'Ouverture and the Haitian situation at the Conversorium School on Church Street in Kingston. Contributions from the lecture went to a worthy cause, the Wesley Chapel Fund. Love was not a prepossessing man but he was an electrifying speaker. The lecture was so well-received that he was invited to repeat it in Kingston and in Spanish Town. Not only was he highly educated, he was articulate. When *The Daily Gleaner* refused to publish his letters on these issues, Love decided to start his own weekly newspaper, *The Jamaica Advocate*, in December 1894. Through his medical practice he could finance this small weekly newspaper which became the voice of the underprivileged.

For the upcoming 1893 general elections, Love and his companions campaigned vigorously but only four coloured men, Charles Campbell, Richard Hill Jackson, George Steibel and J. T. Palache, a Kingston solicitor of mixed Jewish descent, presented themselves as candidates, and only one, Palache, gained a seat. However, the number of black and coloured representatives grew until by the middle of the 1930s they formed the majority in the legislature. But full political control did not come until Jamaica attained independence from Britain in 1962.

Love appreciated the problems of the working-class people in his adopted country, for he had been subjected to his share of discrimination during his early years in the Bahamas and also in the Jim Crow South of the United States. In the republic of Haiti he had witnessed black men in authority oppress their black fellowmen. Change could only come when it was recognised that there was no difference between people of different skin tones.

According to Richard Hart, Love was perhaps the first leader to challenge publicly the assumption that blackness and inferiority were synonymous. He said that anything a white man could do he, the black man, could do as well. His dedication to improving the Jamaican condition earned him a place in W. Adolphe Roberts' *Six Great Jamaicans*.

As an anti-colonialist, Love believed that the primary goal of any black country ought to be self-rule. However, bearing in mind his American and Haitian experiences, he rationalised that possibly "the best hope for black people lay within the British legal and political system". If the Jamaican masses were to take their rightful place within the British political system, they had to resist colonial oppression and strive for self-rule.

Through the pages of *The Jamaica Advocate* blacks were encouraged to assert their equality, express their political views, educate themselves and develop self-esteem and pride in their African heritage. At no time did Love give any thought to severing the British ties.

Love also called for blacks to be appointed to public office as justices of the peace and as members of government boards and commissions. His motto was: "Everything for the people; everything by the people; and nothing without the people."

Until Jamaica could achieve self-rule the best compromise was to adopt the French parliamentary system with representatives from the colonies sitting in the parliament in Paris. He suggested that the British should do the same, but the proposal was never entertained.

The establishment continued to spread rumours that black people were indifferent to politics and that there were no suitable black candidates available. The apparent indifference of the people lay not so much in their lack of interest in assuming responsibility but in their inability to fulfil the high property and financial requirements for political office. They faced severe economic hardships with a declining economy and resultant social pressures, together with job competition with Indian indentured labour. In the 1880s many were left homeless, starving and naked. Natural disasters in succeeding years had also destroyed their provision grounds and many were left penniless. Restrictions placed on employment and advancement of blacks in the police force, the military and the civil service thwarted the ambition of the masses. Top posts in these agencies were filled by whites and near-whites, and blacks could only gain employment in low-paying jobs. The only way to change the system was to keep hammering at the weaknesses and Love persisted in his attacks, writing in the press and speaking from public platforms.

He was branded a racist but he never identified solely with colour, declaring publicly that "complexioned distinctions should be buried in the idea of nationality". Love threw his weight behind anyone, white or black, whom he felt would further his progressive ideals. W. B. Hannan, a white candidate to the legislative council for Clarendon and one of the free thinkers of the day, received his support. Hannan was an Englishman and member of a group of socialists whose ideas had contributed to the establishment of the Fabian Society in 1884. Love and Hannan called for administrative reform and in *The Jamaica Advocate* they attacked the plantation system which they felt "kept the labourer dependent, poor, ignorant, unclean, contemptible and miserable".

In 1894 Love and his colleagues organised the People's Convention, which he claimed was to celebrate "in a sympathetic and useful manner the sixtieth anniversary of the abolition of slavery". It became an annual event at which social issues such as popular education, land distribution, voter registration, taxation and citisenship were discussed and recommendations for improvements made. He hoped that one day blacks would enjoy political recognition just as other white British citizens did, and that through the convention a black nationalist leader with "an attachment to the soil" would emerge whose influence would spread internationally.

Few amendments of any significance had been made to the tax law since 1865 and the law introduced in 1890 continued to favour the few at the expense of the many. In some instances it allowed owners of 1,000 acres and more to pay one pound, sixteen shillings and eight pence annually, or one farthing per acre, while owners of five-acre lots (the small £6 voter) paid two shillings per year. Taxes on draft animals and on drays, wagons and carts remained high. The peasant paid three shillings, six pence for each donkey and six shillings for each cart, wagon, or dray wheel. Higher taxes were imposed on cottages with floorings, so many persons were forced to remove them to avoid the higher rate. Customs duties were fashioned from the same pattern, favouring the wealthy and penalising the poor.

In challenging the system, Love and his colleagues advocated a single tax structure based upon land tax instead of indirect taxes such as customs duties. It was clear that unless blacks could gain the majority in the legislature where they could formulate policy there would be no meaningful change. Love openly advocated self-rule and called upon the public to support his campaign.

His friend and political advocate, Whitfinch, in supporting the call for self-rule, wrote in *The Jamaica Advocate*: "In order to occupy a place of respect among the people's of the earth, it is absolutely necessary that we be entrusted with that which is our birthright, Self-Government. We do not ask a favour, No! we ask for the restoration to us of STOLEN PROPERTY."

As regards fairer political representation under the existing crown colony system, Love recommended one representative for each of the 14 parishes instead of nine for the whole island. The Colonial Office eventually adopted the recommendation, in 1895, but with many reservations, because "the number of black and brown men or even of Kingston Jews and lawyers in the Council" would adversely affect their efforts to attract white investors, and the election of such persons, including "newspaper editors of a low type" would be "unreasonable and very troublesome".

Local newspapers, which were largely supportive of the *status quo*, kept insinuating that "dangerous men were active in Jamaica". Love was their prime target as they feared that if he joined forces with the better educated and more influential brown middle class, the country could rise up in revolt and become another Haiti. As in the case of Governor Eyre, these fears were born of racism.

In order to erase the popular belief that blacks were not interested in politics or would make unsuitable candidates, Love and his associates continued to publicise lists of persons with suitable educational and financial qualifications who might be willing to come forward. They also encouraged local communities to seek out black candidates and support them. On one of their lists, the 21 names included three teachers, two solicitors in Kingston, eight clergymen and eight other individuals.

In *The Jamaica Advocate* of 12 December 1895 Love wrote, "Let the Negroes look around them in their own parish for a representative Negro, gather round him, help him, send him to the Legislative Council." But he cautioned that skin colour was not to be an overriding factor, neither were they to accept candidates blindly or be influenced by their financial status. On two occasions in *The Jamaica Advocate* of May 1895 the following notice appeared, "Don't neglect this. If you wish your country to be better you must help to make it better. Your vote is your power." He also said, "The ballot is our one great weapon of offence and defence. Every Negro who has the vote has the power to help himself." The 1896 elections recorded the highest voter turnout up to that time.

The show of black candidates was, however, disappointing. Only two came forward. They were Josiah Smicle from St Thomas and Alexander Dixon from Santa Cruz in St Elizabeth. They were the first black men since Edward Vickers, a Kingston landlord (1847) and Charles Price, a builder (1849), to win seats in the Assembly. Dixon had appeared on one of Love's lists.

Perhaps because only two men presented themselves, the rumours of black indifference persisted. *The Jamaica Post* newspaper on 6 October 1898 noted with some degree of malice: "We see local elections for board members unattended by a single peasant voter time after time, and when we go among these unsophisticated electors and enquire the reason, it is invariably, 'What good them doing for Black People, Sir?' " This was in spite of the fact that there were black and coloured men already serving on parochial boards.

In 1899 the governor of the day invoked the "official majority clause" to ensure that the elected representatives in the Council could not outvote any proposal with which he was not in favour. No other governor had ever sought to invoke that power before. Love and his supporters challenged the decision and led a series of political protests for several months running.

Conservative elements in the society that were uncomfortable with having elected representatives in the legislature had begun to make representations to have the Jamaica Constitution revert to crown colony status. This retrograde step would have brought further economic and social distress to unfortunate poor blacks, thousands of whom, after more than half a century, were still landless and disenfranchised. Love helped to organise a delegation to Britain to argue against the proposed change.

He kept up his campaign for black representation in local and national councils, offering himself as a candidate and winning a seat in the Kingston City Council in 1898 and 1903, and in the Legislative Council in 1906.

Vassal Calder, a local white planter from St Elizabeth, who was appointed to the Legislative Council spitefully attacked him and his equally caustic response shows how deep the prejudices were on both sides. Calder said, "Dr. Love must remember that his ancestors were my ancestors' slaves, and as such he could never be my equal. He is aggrieved because my ancestors rescued him from the bonds of thraldom and deprived him of the privilege of being King of the Congo . . . enjoying the epicureal and conjugal orgies and the sacrificial pleasures of his ancestral home in Africa." Love replied:

> The men who released my ancestors were not the men who enslaved them. The men who enslaved my ancestors were the Blackbeards and the Morgans, a type of Calder; the men who released them were the Wilberforces and the Granville Sharpes, a different type altogether. After all, slavery is but a preying of the strong upon the weak and all nations have undergone the ordeal in their time, including Calder's nation. The shame is not on the slaves but on the tyrant . . . Mr. Calder boasts that he can trace his ancestry back two hundred years. What of that? I can go back to Adam. When he said that had I not been removed from Africa I would be sitting on the Congo throne I verily believe that, and since "Authority is authority where'er it's to be found" as King of the Congo I would be the equal of the King of England. Calder would have had to approach both of us with due deference which subjects show to royalty. (Sherlock: 1980)

In spite of the fact that thousands of desperately poor people were living under difficult conditions, and were either unemployed or earning extremely low wages, Love did not support confrontationist action. Yet he responded to the call from the Kingston dock workers, when out of desperation they went on strike for four days in 1895, after their efforts to negotiate a pay increase had failed. Love saw this action as a "new departure" in social protest and used it to develop a workable strategy through the formation of labour clubs.

He recognised that a sufficiently large number of people could come together and exert pressure on employers to their own benefit. He also saw that institutions using cooperative methods to obtain financing could assist industrious individuals to "expand their influence in public life and . . . advance their status".

Love conceived of group-based institutions which would reinforce the type of economic and social independence he believed would generate the resources necessary to enable the less fortunate in the society to "expand their influence in public life and . . . advance their status". He put his ideas into practice by forming the Jamaica Advocate Cooperative Association to take over the newspaper when he could no longer run operations.

Love saw Friendly societies as organisations providing healthy social interaction and a modicum of financial stability for the very poor. He founded the Sparks Lodge and became its first master. He had learnt from experience that educational attainment was essential to the achievement of social goals, and so he kept motivating ambitious young people to acquire the necessary education that would help them to fulfil their goals.

Love was not a teacher, but he became an honorary member of the Jamaica Union of Teachers which was formed in 1894. The 1882 Royal Commission had criticised the lack of efficiency in the schools and noted that the increase in simple literacy by no means corresponded with the increase in the number of pupils at school. The Lumb Commission of 1897 criticised the standard of teaching and recommended a 10 per cent retrenchment in the already low elementary school budget. Education was placed on the agenda of the 1898 People's Convention but there was not much that the representatives could do.

In 1905 the Lumb Commission's recommendations "to reduce salaries of all teachers, trained and untrained, good, bad and indifferent alike" as well as to decrease aid for the first- and second-class schools by another 10 per cent were put into effect. The elementary school budget for the whole island was £52,605. After 1865 teachers had been paid by results, mainly in the Three Rs and had apparently become skilled in qualifying for the allowance without any significant improvement in the performance of the students. The report noted that "the curriculum was extensive and the teaching superficial". Education expenditure had risen sixfold between 1861 and 1881 to £23,400, while enrolment (including whites and coloureds) had only doubled to 231,268. At the same time the number of illiterates had doubled.

Out of a black adult population of some 250,000 at that time, it is estimated that only about 22,000, less than 10 per cent, could read and write. The Colonial Office was not prepared to increase the expenditure further.

Love championed the teachers' cause, in the press and on the platform, especially the economic hardships they were enduring as a result of the reduction in their already low salaries.

He had great praise for black women who served as models in their society and were at the centre of family life. In encouraging them to improve their education and become better leaders, he observed that it was by their leadership that the black race would succeed. He also encouraged the education of black girls as he believed that the black race could not rise above the level of its womanhood. He felt that they needed to be protected against the abuse of bookkeepers on sugar estates. Black children also needed to be protected from unfair treatment at school because of the colour of their skin.

When the public holidays legislation was being introduced, Love advocated its extension to include "cooks, housemaids, footmen and field labourers".

Black empowerment could only come with greater black participation in political, economic and administrative life. His hope lay in the spread of Pan-Africanism, because this movement had an obligation to spread black consciousness throughout the diaspora and even to Africa.

The first Pan-African Conference was held in London in 1900 and although Love did not attend, he published the conference proceedings in full in *The Jamaica Advocate*. Pan-Africanism emphasises the richness and diversity of African cultures, and inculcates feelings of self-worth and self-determination among peoples of African descent. For the first time hundreds of African-Jamaicans were exposed to its philosophy and understood the purpose of the movement. Within a month of the publication of the proceedings, more than 500 individuals from across the island joined the Jamaica branch of the association. The mission of the Jamaica branch, as he saw it, was to take the Pan-African message throughout the region, to the United States and as far as Africa.

Love, more than anyone else, influenced the direction Marcus Garvey was to take in championing black consciousness, anti-colonialism and Pan-Africanism. In acknowledging his debt to Love in 1920, Garvey declared, "Much of my early education in race consciousness is from Dr. Love. One cannot read his *Jamaica Advocate* without getting race consciousness." (*The Daily Gleaner:* 1930)

Many of the prejudices Love challenged and the causes he fought for still remained unresolved at the end of his life. His black, literate, middle-class audience never managed to reach out sufficiently to the masses.

Love died on 21 November 1914. He had become seriously ill in 1906 and in 1910 gave up active politics. Garvey's mission was to develop the political strategy conceived of and started by Love, and to take the message of race consciousness into the international arena.

CHAPTER 24

Marcus Mosiah Garvey, 1887-1940

Marcus Garvey remains a vitalising, inspiring force today. He touches Jamaicans closely because he raises questions of race and social commitment with which they still have to come to terms. His message is as relevant now as it was in the 1920s and 1930s, when he formed the People's Political Party. As an independent and predominantly black nation, Jamaicans now have the power to reach decisions on issues he raised.

A study of his life and times shows that he has been urging us to assume a larger role in the scheme of things. He has deepened and enriched our knowledge of ourselves, of our past and our potential as a society. We become aware, also, of a prophet, a man who throughout his life lived his message; and did so through triumph and disaster, in the face of derision and oppression, of imprisonment and of rejection. From the beginning he was driven by a passionate concern for the African-Jamaican people, and indeed for all peoples of African origin throughout the world.

He reminded African-Americans of their background of slavery and of having been let loose in the world without a cent in their pockets or land to settle on that they could call their own. From the beginning they had to fight their own way up to where they are today. Some had done well but the great majority remained propertyless and almost helpless. If they were to improve themselves they had to focus on personal success.

In revering Marcus Garvey as a national hero, Jamaicans pay tribute also to a leader who pioneered a role for Africa and Africans in world affairs. His vision was of black united nations governed by black leaders.

Garvey had a profound respect for books, education and scholarship. He was a philosopher as well as a man of action, a thinker who arrived at his conclusions by analysing the West Indian experience. He grew up in Jamaican colonial society at a time when, as Rupert Lewis points out:

Colonial ideological policy consistently debased Africa as well as people and things African. The future, the coloniser claimed, belonged to Europe. Hence colonial subjects were made to identify progress with the ideals of their master. In the process of the formation of Jamaica as a nation the negation of Africa and blackness has been constant. And so has the resistance to [this negation] by black people. (Lewis: 1987)

The Jamaican people identify with Garvey as one who built their self-esteem, challenged them to affirm their racial identity and reunited them with Africa as homeland. That this should be so is a measure of the cultural and social revolution that has been taking place in Jamaica. This revolution is radically changing the Jamaican self-image to one of assertiveness and racial equality. It has projected Jamaica onto the world stage politically and has moved increasing numbers of black people into leadership roles in their country.

By examining some of his major statements and reflecting on his method of reaching conclusions, we come to understand the magnitude of Garvey's achievement and the quality of his mind. We need to do this because those in the centres of white power and influence in Jamaica, in the United States and Europe saw Garvey as a formidable threat and used all the means in their power, the law included, to obstruct and vilify him. They projected the image of a black racist subversive, a rabble-rouser, a confidence man and trickster.

The Jamaican upper and middle classes of the 1920s rejected his challenge "to formulate a program of racial preservation and to develop a settled racial outlook". In them the terrified consciousness of the sugar-and-slave plantocracy period still lingered. Some kept their distance, not because they disagreed with Garvey's philosophy, but because they feared victimisation if they were seen to be supporting the challenge to the status quo.

In the words of a Jamaican peasant, Marcus Garvey was "not a usual man". Born and schooled in rural Jamaica, he became by his own effort a scholar who understood that nations make, and are made by, their history. He was an educator and an exceptionally gifted communicator of ideas. His richly stored mind linked the particular with the universal, the past with the present, the local or national with the global. To read even a few of his statements and reflections is to encounter a mind that illumines the Jamaican historical experience. In his analysis of colonial society in the 1920s, for example, he demonstrates his methods of basing conclusions on observation and analysis. Writing to the president of the Tuskegee Institute in Alabama in 1916, he said that the Jamaicans were not as racially conscious as the American black because they lived under a common system of sociological hypocrisy. (Hill) He observed:

> We have no open race prejudice here, and we do not openly antagonise one another. The extremes here are between white and black ... The black people here form the economic asset of the country, they number 6 to 1 of colored and white combined and without them in labour or general industry the country would go bankrupt ... The black people have had seventy-eight years of Emancipation but all during that time they have never produced a leader of their own, hence they have never been led to think racially but in common with the destinies of the other people with whom they mix as fellow citizens.

Garvey noted the increase of race consciousness 22 years later, in 1938:

> The West Indians generally, have developed more of the white psychology than of black outlook; but gradually, in some of the islands, the consciousness of race is dawning upon the people which may develop, to place the competent Negroes there in the right frame of mind to be of service when needed. There is much hope for the West Indies as for anywhere else in the outlook of the Negro toward nationalisation and independence.

Garvey's advocacy of a Jamaican national spirit and his critical appraisal of those blacks who regarded England as the mother country were a continuation of the work of Dr Love and his associates who laboured at the end of the nineteenth century to improve the racial consciousness and social conditions of the Jamaican working classes. Love encouraged them to unite, to form themselves into unions and organisations and elect representatives to the legislative council who would be concerned with their welfare. He knew that Jamaica's long overdue political awakening had to come from within, not from without.

Garvey was one of the few of his time who understood how seriously the inner world of the African had been damaged, and in some instances destroyed, by the experience of enslavement combined with alienation; by a transfer of authority and by total immersion in a wholly materialistic society.

George Lamming, in eloquent moving words, describes the outcome:

> The result was a fractured consciousness, a deep split in its sensibility which now raised difficult problems of language and values; the whole issue of cultural allegiance between the imposed norms of White Power represented by a small numerical minority and the fragmented memory of the African masses: between White instruction

and Black imagination. The totalitarian demands of White supremacy in a British colony, the psychological injury inflicted by the
sacred rule that all forms of social status would be determined by
degrees of skin complexion; the ambiguities among Blacks themselves
about the credibility of their own spiritual history . . . Could the
outlines of a national consciousness be charted and affirmed out of all
this disparateness? And if that consciousness could be affirmed, what
were its true ancestral roots, its most authentic cultural base?
(Lamming: 1988)

Lamming's analysis, written long after Garvey's death, underscores
why Garvey challenged African-Jamaicans and indeed all persons of
African descent to set themselves the task of building a racial as well as a
national consciousness, to liberate themselves from colonialism, to build
self-esteem and race-pride. These were, and remain, the imperatives of
decolonisation. Garvey had the capacity for penetrating beyond process to
inner causes and needs and he went beyond anti-colonialism to advocate
a programme of decolonization. (Lewis: 1987)

The irony is that Garvey probably learned the importance of racial
pride, self-esteem and a settled racial outlook from books he used in
elementary school, readers written for English children that built pride
in the English way of life, in the English landscape, in the heroes of
England, in its victories and achievements. With his love of reading and
elocution, young Garvey learned the importance of racial pride from
authors who glorified English achievements; from William Shakespeare's
"This England never did and never shall/Lie at the proud foot of a
conqueror"; or from John Milton's vision of "a mighty and puissant
nation rousing herself like a strong man after sleep and shaking her
invincible locks".

Garvey grew to understand that the key to racial harmony lay in the
open acceptance of racial differences and respect for them. He advocated
racial consciousness but attacked and rejected racial discrimination of
any kind. Race consciousness and a sense of self-worth are important
elements in national development. They are essential for self-respect, for
as Isaiah Berlin emphasised in his essay on nationalism, "To be made an
object of contempt, amused condescension, or patronizing reliance by
proud, successful neighbours is one of the most traumatic experiences
that individuals or societies can suffer." (Berlin: 1981)

Pomp and circumstance are as essential elements in the culture of blacks
as they are for people of all other races. In the same way that other nations
establish their hierarchy of honours, awards and titles, so Garvey established his own system of honours for his Universal Negro Improvement

Association (UNIA): honours such as Earl of the Congo, Viscount of the Niger, Baron Zambezi and Knight of the Nile. In this regard he brooked no condescension.

He was a universalist, concerned with the Africans of the diaspora and of the African continent. He saw racial consciousness as an active and independent program of upliftment. As a result, he never descended to the level of the apostles of white superiority. His vision was Pan-Caribbean, Pan-American, Pan-African.

Two very different groups of Jamaicans have broadened and deepened our understanding of Marcus Garvey. The Rastafarians have consistently given Africa the central place that belongs to a homeland, affirmed their Africanness and revered Garvey. Alongside them stand scholars such as Robert Hill and Rupert Lewis who, on the basis of rigorous academic scholarship, have shown the significance and importance of Garvey's work and of Garvey as a world leader.

Garvey was born on 17 August 1887, in the small rural town of St Ann's Bay. He was christened Malcus Mosiah but early assumed the name of Marcus. At St Ann's Bay he spent his formative years under the influence of two self-educated men, his father, Malcus Mosiah Garvey, and his godfather, Alfred E. Borrowes. From them young Marcus learned certain positive attitudes which guided his life. He was an avid reader and developed a passion for learning. He always carried a pocket dictionary from which he learnt three or four words each day and as a result built up a phenomenal vocabulary. This he utilised to the fullest extent as a public speaker and orator, and as a writer and newspaper editor.

His exposure to a wide range of subjects in his father's and godfather's book collections developed his enquiring mind and an interest in social issues. On his return to Jamaica from the United States at the end of 1927 he owned one of the finest libraries in the island. His collection included works on science, history, African history, religion and art and was consulted by a number of prominent persons in Kingston.

Garvey's first exposure to race prejudice was as a child and it obviously left a deep hurt and possibly more than any other single experience, helped to frame his philosophy on race consciousness. He used to play with a white girl, the daughter of the Methodist minister in the town, until the day came when she was told by her mother that she could no longer associate with Marcus because he was black.

The skills acquired in his godfather's printery equipped him to earn a living wherever he went. Most important of all, he understood the power of the press and never failed to use it to mobilise people of African descent and to lead them to a clearer understanding and appreciation of their black heritage.

Robert Love was one of Garvey's mentors and gave him elocution lessons when he moved to Kingston. From Love, Garvey also learnt much about pride in race and challenging colonialist prejudices. The young man from St Ann's Bay was all the time refining his ideas on racial consciousness. His involvement in the printers' strike in 1908 and his championing of these underpaid workers seemed a natural thing to do, although it cost him his job with the P. A. Benjamin Company, a firm of manufacturing chemists. At that time they were also publishing a small advertising sheet, *The Commercial Messenger*, on which Garvey may have worked. While with the company Garvey made his first venture into publishing. He began *Garvey's Watchman* but this small journal apparently ran for only three issues.

Garvey became a regular contributor to the local newspapers and often addressed social issues affecting the working classes, but the establishment press of the day, as they had done to Love earlier, did not always approve of his radical views and did not always publish his letters.

Garvey began seriously improving his oratorical skills by visiting different churches and observing their preachers; he practised reading aloud, entered and organised elocution contests, and took advantage of every opportunity to appear on public platforms. A contemporary remembers his first visit to the East Queen Street Literary and Debating Society.

> The chairman gave him permission to speak during the "open" half-hour on the topic under debate and as would be expected, this strange awkward looking young man, not so long ago from the country, made us all sit up and listen. (Murray: 1969)

The anti-colonialist National Club of Jamaica attracted him and he soon became a regular speaker at their public forums. Eventually he was elected the club's secretary. The founder was Sandy Cox, a Kingston barrister who had been discriminated against in the Civil Service and was strongly anti-colonialist. Cox advocated that the only way that coloured and black people in Jamaica could better their condition was to unite with other members of the black race in all parts of the world. The club attracted some prominent persons of like views, but after a time it became primarily a platform for Cox, the politicians H. A. L. Simpson and Alexander Dixon, whom Love had supported in his political bid to get into the House of Representatives, and also Marcus Garvey. Eventually out of frustration and disappointment Cox emigrated to the USA. Referring to that period of his life, some 17 years later, Garvey noted: "The people were [then] not sufficiently racially conscious to appreciate a racial movement because they lived under a common system of social hypocrisy that deprived them of that very racial consciousness." (*Black Man*: 1933)

Garvey began reaching out to local artisans, rural peasant farmers, labourers searching for recognition and self-assurance. He awakened in them national consciousness and urged them to shake off their economic oppression. But his vision could not be contained within the confines of the Jamaican society and in 1909 he set out for Central America where thousands of African-West Indians were employed on the Panama Canal and on banana and sugar plantations in Costa Rica.

There Garvey found employment as a timekeeper on one of the United Fruit Company's banana plantations and this gave him first-hand knowledge of the poor working conditions of Jamaican labourers employed there. He was moved to protest to the British Consul in Port Limon on their behalf but his representation was ignored. In his determination to create greater social awareness among the suffering masses in the region and throughout the diaspora, he next took his message to Bocas del Toro, Colón, Nicaragua, Honduras, Colombia and Venezuela and in 1912 he left for Britain in the hope of reaching a still wider audience. There he came under the influence of the Egyptian, Duse Mohammed Ali, whose magazines *Africa Times* and *Orient Review*, discussed Egyptian affairs as well as conditions of Africans under the imperialist powers. From this experience Garvey learned a great deal about African politics. For a short time while working on the docks of London, he attempted to improve his education by attending part-time classes at Birbeck College which had been established by London University to serve working-class students without formal qualifications.

Garvey in Costa Rica

It was during that year in Britain that Garvey developed and crystalised his idea of one great international organisation of black people, educated, financially independent, having pride in race; black people who would take their place as equals on the world stage. Later he explained his vision in these words: "I saw before me even as I do now, a new world of black men, not peons, serfs, dogs and slaves but a nation of sturdy men making their impress upon civilization and causing a new light to dawn upon the human race." (Lewis: 1987)

Garvey returned to Jamaica in July 1914, and on 1 August, emancipation day, he launched the Universal Negro Improvement and Conservation Association and the African Communities League, later referred to as the Universal Negro Improvement Association (UNIA). At first, persons approached the movement cautiously as they were not sufficiently aware of what he was trying to do, and were afraid to speak out on controversial issues.

"Membership was scanty, and hearing was half-hearted. Most people here regarded the young man as an empty dreamer. But he persisted." (Murray: 1969)

The general objectives of the UNIA which were set out in 1914 remained Garvey's guiding principles to the end of his days. They were to encourage material success through individual effort; encourage educational attainment, race consciousness and racial pride. The stated aim was "One God! One aim! One destiny!" The UNIA was also:

> To reclaim the fallen of the race; administer to and assist the needy; assist in civilizing the backward tribes of Africa; strengthen the imperialism of inde-pendent African states . . . establish educational institutions [Universities, Colleges and Secondary Schools] for the further intellectual improvement and cultural awareness of the boys and girls of the race; to develop world-wide commercial and industrial intercourse. (Cronin: 1962)

In 1920 Garvey explained what strengthened his resolve to carry out his dream:

> Just at that time other races were engaged in seeing their cause through – the Jew through their Zionist Movement and the Irish through their Irish Movement – and I decided that, cost what it might, I would make this a favourable time to see the Negro interest through. (Hill: 1987)

The UNIA disseminated Garvey's ideas of African nationalism, and anti-imperialism through political, ethical and practical instructions and provided its membership with opportunities for literary, artistic and creative expression.

Garvey was inspired by Booker T. Washington's achievements at the Tuskegee Institute in Alabama, and began planning a similar facility in Jamaica which he hoped would provide opportunities for the advancement of intelligent, ambitious black people. Dr Washington invited Garvey to Tuskegee and planned to visit Jamaica, but he died in 1915 before the visits could materialise. Washington's successor, Major Robert R. Moton, along with Dr W. E. DuBois, Pan-Africanist editor of *Crisis*, the journal of the National Association for the Advancement of Colored People (NAACP), visited Jamaica for two days in 1916. However, the First World War was then in progress and the British government, perceiving Garvey as a threat to colonial stability, advised Dr Moton not to contact this trouble-maker. (Murray: 1969) Garvey was determined to meet him, and did so at a reception in his honour organised by the Jamaica Union of Teachers at the Mico College. Nothing meaningful resulted from the encounter.

Impatient to get his educational institution off the ground, Garvey decided to seek financial assistance overseas. In 1916 he set out on what was to have been a five-month tour of the West Indies and the United States, but it became instead an eleven year odyssey. The Jamaica Institute he envisaged never materialised.

Garvey continued to refine much of his political ideology and his concepts of self-actualisation. He launched the first American branch of the UNIA in February 1918 in New York and by the 1920's UNIA enterprises were employing more than 1,000 persons in Harlem, New York, and surrounding communities. The movement was also attracting worldwide attention as a black political force.

Garvey gave his first public lecture on Jamaica in Harlem on 9 May, 1916, shortly after his arrival in the United States. It was not well-received because with his unusual appearance and strange accent he seemed out of place in the American environment. His timing was, however, right because the Harlem Renaissance was becoming popular: black intellectuals in the United States and from other countries were then expressing their radical opinions in publications and speeches on the sidewalks of Harlem.

Among these so-called "new negroes" were: Herbert H. Harrison, the well-known black lecturer; A. Philip Randolph, member of the Sleeping Car Porters Association and editor of *The Messenger*; Dr W. E. B. DuBois of the NAACP, and the Jamaicans, W. A. Domingo and Claude McKay. They had all experienced racism and were caught up in the excitement of the Bolshevik revolution and the teachings of Lenin and Trotsky. McKay and others would later denounce communism when they realised that the communist ideals of the citizens' voluntary fulfilment of their duties and their participation in the affairs of society did not replace the state or create a truly classless society.

They crusaded for liberty and equality in American society and challenged their fellow blacks to throw off the yoke of white supremacy. They encouraged them to learn more about their African heritage and "the positive, rich, material content of their Africanity". Their publications challenged social inequality and the injustices meted out to Africans throughout the world and in their homeland as a result of colonial exploitation. Thousands of once prosperous and self-sufficient African people were now starving because great numbers of them had been coerced into abandoning their traditional ways of life to work instead on plantations of cotton, cocoa and groundnut for the European market, while others were being forced to work in miserable conditions in unsafe mines underground from which they received little economic benefit.

Garvey helped to keep the African issue alive as he challenged the falsehoods and misrepresentations of African history spread abroad by

European colonisers. He reached out to American blacks who during the First World War had misguidedly left their farms in the South to work under wretched conditions in factories in the North. Black American soldiers returning from the war also found that during their absence discrimination had grown worse, and that promises of equality and opportunity made by the President of the United States were not being fulfilled. Garvey brought the veterans hope and promoted financial enterprises which it was hoped would provide them with an alternative to a dependency on government largess.

Within four or five years the UNIA became both one of the largest Pan-Africanist movements and the largest international movement of black peoples on the African continent and in the countries of the diaspora. At its peak it is estimated that there were 1,700 groups in 40 countries with 4 million members. The largest concentration was in Harlem.

Garvey was so committed to the use of the printing press as a means of disseminating his message of black upliftment that wherever he went he started publishing ventures even though they were never successful. Henry Rogowski, publisher of the socialist paper, *New York Call,* assisted him with the necessary credit to start the *Negro World,* which first appeared on 17 August 1918, seven months after the inauguration of the New York branch of the UNIA. W. A. Domingo was its first editor and served for a year. He introduced Garvey to the writings of Edward W. Blyden, the West Indian from St Thomas, in the Virgin Islands, who had migrated to West Africa in the 1850s and had become a revered African scholar. Blyden's *Christianity, Islam, and the Negro Race* profoundly influenced Garvey.

In formulating the New York manifesto of the UNIA, Garvey was influenced by Booker T. Washington's body-of-conduct-of-life philosophy. The UNIA emphasised discipline, self-education and a strict code of behaviour. Members learned the UNIA catechism, songs and poetry, attended political and religious instruction and listened to Garvey preach his gospel of success. He motivated them to take pride in self and in race and to develop self-confidence. The same philosophy of moral and intellectual improvement and self-discipline pervaded the movement in Jamaica. The UNIA organised training cells to reinforce the organisation's ideology and paramilitary training for the special guard, the African Legion, which was assigned to protect UNIA officials on ceremonial occasions and was expected to respond to any eventuality in Africa. Members of the Black Cross Nurses Auxiliary received training in elementary nursing care to enable them to minister to the poor and needy. The Universal African Motor Corps, a women's group, received driving instruction and training in motor mechanics.

Wherever he went, Garvey imbued blacks with pride in self and in race, and strengthened their self-esteem. A report in the Baltimore paper, the *African-American* dated 13 December 1918, in highlighting the international aspect of his mission, noted: "In addition to forming a league for political and social improvement of the Negro's condition in this country, the aim is to establish in Africa a strong Negro nation, which could command respect for the Negro, who resides in white countries." (Hill: 1987)

Garvey promoted "nationalist agitation against imperialism" primarily through the *Negro World* which ran from January 1918-1933 and was distributed worldwide as well as through the numbers of other short-lived publications which he edited from time-to-time. In places with a high rate of illiteracy, one copy of the *Negro World* generally served several persons at a time. Jomo Kenyatta, is reputed to have told C. L. R. James that Kenyan nationalists, unable to read would gather round a copy of the paper and listen to articles being read over and over. It was banned at different times in almost every colonial country in Central America, the West Indies and Africa.

In addition to articles on race consciousness, the *Negro World* carried articles by other black intellectuals in French and Spanish aimed at non-English speaking peoples of the region. Subscribers were encouraged to send comments and many came from all over the world. The newspaper's front page editorial by Garvey, was always addressed to the "Fellowmen of the Negro Race". At its peak the paper had a circulation of 50,000 but it may even have reached 200,000 briefly.

Garvey's encouragement of black resistance to discrimination and exploitation, as well as his support of Mahatma Ghandi's and Eamon de Valera's Indian and Irish nationalist activities brought him into conflict with imperialist governments. In 1919 the United States Department of Justice, under J. Edgar Hoover, assigned special agents to monitor his activities, and an attempt was made upon his life that year. Efforts were also made to keep him out of the United States by denying him a re-entry visa in 1921. Garveyism influenced many young African freedom fighters. The Kikuyu employed one of Garvey's "bishops" to train young people and from these schools the Kenyan resistance movement, the Mau Mau, grew.

Garvey never lost sight of the movement's international goal. After his deportation to Jamaica at the end of 1927, he continued to write for the *Negro World* in New York, telegraphing in his front-page editorials every week. These continued to emphathise with the struggles of other colonial nations.

Each UNIA branch was independent of the parent organisation, and had its own Liberty Hall headquarters. The UNIA's flag of red, black and

Marcus Mosiah Garvey, 1887-1940

green denoted "red for the blood of the race nobly shed in the past and dedicated to the future; black for pride in colour of the skin; green for a promise of a better life in Africa". (Cronin: 1955)

From the business section of the movement, the Negro Factories Corporation, grew a number of cooperative enterprises which included groceries, a restaurant, a steam laundry, a tailoring and dressmaking shop and a publishing house in the United States. In all cases, however, management was weak and the businesses under-capitalised. They were also undermined by American bureaucracy, although they were never at any time a threat to the American economy.

Garvey organised the first International Convention of the UNIA in August 1920, at Madison Square Gardens in New York. The commencement date was significantly set for 1 August, emancipation day. The convention led off with three religious services and a parade of 2,000 delegates from 25 countries and four continents. Knowing that they were under surveillance from the Federal Bureau of Investigation, the group marched in silence to the strains of the UNIA band and choristers. The members of the African Legion, 200 Black Cross nurses, the Black Eagle flying corps and members of the Juvenile Auxiliary were all attired in uniform. Officers of the African Legion in their dark blue military-style dress and dress swords created a stir, and strengthened rumours that Garveyites were preparing to overthrow the colonial powers.

Some 25,000 persons gathered on the following day at Madison Square Gardens to hear Garvey's challenge to the black race. In his wide-ranging address he said, "We are the descendants of a suffering people; we are the descendants of a people determined to suffer no longer . . . We shall raise the banner of democracy in Africa or 400 million of us will report to God the reason why . . . We pledge our blood to the battlefield of Africa where we will fight for true liberty, democracy and the brotherhood of man." (Edwards: 1967) He urged the gathering and millions of other Africans to claim Africa for themselves. "It will be a terrible day when the blacks draw the sword to fight for their liberty. I call upon the 400,000,000 blacks to give the blood you have shed for the white man to make Africa a republic for the Negro." (Hill: 1987)

Garvey and the UNIA reviewing a convention parade in 1924

The Declaration of Rights of the Negro Peoples of the World, presented at the convention, protested against the oppressive conditions under which black people continued to labour. It set out 54 demands for black nationalism, political and judicial equality, racial self-determination and a free Africa governed by black people. It established titles and distinctions for officers of the movement. Garvey was declared Provisional President of Africa and President General and Administrator of the UNIA. His official title was His Highness the Potentate. (Edwards: 1967)

In 1921 Garvey returned to the West Indies for what was planned as a brief visit but it took him four months to obtain the re-entry permit to the United States. Thereafter, his militant stance seems to have become more conciliatory, although in that same year he condemned organisers of the Second Pan-African Congress for attempting to amalgamate opposite races, remarking that it was "a crime against nature". He also questioned the hope of achieving social equality in the United States, because it was a white man's country in which the Negro was physically outnumbered and would ultimately lose out.

The Second International Convention held in 1921 was less impressive than the first, possibly because of rumours about the mismanagement of the Black Star Line, his shipping company. But Garvey concentrated upon the African situation and expressed his hope for "a free and redeemed Africa". He hoped to establish a settlement of skilled black persons in Liberia, the "land of opportunity", where black Americans and West Indians would contribute their skills to the development of a great African republic. Several discussions on the matter followed with the Liberian authorities about possible sites for future settlements. Then in 1925 the Liberian government, obviously under pressure from the United States and other outside influences, repudiated the agreement. It issued a statement to the effect that it was "irrevocably opposed both in principle and in fact to the incendiary policy of the UNIA headed by Garvey". (Lewis: 1968)

Garvey had in the meantime purchased and shipped equipment to Liberia to be used to establish a lumber company. The machinery was seized by the Liberian customs and was eventually sold for a fraction of its true value to pay the customs duty.

The Liberian project which came to be known as the "Back to Africa Movement" was not looked on with favour by imperialists and by many black colonials who interpreted it to mean the repatriation of all colonial blacks to Africa. These opponents claimed that Garvey intended to overthrow the imperialist masters who were in fear of their colonial economies collapsing. Garvey later explained that he had not expected all Negroes to leave America and the West Indies for Africa. He only wished to contribute to the building of an independent black nation.

One of Garvey's most ambitious dreams was the formation of a steamship company the Black Star Line. This company was to be owned and operated by black people, in the same way that a white steamship

Garvey makes a farewell address before his deportation from the US in 1927

company was owned and managed by white people. He hoped to build up a fleet of five ships between June and October 1919, "to trade in the interests of the Negro race" and to link coloured peoples of the world in commercial and industrial endeavours. Caribbean and African merchants had been having difficulty getting shipping space on the British Elder Dempster line and it was hoped that the Black Star Line would ease the problem.

The company financed by US$5 shares, sold only to blacks netted about US$750,000. No one was permitted to purchase more than 200 shares. Unfortunately, neither Garvey nor any of his close associates knew anything about finance or the shipping business. They put too great faith in untrustworthy dealers and unreliable crew members, both black and white. Proper records were not always kept and official procedures were often ignored. The first three vessels negotiated for were old and fit only for the scrap heap. They ended up as liabilities, leaving the company to face a deficit of around US$476,000. By 1922 the Black Star Line Shipping Company was bankrupt.

The United States attorney general's office had warned Garvey that it was illegal to sell shares by post for a company that had not yet been properly incorporated. Garvey ignored the warnings and ran foul of the law. Eventually in January 1922 he and three other company officials were indicted on charges of commercial fraud. The charges noted that the company had knowingly used "fraudulent representations" and "deceptive artifices" to sell stocks through the mail and had advertised and sold space on a mythical vessel. (Cronin: 1955) Garvey was indicted on 12 counts, fined US$1,000, held without bail for three months and after an unsuccessful appeal was sentenced to a term of five years in an Atlanta jail. The three other men, referred to as "conspirators", were not charged.

At the trial he defended himself for most of the time and this did not help his case as his often belligerent manner and gerrymandering lost him public sympathy. He appealed the sentence, lost the appeal and was imprisoned in an Atlanta jail on 3 February 1925. Many, especially those who wished to see this black upstart put in his place, thought that he had received his just deserts, but others felt that he had been unfairly treated. The *New York Evening Bulletin*, a white daily, noted on 12 February 1925: "He did many strange things, it is true, but he performed many fine acts, too . . . Had the man been given half a fair deal, his financial schemes might have been successful and he might have been able to avoid the unfortunate disasters which led him into the courts and brought punishment upon him".

The *Buffalo Evening Times* of 24 February, 1925, wrote: "There is still something that is not pleasant about this whole business." It questioned the fairness of the judgment and noted that in the past white men charged with similar offences had received much lighter sentences.

The colonial governments, challenged by Garvey's militancy, were relieved at the news of his imprisonment, but they could not shake his determination or his optimism. His commitment to the establishment of a black shipping line was so fixed that not even the difficulties experienced in the earlier failed attempts could deter him. In 1924, while his appeal was pending, Garvey became involved once again in another shipping company, the Black Cross Navigation and Trading Company, registered in New Jersey. It negotiated for the purchase of a ship in somewhat better condition than the first three and his supporters, anxious to see a black shipping company become a reality, were enthusiastic.

After many delays, this ship, the *General Goethals*, which Garvey had planned to rechristen the *Booker T. Washington*, set out on a voyage round the Caribbean carrying passengers and cargo. Emonei Carter, secretary general of the UNIA was sent along on the voyage to sell stocks at each port of call to raise funds to meet expenses. The vessel reached Kingston on 10 February 1925, but Carter could nor raise sufficient money and the ship was tied up in port for a month until its debts were liquidated. It then sailed for Colón, Panama and spent another month there for lack of funds before it was cleared. It was supposed to have sailed for New York via Kingston but there is no certainty that it ever returned to New York. Garvey was then in prison, the image of the organisation had been badly tarnished and it was difficult to get financial support.

Garvey's dream of establishing a black university was realised if only for a short time when Liberty University was opened in the state of Virginia in September 1926. It too was badly affected by the problems of the UNIA and after three years it closed for lack of financial support.

After the UNIA petitioned President Coolidge in 1927, Garvey's prison term was commuted to two and a half years. He was released in early December 1927, taken to New Orleans and deported to Jamaica. To his second wife Amy Jacques fell the task of clearing up his financial affairs, selling his Harlem property and shipping his possessions home. The reception he received on his arrival in the island on 10 December 1927, was heartening and fuelled his optimism. Cheering crowds greeted him at the docks and thousands lined the streets to watch him pass by. *The Daily Gleaner,* 12 December 1927 reported his arrival as follows:

A short statue attired in a drab suit and wearing a Panama hat was on the second deck. It was Marcus Garvey the idol of the coloured people and his identity could not be mistaken . . . Deafening cheers were raised and remarks heard on all sides in the huge crowd showed the high esteem in which he is held by the ordinary people of this country.

The Ward Theatre which seats approximately 1,000, could not accommodate the gathering which attended the reception in his honour.

At home in Jamaica he organised training courses and cultural activities for adults and children, organised street corner meetings in Kingston and travelled to rural parishes, taking his message of black nationalism to all who would listen and read. Convinced of the Messianic nature of his mission, in 1928 he visited UNIA branches in Central America in the hope of revitalising the movement and he also visited Europe for a short time. Between 1929 and 1931 he published the *Blackman* first as a daily and later as a weekly newspaper. This was followed by the evening daily the *New Jamaican*, from July 1932 to September 1933 and then the *Black Man* magazine which began late in 1933. Where the Negro was concerned, he said, there were no national boundaries, nor would he give up the struggle until Africa was free.

In 1922 the UNIA through Garvey had proposed to the League of Nations that it should take over the former German colonies in Africa, but this was blocked by a ruling which stipulated that petitions could only be considered from existing governments. In 1928 the UNIA presented another petition in which it recommended that the entire regions of West Africa should be incorporated into a commonwealth of black nations under the government of black men. It also condemned the multinational company, Firestone, for its stranglehold on Liberia, the United States for its occupation of Haiti and the American Fruit Company for its undue influence in Central America.

Garvey was also devoting his energies to building up a sense of national pride in Jamaica. Edelweiss Park, an old house and property at Cross Roads in the Corporate Area of Kingston and St Andrew, which he purchased in 1929, became a centre for spiritual upliftment, self-improvement, political indoctrination and purposeful recreation.

Political and religious instruction formed part of the weekly programme, and was intended "to combat ignorance and narrow-mindedness among the masses". Thousands thronged to hear Garvey speak on Sunday nights and young and old journeyed from far off rural places, just to get a glimpse of the man who carried the message of inspiration and anti-colonial solidarity. At these meetings they were given a better understanding of their role in society and the confidence to challenge economic and social oppression. For five years Edelweiss Park gave them the will to achieve but in 1934 it had to be sold for debt.

Garvey decided to enter local politics and in 1929 formed the People's Political Party. It had mass support and fielded three candidates for the 1930 general elections. However as it turned out, many supporters could not meet the necessary voter registration requirements and the party could not command sufficient votes to win a seat. The People's Political Party was the first of what Garvey hoped would have been a number of political parties in the Caribbean championing the cause of the faceless masses.

The party manifesto advocated constitutional change to secure Jamaican representation in the British parliament so that the people might achieve a greater measure of self-government. It called for significant social and economic reform: minimum wage legislation, promotion of native industries, land reform and compulsory improvement of urban areas and public housing; the establishment of a Jamaican university, a polytechnic, a national opera house, and a school for domestic science. It also recommended the building of a town hall in Kingston, the establishment of a legal aid department to assist poor people in the courts as well as legislation to protect voters against those who would seek to manipulate the political process unfairly.

The manifesto also proposed that there should be a law to impeach and imprison judges who, in defiance of British justice and constitutional rights entered into underhand agreements with lawyers and others to deprive ordinary individuals of their rights in the courts. When Garvey elaborated on this particular clause at a public meeting he was charged with contempt of court, sentenced to three months in jail, and fined £100. While serving the sentence he won a seat in the local elections for the Allman Town Division of the Kingston and St Andrew Corporation but the Corporation declared his seat vacant. However, when a by-election was called to fill the vacancy, Garvey was re-elected unopposed. He had by then served his prison term.

Garvey's advocacy of social reform gave the Kingston dock workers the courage to demand better wages and working conditions in May 1929. When they were ignored some 500 of them walked off the job leaving 15,000 stems of bananas on the docks. All they were asking for was four shillings, two pence for loading 100 stems of bananas, instead of the one shilling, nine pence which is what they were receiving. They were also demanding double time on Sundays. Because Garvey was their spokesman he incurred the wrath of the powerful United Fruit Company, which saw the possibility of its profits being eroded.

Discontent was also spreading on the sugar plantations where workers were facing the same social and economic pressures. Their obvious complaints could no longer be ignored and in February 1930 a royal commission headed by Sir Sidney Olivier was appointed to enquire into the situation. Testifying before the commission, Garvey drew attention to the exploitation of the workers and recommended that wage guidelines and set hours of work should be instituted as well as legislation to prevent the exploitation of children in the workplace. He called for health and accident insurance for people working in the banana and sugar industries and attacked the KSAC for paying too low wages.

Garvey's pleadings went unheeded but he continued to call for social change and warned that if conditions were not improved the oppressed would rise up in rebellion. Seven years later, in 1938 as he had predicted, violence erupted on the Westmoreland sugar plantations. Only then did the authorities begin to address better housing and fair employment.

The Sixth International Convention of the UNIA in Kingston in August 1929, emphasised international outreach and revitalisation of the UNIA. Representatives were invited from all social organisations in the island, including churches, benevolent societies and lodges. On this occasion overseas delegates came from the United States, Central America, Cuba and the Bahamas. The Carib International Association from Guatemala was refused entry and one delegate spoke on behalf of Nigeria.

The convention discussed international issues affecting the conditions of black people. It recommended that the political arm of the movement should be revived and given a new mandate to secure the enfranchisement of the black American population; that the UNIA should engage in large-scale agricultural enterprises in the West Indies, Africa and the United States; and that negro consuls should be located in centres of large black populations. The matter of proper black representation at the League of Nations in Geneva was raised but because of the expense involved it was abandoned. In spite of past difficulties with failed shipping ventures, it was recommended that the Steamship Company should be revived and renamed the African Steam Navigation Company, but that was not to be.

Because education for blacks was so inadequate, the convention urged that a school building programme should be instituted, especially in isolated communities with predominantly black populations. Departments to oversee health and public education were also to be instituted. A target of $600,000,000 was set for the establishment of three Negro universities in the West Indies, West Africa and America. Daily newspapers were to be strategically established in several European capitals, in West Africa, Cape Town and in important West Indian islands so that they could shape sentiment in favour of the entire Negro race. 1 October was designated Health Day, when emphasis would be placed on personal hygiene and sanitation of the surroundings.

Among the social activities arranged during the convention was a debate between Garvey and Otto Huiswood, a representative of the American Negro Labour Congress. The topic was cooperation between black and white workers. Garvey's emphasis on racial solidarity and self-preservation as the first law of nature received overwhelming support from the audience.

On the closing night, 22 August, there was a re-enactment of the court life of Ancient Africa before some 10,000 persons at Edelweiss Park.

The high dignitaries of the UNIA, accompanied by their bejewelled ladies, appeared resplendent in their rich robes of state, while the officers of the African Legion fairly dazzled the excited black multitude with their dapper uniforms, shiny Sam Brown belts, and gleaming swords . . . As the President General of the UNIA and Provisional President of Africa passed between lines of erect legionnaires holding aloft drawn swords, the vast assemblage gave a mighty roar of greeting. Accompanied by his wife and the High Potentate of the Association, Garvey made his way to a lavishly decorated stage where he informed his audience that they were but celebrating what had gone before in the noble court of Ethiopia, the grandeur of past ages. (Cronin: 1955)

One regrettable occurrence at the convention was the split in the UNIA between the Jamaican and the American representatives. Garvey accused some members of the movement of dishonesty and disloyalty over the failed shipping company and the events which led to his imprisonment. He and some of those loyal to him preferred to start a new organisation but Henrietta Vinton Davis and some of the other Americans did not agree. This dissension lost the UNIA much public support.

The African nations were by this time awakening to the importance of unification and in that same year the National Congress of Black West Africa was convened in Lagos, Nigeria. Jamaica was not represented but Garvey published J. B. Danquah's seminal address to the conference in the *Blackman* and so subscribers were kept abreast of this important international happening.

Garvey continued to broaden the perspective of his audiences at both local and international levels. Edelweiss Park became the mecca for cultural events in Jamaica. One music competition is described thus by a contemporary.

> Over 2,000 listeners were packed on the ground floor and in the galleries . . . Contestants were classified into solos, duets, quartets and choral ensembles. All the items offered were serious, rather than popular music. They included selections from Haydn, Tchaikovsky, Arditi, Eli, Handel; offerings which ordinarily would hardly appeal to the musically unsophisticated. At the beginning Garvey described how polite society here and abroad behaved at concerts, and asked the listeners to show the same polite and encouraging behaviour to the contestants. Throughout the long programme . . . there was polite, considerate and appreciative reception by the large mixed audience. (Mills: 1969)

By including classical music Garvey was demonstrating that there was no difference between black and white people, and that poor people were just as capable of appreciating the finer things of life. His audiences understood his message and responded appropriately.

In the *Negro World* of 26 June 1931, Garvey pointed out the need for a code of ethics for black children which should be no different from that for white children. He said that in the same way that white children had a philosophy, a set creed to guide their lives, so black children needed a similar code. (Hill: 1987)

The Seventh International Convention of the Negro Peoples of the World was convened in Kingston on 1 August 1934, the centenary of the abolition of slavery. Garvey had by then softened his political stance from militancy to popular mobilisation and compromise. At the convention he said, "Others are learning that they cannot gain much today by being too aggressive; we have to be more compromising than other peoples. It is because of our peculiar position – a position that we have invited upon ourselves." (Hill: 1987)

A five-year plan stressed the international aspects of the movement and reiterated some of the recommendations from the Sixth Convention dealing with the development of shipping, manufacturing, mining, agriculture and other industries in the West Indies, Central and South America and Africa. It approved the adoption of a standard African language, discouraged nonconformist religions and cults with passing reference to the Rastafarians. It condemned birth control.

The UNIA had by now lost much of its earlier dynamism and the Jamaican colonial administration added to the pressure by attempting to enforce a US$30,000 judgment handed down against the old UNIA in a New York court. Creditors auctioned the Kingston headquarters, Liberty Hall, at 76 King Street, although it was later restored to the organisation. They levied on Garvey's printing press and office equipment, and other items. These adversities broke the organisation financially, but not Garvey's fighting spirit, or his vision of a mighty black race, triumphant.

He did not give up his vision of a vigorous UNIA with international outreach and continued to prepare UNIA officers for leadership roles. He continued to write the front-page editorial of the weekly *Negro World* in New York and maintained contact with UNIA branches in the West Indies, Central America and Canada, confident that black nations would eventually take their rightful place in the world.

In 1935, in the face of financial and political adversities, Marcus Garvey decided to emigrate to Britain where he would be nearer the centre of world influence. For the next five years he maintained his international associations and worked steadfastly for the political unification of the black race. He lectured regularly on black nationalism, attended UNIA conferences in St Kitts, in other West Indian islands and in Canada. He continued to publish the *Black Man* journal but at six pence per copy and a small circulation, the journal was not viable. It ceased publication in 1939.

After attending a UNIA conference in Toronto in 1936, Garvey decided to open a School of African Philosophy in Toronto with lessons prepared in London. The main objective was to train blacks for world leadership in the UNIA. The course started in 1937, and was available "only to Negroes". Applicants were expected to have a high school education. Of the nine students who enrolled, eight graduated. Two years later a second correspondence course was offered in London at a cost of US$25. The advertisements named Garvey as principal. He had hoped to attract 1,000 students but only 11 registered. They came from the United States,

Nigeria, Uganda, Cape Province and South Africa. The training course had its greatest influence upon the Africans. Most of them were later involved in the liberation of their countries.

The university and technical institute which Garvey had envisaged for Jamaica materialised after his death. The University College of the West Indies was established in 1948, and the College of Arts, Science and Technology, in 1958. Social and educational programmes such as public high schools in rural areas, legal aid clinics and the beautification of public parks were all instituted after the island attained political independence in 1962. Poor health drained Garvey's energies in England, and in January 1940 he suffered a stroke. He died six months later on 10 June, in straitened circumstances.

In spite of his many frustrations and reversals of fortune, Garvey accomplished what no other black leader had done before. He created an international awareness of the right of the black race to coexist with other peoples of the world as equals. He awakened race consciousness and race pride in millions of working-class blacks in Africa as well as in the diaspora. He taught them to respect their own worth and to demand their rights as human beings.

Shortly before his death in 1940, the *Boston Guardian* wrote: "Already his name is legend, from Harlem to Zanzibar". The African, Mazilinko, pointed to his Messianic role when he said, "After all is said and done, Africans have the same confidence in Marcus Garvey which the Israelites had in Moses". (Hill: 1987) He fought for freedom, justice and equality and remains a source of inspiration to all popular movements for black people and to all who would aspire to lead the black race.

Twenty-four years after his death, in 1964, the Government of Jamaica honoured his name by declaring him Jamaica's first National Hero. His remains were brought from England and interred at the National Heroes Park. Even a quarter of a century after his death the controversy generated by the government's action revealed that a substantial core of middle-class Jamaicans still were not comfortable with Garvey's message of decolonisation and physical return of black people to Africa. It was left to a handful

Marcus Garvey's grave at National Heroes Park

of liberal journalists to convince their fellow-countrymen that "Garvey's greatness lay in the massive psychological warfare that he deployed to wipe out the inherited inferiority complex and the facelessness of the Negro in a white world". (Lewis: 1968)

Time, the judge, has gradually adjusted the balance. In 1983 the polls ranked Jamaica's national heroes as follows: Bustamante 37 per cent, Bogle 19 per cent, Garvey 15 per cent, Manley 14 per cent. By 1987 Garvey had soared to 56 per cent, Bustamante was at

20 per cent, Manley 16 per cent and Bogle 5 per cent. A January 1988 survey showed that 88 per cent of those polled agreed that Garvey's life and work should be taught in all schools.

Throughout his crowded, often difficult and tempestuous life, Marcus Garvey was above all, a champion of blacks, the one who fought fearlessly for their rights. As a young man, he lost his job at the Benjamin Company for supporting a strike of underpaid employees; at the beginning of his career as a race leader, he protested to the British consul in Port Limon about the victimisation of black banana workers by the American Fruit Company. Throughout his life he championed the cause of people of African origin worldwide, and more than any other African-American leader, he attacked the European partitioning of Africa. To this day African leaders pay tribute to him.

The statue in honour of Garvey erected at the St Ann Parish Library

In 1939, the year before his death, he expressed his vision of a liberated Africa. He saw it as "a country of the future. Her inhabitants, her everything tend toward an Africa of the natives, where they will rise to govern as other men are governing". (*Black Man*: 1939) That dream of black supremacy, at first slow in realisation, has taken on momentum with the dismantling of apartheid in South Africa in April 1994, through the exercise of the ballot by black South Africans for the first time, and the appointment of the first black president in that nation's history.

Today, more than ever before, Jamaicans honour Garvey as a black world leader and as a great national hero who gave his life to guarding over and protecting the rights of blacks.

CHAPTER 25

Building a new society: People from India, China and the Middle East

The accepted forms of Jamaica's institutional and social life are of European derivation, but African ways are commonly observable. On the one hand Europe provides a model for government, religion, law, property, education and language. On the other, there are African survivals in social customs, eating habits, the role of women in the family, in cooperative efforts for planting and reaping crops, in practices related to death and burial, in magical rites, in African words and phrases, tone and flavour of speech. There are African drum-beats and rhythms every-where and growing evidence that Africa is now the central force in Jamaica's great cultural movement. We have also seen that under European domination the attitude of the ruling minority was one of exploitation and repression to others of whatever race. Cheap labour was required to work the plantations whether that labour was provided by slaves from Africa or by indentured servants from Europe or Asia. The main difference between the slave and the indentured servant was that one was condemned to perpetual bondage whereas the other was freed after serving a specified period.

The Jews were among the first ethnic groups to settle in the island. They were brought as indentured servants in the early sixteenth century because of their skills in sugar manufacturing. Sugar led to the establishment of the plantation society which required vast capital and an unlimited supply of labour. After serving out their apprenticeship the Jews became traders, selling local dyewoods and other products to the Spanish mainland, and importing wines and European goods for the Jamaican and West Indian trade. Their business dealings continued under the English and helped to lay the foundations for the island's internal and external trade.

The English found it expedient to grant the Jews freedom of worship. Their presence was needed to maintain the statutory ratio between the white minority and the overwhelming black majority. The Jewish community has remained numerically small but their influence in trade and in the professions has been considerable.

Deficiency in the white population had always been a concern under the plantation system. Consequent upon emancipation the government and the white ruling class were faced with the possibility of a drastic reduction of labour supply and with the fact that being so greatly outnumbered by the black population, they could face extinction.

The need for adequate supplies of cheap labour to replace those who had begun to move away from the plantation, and also the need to maintain the ratio between blacks and whites led, in the first instance, to the importation of white indentured servants from Germany, Scotland, England and Ireland. Beginning in 1834, some 450 Europeans were recruited to establish villages in the mountainous interior. The Germans who were the first to arrive were expected "to introduce new methods of cultivation and to have in general a favourable influence on the Negro worker". They were given material and financial assistance in the hope that they would settle down as small farmers. Others were allocated in twos to the plantations where they were employed mainly as artisans on coffee plantations and cattle pens. A few were employed in the police force.

Mention has already been made of one German community that has survived into the twentieth century but generally the project was not successful. In all about 4,100 Europeans, hoping to escape famine and other hardships at home, came during an eleven-year period, between 1834 and 1845, in spite of strong discouragement. Anti-emigration groups such as "the friends of humanity" and local missionaries, including William Knibb, claimed that the climate was unhealthy, planters were cruel and the emigrants would be reduced to a state of near slavery.

The Europeans at first loved the climate and the easy lifestyle, but enthusiasm soon waned when they were faced with having to perform manual labour. They had signed a civil contract but found that a breach could land them in jail with a fourteen-day sentence. Many left the plantations for the city. A few, assisted by benefactors, migrated to the United States, and yellow fever and other tropical diseases reduced the numbers of those remaining. Of 127 persons who arrived early in 1841, only 24 were still with their original employers at the end of 1842.

The Jamaican Government's request to the Colonial Secretary in London to recruit Africans was not received favourably, because it was feared that this could be viewed as another form of African enslavement. Nevertheless, between 1841 and 1867, 10,000 Africans were recruited mainly from St Helena, Sierra Leone and adjoining coastal areas. Many of them had been liberated from slave ships by the British navy. As mentioned earlier, in the period leading up to and following the Morant Bay Uprising, several of these African labourers joined the African-Jamaicans in their struggles for social improvements.

Having failed to attract adequate numbers of cheap labour from Europe, North America and Africa, the government turned to India and China. Indian labour had already been tried in Mauritius and seemed to be successful. It was therefore thought that Jamaica and the other sugar producing British West Indian colonies could benefit similarly. Indian immigrants were however treated with great disrespect. They were paid lower than the African-Jamaican workers, and were therefore relegated to the bottom of the Jamaican society. Because their form of dress, lifestyle and language were unfamiliar to African-Jamaicans, they were singled out for ridicule and were often referred to as "slave coolies".

The Indian Government took care to protect those who had signed up for the indentured labour programme. It monitored recruitment, stipulated conditions under which the recruits should be employed, set the period of indenture, laid down guidelines for their transportation and repatriation, and appointed a Protector of Immigrants to see to their welfare in the country of destination. In Jamaica the Protector of Immigrants was not an Indian national. He was appointed by the Assembly and, as was to be expected, apparently showed more concern for the interests of the employers than for the welfare of the Indian labourers.

No emigrant contracted for service could be taken on board a vessel if he did not have in his possession a government permit. Theoretically, this permit was issued only after the emigrants and the contractor had appeared in person before a magistrate, and the details of the contract explained to the emigrants. The problem was, however, that the contract was in English and the vast majority of the recruits could not speak or understand English. Thousands of illiterate unsuspecting persons lured by rumours of prosperity and a better life in the West Indies, put their thumb marks to documents they did not understand. By so doing they signed away their independence for a fixed number of years. At first contracts were for one year, then they were set at two years and afterwards for five years.

Recruiting depots were opened in Madras and Calcutta and agents were paid up to £7 for every recruit. This sum was less than one-third the amount paid for European indentured labour. A few higher caste and better educated Indians joined the emigrants to Jamaica. They found, however, that on arrival they were treated as common labourers.

In 1845, the first 261 East Indians landed at Old Harbour Bay. There were 200 men and 28 women, mainly between the ages of 20 and 29 years, as well as 33 children under the age of 12. Another 1,851 arrived in 1846 and 2,439 in 1847. After that the Indian Government suspended immigration for the next 11 years while it re-examined this form of contractual labour. The immigration programme resumed in 1859 and continued regularly until the First World War when reduction in available shipping space halted the programme and it was eventually terminated.

Re-enactment of the East Indian arrival 150 years later, 1995

On arrival in Jamaica the Indians were distributed in groups of 20 and 40 to plantations contracting for their service. They went mainly to the parishes of St Thomas, Portland, St Mary, Westmoreland and Clarendon. They were transported in mule-drawn carts and later, after the introduction of the railway, in overcrowded freight cars without seats. They were taken to the nearest railway station, then had to walk the rest of the journey to the plantation. The conditions of their indenture were almost as debasing as slavery.

Little thought was given to their personal welfare. They were herded into dingy, overcrowded barracks, without proper flooring, often with no water supply or sanitary conveniences. A barrack of three or four small rooms accommodated several individuals or families in each room without respect for privacy. The detached kitchen, the crudest of broken down huts, usually served the occupants of more than one room. If the labourers worked "with only ordinary exertion" for the required five and a half or six days a week, they were paid one shilling a day and slightly more if they worked "with extraordinary exertion".

On arrival each immigrant was provided with a suit of clothing, agricultural implements and cooking utensils, at their employer's expense. The only deduction from their wages was two shillings and six pence for their weekly rations of rice, flour, dried fish or goat's flesh, peas and seasonings. Children were supplied with half rations at one shilling and threepence per week. Employers were instructed to pay them weekly, and not to treat them harshly. They were to receive quarterly checks by a doctor, and if they became ill they were to be taken to the nearest hospital for treatment.

Indentured workers are taken to estates on dray carts

These labourers kept poor health and suffered from tropical diseases such as malaria, yaws, and hookworm. Malaria was at that time incurable but could be prevented by administering regular doses of quinine. Employers were encouraged to supply them with the drug but this was not always done.

In order to ensure that employers received the maximum benefit from their labour, the Indians were confined to the plantation and could not leave the precincts unless they obtained a permit to do so. This applied even when they were on their annual two-week vacation leave. Like the Europeans, if they failed to work because of ill-health or for any other reason, or if they left their place of employment without permission, they could be fined or face a jail sentence.

On completion of their contract, they were issued with a certificate of freedom which enabled them to move freely about the country. However, they could not apply for their return passage until two years after the contract had expired. In addition, they had to have lived in the country for a total of ten years before they could be repatriated.

A ship was chartered periodically to transport the repatriates. However, by the time it arrived there were usually more passengers than could be accommodated. The healthier individuals were therefore left behind with the expectation that they would continue to work on the plantations. Those with families were required to pay the fares of the other family members. If they could not, they were forced to remain in the country.

In an attempt to reduce the numbers applying for repatriation, the law was amended so that after 1903 time-expired Indians had to apply for this facility within two years of completing the contract or forfeit their claim. Contracts could be renewed for one year, but these "second term coolies" were treated as if they were first-term labourers. Very few took up the option.

Their inability to understand and speak English placed them at an even greater disadvantage. Indian names were transposed at will by officials and many an individual ended up in Jamaica with a different name from the one he had been assigned at birth.

Recruitment areas in India

The first Indian labourers had come mainly from Northern India. Later others came from Uttar Pradesh, Bihar, the Central Provinces, Punjab and the North West Frontiers. Most may have been illiterate, but their cultural traditions and established religions predated Christianity and other Western cultures by three or four thousand years. In India magnificent temples intricately decorated with sculptures, paintings and precious stones dominate the countryside and dictate an ordered way of living. The people commemorate their social customs, their myths and legends in song and dance especially on occasions such as marriages, births, deaths and changing of the seasons. Most Westerners were ignorant of these traditions and employers unfamiliar with them described the Indians as heathens.

THE STORY OF THE JAMAICAN PEOPLE

No thought was given to accommodating their customs and beliefs. Indeed, non-Christian religions were outlawed and devout Hindus and Muslims were forced to congregate whenever and wherever was convenient. Some met by the riverside where they went to bathe and wash their clothes on weekends. Others kept little shrines in their homes where they could.

The Jamaican Government refused to recognise non-Christian marriages. The Indians were obliged to perform Christian ceremonies in addition to celebrating their traditional marriages or stigmatise their children as "bastards" who were unprotected under the Inheritance Law. It was not until 1957, more than 110 years after the first East Indians arrived, that the law was amended to permit non-Christian marriages.

Deliberate efforts were made by Christian religious organisations to convert them to Christianity. They coerced them into Christian marriages although they knew that the participants were often not Christians. They persuaded them to give up their children for adoption, or place them in orphanages with the excuse that the children would have better opportunities in the Jamaican society. In spite of these efforts, some Indian traditions survived. These include arranged marriages, the celebration of certain traditional festivals and community administration by the Council of Five (*panchayat*).

> In spite of modifications in the family system the words "family" and "relatives" have not lost their magic or magnetism in arousing traditional loyalties and emotions. The feeling of closeness between parents and children, brothers, sisters, cousins and uncles, and the concern for each other's welfare still exist. The elders may not be able to dictate, yet feel responsible for the welfare of younger ones."
> (Mansingh & Mansingh: 1976)

About 80 per cent of the Indian immigrants were Hindus and many of the rest were Muslims. Religious practices precluded Hindus from eating pork, chicken or fish and Muslims from eating beef. These dietary habits helped to set the Indians apart, so did the deliberate segregation of Indian and African-Jamaican dwellings by employers afraid of African-Jamaican influences upon the Indians. The Indians were treated by the African-Jamaican with the same prejudice and suspicion as the slaves had been treated by their white masters. The more successful they were at their tasks, the more they were resented by their fellow workers who saw them as threatening their livelihood.

For the most part the Indians were poor and knew nothing of the land the problems of the land to which they came. Their highly developed cultures and fixed caste systems, in which skin pigmentation and type of employment determined social status, caused the Indians to view the darker complexioned African-Jamaicans as socially inferior. They referred to them disparagingly as *kafari* or infidel. Even into the twentieth century some Indians refused to allow their children to attend the same schools with black children.

In 1938, almost 100 years after the arrival of the first East Indians, a survey revealed that on the major sugar estates living conditions were still cramped and unhealthy. Only one in every eight barracks was supplied with water from either pipes or wells; 38 per cent had no provision at all and about half took their water from rivers and ponds. Even when the river was some distance away, women had to trudge back and forth carrying pails of water and laundry.

Provision had been made for persons who so desired to commute the unexpired portion of their contract. They were required to repay, in cash, one-fifth of the sum outstanding, depending on the number of years or portion of a year remaining. They could also be released from the contract if the individual was suffering from some permanent disability or infirmity and the employer had requested his release. The indigent person could then be sent to hospital or be repatriated if and when shipping space was available.

Not all those who commuted their contract or completed the time returned to India. Between 1910 and 1911, for example, only one-fifth of the number eligible chose repatriation and overall only about one-third were repatriated. The others remained in the island.

Repatriation was not encouraged by either the Jamaican or the Indian Governments. The Jamaican Government found difficulty in paying all the return passages, and also saw repatriation as depleting the labour force. Contracting plantations assisted with the cost of the return fares but the sums collected were often insufficient. Also, many more Indians sought repatriation than was expected and ships were reluctant to take returning passengers from Jamaica because of the high death rate at sea.

The Indian Government claimed that too many returned as invalids and destitutes and had become a financial burden on the government. Often those returning had lived for such a long time away from their homeland that their relatives could not be located, and they had lost touch with their culture and traditions. They had become strangers in their own land. The Jamaican Government was only too pleased with the Indian Government's attitude as it saved the cost of the return fares.

Beginning in 1873, time-expired Indians were encouraged to remain in the island with the offer of a bounty in lieu of passage. They could choose to take either £12 in cash or 10 acres of land. Hindrances were also placed in their way to prevent them from taking advantage of the return passage and the compensation. For instance, one man married to a Jamaican-born

Indian woman was denied passage for his wife because she was a "foreigner".

Crown lands selected for allocation were usually to be found in the mountainous interior, infertile, of marginal value, and often without proper water supply. If the time-expired Indians refused to accept these allotments, the lands reverted to the Crown and they had to find lands of their own choosing, at their own expense. On rare occasions, as happened in Hayes, Clarendon, some succeeded in having basic infrastructure installed before they would accept the lands. In 1879, the land grant incentive was withdrawn, and in 1906 land grant in lieu of repatriation was discontinued. Those wishing to return to India now had to pay part of their return fare as well as purchase warm clothing and blankets for the journey.

In the 1880s when economic conditions in the island were at a low level because of the continued fall in sugar prices, thousands of rural unemployed, having no other means of earning a living, began the great trek to Central America in search of employment and better wages. They worked on the Panama Railroad and on the Panama Canal project. Others, including the Indians forsook the plantations hoping to find employment in the towns mainly in Kingston, but work was equally difficult to come by as there were no industries to absorb them.

Some Indians with skills practised their trade as jewellers, fishermen, barbers and the like. Others established themselves in villages as shopkeepers, first with a few basic items needed by the community; then as the

An Indian family in Golden Vale Plantation in 1896

Building a new society: People from India, China and the Middle East

business prospered they added additional services supplying dry goods and hardware. Beginning in the twentieth century, increasing numbers continued the migration to the towns, especially to Kingston and St Andrew, where they found it difficult to compete with the African-Jamaicans for the scarce jobs. They were forced to turn to what they knew best, agriculture. They became market gardeners.

They huddled together in shacks on the outskirts of the city, without amenities – light, water, roads or sanitary conveniences. They rented small plots of land, half-an-acre and less, planted vegetables and sold them from door to door in residential areas of the city. They managed to eke out a living and at the same time provided a valuable service to housewives who learned to eat healthier by including in their diet, the fresh vegetables supplied by the Indians.

The government, conscious that the growing worldwide depression, which began in the late 1920s, would have an even more disastrous impact on the already battered Jamaican economy, discouraged rural migration and the practice of market gardening. In 1931 a law was passed prohibiting the sale of items from door to door. The hope was that the market gardeners would be forced to return to the plantations and so help to save what was left of the sugar and banana industries. In response to public protest this law was amended to permit the sale of poultry, game, fruit and ground provisions to continue, but restriction on the sale of vegetables, which was almost entirely an Indian monopoly was not removed until 1945.

A few industrious Indians went into rice planting, the growing of vegetables and other crops on a large scale. Rice was the crop of preference but suitable lands were difficult to come by. They were to be had mainly on the plains of Westmoreland, where rundown sugar lands were selectively leased only to those willing to work three or four days a week on the plantation. However, successive years of drought and hurricane during the late 1890s brought the sugar planters to the brink of ruin, and they were obliged to lease more lands for rice planting. The arrangements were deliberately kept loose. Price per acre varied, so did conditions under which the lands were made available, and as soon as conditions began to return to normal and the sugar industry showed signs of reviving, owners took over the leased lands and put them once again into sugar cane cultivation. The acreage in rice was drastically reduced and an industry which could have been productive was stifled. Experiences such as these caused Indians to lose faith in Jamaican institutions and Jamaican justice. They bypassed the normal banking systems, preferring to entrust their savings and valuables to the care of some reliable member of the Indian community.

After the takeover of the rice lands, more displaced and unemployed

Indians joined the trek to the towns in search of employment. They added to the rapid urbanisation of Kingston, and lands once available for market gardening grew scarce and more expensive. Productive market gardens gave way to slums and housing projects. The already poor East Indian gardeners became poorer. The East Indian Progressive Society which was formed to protect their welfare, appealed to the government to make lands available in the Molynes Road, Waltham Park and Four Miles areas of St Andrew. However, the government, preferring to see the Indians back on the estates, declared that these lands were too expensive and advised the Indians to apply to land settlement schemes in the rural areas.

Economic conditions did not improve as sugar prices fell even lower in the face of worldwide recession beginning in 1929, and banana production was reduced as banana fields were rapidly wiped out by the Panama and leaf spot diseases. Sugar and banana were the only two major industries employing large numbers of persons. Independent small farmers in the rural communities were also suffering as they were losing more and more of their banana crops to disease.

Money became a scarce commodity. The labouring classes especially in Kingston faced starvation and the government was forced to institute relief work to avert a crisis. There were too few jobs for the numbers seeking employment and as a result, the jobless African-Jamaicans unwilling to share the few jobs, turned their hostility on the East Indian minority. They were forced out of the queues and Government Relief Programme selectors refused to employ them claiming that they were not capable of doing anything other than agricultural work. Those who remained on the banana plantations were employed for only two days a week throughout a whole crop season.

The Second World War caused severe restrictions of imported goods and this encouraged some Indians to enter into large scale rice cultivation once again. However, as soon as the war ended, they were once more forced out of business by the importation of cheaper foreign rice and the termination of their leases by landowners hoping for improvement in the sugar industry. The Indians found difficulty acquiring lands for purchase. Of 17,318 East Indians owning approximately 11,600 acres in 1926, two high caste Indians owned 4,037 acres. The remaining 7,563 acres had to be shared for the rest of the Indian population: an average of less than half-an-acre per person.

Striking aspects of Indian contribution to Jamaican culture are in the festivals and in jewellery. African-Jamaicans participate in the *hosay* and *divali* festivals although few fully understand their symbolism. The *hosay* is a Muslim celebration re-enacting the war between two brothers, sons of Mohammed, their death and burial. It stretches over nine nights of

A *hosay taj*

mourning. The sword fight and replica of the tomb of the slain brothers are central to the festival activities, the processions and the dances. Where there are significant numbers of East Indians, for example, in the parish of Clarendon, African-Jamaicans have helped to keep the *hosay* festival tradition alive. They build the *taj*, the replica of the tomb, perform the sword dances and participate in other activities. The dances associated with the festival have lost much of their significance and in recent years have begun to evolve into a western-style dance.

Divali is a Hindu celebration which takes place usually in late October or early November, on the darkest night of the year. It is associated with the reaping of grain and celebrates in song and dance, the victory of good over evil. It also celebrates the return of Prince Rama after 14 years of exile. At the time of *divali* houses are cleaned, everywhere is brightly lit and everyone is in good spirits.

Elements of Indian dress have been incorporated into the jonkunoo dance, adapted from African dance forms and performed usually at Christmas time. Indian jewellery has significantly influenced the Jamaican jewellery trade, especially the style of bangles which are sometimes referred to as slave bangles.

The recruitment of indentured labour to work in foreign countries was never popular in India. The Indian Government had from 1875 opposed the scheme because of the oppression of the Indians in the Caribbean. Faced with mounting opposition, the British Colonial Office put an end to the programme in 1917, in spite of pressure from colonial governments

Celebrating *Satnarine pujah*

THE STORY OF THE JAMAICAN PEOPLE

to continue the traffic. Lack of transportation during the First World War was also a contributory factor, as three of the six ships normally engaged in transporting the labourers were commandeered for war service. The last set of Indians to be brought to Jamaica arrived in 1914. The last repatriates left in 1929 and legal repatriation ended in 1930.

Over a period of 70 years, more than 36,400 East Indians were brought to Jamaica and approximately one-third returned to their homeland. The estimated number of Indians living in Jamaica today is about 70,000, double the number who came under the indenture programme. The majority are still engaged in agricultural pursuits although in recent years some have moved into business and commerce and the professions.

The Chinese also constitute a separate racial group "which serves as a cushion between whites and blacks". Compared with the East Indians, their numbers are small and of little or no political significance. They were first brought to the island as indentured labourers between 1854 and the 1880s. The first Chinese to the West had been brought to work in the gold mines of California in 1848. Two years later, another group of workers was brought to Panama to help with the construction of the Panama Railroad, but they fared badly in the equatorial forests and mosquito infested swamps through which the railroad passed. Large numbers died from malaria and other diseases, from starvation and from physical abuse.

They insisted on leaving the country and in 1854, after some negotiation, 472 were sent to Jamaica in exchange for Jamaican labour. These Chinese were in such poor physical shape that most of them died within a short while. The government then brought in approximately 328 from Hong Kong but again the losses were high. Of a total of 800 from Panama and Hong Kong only 200 were still alive at the end of eight months. This possibly gave rise to the rumour that Chinese men were weak, and were therefore counted "two for one". Between 1864 and 1870, an additional 200 were also brought from Trinidad and British Guiana. They were apparently in better condition than those who had come earlier.

Chinese labourers were given three-year contracts which included the repatriation clause. They were housed in the same stifling, insanitary conditions, in overcrowded barracks as the Indians were allotted. They carried out the same menial tasks as other field labourers, worked for the same low wages of one shilling six pence a day, six days a week.

They protested about the long working hours and some Chinese labourers in St Thomas took strike action and refused to work the twelve-hour day. The time was reduced to nine hours per day. This is one of the earliest recorded strikes in Jamaica. As harsh as their conditions were, most Chinese served out their period of indenture although a few deserted to the towns.

They found openings in rural villages, set themselves up as grocers and at one time had almost complete monopoly of rural grocery shops so much so that the phrase used to describe a grocery store was "Chinese shop". This was a significant contribution to opening up the interior of the island and also to providing a vital service to villagers, at first bringing them basic necessities and as time passed, a wider range of goods. The average rural dweller was poor and usually had no fixed income. The Chinese shopkeeper accommodated his customers with credit, by selling in small quantities and by barter. A customer could barter a few pounds of ginger, pimento, annatto, coffee or other economic crop which would be weighed, valued, and the equivalent in groceries exchanged. Any balance due to the customer was paid in cash. From time-to-time the shopkeeper would also lend small sums of money to a client, with the assurance that the debt would be repaid in due course.

During the 1880s when the departure of African-Jamaican and East Indian labour from the plantation appeared to pose a threat to production, the Jamaican Government turned once again to Hong Kong for more cheap labour. News had by then spread of the success of some of the earlier Chinese immigrants. Some 680 farm labourers, lured by prospects of prosperity took up the offer. Not all of them were indentured labourers. Some borrowed the passage money, and relatives in Jamaica sent for others.

They set out from Macao on the South China coast and, after ten weeks at sea, arrived in Jamaica on 12 July 1884. Their wooden vessel, driven partly by steam and partly by sail, was so badly battered in a typhoon that it had to be abandoned at the first Canadian port of call and the passengers transferred to another vessel to continue their onward journey to Jamaica. Among them were 501 men and 105 women, 84 boys and girls including three babies born at sea. There were also on board a translator and a herbal doctor. The ship was provisioned with familiar Chinese foodstuffs: salted eggs, salted vegetables, rice, cooking oil, vinegar, soybean sauce, fowls, pigs and other livestock as well as medicines. (Lee: 1957)

Their first experience in Jamaica was most disheartening. On disembarkation they were taken to the Spanish Town prison and kept there under armed guard until they were shipped out in mule carts to the various plantations which had contracted for them. They were treated with the same distrust and faced the same discrimination which earlier Chinese and Indian labourers had experienced.

Most of them were Hakka people, farmers from Kwang Tung province in South East China with a climate similar to that of Jamaica. In Jamaica they found familiar medicinal herbs, fruits and vegetables which included sugar cane, bananas, plantains and dasheen. They had all come with one goal in mind, to acquire wealth and return to build China.

Once they had fulfilled the contract they left the estates and sought employment with their sponsors and with other established members of the Chinese community. They were prepared to perform menial tasks until they could acquire a sufficient amount of money to set themselves up in business. Some obtained small loans; others received their start from "fwee chen", the equivalent of the African-Jamaican "partner money" or "susu". "Fwee chen" required each participant to contribute an agreed amount regularly, whether it was weekly or monthly. When it was an individual's time to be paid, he or she received the draw for that week and this continued until all participants were re-paid.

In 1888, some 800 other immigrants arrived from Hong Kong. By then Jamaica was becoming a popular destination for Chinese immigrants. No doubt with prodding from the local business community, fearful that the Chinese were taking over the retail grocery trade, the government, in 1905, began to restrict their entry to the island. Immigrants then had to apply for registration with the immigration authorities, be recommended by some member of the local Chinese community who had to give an undertaking that they would not become a burden on the society and guarantee their good conduct. An official permit was then issued which the immigrant had to produce on arrival.

There was no Chinese consular representation on the island and the immigrants had little recourse in law. Their only official contact and source of appeal was through the Chinese Embassy in London, and it took a very long time for them to get action. They therefore established their own social institutions which are still in operation today. The Chinese Benevolent Association offers humanitarian and social services; the Chinese Sanitarium takes care of the sick, and an old folks home provides for the aged and indigent.

During the latter part of the nineteenth century and the early years of the twentieth century, a halfway house was established in Panama where prospective immigrants to Jamaica could await clearance. They could wait for as long as five years and more. Sometimes the permit was not forthcoming as unscrupulous agents, having taken money from sponsors in China and in Jamaica had no intention of troubling themselves any further. Those stranded in Panama could not return home or they would lose face. Some took the only honourable way out and committed suicide.

In 1910, the immigration law, as it affected Chinese and persons from the Middle East, was further amended. It required them to deposit £30 on arrival, which was returnable after one month. They were also required to demonstrate written and spoken familiarity with at least 50 words in either English or French or Spanish, as well as undergo a physical examination.

The literacy requirement was not always rigidly enforced and at times immigrants were admitted who could only sign their names in English.

Up to 1894, it was illegal for Chinese nationals to leave their country. But those who came to Jamaica were prepared to take the risk, in the hope that they could amass sufficient wealth and return to China with dignity. They were discouraged by relatives at home from acquiring property in Jamaica lest they be tempted to settle permanently in the island. They therefore rented land instead of purchasing it. Not many, however, worked the land although they were originally farmers.

Because of the language difficulty, some Chinese were cheated in land transactions just as the Indians were and they were made to believe that it was the government that had taken their land away. They lost faith in the official institutions and just as the Indians did, they selected a reliable Chinese shopkeeper to serve as banker.

As soon as they could they branched out into new business ventures, into laundries and restaurants and bakeries in addition to the usual retail and wholesale grocery trade. Though few in number, they have contributed significantly to Jamaica's commercial and industrial growth. They became general importers and distributors of rice, saltfish, saltmeats, flour and cornmeal and made these commodities staples in the Jamaican diet.

In the early years, because of ignorance of Chinese dress, African-Jamaicans referred disparagingly to the black, silk outfits worn by the Chinese as "oil-skin". When the thrifty Chinese turned flour bags into suits, they were criticised. They were disparaged and insulted by the local village bullies who thought that they did not understand what was being said. Jamaicans were suspicious of Chinese customs relating to death as they did not understand the Chinese traditions and the philosophy that only those who gave life should first look on or touch the dead. No one else was allowed to view the body until all the rituals were completed.

The myth about Chinese men being weak was attributed to the amount of rice they ate. The truth was that the Chinese ate much larger quantities of vegetables and meats and had a much more varied diet than the average

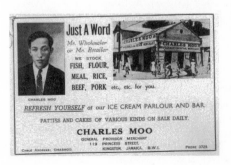

Jamaican. Mixed marriages were frowned upon by both sides and even today are accepted with some reservation. If anything unfortunate happens in such a marriage, the Chinese relatives tend to blame the bad luck on the fact that it was interracial. Children born to Jamaican and Chinese parents are "not quite good enough". Chinese mockingly refer to them as "half Chinese" or "eleven o'clock children": "not quite there, not quite twelve o'clock".

Gradually these prejudices have faded as African-Jamaicans developed familiarity with some of the Chinese customs and the Chinese have adapted to some Jamaican lifestyles. Their economic success has caused some African-Jamaicans to envy their good fortune without appreciating the amount of hard work that has gone into their endeavours. During the 1930s riots, the disaffected in the Jamaican society vented their envy and frustrations on the more successful members of minority groups, especially the Chinese. Their business places were frequently robbed and in extreme cases, owners were murdered.

One member of the Chinese community expressed it this way:

Chinese Free
Mason Society
participating in
Jamaica's
Tercentenary
Celebrations,
1955

The reason for the apparent discrimination is not racial but economic, because these small concerns are profitable only when operated on a family basis. These concerns pay no salaries and money is withdrawn only for the necessities of operation and living expenses. Consequently, the meagre profits accumulate and the capital grows until it is sufficiently large to provide a good standard of living for the operators. (*The Star*, 8 August, 1936)

For a long time the colonial government continued to discriminate against the minority groups by introducing laws restricting daily opening hours of business places, compelling them to curtail their operations although the businesses were operated by family members and were therefore not affected by the law. Chinese and Jews were singled out for additional taxation. Chinese, whether new arrivals or returning residents, were required to pay an additional head tax of £5 although other foreigners were exempt.

Nevertheless, the rate of new arrivals kept increasing. In a 70-year period (1854-1924), 4,000 Chinese emigrated to Jamaica. In the next six years (1925-30), an additional 2,000 arrived. Compared with the African-Jamaican population and even with the number of Indians, the figure was relatively small but the Jamaican Government, facing economic pressures of the depression years with thousands of unemployed having no prospects of jobs in the immediate future, decided to close its doors to Chinese immigrants. After 7 January 1931, only children under 14-years-of-age were allowed in on a student permit. Returning Chinese residents were required to produce a re-entry permit which had to be obtained prior to departure. Restrictions were tightened further in 1940 when only diplomats, tourists and students with permits were allowed entry. Sometime later limited quotas were granted for wives, children and parents. Jamaican-born Chinese had to show proof of birth.

A school solely financed and operated by the Chinese and established in the latter part of the nineteenth century which prepared Chinese children for a prolonged stay in China, was excluded from government financial assistance although Christian denominational schools all qualified for grants.

Chinese immigrants were mainly farmers but only a few appear to have gone into farming. However, when foreign trade was restricted during the Second World War, some turned to rice cultivation but abandoned the rice fields as soon as the war ended, because of government policy to allow the importation of cheaper rice in competition with the locally grown product.

The Chinese custom of using fireworks to celebrate special occasions became a favourite Jamaican attraction, especially at Christmas time. It was however banned in the middle of this century when elements in the society began using it for antisocial purposes. In more recent times Chinese celebratory dances such as the lion dance have been included among the annual National Festival events. This is one area of the creative arts which demonstrates the integration process.

Chinese industry and their disciplined approach to work, their care and nurturing of children and the emphasis they place on education and on family life, set examples for the Jamaican society. The tradition of the extended family in Chinese culture parallels that in African cultures. So is respect for age whether it be to a member of the immediate family, or to an outsider. In these ways the Chinese have helped to preserve such values in the Jamaican society.

A much smaller number of immigrants from the Middle East have also made their contribution to the building of the Jamaican nation. In the early years of the twentieth century, some Jews, Lebanese and others from the Middle East began arriving. We will recall that Jews helped to finance Columbus' expedition to the West; a few had come with the first Spanish explorers to Jamaica, and others had been brought as indentured servants to help establish the sugar industry in the sixteenth century. Since the beginning of the sixteenth century there has always been a Jewish community in Jamaica.

Religion has been a bond. Although non-Christian religions were not tolerated for a very long time in this predominantly Christian society, the Jews were allowed to establish their own places of worship. They, like other minority groups, faced discrimination but they had early established control over the Jamaican economy and because of their financial strength they could not be ignored. Over the centuries small numbers have come and joined the already established merchant class. They have prospered and in times of crisis have often come to the rescue of the insolvent plantation owners.

Elias Issa, (back row, centre, a Lebanese who migrated to Jamaica in 1894), with his family

Building a new society: People from India, China and the Middle East

The more recent arrivals from the Middle East left their homes in Palestine and Lebanon, then part of the former country of Syria, to escape political and religious discrimination and to seek a better way of life in a new country. In the redistribution of power after the First World War, Syria was carved up politically. The new geographical and political boundaries, some of them under European "protection", uprooted generations of settled people and bred animosity among communities which normally had lived together in peace for centuries.

Jamaica became a stopover point for many en route to the land of opportunity, the United States. Others encouraged by success stories of relatives and friends on the island, chose to remain. They did not come as indentured servants; this was "chain" migration where prospective migrants learn of opportunities, are provided with transportation and have initial accommodation and employment arranged by means of primary social relationships with previous migrants. (Nicholls: 1956) A few came by accident. Having bought passage on a westward bound ship, often from Marseilles, they disembarked whenever the ship reached what they considered might be a suitable destination. Sometimes that place happened to be Jamaica. Many were farmers, some were professionals but in the beginning they were prepared to take any form of employment.

Some Lebanese, (often referred to as Syrians) at first went into banana production but found difficulty breaking the entrenched cartel of the fruit companies. They therefore followed members of the older Jewish community and became merchants and traders. One of the easiest ways of getting started was to become a pedlar. The future pedlar would identify an area, survey the possibilities, obtain a loan from one of the more established members of the "Syrian" community, acquire a modest amount of merchandise that was likely to find acceptance in the area, then sell his wares of cloth and household items from door to door. As business improved, the pedlar would acquire a donkey to transport the goods, then later upgrade his status with a buggy and still later to a motor vehicle. Householders greatly appreciated this convenience although their choice was limited. The fact that they could purchase the goods at home and pay in small instalments made the arrangement even more attractive. Eventually when a pedlar amassed sufficient money, he opened a small dry goods shop and gave up travelling on the road.

Because of European interest in the Middle East, the immigrants from Palestine and Lebanon were usually familiar with some European language, particularly French or English. They therefore did not have the same difficulty in communicating as the Indians and Chinese before them.

They were thrifty, worked hard, and where they could, paid periodic visits to their homeland to ensure that their children retained the culture and language of their ancestors. The Second World War disrupted this practice. Fewer individuals were able to share this experience, and so the younger generation became more rapidly integrated into the Jamaican society.

Whereas African family structures were seriously eroded over 300 years of British rule, the later immigrants from India, China and the Middle East were not subject to such a long and intensive period of deculturisation. As a result they have retained more of their original cultural values while at the same time integrating into the Jamaican society. They have retained religious rites and festivals and art forms which have enriched the emerging Jamaican nation while the Rastafarians were displacing Babylon.

CHAPTER 26

Day da light, oh

There are mountain-top times in the Jamaica story when "day da light" and sunrise comes, as if we were standing on the peak on a clear dawn when:

> The innocence of daybreak revealed the island like a cut beryl set in a glassy sea. The sharp ranges were of precious stone. The white clouds were intense drifts of the pure cold atmosphere. The rivers lay veiled in motionless slumber like opal serpents. Port Antonio shone in the ring of its harbour like a snowy lily in an azure jug. And far away to the north-east the thin lake line of Cuba was steady against the paler blue of sky and sea. (Pringle)

The Jamaican finds his story in the landscape; the lake line of Cuba and the harbour of Port Antonio summon up ancestral memories of a separating sea, of slave ships and perpetual exile; the mountain ranges tell of places of refuge for blacks in search of freedom; the plantations on the coastal plains speak of having been for 300 years the battlefields of Africa's conflict with Europe; of blacks stripped of the rights of ownership, of rights to the labour of their bodies or to the possession of their own children, of blacks in conflict with whites who had everything; a political monopoly, control of the legislature, the guardianship and protection of Britain.

The struggle lasted for just over 300 years, from 1655 to 1962. It covers four phases. At the end of the first phase, in 1739, England recognised the right of two bands of maroons to freedom and independence. A century later, in 1834, the second phase ended when Britain passed the Act of Emancipation by which all slaves in the British empire were set free.

But the conflict was far from over. The blacks soon found that slavery did not die in 1834 and that full freedom did not come in 1838. The complete mastery of one man over another was no longer legal, but the economic mastery of the estate owners over landless free blacks still prevailed, the mastery of the educated over the illiterate, of the white and the brown over the black. The third phase came to its climax with the Morant Bay Uprising in 1865.

In that year the character of the conflict changed. The objectives sharpened: the right of the black labour force to a better way of life, their right to representative government and to racial equality. This claim made with increasing urgency by Robert Love and by Marcus Garvey in the first quarter of the twentieth century transformed a riot at Frome in 1938 into a critical turning-point in a cultural and political revolution that swept the Jamaican people to independence in 1962, when white authority transferred the seals and symbols of power to duly constituted black authority. The empowering forces were race consciousness and an emerging nationalism.

Neville Dawes in his *Prolegomena to Caribbean Literature*, spoke of this aspect of Garvey's work: "There is one element in the African's experience of the New World that does not seem to have been given much attention and that is his attitudes, changing attitudes, to Africa as Mother and to the African continent. I consider this to be vital to an understanding of what is going on in the Caribbean not simply in the creation of literature but in the general area of culture and cultural development."

Dawes spoke of various changes in our attitude to Africa.

> The first phase was one of pure plangency, one of the pure bereavement of the child dispossessed of its mother – the cry echoed on the shores of Hwyidah, perhaps in the Ewe language, as the slave ships, full of Africans who had been tricked aboard, pulled away to the dark sea-journey. Our brothers and sisters have gone, the dirge said. On what shore will they land? The second phase was characterised by the gradually darkening memory of Mother Africa, as my forefathers of the Diaspora began to learn new ways of necessity.

At the third phase, the process of colonisation became Europe's battle for control of the African-Jamaican's mind. Dawes pictured it; at this point the real Mother Africa was almost dead in the mind of the diaspora and the colonisation of the African in the Western world was almost complete. At this point Africa became "the fully dark continent of cannibals and snakes and powerful juju and not as a source of democratic forms of society of justice of the realistic understanding of the divine".

In this setting Garvey's trumpet-call to racial pride and an affirmation of racial identity set African-Jamaicans to the task of reclaiming their identity and their heritage. The national movement and the cultural revolution initiated by Garvey were the revolutionary forces that released Jamaicans from colonialism.

The process began in the mind, with self-discovery and self-liberation. It was often painful and distressing. We who belong to later generations need to enter for a moment into the inner world of two of our griots, Claude McKay and Una Marson, in order to understand the significance of this affirmation of a racial identity and the recognition that the basic heritage of the African-Jamaican people is African.

Claude McKay was from the James Hill area in North Clarendon, with its glorious landscape, its superb view of the Bull Head Mountain and its independent country folk, amongst whom he grew up, the son of a small farmer. He described rural Jamaican society in *Banana Bottom*, which was published in New York in 1933, but which pictured rural Jamaica in the early 1900s. For a brief period McKay served as a policeman in Kingston and then emigrated to the United States where he became a leading figure in a distinguished group of black American writers during the Harlem renaissance. Una Marson was a black middle-class Jamaican whose *Heights and Depths* and *The Moth and the Star,* established her as Jamaica's outstanding woman poet of the 1920s and 1930s.

McKay and Una Marson write as Jamaicans with anguish and triumph about Africa as mother country and African-Jamaicans as kinsfolk. Before journeying with them through that experience let us remind ourselves that our own conflict is a part of the larger story of African-Americans, our island struggle of Africa against Europe, black against white, a part of a story hemispheric in scale and unbroken in sequence from the 1520s, when black maroons took to the mountains of Hispaniola. Further, just as the creative dynamic in Jamaican history came from the African and not from the European so throughout plantation America "all along it was the people who had African slave forbears and had suffered the anguish of the early plantations, who were giving the new Caribbean society cultural shape and purpose as they once brought, through their labour, economic significance and prominence to the sugar-producing region". (Nettleford: 1978) We bear in mind also Rex Nettleford's warning that:

> It is a mistake to sacrifice in all this the specificity of racial cultural concerns which are self-evident in every single territory of the Caribbean. Not only have the vast majority in places like Jamaica been the survivors of an oppressive system, they are still being the survivors of a global conspiracy to keep the Black in his place, whatever his demonstrated potential as a creative resourceful being. (Nettleford: 1978)

We will spend time in the company of McKay and Una Marson because their message remains relevant. Their work, their suffering, their confirmation of racial identity, of historic achievement, their example of intellectual integrity, enable us as their successors and kinsfolk "to chart our own courses along universal paths to freedom and dignity for the people".

McKay's *Banana Bottom* stated the African-Jamaican position. It is Jamaica's first self-portrait and the first classic in Jamaican and West Indian prose. The author holds a place of honour in our history for he led the way in creating a Jamaican literature that draws its inspiration from the African-Jamaican historical experience. He wrote as eyewitness, novelist, chronicler and interpreter, realist and visionary. McKay introduced us also to an elderly Englishman, Walter Jekyll, who is Squire Gensir in the story. Jekyll taught him that the folklore of the Jamaican people is:

> Your spiritual link between you and your ancestral origin . . . My mind is richer because I know your folk-lore. This man was the first to enter into the simple life of the island negroes and proclaim significance and beauty in their transplanted African folk tales and in the words and music of their native dialect. Before him it had generally been said the Negroes were inartistic. But he had found artistry where others saw nothing . . . wherever the imprints of nature and humanity were to be found, there also were the seeds of creative life.

Models of greatness were absent from that colonial society. The past was forbidden. Africa was taboo. A black minister, the Rev. Lambert, in *Banana Bottom* urged his predominantly black congregation to reject Africa, for "there are no people so addicted to sorcery (Obeah) as we negroes. The continent we came over from is cursed and abandoned of God because of magic. We brought along the curse from there . . . Give up our ancient God of darkness. Throw the jungle out of your hearts and forget Africa".

Claude McKay

Self-rejection was the doctrine the Euro-African preached. Self-fulfilment was to be found in Europe. In consequence there were neither heroes nor any unifying memory of great achievements in Jamaican society. "Greatness could not exist in the backwoods. Nor anywhere in the colony. To them and to all the islanders greatness was a foreign thing. The biggest man in the colony was the governor. But not even the most ignorant peasant thought him great."

Banana Bottom is novel and allegory. The central character, Bita, is a symbol of the African-Jamaican seeking for and assenting her African identity in a colonial society. It is also a shattering indictment of a colonial system of education based on the principle of black inferiority: "Too bad she should have been taken and educated above her station," Busha Glengley said of Bita, and "Anyway, look out about teaching them wrong ideas. They may use them against us some day . . . Yes, us, of the white race . . ."

Bita, who had been grievously wronged in her childhood, symbolises the uprooted African-Jamaican, who somehow preserves that unsurrendering element of personality that manifested itself in the long series of liberation struggles. Although educated in Britain, she remained African:

> Let me tell you right now that a white person is just like any other human being to me. I thank God that although I was brought up and educated among white people I have never wanted to be anything but myself. I take pride in being coloured and different, just as an intelligent white person does in being white. I can't imagine anything more tragic than people torturing themselves to be different from their natural unchangeable selves.

Bita knew that in Jamaican society colour dictated standing. She took this into account without passion or anger:

> What could a cultivated Negro girl from the country hope for better than a parson. Marrying a good parson was a step higher than marrying a schoolmaster. If she had happened to be born a light brown or yellow girl she might, with her training, easily get away with a man of a similar complexion . . . but she was in the black and dark-brown group and there were no prospects of her breaking into the intimate social circles of the smart light-brown and yellow group.

In the end, Bita moved from living with the missionaries who had adopted, reared and educated her, and went back to her own father and his peasant home. "She had grown out of that soil, his own soil, and had gone abroad only for polishing. Her choosing of her own will to return there filled him with pride, so strong was his affection for the land."

The symbolism of Bita's return was highlighted by a brown-black controversy that raged at the time over a switch in civil service requirements; "Some of the strongest support for the change had come from a group of black men, most of whom had near-white or white wives and light-coloured children; among these was a black clergyman with a large family of freckled reddishly-coloured children." McKay derided the idea that civil service posts should be given to peasant youths fresh from the huts who possessed no background but were clever enough to pass the examinations. There were in *Banana Bottom* aged white-headed blacks who remembered that "the honorable and reverend black legislator had not even had the benefit of a hut as background but that the roof over his head had been the trash-house of the sugar-cane plantation and his bed the trash-heap".

Una Marson, (centre) at the BBC

Bita carried her affirmation of identity and of kinship with other African-Jamaicans further by marrying one of them, the drayman, Jubban. The browns and whites saw her as "only a nigger gal", but "she was proud of being a Negro girl. And no sneer, no sarcasm, no banal ridicule of a ridiculous world could destroy her confidence and pride in herself and make her feel ashamed of that fine body that was the temple of her high spirit".

Bita moves against a richly tapestried background of African-Jamaican people; a gregarious, often raucous yard and village society with its own art forms and cults which it preserved against the preachings of the church and the hostility of the powerful. Just as African-Jamaicans finally achieved freedom and justice by their own long-sustained efforts, so throughout rural Jamaica the African-Jamaican people drew on their African cultural heritage. They were a part of a deeply segmented society but culturally they belonged to Africa. McKay emphasised this by showing that it was Africa that called most powerfully to British-educated Bita. At the market Bita,

> mingled in the crowd, responsive to the colour, the swell and press of it. It gave her the sensation of a reservoir of familiar kindred humanity into which she had descended for baptism. She had never had that big moving feeling as a girl . . . if she had never gone abroad for a period so long . . . she might never have had the experience . . .

Accents and rhythms, movements and colours, nuances that might have passed unnoticed if she had never gone away were now revealed to her in all their striking detail.

Bita loved the harvest festival, Sunday school, picnic, a tea meeting at Kojo Jeems yard where she delighted in "dancing down the barrier between high breeding and common pleasures under her light-stamping feet until she was one with the crowd". She could easily understand the pungent perfume of the pimento exciting love with the pickers up to their necks in it, squatting upon the leaves with stems and berries in their hands, which dominated the atmosphere with their odour; and the old-time revival with a thin little black woman with a bright bandana upon her head, beating a drum and followed by other women and a few men all bearing supple-jacks and singing

> Rolling, rolling, rolling down
> Ages rolling, rolling ages
> Rolling along for a golden crown
> Silver shoes and silver clothes . . .

Then the dancing began. These bodies poised straight in religious ecstasy and dancing vertically up and down while others transformed themselves into curious whirling shapes, seemed filled with an ardent nearly-forgotten spirit, something ancestral recaptured in the emotional fervour, evoking in her memories of pictures of savage rites, tribal dancing with splendid swaying plumes, and the brandishing of the supple-jacks struck her as symbolic of raised and clashing spears . . . Magnetised by the spell of it, Bita was drawn nearer and nearer into the inner circle until with a shriek she fell down.

When Bita had recovered her senses under the mimosas where she had been taken, she was at a loss to explain what had happened to her. She remembered experiencing an overwhelming mesmeric feeling and a sensation of becoming a different person in a strange place and suddenly there was lacuna and she was conscious of nothing more.

Herein lies the message of *Banana Bottom*, with its portrayal of the great cultural achievement of the disenfranchised mass of the African-Jamaican people, who in their pulsating, gregarious way responded to Africa, preserved their tradition of open spaces, and dance, drumming, songs, proverbs, riddles, spirituals, kumina, myal and other cults, and the yard, road, village, their theatre, where they developed an indigenous Jamaican culture.

Even where the forms or phrases were copied from the great house, even where European-style dances and rituals were taken over, something African was retained. The spirituality that existed before the missionaries came had its source in Africa, in ancestral memories of communication with God or the gods at any time and in any place, all a natural part of the African way of life.

Looking, then, at the folk culture and the African way of life, we learn respect for the inner thoughts of the African, whose concepts of the individual human being and of the child, stand in sharp contrast to white plantation society's example of social irresponsibility and sexual promiscuity. These are embodied in McKay's Marse Arthur, with his "healthy pink face, betraying not the slightest sign of mind, restless eyes and fleshy mouth, known for his amorous embodiment of social irresponsibility". In opposition to this, we have the African concept of a child:

> In African societies, the birth of a child is a process which begins long before the child's arrival in the world and continues long thereafter. It is not just a single event . . . Nature brings the child into the world, but society creates the child into a social being, a corporate person. For it is the community which must protect the child, feed it, bring it up, educate it and in many other ways incorporate it into the wider community. Children are the buds of society and every birth is the arrival of 'spring' when life shoots out and the community thrives. (Mbiti: 1970)

We continue in the company of Claude McKay as the outstanding Jamaican poet of his generation. He and Una Marson rooted Jamaican literature in the Jamaican experience in a way that had not been done before. He stripped away the hypocrisies with which Jamaicans of that period habitually shrouded the colour bar and race hatred. By portraying his own experience he revealed the crippling effects of self-contempt, self-doubt, self-rejection, the haunting uncertainties and anxieties caused by a feeling of inadequacy. At a critical moment in our history his works set Jamaicans on the road to self-liberation, to the discovery of a country that was theirs, of a nation and race that were theirs.

Angry at racial separatism and colour discrimination and "a social system characterized by strongly entrenched class-colour differences", McKay pictured the contrast between Backra's world and Quashie's world, to which he belonged:

> You tase petater an' you say it sweet
> But you no know how hard we wuk fe it . . .
> De sun hot like when ketch a town;
> Shade tree look temptin, yet we caan' lie down . . .
> You see petater tear up groun', you run

McKay felt the contrast deeply. He rebelled against Backra's view of the picturesque peasant life.

Watch how dem tourist like fe look
Out 'pon me little daughter,
Wheneber fe her tu'n to cook
Or fetch a pan of water:
De sight look gay;
Dat is one way,
But I can tell you say,
'Nuff rock'tone in de sea, yet none
But those 'pon lan' know 'bouten sun.

McKay's inner conflict worsened when as a policeman he had to enforce
the laws of the white world against people of his race. The conflict became
an agony when he had to witness the flogging of a black prisoner.

I dared not look at him,
My eyes with tears were dim,
My spirit filled with hate
Of Man's depravity,
I hurried through the gate.

But he could not separate himself from the system he served by hurrying
through the gate. He returned – to comfort the prisoner and affirm his
brotherhood with him. Then, making his exit from his country to
America, he came face-to-face with racial hostility, symbolised in the
White House:

Your door is shut against my tightened face,
And I am sharp as steel with discontent,
But I possess the courage and the grace
To bear my anger proudly and unbent . . .
Oh, I must search for wisdom every hour,
Deep in my wrathful bosom sore and raw,
And find in it the superhuman power
To hold me to the letter of your law!
Oh, I must keep my heart inviolate
Against the potent poison of your hate.

As Lloyd Brown points out in his study of Claude McKay's work, the
poet was searching for a distinctive identity that harmonised West Indian
folk culture and his African heritage with "the countervailing weight of a
Western heritage". Reflecting on McKay's experience, we see that there
were two emancipation struggles, one from physical bondage in 1834 and
the other an emancipation of the spirit, towards which Claude McKay and
Una Marson were striving.

Una Marson, like Claude McKay, has an important place in the story
of the Jamaican people, a story that goes beyond a recital of battles won,
beyond a catalogue of political events. It penetrates into the ways in which

black and brown Jamaicans see themselves, other Jamaicans and their world. She is important as a poet whose works "were concerned, to a considerable degree, with the situation and identity of the Jamaican woman . . . the sexual perspectives of the woman are integrated with the cultural and racial themes which she clearly shares with Claude McKay". (Brown)

There is the personal agony of frustration, of the prisoned pain of conflicts engendered by colour prejudice and self-rejection.

> Rest then my heart, thou knowest but too well
> How strong and fierce relentless winds can blow.
> For hearts do not upon the wild rocks break
> They only know deep hurt and ache on ache.

She turned from the theme of the picturesque, exotic tropics to the experience of an African-Jamaican woman.

> We who see through the hypocrisy . . .
> feel the blood of black and white alike
> Course through our veins as our strong heritage
> Must range ourselves to build the younger race.

But the realities of self-rejection tormented her.

> I like me black face
> And me kinky hair
> I like me black face
> And me kinky hair
> But nobody loves dem,
> I don't think its fair
> Now I'se going press me hair
> And bleach me skin
> I'se gwine press me hair
> And bleach me skin
> What won't a gal go
> Some kind of man to win.
> Your mama does love you
> And you colour is high.

Our time spent with Claude McKay and Una Marson opens up the inner dimensions of the story of the African-Jamaican people. In a white-dominated society in which blackness was despised, educated Claude McKay denounced the potent poison of race hatred, and Una Marson affirmed her liking for her black face and kinky hair. In them we see the movement towards a Jamaican culture, beginning with an affirmation of racial identity.

CHAPTER 27

The birth of a national
consciousness, 1920-44

The final conflict between African-Jamaica and Britain began in the 1920s at the bidding of Quashie, the most underrated character in Jamaica's history, and of Marcus Garvey, the most feared and derided black leader of his time.

So decisive, so far-reaching were the results of this conflict that we refer to it here as the Jamaican revolution. It brought about the enfranchisement of all adult Jamaicans, set the feet of the people on the path to independence, speeded up the rapid growth of racial and national consciousness, the emergence of a Jamaican culture, the development of ties with Africa and the modernisation of the Jamaican economy.

Early in the 1920s the rural unemployed began to lay siege to the outworks and lower bastions of the citadel of Euro-Jamaican power in Kingston and lower St Andrew. So it comes about that the African-Jamaican peasant stands with Garvey, Alexander Bustamante and Norman Manley as heroes of that final conflict which began with the start of urbanisation (1920s) intensified during the Garvey years (1927-35), reached a decisive turning-point in the Frome years (1938-44) and moved into the period of consolidation and development in the period 1944-62.

The first phase of the revolution began early in the 1920s when the rural unemployed began to move to Kingston and lower St Andrew, the only places in the island where there was the remotest chance of finding work. By doing this they set in motion the process of urbanisation which, being so all-embracing, functioned as catalyst, incubator of ideas and generator of social discontent. By the time that Garvey returned to Jamaica in December 1927 a proletariat had begun to emerge.

In this chapter we focus on the urbanisation of Kingston and St Andrew in the years 1920-44 with indications of ways in which urbanisation contributed to fundamental social change. The chapters that follow focus on the political and socio-economic aspects of the revolution, the leaders of which were Alexander Bustamante and Norman Manley, and on the period of consolidation that followed the climactic years 1938-44. The final chapter gives an account of the extraordinary upsurge of creativity that followed the emergence of racial and national consciousness in the 1930s. These aspects belong together, are interdependent and interact upon each other.

The great ennobling themes of the story of the Jamaican people come together in this period of revolutionary ferment. The long struggle of the mass of the people for betterment and for freedom from economic oppression, the 1832 uprising for liberty and for human rights, brown George William Gordon's alliance with black Paul Bogle in the Morant Bay rejection of serfdom, find their champions in Garvey and later in Bustamante and Manley.

By treating the revolution in this way, by seeing that it grew out of the struggle of the mass of the Jamaican people for a better life, and out of the vision of Jamaican leaders, we link past generations with our own in an empowering experience of achievement.

So powerful a force as urbanisation calls for fuller consideration. It has been defined as the process and effects of gathering people in cities and towns. The concept covers urban expansion in area and population and the resulting changes in land use, ways of life, landscape and the geographical and occupational distribution of people. Of course urbanisation was not a uniquely Jamaican phenomenon. "The unprecedented scale and speed of urbanization in the 20th century – the majority of mankind will soon be living in urban places – has brought a host of urgent needs . . . and has made it a major concern of our time." (*Dictionary of Modern Thought*: 1977)

Linked with the process are the words "proletariat" and "bourgeois", which came into current use in the early twentieth century. It was Karl Marx who, in the opening passage of his *Communist Manifesto* (1848) drew attention to the message of conflict which these words conveyed: "The history of human society, past and slave, patrician and plebeian, lord and serf . . . the bourgeois age . . . has simplified class antagonisms . . . society is splitting into two great hostile classes . . . bourgeois and proletariat."

Marx was often more specific, using terms such as "wage labourers", "factory hands", the "working class". The word "proletariat" nevertheless became an important concept in the communist literature of the 1920s. In earlier times, such as the fifteenth and sixteenth centuries, "proletariat" had referred simply to landless men whose only means of livelihood was selling their labour. In our time it conveys also a suggestion of class conflict.

The word "bourgeois" was used in Europe in the Middle Ages to denote one who was neither a peasant nor a lord. Later it was applied to the master or employer in relation to the worker, with the result that gradually it became synonymous with the middle class. Since the nineteenth century the word has been used to express two contradictory judgments. Marx went on to say in the passage quoted above that the bourgeoisie historically had played "a most revolutionary part . . . .The bourgeoisie cannot exist without constantly revolutionizing the instruments of production . . . and with them the whole relations of society". Opposed to this judgement is that which portrayed the bourgeois or middle class as avaricious, mean and reactionary. Whereas "economic and political historians tend to see the bourgeois class as tearing up the roots of traditional society and its fixed ways, cultural historians . . . have tended to write from an aristocratic point of view and to decry the breakdown of standards when all culture becomes a commodity". (*Dictionary of Modern Thought*: 1977)

We turn now from the concept of urbanisation to the process, its scale and the numbers involved, and then we place it in the Jamaican historical context, for although the process is at work in all developing and developed countries, it is shaped in each country by that nation's history, needs and way of life.

In the preceding chapter we saw that between 1880 and 1920 more than 146,000 Jamaicans, practically all from rural Jamaica, moved overseas in search of employment. Emigration was their response to poverty at home.

In Jamaica, although the First World War (1914-18) had brought higher prices for sugar and had increased a demand for logwood to replace the German synthetic dyes, conditions had worsened. The entry of the United States into the war had reduced the demand for bananas. Four hurricanes in the period 1911-21 had ravaged the banana plantations. These disasters had been followed by the Spanish influenza epidemic of 1918, which caused heavy loss of life, inflicted great suffering on the rural poor and deepened the widespread gloom and the general feeling of despair.

But hope remained. In 1920 Cuban sugar was selling on the New York market for 22 cents per lb. Jobs were still available in the United States and in Cuba.

Then the blow fell, removing all hope. The great depression set in. By 1929 the price of Cuban sugar was down to one cent per lb on the New York market. Word spread throughout rural Jamaica that "no entry" signs were up in Panama, Honduras, Costa Rica, Cuba and the United States. No jobs were available. The "pull-factor", a demand for Jamaican labour, no longer operated. Cuban cane fields were no longer the mecca they had been for Jamaicans. Lengthening bread lines in the industrial cities of the United States and closed factories told of rising unemployment. New restrictions on immigration to the United States and other countries reversed the inflow of Jamaican labour, so that it became a return flow from the host country to the home country. In Jamaica in the late 1920s the picture was bleak. More people came than went, fewer babies died, more people lived longer, sugar prices were down, banana trees were dying from the Panama and leaf spot diseases.

By the early 1930s the situation was desperate in Jamaica and through-out the West Indies. In the words of Arthur Lewis, "It is generally agreed that bad conditions which have ruled in recent years are a major predis-posing factor (to economic distress). The prices of the principal West Indian exports were on the average almost halved between 1928 and 1933 and workers were forced to submit to drastic wage cuts, increased taxation and unemployment." Even in relatively prosperous Trinidad, there was a steady drift of unemployed workers from the plantations to the towns.

In Jamaica the rural unemployed responded to the no-entry barriers overseas and aggravated poverty at home by initiating a transfer of popula-tion from rural to urban Jamaica. L. Broom in a 1951 study noted that the most significant trend in the present-day Caribbean was the urbanisation of agricultural populations and the progressive concentration of people in the major city. They did this without the inducement of industrial devel-opment in the city. Their target was the island's major urban areas, Kingston and St Andrew. There were four currents, the two major ones being the northern and the southern currents and the two minor ones representing additions to Kingston and St Andrew from Portland and St Thomas:

Southern current	35,000
Northern current	27,500
Portland current	4,200
St Thomas current	2,300

The heaviest flow, made up of 37,300 people, came from the southern parishes. (Roberts: 1957)

The figures provide evidence of increasing economic instability in these years. The general restlessness of the rural population also indicated this. About one-fifth of the total population, 90,200 males and 108,900 females, moved from one parish to another in that period. Suburban St Andrew became the favoured location for about 47,500 persons. Of this number 11,300 were from Kingston, which "emphasises the shrinking importance of Kingston as a residential area". (Roberts: 1957) This general movement of people led to the growth of other urban centres in the island. As Roberts points out, "The parishes showing appreciable gains from neighbouring parishes were St James, St Catherine, St Thomas and Clarendon. St James was the chief beneficiary, through the pull exerted by the expanding Montego Bay area which, ever since the 1920's, had been displacing Port Antonio as the chief centre of the tourist industry." (Roberts: 1957)

This large movement of male and female unemployed workers from every part of Jamaica to Kingston and St Andrew gave rise to a proletariat that grew in numbers year by year. At the same time jobless veterans were returning from the First World War, bitter at the racial insults they had suffered at the hands of those for whose countries they had fought. Greatly shocked and hurt at the scant welcome given to them, many joined the ranks of the disaffected. Later in the 1920s, thousands of immigrants returning from the United States were dismayed at the conditions they found in Jamaica. Many were strong anti-imperialists, and others were active nationalists, sympathetic to racist and radical movements. This strong inflow of disaffected, educated, unemployed people from Europe and the United States reinforced the ranks of both the proletariat and the radical bourgeoisie, whose leaders were drawn from the Jamaica Union of Teachers, the Jamaica Agricultural Society, followers of Sandy Cox, Bain Alves and Garvey. They injected into a sector of the middle class that revolutionary force of which Marx wrote. They were reinforced by the anti-colonialists and the nationalists of the 1930s and 1940s, among them such pioneers as W. A. Domingo, W. Adolphe Roberts, O. T. Fairclough, H. P. Jacobs and Ken and Frank Hill. They made the political education of the people one of their chief objectives.

By 1930 it had become clear that by initiating and accelerating the urbanisation process, the powerless, landless, jobless African-Jamaican people had yet again started another social and political revolution. There were now groupings at work in the society that had not been there in the times of Sam Sharpe, George William Gordon and the banana smallholders of the 1880s and 1890s. Two of the most significant were the easily inflamed proletariat in Kingston and St Andrew, with their linkages to other new urban areas, and a radical sector of the bourgeoisie committed to a nationalist, African-Jamaican ideology.

In those years urbanisation began to transform the Liguanea landscape and emphasised the concept of Jamaica as being two societies. The contrasts stood out large and bold, without cover-up, all in the open air: the Jamaica of the black and poor, of Trench Town, Dungle, Back O' Wall, and on the surrounding hills the Jamaica of the rich and powerful white and brown minority.

This landscape mirror brought Jamaicans face-to-face with the reality that M. G. Smith, Jamaican scholar and poet, analysed in his *Plural Society*. His theoretical analysis was invaluable in opening Jamaican eyes to the need for understanding and taking measures to solve their gravest problems, massive black unemployment and a deeply divided society. It was confirmed by one of Jamaica's first and finest novelists, Roger Mais, who told in *Brother Man*, of entering into the slum culture, a divided and split world, the division not being just a question of colour, nor yet of rich and poor, but also "of differences that involved widely different acceptances and rejections of values, that involved different interpretations of reality, that involved the use of identical words to express different concepts and understandings . . . that other world to which the majority belong". (Manley: 1966)

A Rastafarian poet, Sam Brown, pointed to the lightning hidden in the hurricane cloud.

> Some young desperates look to the hills,
>   see the seat of their distress,
> They see the dwellers of the hills as them
>   that do oppress . . .
> Men, women and children stark naked,
>   lunatics of wants, reformatory.
> Executives in horseless chariots
> Sometimes pass through
>   hold their noses,
> Hapless poor look with vengeful
>   eyes, for them no bed of roses . . .

The executives in horseless chariots, holding their noses in disgust, were passing through a world that they had brought into being. The young desperates, the naked and afflicted, had built the shacks and slums, but the massive rural unemployment that had driven them from the rural to the urban areas of Jamaica was a result of economic and social policies adopted by the colonial government in alliance with a white-brown upper class.

The League of Coloured People in London, which had been founded by a black Jamaican, Dr Harold Moody, and which had a future Nobel Prize winner, W. Arthur Lewis, as one of its members, made this point in its analysis of the 1945 Report of the Royal Commission under Lord Moyne. The league held the predominantly white political leadership responsible for existing conditions and stated bluntly that many of the Royal Commission's proposals for welfare and development had been made for years but had been blocked by the local ruling classes who held a political monopoly and who were backed by the system of Crown colony rule. Lewis in particular emphasised that until radical political and constitutional changes had been made there would be no end to agitation and little prospect of development.

The poet's image of "the dwellers of the hills as them that do oppress" captured in a few words the harsh penalisation endured by African-Jamaicans. It brought to mind Gordon's attack on Eyre and the white magistracy for oppressing the peasantry, the complaint of the St Ann peasants about oppressive estate owners, the heavy emigration of rural unemployed between 1911 and 1921, and Garvey's blunt assertion in 1938 that the African-Jamaican people had no reason for patriotism to Britain since it had done nothing for them.

In substance the Moyne Commission's report was an indictment of Crown colony rule. It confirmed the charges made by Garvey, the League of Coloured People and Arthur Lewis. Through the policies they followed, the government and the upper-middle class discouraged industrialisation and manufacturing, used systems of taxation that burdened the poor and eased the prosperous, denied educational opportunity to the lower class, the blacks, and created a type of caste system that kept blacks at the base of the social pyramid. These measures, designed to retain a low-cost black labour force, burdened the available land with too many people and increased rural unemployment. Crown colony and upper-class rule created the urban slums.

To test the validity of this statement we turn to a comprehensive study of Kingston, Colin Clarke's *Kingston, Urban Change and Reform*, which covers the period 1692-1962. Clarke's findings reveal that during the week ending 12 December 1942 one-fifth (21 per cent) of black wage-earners in Jamaica were unemployed. Underlying and reflecting this poverty was their poor educational level. A large number of the black population of Kingston and St Andrew was illiterate. The black:

> was caught in a vicious circle in buying a secondary education for his children and keeping them at school for regular intervals . . . In 1943 fewer than 2.5 percent of the blacks in Kingston had received or were receiving secondary education . . . coloured men had achieved much greater success than blacks in obtaining white collar jobs in the civil service and the professions and in acquiring artisan and technical skills. (Clarke: 1962)

The figures for the island showed that almost 60 per cent of black wage-earners earned less than ten shillings per week, and the greater part of the population in Kingston remained desperately poor.

The link with educational opportunity was clear. "The social system was largely regulated by the educational institutions of the colony.

Consequently, the financially well-entrenched white minority could easily dominate the social and economic scene, while insisting that a free society existed without a legal basis for racial discrimination." (Clarke: 1962)

Clarke found that the burden of the caste system fell heavily on the blacks in the period 1820-1943. By the end of the nineteenth century some were filling minor posts in public departments and others were qualifying as physicians, solicitors, barristers, teachers, journalists and nurses, but the greater proportion in Kingston were employed in semi-skilled trades, in unskilled labouring jobs or in domestic service: "Although the white bias of the society and inferiority complex of the Negro were inherited from slavery both features became a continuing part of the social system in Kingston." The statistics show that in the 1930s unemployment had become characteristic of the labour situation. This critical condition was aggravated by an educational system that barred the way to vertical mobility and neglected even those areas for which it was supposed to fit the people: craftsmanship and the mechanical trades.

The Europeans defended colonial rule as being the trusteeship of an inferior race by a superior one, and it maintained that black poverty was proof of that inferiority. Their doctrine manifested itself in Eurocentricity, which so distorted their vision of mankind that they saw all other races and cultures as inferior. Isaiah Berlin, for example, points out that in the nineteenth and twentieth centuries even the most imaginative and radical political thinkers saw Asians and Africans almost exclusively in terms of their treatment by Europeans.

> Imperialists, benevolent paternalists, liberals, socialists discussed the people of Africa and Asia either as wards or as victims of Europeans, but seldom, if ever, in their own right, as people with histories and cultures of their own; with a past and present and future which must be understood in terms of their own actual character and circumstances, even if the existence of such indigenous cultures is acknowledged . . . it tends to be largely ignored. (Berlin: 1981)

In consequence, as late as the 1930s upper- and middle-class Jamaicans, white, coloured and black, having been educated in schools which nurtured Eurocentricity, were Jamaican by residence, British in attitudes and values and very British in their contempt for Africans and other African-Jamaicans. Eurocentricity was pathological, a first phase of that racial and national fanaticism called Fascism, that made Benito Mussolini invade Ethiopia and under the evil name of Nazism drove Adolf Hitler to exterminate some 6 million Jews and to plunge the world into a war that wiped out some 50 million men, women and children worldwide. Religious, racial and national fanaticisms, through holy wars, the slave trade, genocide, the holocaust and the Second World War were the great scourges of mankind and remain the most shameful chapters in the history of the world.

Racial and colour discrimination created the two Jamaicas described by Richard Sheridan as well as by M. G. Smith and Madeleine Kerr, from whom we quote below. Their message is as relevant for independent Jamaica as it was for Jamaica the colony.

Smith described the traditional cultural differences between the upper and middle strata of Jamaican society and the lowest stratum. He stressed that the moral axioms and values of the upper and middle strata were very different from those of the lower class: "Materialism provides the formative principle or reference point in the value system of the intermediate section, spiritual as well as secular values reflecting these principles." (Smith: 1974)

Kerr, as a social psychologist, was more concerned with ways in which social values and structures inhibited development. Her conclusion was that in the Jamaican society of the 1940s it was extremely difficult (indeed virtually impossible) for a Jamaican to move upwards from the lowest stratum. The value systems and class structure hindered acculturation.

> The fact that people are trying to adjust to a pattern which in itself is an economic impossibility, the fact that children are brought up to adjust to a family situation in which the mother is basically the most important person yet the father has to be respected as if he were; the fact that a coloured man knows that he will have more difficulty than his white neighbour in reaching posts of responsibility; the fact that whiteness was identified with 'good' and 'desirable' and 'black' with 'bad' and 'undesirable'; the fact that the majority of people know that it is unlikely that they will spend their lives at anything more than subsistence level, all these cause the most far-reaching psychological reactions. (Kerr: 1963)

Fifty years have passed since Kerr's work and her findings show that great progress has been made in changing the image of "blackness" as well as in transferring political and economic power from Europeans to Jamaicans. But as long as the landscape reflects two deeply divided societies, as long as it remains true that the value systems and educational system hinder acculturation, so long will the findings of Smith and Kerr deserve study. Indeed, the rise of a counter culture based on drugs and on murder as a purchaseable commodity makes some of their findings more relevant now than they were in the 1940s.

We turn at this point from the social scientists and enter the shanty town world of the 1930s and 1940s. Two remarkable street singers of the

1930s, Slim and Sam, are our guides. They respond with deep understanding and sympathy, with a defiant wry humour and self-mockery, to the grim challenges of desperate urban poverty, chronic unemployment, colour discrimination and political disenfranchisement.

Keeping company with Slim and Sam, we enter a vigorous, violent world, bawdy, full of "ginnals", of the young scuffling for a meal, a place of rascality and heroism, of cruelty and tenderness. All the characters in folklore, the Anansi stories, proverbs, the folk vocabulary, flourished in the merciless sunshine of West Kingston, among them the "cubbitch" man, Mr Cramouchin, deceitful and sly, who brought hard times to all.

Slim and Sam

> Annotto can't sell, the price is unfair
> Pimento a blossom an' drop
> Hard time, hard time
> Hard time a carry the day.
> For they won't put Cramouchin away.

Close beside him walked Mr Geechy, the stingy man with the "tight han", domineering "trong-eye Joe" and the "boasify" lady who "shake up dem hip". The vices were greed, selfishness, covetousness, stinginess, while the fault-finding "fenky-fenky" customer and the clumsy, stupid "buffootoo boy" were objects of derision. The dramatic characters of the great markets of West Africa moved besides these, the formidable women traders who show "dat dem no peaw-peaw, dat what dem say is law; the trickify Anansi-man or sam-fie man and the boisterous 'trong-mout' male trader selling livestock and jackass rope".

Through this raucous, clamorous world moved the folk-singers poking fun at the returned immigrant from Panama.

> Colon man dah come.
> And de brass chain dah lick him belly
> Bam bam bam, . . .
> You ask him for de time an' him
> look upon de sun;

Hard times brought laments from the market traders.

> Carry me ackee go a Linstead Market,
> Not a quattie wut sell
> Everybody come feel up, feel up
> Not a quattie wut sell

The two ballad singers, tall, "mauger" Slim who sang first voice and short, stout guitarist Sam, told in one of their favorite songs how:

> Up Constant Spring road dis time
> Right a number one-sixty-nine
> A gang a coolie duppy combine
> Fi stone Isaac
> Run Isaac, run fi you life
> Run Isaac, run wid you wife
> You gi de duppy dem food an ting
> Di more you give dem di more dem sing
> Di more you give dem di more dem sing,
> So tek you body from Constant Spring
> An' run Isaac

Slim and Sam sang of "duppy power" in a world in which every night peopled the countryside with duppies, rolling calves and a headless woman carrying a baby on her right shoulder and every day brought unemployment.

> A went to Sandy Gully fe go get a bite
> Dem set dung me name and a feel alright
> De very day a start to work di man dem strike . . .
> If I had a gun a would a hang myself,
> If I could a swim I would a shoot myself,
> If a had a rope a would a drown myself,
> Waai.

Though Slim and Sam could lighten the passing hour, they could not banish the reality that Sam Brown portrayed, the brutalising experience of ghetto life for all who endured it.

> Tin can houses, old and young, meangy
> dogs, rats, inhuman stench,
> Unthinkable conditions that cause the
> stoutest heart to wrench
> Tracks and little lanes like human
> veins, emancipated people . . .

Slim and Sam's self-mockery and Sam Brown's anger were protests against the enfeebling impotence of the poor, their paralysing powerlessness, their helplessness. But saddest of all was the general blindness of the rich and powerful to the condition of both urban and rural poor. It was little wonder that the Royal Commission commented that the general insanitary environment gave rise to malaria, worm infestation and bowel disease, tuberculosis and other diseases. It also went beyond a listing of diseases brought on by insanitary conditions and condemned the levels of the health services and of the housing of the people as grossly inadequate, the status of women as wholly unsatisfactory, and declared that the children were the most exploited of all West Indian people. The Commission spoke in scathing terms of British colonial society. It regretted the absence of those factors and traditions which elsewhere make for social cohesiveness and a sense of membership of a community. "The whole West Indies are practically devoid of all the multifarious institutions, official and unofficial, which characterize British public life and bring a very large proportion of the population into some living contact with the problems of social importance." (West Indies Royal Commission [1938-39]: 1945)

The Commission was looking at the product of very nearly three centuries of British rule. During that period the moulding forces had been utterly divisive and the upper classes had established a tradition of social irresponsibility. Their policies had created the slums and their racial prejudices had blinded them to the needs of all but themselves. Their Eurocentricity had hindered the growth of anything like a sentiment of national unity, for "the European mind failed to apply the idea of equality – so much at the centre of European liberalism – to the subject Caribbean peoples. There is hardly a single outstanding mind in the history of that liberalism which felt able to accept the Negro as the equal of the white person." (Lewis: 1968)

Had the Royal Commission known where to look they would have found the network of associations for which they were searching in the lowest stratum of the society in the neglected black rural communities clustered around church and school. There they would have found the folk organisations, the friendly societies, the lodges and burial scheme societies, the leaders' meetings, class meetings, prayer meetings, the informal labour-sharing morning diggings, the day-for-day groups, the informal saving unions known as "susu" and "partner", the folk-leaders and counsellors that included parson, teacher, village druggist, Aunt Eliza, Tata Joe, Busha Tom, Cousin Mattie, key figures in islandwide networks for counselling, guidance, comfort, father-figures, mother-figures for the people and their children.

Looking back across the post-emancipation century, 1830-1929, we see that, inspired by the churches, by their parsons and teachers, the African-Jamaican labouring folk created the social and economic linkages and associations that encouraged social cohesion and built a tradition of social responsibility, of caring, of brotherhood and sisterhood. Here were to be found a unique blending of Christian and West African religious concepts, a sense of family as involving also kinsfolk and community, of authority as being rooted in morality and not in the use of force, of religion permeating all the departments of life, of human beings as living in a religious universe in which natural phenomena are associated with God. The formative principle was religious, not political; and it was religion in the form of Christianity, with its central message of love. To Eurocentricity and the assertion of authority through violence, the common people offered the alternative of caring and of fellowship.

Whoever knew that impoverished rural community in the late 1920s cannot forget the common pot of the tenement yard shared with migrants from other villages. Or who, brought up in a country district, can forget the sight of four men carrying on their shoulders a homemade stretcher with two bamboo trees as the two poles, and on the stretcher a woman or child, setting out on ten miles of unpaved country road from Glengoffe to the hospital at Linstead. Listening to them and their accompanying friends singing "Abide with me, fast falls the eventide" and "Jesu, Lover of My Soul", or listening to Bedward's shepherds and shepherdesses singing of Zion on their way to the healing waters of the Hope River, was to understand the reality of religion to the Jamaican folk. The churches, the parsons and the teachers, by implanting the Christian message of love, reinforced the memories of African tribal life with its tradition of social responsibility.

"The African influence is strongest in Revival, which is more than 200 years old and includes two traditions, Revival Zion and Pukumina. Women play a leading part as members, healers, preachers. In religion there is a deep tradition of women serving as healers . . . in our religious tradition women serve in virtually all capacities, evangelists, missionaries, deacons, ushers, secretaries. If women as a group were to withdraw their membership all churches would cease to function as viable social entities . . . Women play a major role in the maintenance of values shaped by religion." (Chevannes: 1995)

Chevannes refers to a very significant feature of Revival, which is that there is no dichotomy between this world and the next.

> Among the European religions the next life is seen as that world where everything that is not right will be rectified . . . However, in the Jamaican tradition God's justice, His regard and love are made manifest in this life. Such beliefs make religion a potent force in the drive of the people for self-improvement and upward mobility. As the leading social force in religion women are therefore the leading force in self-improvement.

The women African- and Euro-Jamaicans leaders pioneered the way for the women's movement that developed in the 1930s and 1940s. The demographic setting is provided by George Roberts. His analysis reveals the distance the women had travelled from the immediate post-emancipation period when 80 per cent of all gainfully occupied women were in agriculture. This proportion declined slowly, standing at 64 per cent in 1921 and 47 per cent in 1943: "It is the large scale withdrawal of females after 1921 that has in the main resulted in the great reduction in the numbers of persons engaged in agriculture." (Roberts: 1957) Between 1921 and 1943 the number of females in agriculture declined from 125,400 to 45,600. Roberts points out that changing definitions of employment may explain some of the reduction but that this diminishing dependence of females on agriculture as work in this period appeared also in other West Indian populations. This reduction in female employment marked a break with slave society in which "every adult was potentially a work unit". Another important feature was the growth in the proportion of women in domestic service, but most significant of all was the increase in the number of women in commercial occupations. This grew from 2,800 in 1891 to 51,200 in 1943, the increase "being consistent with diversification of enterprises, growth of service occupations attendant on enhanced urbanization and improving standards of living". (Roberts: 1957)

The increase in the number of women in domestic service in the urban area was itself a sign of trouble, being an indication, as Arthur Lewis has pointed out, that there were more women competing for a limited number of jobs. And urbanisation did not screen poverty behind the picturesque. It stripped away the easy phrases about a "happy smiling people". It showed poverty and joblessnes for what they were, stark and ugly, and by the 1930s some educated middle- and upper-class Jamaicans began to respond to what they saw.

That fact was in itself significant, for there were no mother-figures, no female symbols of compassion in plantation great house society. These were to be found among the African-Jamaican labour force, among the slave nurses, the higglers and traders and common-law wives. Plantation society marginalised and degraded all its women, black, white and coloured.

For this reason it was especially significant that in this period in response to the evidence of increasing unemployment among women and widespread suffering amongst children, a redoubtable group of concerned women leaders emerged. Some had come into prominence as members of the Jamaica Union of Teachers, others as public-spirited upper-class citizens, yet others as writers, feminists, champions of the rights of children. They included Mary Morris Knibb, Amy Bailey, May Farquharson (Miss Amy and Miss May), Edith Dalton James, Ethlyn

Rhodd, Marjory Stewart, Edris Allan (later Lady Allan), Lilly Mae Burke, Gladys Longbridge (later Lady Bustamante), Una Marson and Carmen Lusan. These were among the women pioneers who led the way in establishing a tradition of social concern. By reaching out beyond the dividing lines of colour, race and class they charted a worthy and indispensable role for women in Jamaican society. The women leaders of the 1920s and 1930s, black, brown, white, African-Jamaicans and Euro-Jamaicans, set about putting an end to the marginalisation of women in Jamaican society. These women understood that it was their task to invest womanhood with its proper meaning and dignity.

Another indicator of increasing concern for the welfare and advancement of the African-Jamaican people was the founding in 1936 of the Jamaica Welfare Ltd. Arising out of a discussion between Norman Manley and the president of the United Fruit Company, Samuel Zemurray, the company established a fund to be used for the welfare of the people of Jamaica, with emphasis on the rural people. Manley was to form a competent board and report annually. The board was free to plan as it thought best. Zemurray was of Armenian peasant stock. He had begun his working life peddling bananas on the New Orleans wharves. It may be that he was struck by Manley's account of the plight of the Jamaican peasantry. The funds provided by the company were used to finance the work of Jamaica Welfare Ltd, Jamaica's first community development non-government organisation, founded in 1936. An account of the work is given in *Working Together for Development,* edited by Norman Girvan, which documents Jamaica's rich experience in grassroots development from the late 1930s to the 1960s. The book represents a major contribution to the social history of Jamaica. The philosophic concept that governed the work of Jamaica Welfare was that development is a process which begins with "the unfolding of what is in the germ" (dictionary defintion), and leads to the release of the creative potential in an individual, a community, a nation.

Within ten years of its foundation, Jamaica Welfare had become a model for developing countries in Africa and Latin America. In that period international agencies began recruiting from it as consultants and as officers leaders such as Thom Girvan, Eddie Burke, Arthur Carney, Chester Dowdy, Marjory Stewart and Sybil Francis.

The three guiding principles were: to enable people to make the best use of the opportunities that exist or that they can create, for betterment; the creation of a dynamic for action by inspiring desire, hope, self-confidence; and to keep the action moving by a combination of planned activities leading to the constant regeneration of energy at the start. These tasks can only be carried out through education, "not the education of books but education related to living problems and derived from the action taken to solve them." (Manley: 1971)

The affirmation of racial identity, the emergence of women as advocates of social responsibility and the formulation of a Jamaican theory of social development based on an analysis of the historical experience of the people and their needs, signified a rejection of colonial dependence and a movement towards self-government.

Central to the process was the liberating force of a discovery of personal and racial identity. This force manifested itself in political, economic and cultural developments. The change began within the Jamaican society a decade or more before the British Government announced its policy of self-government and colonial development. A Jamaican theory of social development and its methodology influenced British colonial development and welfare policy in the 1940s.

CHAPTER 28

The founders of the nation: Marcus Garvey, Alexander Bustamante, Norman Manley

The founders of the Jamaican nation are Marcus Garvey, Alexander Bustamante and Norman Manley. They belong to the same period in history, were country-bred, lower-middle class and working class. Marcus Garvey was black, Manley and Bustamante were coloured. Each was a leader in his own right, and each contributed in his own unique way to the creation of the Jamaican nation. Their vision of the Jamaican people still shapes our way of life. The work of each is incomplete when isolated from the work of the other two. Though Garvey was senior, the three belong together, not as a team, but each as a leader of heroic quality, whose special contribution expressed his deepest convictions.

Garvey's liberating call to African-Jamaicans was to an affirmation of racial identity, to racial pride, self-worth and to claiming their African heritage. History has vindicated him. He broke new ground by founding a political party to contest the Jamaica election of 1930 and by publishing a political programme. His election message was not forgotten: "My opponents say I am against white and fair-skinned people. This is not so. I am against the class system here which keeps the poor man down, and the poor mostly black people. It is only natural therefore that their interest should be nearest and dearest to my heart . . . Let us all work together as fellow-Jamaicans and ring in the changes for a new Jamaica."

To the liberating force of Garvey's insistence on racial consciousness and on an African identity Manley added the empowering force of a feeling of national unity. He declared:

No amount of economic good will make our people a real unity. All efforts will be wasted unless the masses of the people are steadily taken along the path in which they will feel more and more that this place is their home, that it is their destiny . . . (Manley: 1971)

Manley's work was made possible by Garvey, who gave to blackness a new dynamic personality, animated the great majority of the people with hope and confidence, kindled their interest in changing their condition through organised political activity, insisted on self-help and intellectual effort as a foundation for progress, and pointed the Jamaican away from his isolation to a larger brotherhood that linked Africa and the Americas. Paying tribute to him ten years after his death, the editor of *The Daily Gleaner* wrote: "It would be true to say of Jamaica, and to a lesser extent of the other British West Indies, that national consciousness received its main stimulus from the movement associated with the still revered Marcus Garvey." Manley spoke to many whose ears had been unstopped by Garvey, whose eyes had been opened by him, whose faith in their future and in their country had been kindled by him.

To these liberating messages Alexander Bustamante added a direct and powerful call to the great mass of the African-Jamaican people, for a better life here in a country where they were the majority, but from whose society they had been excluded. The three messages covered the primary requirements for transforming the colony, Jamaica, into both nation and homeland. To ideology Bustamante added a visual image of compassion, of shepherd and provider, qualities that John Dunkley, the first leading intuitive painter of modern Jamaica, portrayed in one of his best-known paintings. Bustamante contributed to the ideologies of racial and of

The Shepherd by
John Dunkley

national consciousness the compassionate feeling of a leader for his people. Jamaica was singularly fortunate in its founding fathers, each one speaking in his own way with a prophetic assurance and authority, as when Garvey, receiving news of his defeat at the polls in 1930, declared, "The voters (not the people) have turned back the clock of progress for another ten years, but party system is well established in your minds and it will come, it is bound to come." (Edwards: 1962)

A Caribbean-wide revolution entered into an explosive phase in 1933, when Fulgencio Batista and the Cuban army drove the dictator Machado from Cuba. There followed strikes and disorders in Puerto Rico's sugar-belt. In 1935 sugar workers in

St Kitts led by Robert Bradshaw struck for higher wages. Disorder broke out and some of the strikers were killed. In the same year workers in British Guiana rioted and set fire to canefields. Tension mounted in St Vincent where a workingmen's association was formed to demand land and a new constitution. In St Lucia coal carriers went on strike. Also in 1935 a fiery Grenadian, Uriah "Buzz" Butler, led a march of unemployed into Port-of-Spain, formed a militant Workers' Home Rule Party and, in 1937, called a strike in the oil-fields. Two oil wells were set ablaze. Two of a party of policemen were killed when they attempted to arrest Butler. In Barbados a follower of Butler's from Trinidad, Clement Payne, attracted large crowds with his attacks on the government and his demand for trade unions. A showdown followed. The governor ordered that Payne be deported. He was taken before the court, tried and ordered to be deported, but a young Barbadian lawyer, Grantley Adams, won an appeal against the verdict. He was deported, nevertheless. The people rioted. Fourteen were killed and 59 wounded.

In Jamaica Alexander Bustamante and A. G. S. Coombs formed the Jamaica Workers' and Tradesmen's Union in 1934 and started holding mass meetings protesting against low wages and working-class poverty. Crowds gathered in the streets demanding work. Bustamante and Coombs led marches. From time-to-time the police broke up crowds of unemployed, and Jamaica learned something about the destabilising power of an angry unemployed proletariat.

Bustamante, originally Alexander Clarke, was born in Hanover on 24 February 1884. He left the island when he was about 20, returned in 1934 at the age of 50 and settled in Kingston. Tall, thin, with a striking face and a great shock of hair, dramatic in speech and appearance, Bustamante took the centre of the stage wherever he went. He was greatly disturbed at the poverty in Kingston, the ineffectiveness of the Legislative Council and the lack of concern amongst the employers. He wrote trenchant letters to *The Daily Gleaner* and, always a man of action, led street marches and protest demonstrations. To *The Daily Gleaner's* criticism of the demonstrations he replied, "Hungry men and women and children have a right to call attention to their condition and to ask of people fulfilment of promises made to them so long as they do so without using violence." To someone asking in the columns of *The Daily Gleaner*, "Who is Bustamante?" he replied, "Bustamante is a lonely fighter." Thus he stamped his image on the minds of the people. He conjured up vivid pictures, for example, the prospect of having the supine Legislative Council in power for another three years was like having an elephant on its back with its trunk full of water; or, in Jamaica the rich man had his stomach growing out day after day until it ripened while the stomachs of the poor were shrunken like loofahs.

Unemployment was widespread among the rural folk in these years, but a glimmer of hope came with the building of a large sugar factory at Frome in Westmoreland, where the West Indies Sugar Company (WISCO) had acquired control of 30,000 acres of fertile land. The British firm of Tate and Lyle, which had a controlling interest in WISCO, also owned the island's other major sugar producing complex, Monymusk in Vere.

Reports of high wages attracted thousands of unemployed to Frome. Their presence aggravated an already tense situation caused by wage deductions and inefficiencies in the pay office. On 1 May 1938 the workers struck, police were rushed in, rioting broke out, four people were shot by the police, some 15 were wounded and 105 were arrested for rioting. Three weeks later violence broke out in Kingston; on 21 May dock workers went on strike and the mob brought Kingston to a standstill.

On 23 May, Manley, the island's most brilliant lawyer, was in Savanna-la-Mar, attending an official inquiry into the Frome riots, when news reached him of rioting in Kingston. He hurried back to the city that afternoon. Kingston was strangely still.

> Everywhere was shut up. The crowds had seen to that, and soldiers moved around, passing at street corners knots of silent, sullen people waiting in an ugly frame of mind. I did not at all like what I saw . . . I heard that there was trouble at the fire brigade headquarters . . . He and his faithful friend of those days, St. William Grant, had been arrested . . . When I heard that they were to strike that afternoon and that Bustamante had gone there to address them. I went home deeply persuaded by all I saw and feared that with Bustamante arrested and all workers in the Corporate Area [city] on strike we were in for a serious time and that violence, disorder and bloodshed would be the final result. (Edwards: 1967)

That evening and far into the night Manley and his wife Edna, confronted with this grim tangle of despair, discussed the situation.

The following morning he told the governor of his intention to put aside his legal work for the time being and offer his assistance to any group

of workers who had grievances and wished him to negotiate on their behalf. The governor welcomed his intervention. William Seivright, who later became mayor of Kingston, offered his support. A group of women workers sought his help. Then, later in the day, a critical meeting took place. A delegation from the waterfront called on him.

> The men knew exactly what they wanted both as to straight time work and as to overtime. They had a straight position for which they were fighting and had been offered very little on their demand. But over and above all that, there was an intervening problem. They insisted that they had struck without any advice from Bustamante. As they explained, he had intervened on their behalf and told them what the employers were prepared to do but had been careful to say that he was not advising them to strike . . . they were certain that Bustamante had been arrested because they had struck and they told me that they had no intention of going back to work unless Bustamante was released from jail. (Manley: 1938)

The governor then appointed a conciliation committee, accepting Manley's advice about members. The shippers agreed to grant the demand of the wharf workers for increased day pay but would not budge on night time. Eventually, under pressure from the conciliation committee, the shipping association agreed to all Manley's terms, thinking these would eliminate the demand for Bustamante's release. The stand Manley took determined the course of events and made this a point of confluence of the workers' protests with the anti-colonial movement.

Alexander Bustamante makes a final address before leading the historic protest march

They expected me to agree with their view. I did not. I told them bluntly that I would not be responsible for what happened to the Corporate Area if the week-end passed and Bustamante was still in jail. There were, I said, active plans to start a graver level of trouble. True, I said, the fire brigade issue had been settled by me but there were plans to start on Sunday a scale and range of fires that would leave the brigade helpless . . . I spoke strongly. I had it in mind that only pressure from the committee could make the Governor change his mind. I did not advise them . . . The move had to come from within the body itself. (Manley: 1938)

The mayor of Kingston, Dr Oswald Anderson, made an emotional appeal to the committee to save the city of Kingston, which urged the governor to release Bustamante. The governor agreed. Bustamante and St William Grant were released on bail.

In the weeks that followed the island was rent apart by widespread turmoil and labour unrest. Bustamante and Manley travelled throughout the country urging calm and promising their support. By the time quiet was restored, eight lives had been lost, 32 people had been wounded and another 139 injured, and some 400 imprisoned for rioting. There followed the Orde Brown Inquiry into labour conditions and the appointment of the West India Royal Commission with Lord Moyne as chairman. Bustamante and Manley were now recognised as national leaders committed to building a new modern Jamaica. Bustamante forged ahead with developing the Bustamante Industrial Trade Union while Manley announced at the end of May 1938 that he had accepted the invitation of a delegation led by O. T. Fairclough to form a national political party. The immediate aim was to set about organising a party committed to self-government.

Alexander Bustamante was among those present at the historic meeting of 1938. He was by then the acknowledged leader of the Jamaican working class, their leader in the way that Garvey had been in the late 1920s. He politicised the great mass of the people and through the Bustamante Industrial Trade Union organised them into a formidable force which soon won the respect of employers and of the public. So by 1940, through the leadership of these two men, organised labour and a political party had become powerful realities.

Manley's words at the launching of the People's National Party in 1938 indicate the strength that the national movement had gathered during the 1930s: "Anyone looking at the past ten years will realise that we in this country have been more and more concentrating upon our own affairs. We have thought more of Jamaica, spoken more about Jamaica, breathed more of the atmosphere of Jamaica than ever before." He spoke of the dawn of the feeling among Jamaicans that Jamaica should be their country. "There is a tremendous difference between living in a place and belonging to it and feeling that your own life and your destiny is irrevocably bound up in the life and destiny of that place. Radical change was under way."

These events were overtaken by the Second World War which began in 1939. When the war ended, only the United States, whose money and industries had through land-lease, sustained and augmented the war economies of her allies, seemed the immediate and real victor. Anti-Semitism and the doctrine of a superior Aryan race had been rejected.

The British Government understood this. They saw that the concepts of empire and of the trusteeship of a superior race were dead. They knew that in the war young West Indians were flying and dying with their own pilots, that West Indians were serving in France and were with Field-Marshal Montgomery at El Alamein; that black and coloured West Indians were working in the munitions factories in the Midlands. A new spirit of understanding replaced the old colonial relationship. Jamaicans recall that even when the Battle of Britain was at its fiercest, Britain met the Jamaican representation for the introduction of universal adult suffrage, and granted self-government by reforming the constitution in 1944. It went further and signalled the end of the colonial policy of economic exploitation by adopting a policy of colonial development and welfare, by setting up a colonial development fund of £10 million in 1942, when the country was virtually bankrupt, and by doubling that amount in 1945 to £20 million.

But it remains a question whether the demand for self-government having been met, the period of tutelage need have been spread over as long a period as 18 years. What was granted was diluted self-government in doses graduated to suit the imperial interests. This was further evidence of the extent to which the colonial system of education bred a lack of self-confidence among blacks in their own ability to manage their affairs and confirmed among whites the sense of superiority in their dealings with colonial peoples. This persistence of a colonial mentality explains why Garvey continually appealed to history and pressed for a system of education that included higher education. Many of those who had the vote opposed the demand for universal adult suffrage, and proposed instead the introduction of a literacy test.

The central issue went beyond administrative efficiency to the restructuring of Jamaican society and the full liberation, through education and knowledge, of the Jamaican working class. Garvey foresaw that.

It is for this reason that in the closing paragraphs of this chapter we now return to Marcus Garvey, to Africa and to the African heritage, and to Garvey's insistence on blacks of every class having the opportunity to develop to the full their intellectual ability. Culture, self-liberation and self-discipline were essential parts of his message.

In the 1920s when the revolution began, the black Jamaican man, heavily burdened with a tradition of discrimination and trapped in a society still dominated by the white-based values of the sugar-plantation system, stood in need of a vision and a voice. So did the black man of the United States, who began to discover after the First World War that the American dream was not dreamed for him, that the American promise had not been made for him. So also did the black man of the European colonies of Africa, who was beginning to perceive that the right of self-determination, the great slogan of that war, did not apply to him.

The African-Jamaican, in common with blacks throughout the world was in desperate need of a voice and a vision. Marcus Garvey became the voice and, like a prophet, communicated the vision. He generated within blacks the will to free themselves and to fit themselves, intellectually and through self-discipline, to play a part in history that would earn respect for Africa, their own people and for Jamaica, the land of their birth, their homeland.

CHAPTER 29

From colony to nation:
Political progress and economic growth

For more than three centuries we have travelled with the African-Jamaican people as they struggled towards freedom. Only occasionally did we come to gentler country and green pastures; always mountains lay ahead and there were rivers to cross. For the first time, however, in 1944, all the Jamaican people became involved in making the decisions, setting the directions and implementing them.

With the granting of a new constitution on 20 November 1944 the Jamaican people took the first steps towards independence. They had always chosen the difficult road no matter where it led, to Accompong and the Land of Look Behind, to Nanny Town and to the mountains in St Thomas that looked down on Paul Bogle's chapel. The coastal plains were still backra's property.

Jamaica's first general election took place on 14 December 1944, soon after the granting of the new constitution. The People's National Party (PNP) and the more recently formed Jamaica Labour Party (JLP) contested it. Alexander Bustamante had broken with the PNP in 1942 and founded the JLP in 1943. In Norman Manley's words:

> There came the time when Sir Alexander made what history may come to regard as his greatest contribution to democracy in Jamaica, and this was the formation and creation – for it really was an act of creation – of the Jamaica Labour Party which led to the establishment of the two-party system in Jamaica . . . It is said that when God was creating the world, God said "Let there be light" and there was light. And when Sir Alexander was creating the Jamaica Labour Party, Sir Alexander said 'Let there be a Jamaica Labour Party', and there was a Jamaica Labour Party. (Nettleford: 1971)

Time has confirmed Norman Manley's judgment that by creating a second party this man, his cousin, "Originally by nature and temperament autocratic, who had very strong and firm opinions of his own, was able to grow in a democratic world and to contribute to it because he was able to face the fact that, having said, 'Let there be a party' and there was a party, it had to become an organised body." (Nettleford: 1971)

The JLP swept the board with 25 elected members as against the PNP's five and two independents. Norman Manley lost to a relatively unknown Dr Edward Fagan, so strong was Busta's gravitational pull. Manley took defeat like the democrat that he was. When the news reached him in the Half Way Tree Court House that he had lost to Dr Fagan, he said, "Vox Populi, Vox Dei, the people have spoken. Moses never saw the promised land." With the assistance of Ivan Lloyd of St Ann, who led the opposition in the House, he built the PNP into a formidable opposition party. He gained his seat in the second general election which took place in 1949.

Before carrying our story any further, we turn to the people themselves. "I cast my vote at a polling station in one of the poorer suburbs of Kingston. As clearly as though it were yesterday and not more than half a century ago, I saw a friend, old Ebenezer Brown, a small cultivator, coming towards me, his black wrinkled face gleaming with pride and happiness. He greeted me by holding out the forefinger of his right hand which had been dipped in a scarlet dye to show that he had voted. 'I feel big,' he said, 'and now all we is one.'"

Africa remains at the centre of our story. Ebenezer Brown, as deep-rooted in the Jamaican soil, as tough and gnarled as the lignum vitae tree that sheltered his yard, symbolised the majority of the Jamaican people, all of them laden with buried memories of the terrible plantation years and of tribal relationships, of the presence of the ancestors, of a hierarchy of rulers whose business it was to protect and be the fathers of the people. The ancestral sense of self-worth and tribal fellowship had been grievously damaged by the psychosocial controls of the sugar-and-slave plantation but, by exercising the right to vote, Ebenezer had affirmed his personal worth and his membership of the Jamaican community. How would he fare during the crowded years that led to independence?

We will continue our journey with Jamaicans like old Ebenezer during these tumultuous years of early nationhood in our attempt to join him in his inner world. Pandit Nehru of India used to explode at nonsense about the idealisation of the simple peasant life. "I have almost a horror of it . . . what is there in the man with the hoe to idealise over? Crushed and exploited for innumerable generations, he is only little removed from the animals that keep him company."

Nehru was attacking the class view of the peasant. So as to keep close to the people, we interweave events with reflection, chronology with leaps from one generation to another, believing with historians such as John Plum and Simon Schama that history should be synthesis as well as analysis, chronicle as well as text; and having learned also that throughout our history the enslaving forces have come from those in power and liberation from the peasantry.

Nor is the phrase "laden with Africa" used lightly. Africa lived on in religious concepts, traditional codes about family relationships, kinsfolk, family spirits, ethical values, modes of expression, physical gestures, and it lived on also in deep-buried memories, frustrations and anger carried over from two centuries of plantation life into our own time.

Society, as in plantation times, fell into three classes, differentiated by race, colour, education and means. The upper class of whites with a discreet sprinkling of light browns, and a middle class of propertied browns, on the basis of a limited franchise, exercised a political monopoly and buttressed the governor who, as the Crown's representative, ruled the colony. The lower class, predominantly black and dark brown, mostly illiterate or with some elementary schooling, formed an exploited, controlled labour force, underpaid, despised, whose only means of change lay in occasional outbursts of violence.

In the period 1938-62, Jamaica moved from the colonial condition to full and sovereign nationhood. Unemployed peasants, by riots at Frome, the unemployed proletariat by islandwide disorders expressed through a group of nationalists drawn from the middle and lower classes, and a group of disaffected trade unionists, set the forces of radical change in motion. At the same time a combination of educated, politically motivated, African-Jamaicans, black and brown, by organised political action ensured that the violent protests of 1938 would be translated into political progress and economic growth. We watch in these often tumultuous years a transfer of political power from a predominantly white-brown minority to a predominantly black majority and we watch also with growing excitement and wonder the release of an astonishing and unexpected creativity that commanded international attention and respect.

In this chapter we tell the story of that release of creative energy in the fashioning of a constitution that began as a tepid Colonial Office version of "embryo ministers", then advanced to full internal self-government and finally to sovereignty as a nation in 1962. In the same period we move from a rejection of a Colonial Office economic dominance in 1944 to the development of a diversified and vastly more productive economy.

The first phase of the movement towards self-government and independence included the launching of the PNP in 1938, the PNP's campaign for universal adult suffrage and self-government, Alexander Bustamante's founding of the Bustamante Industrial Trade Union (1943) and then of the JLP. In this first phase Bustamante concentrated on organising labour as a political force. He was not yet convinced of the need for self-government.

The start was difficult. It took the constant pressure of Norman Manley and the PNP to keep universal adult suffrage and self-government on the Colonial Office agenda. They did this with the support of the Jamaica Progressive League in New York and of Sir Stafford Cripps, Creech Jones and other members of the Fabian Colonial Bureau in Britain. When, following the 1938 riots, the Moyne Commission's proposals were tabled, the Rev. Ethelred Brown of the Jamaica Progressive League in New York found them so unsatisfactory that he exploded, scattering brimstone and ashes upon the governor in Kingston and the Secretary of State in London.

As a result of this increasing pressure from within Jamaica, the United States and Britain, the British Government in 1944 granted a constitution which provided for universal adult suffrage and an elected majority in the legislature. It provided for a legislature made up of an elected House of Representatives and a Legislative Council which included official and unofficial members, and an executive council under the governor as chairman, with three officials, two nominated members who were not officials and five ministers from the House of Representatives. Creech Jones, a leading member of the British Labour Party, regretted that Jamaica would still be answerable to the Colonial Office. This meant, he pointed out, that Jamaicans would not learn the practical work of government.

The first five years (1944-49) were a charade. Ministers had to report on various departments but were not responsible for seeing that action was taken by them. They had no executive responsibilities for the departments. The constitution provided for "partnership" between the governor and official members and the "ministers", but not for a ministerial system. In his presidential address of 1945 to the PNP, Manley emphasised that the greatest defect of the constitution was that in their [the Colonial Office's] efforts to play safe they gave great power but they failed to give a corresponding responsibility. "The house can pass any resolution and nobody can stop them." But in the executive council the governor had the casting vote and so "When it suits him the leader of the majority party comes in the House and says 'I am only half government – in fact I am not government at all . . .' and you can't pin them with any responsibility at all." (Nettleford: 1971)

The two fundamental changes had been made, however: the granting of universal adult suffrage and an elected majority in the legislature. These were great cornerstones for the erection of a democratic system of government. The second phase began with Manley's motion in the legislature, in cooperation with the JLP government, for the introduction of a ministerial system. In 1953 the amended constitution increased the number of House of Representative members in the Executive Council to eight. This gave them a majority over official and nominated members, so that ministers now had the responsibility for carrying out decisions reached in the House. Under the new system Alexander Bustamante became Jamaica's first chief minister. He was succeeded by Norman Manley in 1955, when the PNP won the general election for the first time.

Constitutionally, the next advance in self-government came in 1957 when the Executive Council, over which the governor presided, gave way to a Cabinet, at that time called the Council of Ministers, over which the chief minister presided. The Council was made up of eight members from the House of Representatives and two or three from the Legislative Council, these being appointed by the governor on the nomination of the chief minister. Officials were no longer members of the government.

In 1958 Jamaica became an independent country in all internal matters, with only bills relating to defence and international affairs being reserved for the Queen. The governor's veto powers were retained but could be exercised only on the advice of the Cabinet. A Minister of Home Affairs took over matters formerly dealt with by the Colonial Secretary and, in some measure, by the Attorney-General.

Throughout their history the black majority had learned to judge the upper- and middle-class people by their actions and conduct, not by their words. Reports of constitutional change became reality only when they saw that where backra alone had walked, blacks and browns now walked. The people saw social change painted in skin colour, black and brown ministers of government walking through King's House as of right, and receiving the salutes of white soldiers. In 1957 they hailed Florizel Glasspole's educational reforms that gave their children greater access to secondary education. They greeted with affection and acclamation, as their own, a new generation of political leaders, black, brown, white, among them Donald Sangster, Noel Nethersole, Hugh Shearer, Robert Lightbourne and Clifford Campbell. They gained an understanding of democratic principles from the way in which their two leaders behaved, the respect they showed for each other and from the way in which each accepted defeat at the polls, Manley in 1944 and 1961, Bustamante in 1955 and in 1959. From the conduct of these two leaders they learned the underlying principles of two-party government, that differences of opinion did not have to mean hatred and vindictiveness, that Busta could invite a political opponent to have a drink and swinging to the vernacular would say with a laugh, "You is only a damn PNP." Manley for his part could declare to the

Bustamante
and Manley,
cousins and
friendly political
rivals

annual conference of the PNP in 1961: "On matters where I am consulting with the Opposition, I think it is right that I should treat them with
the greatest respect and discuss no details until I have discussed details with
them." (Nettleford: 1971) In 1964 he declared to another annual conference, "I will be no party to inciting people to physical violence as a means
of progress in this country." (Nettleford: 1971)

Bustamante and Manley, by example and by words, demonstrated their
full acceptance of the two-party system, "in a general way the foundations
of their society, so that neither consciously desires or intends or will be
forced to destroy the other". Furthermore, he emphasised that the opposition's great role is "to preserve democratic procedures and fundamental
human rights; in a word, to protect society from the excesses and corrup-
tions of power that will always be found wherever power finally resides".
The central change in the introduction of Crown colony government in
1865 had been that it transferred power from a white minority to the
crown; in 1944 there was set in motion the transfer of those powers from
the Crown to the whole society in 1962. Manley, in his moving tribute to
Busta in 1968, in a characteristic spirit of fair play and with a profound
respect for history, said:

Jamaica was fortunate in throwing up among its leaders one man, Sir Alexander, who gave confidence to the masses of this country, who won their affection and love to the most extraordinary degree and their loyalty and who proved afterwards by the whole course of his life that he had accepted the responsibilities of that time, and grown in stature with them as the years passed. And in considering Sir Alexander's rightful claims to the growth of democracy in Jamaica, I think that is the first thing to be said. (Nettleford: 1971)

We see the years 1927-62 as a period when the three great founders of the nation, Garvey, who left Jamaica in 1935, and later Bustamante and Manley, by word and example, taught that:

Democracy means recognition of the rights of others. Democracy means equality of opportunity for all in education, in the public service, and in private employment . . . Democracy means the protection of the weak against the strong.

Democracy means the obligation of the minority to recognise the right of the majority. Democracy means the responsibility of the government to its citizens, the protection of the citizens from the exercise of arbitrary power and the violation of human freedoms and individual rights. Democracy means freedom of worship for all and the subordination of the right of any one race to the overriding right of the human race. Democracy means freedom of expression and assembly of organization. (Williams: 1981)

These words were spoken by another great West Indian nation-builder, Eric Williams, in his Independence Day speech as prime minister of Trinidad and Tobago on 31 August 1962. The Jamaican people, by their voting record, by their support of the trade unions and by their demand for greater educational opportunity, showed that they greatly valued the vote and the two-party system. But they also regarded bread and jobs as basic issues. Crown colony rule had doomed the mass of the people to poverty and unemployment. What change would self-government bring?

That the British government should have taken these two critical decisions at this time deserves special notice, because the Second World War was then at its fiercest. Although poverty and government neglect had caused great distress amongst West Indians and although the demand for self-government was pressed with vigour, the debate was conducted with great respect and consideration on both sides, without racial or class rancour, and certainly without hatred. In the West Indies and in Africa, Britain won both affection and respect from her former colonists in these years of the triumph of the various national movements.

In the 1940s, also, international developments and the general climate of opinion were helpful to countries which, like Jamaica, were moving towards independence. Many of the major institutions of the United Nations, for example, were established at this time: the Food and Agriculture Organisation in Rome in 1945, the International Monetary Fund and the International Bank for Reconstruction and Development in the same year, and UNESCO and the International Labour Organisation in 1946.

Even during the havoc and gloom of the Second World War, green shoots of hope and brightening skies moved mankind to start building again, and to do so with the needs of non-industrialised nations in mind. Even a brief sample list of some of the chief events that took place in the five or six years following the grant of self-government to Jamaica indicates the beginning of a new age: the winding up of the old League of Nations in 1946 and the meeting of the United Nations General Assembly in London and then in New York, which became its permanent headquarters; the establishment of a General Agreement on Tariffs and Trade in Geneva by 23 countries (1947); President Harry Truman of the United States' call for a programme of technical aid to underdeveloped countries (1949); and the production of electricity by atomic energy (1951).

Events such as these strengthened the feeling amongst Jamaicans that they were entering an age of which interconnectedness and interdependence were the chief features. Small islands were no longer remote or wholly on their own. Science and technology, now the foundation of civilisation, were transforming our globe into an electronic village in which technology transfer and the dissemination of new knowledge could be used to help bridge the gap between rich and poor, developed and underdeveloped.

In this new age the trained human intelligence was recognised as being a nation's most precious asset. The social scientists, and especially the economists, sociologists and anthropologists transformed attitudes and influenced government policies in the way that Adam Smith's *Wealth of Nations* had done in the eight-eenth century. Our own Arthur Lewis, who wrote a seminal work, *The Theory of Economic Growth*, in the 1950s, noted the role of culture in impeding or furthering economic growth. Gunnar Myrdal's fuller treatment of this subject in his study of poverty amongst the peoples of South-East Asia, John Kenneth Galbraith's work *The Nature of Human Poverty* and John Maynard Keynes' work in economics helped to shape the thinking of the industrialised nations, especially in such areas as international aid, the internationalisation of trade, modernisation and the role of governments in promoting industrialisation and restructuring developing societies.

In such a world the key-word was "development" and the development of human resources was the top priority. International and national funding agencies made funds and training available. In these critical years the Jamaican people moved along the road from dependence to full internal self-government, their tutor being Norman Manley. Like Garvey and Eric Williams, he believed passionately that the ultimate powers of society should rest with the people and that – to echo Thomas Jefferson – if we think them not informed enough to exercise their powers with discretion, the remedy is not to take their powers from them but to inform their discretion with education.

Garvey did this throughout his life, instructing blacks in the history of Africa and in the need for social change through a representative, organised political system. Eric Williams pointed with justifiable pride to his programme of political education based on the "University" of Woodford Square, where he sought "to open the door behind which our dynamic energies are at present confined". Manley's testament is the body of speeches edited by Rex Nettleford under the title *Manley and the New Jamaica*. These four leaders, two of them Jamaican, in the first quarter of a century of West Indian nationhood provided the West Indian people with a theory of West Indian (or indeed Caribbean) political philosophy, which was rooted in the West Indian historical experience and aimed at the intellectual and spiritual liberation of the West Indian people. They rejected the Eurocentric mode of thinking, and "accepted the principle of parliamentary democracy and of belief in the essential importance and value of the individual man". (Nettleford: 1971)

We have taken account of global trends which favoured the efforts of poor countries to develop their natural and human resources, and indeed regarded such efforts as conditions for social and economic assistance, and we have referred to the creation of a West Indian system of political philosophy as a West Indian counterpart to constitutional advance. Hitherto, the primary consideration had been the best interests of the British empire. The changes in decision-making, in the guiding principles, constitutional goals and economic development were defined by Jamaicans. This explains why these years are so vital in our history.

When Bustamante and the JLP came to power and Ivan Lloyd and the PNP elected members took their places in the House, they all knew that they were on test as representatives of all the people, all the unemployed, the squatters and the vacant-eyed youth. They had to create bread and jobs. It was for these that Bustamante had marched through the streets of Kingston. The governor also knew that he would be held responsible if social discontent erupted, for under the 1944 constitution he, and not the ministers, was ruler.

In 1944 he set up an economic policy committee under a British economist, F. C. Benham. It turned out to be like consulting Queen Victoria. The committee laid it down that Jamaica should not use tariff protection to encourage local manufacturing. Benham advised that Jamaica's future lay in agriculture and in providing a market for British manufactured goods. But the development economists of the period, the West Indian Arthur Lewis among them, urged that countries like Jamaica, with surplus labour, a small home market, limited natural resources, too many people on the overburdened land, had no choice but to manufacture for export, to use tariffs for protection and to attract overseas investors by tax incentives. Trade was to include manufactured goods as well as agricultural products and raw materials.

Next door Puerto Rico was setting an example. The leader of the Populares, Muñoz Marín, who had campaigned in the 1930s under the promise "Land and bread", confronted by slum-ridden cities and rural distress, had worked out an agreement with the United States for Puerto Rico to be granted the status of Commonwealth in free association with the United States, and so had opened the way for emigration and for industrialisation through a planned programme of economic growth.

In Jamaica unemployment and rising social tension were also warnings that there was no time to lose. In 1945 Norman Manley said: "There is on the part of the masses, standing on one side of the dividing gulf, a deep resentment and urge to end and change it all. On the other side are the privileged few. These cannot escape the fear that secretly haunts them." Bustamante, an expert in sensing social tension, in breaking with colonial tradition, lost no time and moved ahead with the development of natural resources and the use of incentive legislation to encourage industrialisation.

Suddenly rays of sunshine broke through the dark clouds. The rumour spread that bauxite had been found in Jamaica. The incredulous Jamaican peasant shook his head and proclaimed his suspicion of backra, that trick-ified man: "Dem did know something long time", "Dem did know long time but didn't want fe share it", and "Ah nuh so it go. Dem a play dem tricks. You see dem too trickify."

But it was true. Jamaicans were sitting on a fortune, bauxite, red earth, which changed its name to alumina hydrate as it was purged of its redness and moved up the social scale to whiteness, and then to the summit and so gleaming a metal that not even whiteness could attain to it.

It was true, and every small upland farmer began to look at his patch of red earth and recalculate its worth. In 1868 a government geologist had found that Jamaica's red earth was largely a mixture of iron and alumina, but 19 years were to pass before the commercial development of the metal aluminium began in France and the United States, and another 50 years passed before Jamaica's bauxite attracted overseas attention. The demand soared for a light, strong, pliable metal for aeroplanes and for prefabricated, strong yet light, metal shutters, cookery ware and furniture of a hundred types. The demand was for the strongest, most pliable, most durable of them all, aluminium. So the world broke in on Jamaica, to buy its bauxite.

In 1942 a Jewish Kingston merchant and St Ann penkeeper, Alfred D'Costa, had some of the red earth on his property near Claremont analysed because it was so infertile. Bauxite was found to be present. A survey of Jamaica's bauxite reserves followed and soon afterwards negotiations began between the government and Canadian (Alcan) and United States companies (Reynolds and Kaiser). The 1942 estimate of 5 million tons was revised after more extensive surveys to between 500 million and 600 million tons. In the 1950s the three companies were extracting more than 5 million tons a year and Jamaica had become one of the world's major producers of bauxite. In 1957 the original agreement between the government and the companies was modified, with the result that the revenue paid on bauxite that had been mined increased tenfold, from a total of £352,000 per year to £3,700,000 in 1960-61.

Jamaica learned much from the bauxite companies, who from the beginning set an example of good citizenship. It could easily have been otherwise, for Jamaicans love their upland pastures and the sight of bulldozers tearing up the grass dramatised, often in a painful way, the extractive nature of the industry. In addition, these areas were often those most suitable for cattle rearing. Agricultural land is in short supply in Jamaica, as the process of urbanisation and the frequent waves of emigration show. By law the bauxite companies were required to keep agriculturally productive land in production until it was needed for mining, and to restore the mined-out land as far as possible to its original level of agricultural productivity. In response, the companies increased and improved the herds of cattle and gave particular attention to afforestation. Further, by skilled and sympathetic programmes of industrial relations and of community development, with special attention to education, and by ensuring that employment was open to qualified Jamaicans, men and women, at all levels, the bauxite companies eliminated racial discrimination in the industry and contributed both to the building of self-esteem and of a sense of national unity.

Jamaica's red earth from her upland pastures and her gleaming beaches of white sand became in the 1950s two of her chief money-earners. Dust-covered rust-coloured containers loaded the earth onto ships bound for the United States and freight cars laden with alumina hydrate loaded ships

bound for Canada, while some of the largest cruise ships in the world
discharged their passengers at Ocho Rios and Montego Bay, already the
two major centres of tourism on the north coast.

Montego Bay was the pace-setter. In the 1930s Doctor's Cave had been
nothing more than a gracious curve of sand leading to a small, friendly
cave, popular with the local people because the water was so buoyant, with
a constant, pleasantly warm temperature all year round. Doctors recommended the safe, healing waters; and after the Second World War, when
tourism became a global industry, Doctor's Cave began to attract the
wealthy and achy.

In the early 1950s, with Abe Issa as chairman of the Jamaican Tourist
Board, Jamaica set out to woo the tourists, and under his leadership and
that of John Pringle, both gifted entrepreneurs, tourism became one of
Jamaica's most important sources of revenue. In 1950 just under 75,000
tourists came to Jamaica. Three years later the arrivals had trebled.
Between 1950 and 1954 the revenue from tourism almost doubled, rising
from very nearly £3 million to £5,750,000.

There were losses. Jamaicans felt squeezed off their own beaches. In
response, in 1955 the government established the Beach Control
Authority with powers to declare any beach a public recreational beach.
There was concern that coloured and black Jamaicans might be unwel-
come in north-coast hotels. Generally, it was cash, not colour, that made a
difference. All in all, good sense prevailed and in the 1950s tourism
became a vital industry.

Courtesy of Jack Tyndale-Biscoe

Aerial photograph of Ocho Rios

Bauxite and tourism would ease, but could not solve, the problem of unemployment. Driven by intensifying social discontent, encouraged by the urging of the economists and by the example of Puerto Rico, the government decided to move ahead with a programme designed to create new jobs by encouraging manufacturing and industrialisation. In 1944 the Textiles Industry Law and the Hotel Law were enacted, followed by the Pioneer Industry Law in 1949, described as "the fountain head of subsequent industrial development", because, like the Puerto Rican model, it applied to any industry that qualified as a "pioneer", and not to one particular industry. The purpose was to encourage local entrepreneurs to become manufacturers. This was followed in 1952 by the creation of the Industrial Development Corporation, "to stimulate, facilitate and undertake the development of industry". The drive for industrialisation gained strength with the passing of these laws, and with the recruitment of a black Jamaican entrepreneur, Robert Lightbourne, who had established himself in Birmingham, England. He returned to Jamaica to direct the Industrial Development Corporation.

Manley welcomed the foundation of the Industrial Development Corporation, which had indeed been on the PNP's agenda: "We who welcomed this part of a series of essential measures for the beginning of a planned economy have done so because we recognize that without measures of this sort we cannot attempt to solve the problem which grows greater year by year."

After the PNP took office in 1955 the government supplemented earlier legislation with the Industrial Incentives Law of 1956 which, along with the Export Industries Law of the same year, sought to make Jamaica a major manufacturing centre by granting tax concessions during a "holiday period". The law was designed to attract foreign investors who already had foreign outlets for their goods in countries within easy reach of Jamaica, by granting tax concessions on initial imports of machinery and all imports of raw materials and fuel. The finished products were exempt from duty, but they all had to be exported.

Planned social and economic growth required the modernisation of the Civil Service, and its transformation from a Eurocentred law-and-order civil service ornamented with ceremonial swords and helmets into an innovative, creative public service of bright young Jamaicans eager to develop their country's natural resources, to build a strong economy and a united nation. The new group included leaders such as Egerton Richardson, John Mordecai, G. Arthur Brown, Don and Gladstone Mills. Working hand-in-hand with these was an English development planner, George Cadbury. Dedication to Jamaica and the Jamaican people was the motivating force. Whatever the political party in power, Jamaica was the cause to serve. The creative energy of young, trained Jamaicans working harmoniously and loyally with the political leaders and the appreciation the politicians showed for their advice, explain the extraordinary record of the 1950s in transforming Jamaica into a dynamic, patriotic self-governing community. They worked with the political leaders to create a range of specialised agencies and organisations such as the Industrial Development Corporation, the Agricultural Development Corporation (already mentioned), the Bank of Jamaica, the Central Planning Agency, the Central Bureau of Statistics and the Jamaica Broadcasting Corporation. This was the silent revolution which enabled Jamaica to develop a range of successful programmes for economic growth and to perform the monumental task of meeting the multiplying demands of an expanding and greatly diversified economy.

This drive for industrialisation and manufacturing, directed alternatively by the JLP and the PNP, was the single most important economic initiative of these years of extraordinary achievement.

Instead of recounting the events in order, we will treat the programmes as a case-study, for these years have much to teach us about the development process, social change, the liberating power of affirming a racial identity and about the persistence of colonial stereotypes.

We begin with the historical significance of the programmes. For the first time in their history of struggle, black Jamaicans joined in the process of electing their representatives, and for the first time the elected representatives of all the Jamaican people made employment, bread and jobs their major concern. By setting this priority the first elected government of all the people rejected the colonial imperatives and set a Jamaican agenda. They broke the stranglehold of the planter class on political power. For the first time the government of Jamaica stopped being a struggle between planter interests and a British governor, and became a democratic exercise in selecting political and social goals.

For the first time also, the Jamaican legislature examined the experience of another Caribbean society in order to learn from it. It is one of the ironies of our history that Jamaicans emerging from British colonial rule turned to Puerto Rico, which as a Spanish stronghold, had repulsed Francis Drake's attempt at landing in the seventeenth century. La Fortaleza, once the seat of the Spanish governor, became the residence of the American governor, Rexford Tugwell, one of Franklin Roosevelt's New-Dealers. The political leader of Puerto Rico, Muñoz Marín, was leading his people's struggle against the very poverty and degradation with which Bustamante, Manley and African-Jamaicans were struggling. The Puerto Rican techniques for encouraging industrialisation were reflected in the Jamaican legislation, and contributed to the success that attended Jamaica's effort.

For the first time in their history the Jamaican people experienced the exhilarating effect of achievements and of growing confidence. The government by its sense of purpose and increasing competence soon won the support of leaders of the private sector such as the Hannas, Issas, Matalons. Carl Stone draws attention to this growing sense of direction and of achievement in an important analysis of this period.

> Between 1944 and the mid-1950's this policy perspective on economic strategies changed radically as elected politicians came into full control of domestic economic policy. Greater self confidence was infused into the business class as the political system was democratized. Urban merchant interests took on the challenge of shifting from being commission agents of manufacturing companies to creating a local manufacturing sector with state support and protection.

Writing with reference to the expansion of industry between 1956 and 1967, and to the parallel expansion in bauxite, tourism and other services, he noted the consequent rise of

> a vibrant, new and increasingly wealthy and influential entrepreneurial class. The political directorate treated the interests of the new entrepreneurs as equal to the interests of the economy as a whole as the country's economic future seemed hinged on their continued

expansion. They had easy access to the corridors of power . . . They effectively replaced the planters as the dominant owning interests after the earlier decline in plantation agriculture in the first two decades of the twentieth century.

The record of economic growth for the period 1945-60 is impressive by any standards. Between 1954 and 1960, the sale of electricity to industry doubled to 50 million kilowatts. Between 1943 and 1960 national income per head at current prices grew from £32.50 to £128, while gross domestic product increased from £70 million in 1950 to £230 million in 1960. This rate of growth was exceeded only by two other countries, Puerto Rico and Japan.

This extraordinary achievement had a minus sign attached to it. The gap between the general mass of the people and the new entrepreneurs widened. Edward Seaga voiced the general concern when, as one of the leading young politicians of the 1960s, he pointed out that the "haves were getting richer and the have-nots were getting poorer". A week later Bustamante declared that Jamaicans were sitting on the brink of a volcano.

The figures did indeed point to serious social dislocation. Clarke's analysis showed that "despite the economic changes which had taken place the pattern of employment in Kingston in 1960 remained basically similar to that in 1943" (Clarke: 1973); and Volker's study indicated that "manufacturing concerns with ten or more workers employed only 17,000 persons in Kingston in 1960 . . . and race and colour were important outward symbols of the social situation".

It was a time of growing anger among the urban poor. Alongside Carl Stone's portrayal of the wealthy entrepreneurs we place Simpson's description of the rural poor arriving in Kingston.

> Everyday young people arrived from country districts; many of them gravitate to West Kingston . . . Some men come with the hope of finding work, fewer girls than men arrived, some to work as domestic servants, others to become prostitutes or scuffle for a living. Many of the incoming men fell into the practice of "living around", of gambling and stealing, and if they had no friends, money or relatives they had to "live hard", to cotch, or start squatting or living on the dungle, all these being signs of extreme population pressure and over-crowding.

By 1960, during the period of economic growth, more than one-half of all unemployed Jamaicans were residing in the Corporate Area, and overcrowding increased, with the result that "although some rehousing had been effected in these areas, in general they were characterized by population increase and social stagnation . . . By 1960, therefore, the distinction between the slums and the better areas was as marked as, if not more marked than, it had been in 1943. Gross population densities at the two dates support this contention." (Clarke: 1975)

Norman Manley described the problem in anguished terms: "And what do we do? We have to move from an economy wholly dependent on agriculture; we have to answer the people hammering on the door for bread; we have to find more jobs, to take more people off the land, to open more schools, to generate more capital, and we remain wholly dependent on external markets."

Equally disturbing was the insidious disease of class-blindness which focused judgement only on what was happening within one's class and made it appear to be universal. Even Norman Manley, the most scrupulously fair of men, fell victim to this form of selective blindness when he described West Indian society, and Jamaican society in particular, as "made up of people drawn from all over the world, predominantly Negro or of mixed blood, but also with large numbers of others, and nowhere in the world has more progress been made in developing a non-racial society in which colour is not significant". (Nettleford: 1971) But in this very period Negro racist organisations in Kingston were becoming increasingly belligerent.

As Clarke reports, some Rastafarians vilified the brown population in particular, describing them as mulattoes, quadroons and spittoons; and there was a group which cried out during their meetings, "Manley is Pharaoh! Pharaoh, let my people go." And they used to chant "He layeth me down to sleep on hard benches, he leadeth me by the still factories." (Clarke: 1975)

Many Jamaicans had hoped in the 1950s for a lessening of social tension and, most pressing of all, for a coming together of the "two Jamaicas" in preparation for the setting up of the Federation of the West Indies. They were grievously disappointed to find that the rapid growth of the economy had widened the cleavage and added to the anger of the have-nots.

Things had gone otherwise in Puerto Rico. Slums had been cleared, income levels lifted, high rates of economic growth achieved and social tensions eased. The difference lay in the fact that whereas Jamaica concentrated on economic growth through incentive legislation, Puerto Rico made this a part of a larger programme for social change. The University of Puerto Rico, which had been revitalised and modernised, was entrusted with the task of becoming a vigorous centre of education and research and of developing a profound sense of unity in the Puerto Rican people. The school system was strengthened with an efficient network of technical and vocational schools, and a number of reorganised second-unit schools enriched the Puerto Rican children's knowledge of their physical and cultural environment. As in the American tradition, every effort was made to increase social mobility through equality of educational opportunity. The result was that social cohesion was strengthened and a sense of unity enforced by the impressive rate of economic growth.

Here we come to a major cause of the dislocating impact of Jamaica's industrialisation drive of the 1950s. The goals, values, methods, outlook of Jamaica's system of education remained colonial and generated split loyalties. Evan Jones' description of one of the most prestigious of Jamaica's schools in 1940 reveals how, in the period we are considering, while the Puerto Ricans were striving to develop through education a deep sense of unity in the Puerto Rican people, and while Jamaica's nationalists were campaigning for national unity, Jamaica secondary education was rooting the country's élite children in Europe. The greatest and most debilitating split in society was not that which was reflected in the urban landscape, but that which revealed split loyalties. The educational system was the chief barrier to social development.

It was years later, in 1958, that Jamaica's ministry of education referred to the general criticism of the secondary schools for their lack of concern about Jamaica and lack of knowledge about its people.

As for primary education, the colonial administrators and the ruling élites had one set of objectives, that of maintaining the *status quo*, while the people sent their children to school "with the intention of changing their socio-economic position, that is, changing the *status quo*. This cross-purpose is the source of dysfunctionality in the Jamaican educational system." (Miller: 1989) As late as 1989 Miller pointed out: "In a real sense the ideas that have informed educational developments in independent Jamaica have been those that were formulated by the colonial administration in the 1940's." As a result, while Jamaicans were driving ahead with industrial development, their system of education was weakening, their efforts splitting the society culturally as well as economically.

Puerto Rico and Jamaica, in contrasting ways, drove home the lesson that development involves political, social and economic factors, that it centres on the human being and is "an unfolding of what is in the germ", a release of creative potential.

It remains for Jamaican society to recognise the centrality of Africa, and to translate Sheikh Anta Diop's message into a system of education. As he said, "The Negro must be able to grasp the continuity of his nation's history and to draw from it the moral support he needs to recover his place in the civilised world."

The teachers are the heroes in our account of Jamaica's colonial system of education which endured for some years after independence. "Teacher" was one of the heroic community builders, along with the country parson,

the village nurse and "Doc" the druggist. These by their dedicated leadership, made the school a way of escape from rural poverty.

CHAPTER 30

Culture and nationhood

Division, separation: these were the key words during the three centuries of British rule. Always, decade after decade, from 1655 to 1940, there were two groupings of people in Jamaica, "two Jamaicas" separated by race, colour and political power.

There were no overarching loyalties, no collective memories, no sense of a community that for long had shared the same soil. For Africans the plantation was a place from which to escape. There was no common creed, no common language, no common culture. The term "Jamaica" was little more than a label, a name on a map. There were Africa and Europe; and Europe, the dominant power, dedicated itself to maintaining difference, not to nurturing unity.

The badges were stark, unequivocal, irreversible. "White" meant "good" and "black" meant "bad", although the African experience was that Europe meant guns, slave ships and the Middle Passage for hundreds and thousands and indeed, in total, for 10 million African men and women.

"White" meant "good" and "black" meant "bad", even though Governor Eyre was never charged with the murder of George William Gordon, nor the Colonial Office charged with using an unfair system of taxation to compel the African-Jamaican to bear the tax burden, nor for using legislative power to safeguard the political power of the white and brown minority.

The British Crown was the only symbol of unity. For the upper and middle classes it represented protection and the preservation of privilege. For the working class it meant persistent poverty. The chief dividing factor was race, but Euro-Jamaica masked this fact with a ritual of pretence. There was a carefully preserved picture of a multiracial society in which "racial issues tend to be avoided in political discourses. No one who is progressive talks about racial consciousness. Class consciousness is acceptable, either from the standpoint of radical politics or as a reflection of social mobility. In Jamaican history since Garvey the only sector to consistently challenge the false multi-racialism has been the Rastafarians". (Lewis: 1987)

The picture presented by traditional historians is of a colony united under British rule, moving gradually in the 1940s towards self-government and finally to independence. In reality, the divisions and differences were so many, so deep, that in recent years scholars such as the Jamaican sociologist M. G. Smith described it as a plural society. Up to the 1920s there was little sentiment of national unity and little that could be described as a Jamaican culture. How could it have been otherwise when for two centuries and up to the abolition of the slave trade freshly arrived Africans were separated from each other and distributed to different plantations? Or when many Euro-Jamaicans saw Britain as home and Jamaica as a place of exile?

Jamaica's nationhood, then, did not grow out of memories of an earlier tribal unity. Its social heritage reflects its history of racial and colour discrimination. Its educational system was designed to perpetuate social and economic differences. If we define culture as the social heritage of a community, the total body of material artefacts, the mental and spiritual artefacts (systems, ideas, beliefs) and the distinctive forms of behaviour, then up to the 1930s the colony's social heritage could not exercise a powerful cohesive force because it was itself split.

To a Jamaican what happened in the 1930s and 1940s is nothing short of a miracle, for the political revolution described in the preceding chapters was attended by a powerful surge of creative energy that impelled Jamaicans of all classes to think of Jamaica as "my country" and of Jamaicans of all colours as "my people".

Norman Manley made this point when he launched the People's National Party.

> Anyone looking back on the past ten years (1928-1938) will realise that we in this country have been more and more concentrating upon our own affairs. We have thought more of Jamaica, spoken more about Jamaica, breathed more of the atmosphere of Jamaica than we can recall before in this country. And it has been symptomatic of the existence of an increasing number of organisations in all classes of the community . . . and most marked in the growth of opinion among the young men of this country, of the dawn of the feeling that this should be their home and their country . . . There is a tremendous difference between living in a place and belonging to it and feeling that your own life and your destiny is [sic] irrevocably bound up in the life and destiny of that place. (Nettleford: 1971)

Marcus Garvey had challenged the people to claim the African heritage and to cherish self-esteem and nationalist Jamaica was rejecting imperial domination. With one touch of creative intensity, generated by self-discovery and self-emancipation, the desert flowered.

The change came as silently, as magically as spring comes in upland Jamaica, with its delicate greens and the glowing purple of new leaves on the pimento trees, and on the Liguanea Plain with the tender translucent green of the lignum vitae trees. The impulse came from the people's discovery of their identity and this was accompanied by a surge of creative energy unparalleled in their history. Animated by these creative forces, Jamaicans brought into being a literature, an art movement and wide-ranging activities in sports and athletics, the whole comprising a burgeoning, distinctive culture.

The extraordinary achievements in athletics, sport and in diverse cultural movements, including Rastafarianism and the women's movement, brought the two Jamaicas nearer together. After considering the cultural revolution in sport, athletics and the creative arts, we will reflect on the role of education and culture in making nationhood the meaningful reality that it should be.

Our story of cultural achievement is one that inspires pride and confidence in all Jamaicans. African-Jamaica's first breakthrough in one area of British supremacy came in 1930 when young George Headley, not yet 21 years of age, "completed his fourth century in four tests, with a record West Indian Test score of 223 in the first test ever played at Sabina [Park]". (Carnegie: 1996) The time came when the British cricketing world rose to its feet to acclaim George Headley's entry into the world of cricket's immortals with a century at Lord's in each innings of the match. The famous West Indian tour in England in 1950, with two of the world's great spin bowlers, Alfred Valentine and Sonny Ramadhin, and three of the world's great batsmen, Everton Weekes, Frank Worrell and Clyde Walcott, further demonstrated that West Indian cricket had achieved world levels.

By 1950 Herb McKenley had also announced the entry of Jamaica into world athletics. In 1947 McKenley had managed to:

> set the first time-measured world record by a Jamaican, or any other English-speaking West Indian, for that matter. In 1948 he set another world-record for the quarter-mile of 46 seconds

Herb McKenley

Arthur Wint

flat, and ran 45.9 for the metric equivalent 400 metres, feats that had been set down as impossible barriers by experts in the sport years before. In that same year he was beaten for the Olympic 400 meters title by his countryman, Arthur Wint . . . The two gave Jamaica the first ever such triumph in the entire history of the Olympic games over athletes from the United States of America (USA) in a male sprint event. (Carnegie: 1996)

Another of the pace-setters in athletics was Keith Gardner, gold medalist in the hurdles in the Commonwealth Games of 1954 and 1958. These triumphs, coming as they did in this period of nat-ional awakening, in competition with the rest of the world, were of pro-found importance. By winning instant worldwide recognition in competition with people of all races and cultures, they lifted Jamaica's self-esteem, opened the eyes of Jamaicans to the potential of all Jamaican youth and shattered the myth about black inferiority.

By great good fortune, through the foresight of a British governor of the Crown colony period, Sir Anthony Musgrave, Jamaica had the institu-tional underpinnings for nurturing and extending a cultural revolution, the Institute of Jamaica and the National Gallery. They are reminders not only of Sir Anthony Musgrave, who established the Institute for the encouragement of literature, science and art, but also of an Englishman, Frank Cundall, who almost single-handedly built up the West India Reference Library into one of the finest collections of its kind in the Americas, and of scientists such as Sawkins and, in more recent times, Bernard Lewis, who built up the Natural History Museum with its price-less collection of Jamaica's fauna and flora. In the 50 years between the founding of the institute and the revolution of the 1930s, the institute was the only agency in Jamaica dedicated to studying and preserving the country's political and natural history and encouraging an interest in indigenous Jamaica.

Institute of Jamaica

In the 1930s the institute became both catalyst and activator for Jamaica's burgeoning art movement. It brought together young Trelawny-bred Albert Huie, mature master-barber John Dunkley back from his travels in Central America, Edna Manley who was London-trained in the cubist style, realist-romantic Ralph Campbell, lonely Henry Daley and the questioning social satirist Carl Abrahams, all individualists working on their own with absolute certitude as if they had been tutored in five centuries of an artistic tradition. Edna Manley had returned to Jamaica with her husband Norman in 1922, and had produced her first piece of sculpture, "The Beadsellers", a year later. She then spent ten years grappling with the technical problems of carving in mahogany in the place of stone, and learning how to create an authentic Jamaican icongraphy out of the body gestures, arms akimbo, vital dancing bodies and defiant heads of Jamaicans. Soon, groups of Jamaican sculptors, painters, poets were busy portraying the historical experience of the African-Jamaican people. Where will one find a more powerful, more moving portrayal of a poor, elderly black woman than in Albert Huie's "Woman in the Sun", a more African and Jamaican interpretation of revivalism than in Carl Abrahams' "Backyard", urban squalor more disturbing than in the darkness of David Pottinger's "Street Scene" or find more intensely African carvings than David Miller's "Rasta Man" and "Mask"?

Albert Huie

Edna Manley's "Negro Aroused", and Dunkley's portrayal of what the negro protest was about, marked the beginning of the Jamaican art movement. The carvings, "Negro Aroused", "Young Negro", "The Diggers", "caught the inner spirit of our people and flung their rapidly rising resentment of the stagnant colonial order into a vivid appropriate sculptural form". (Smith: 1974) David Boxer enlarged the theme: "With their powerful insistent rhythms which frame the essential leitmotif of the head turned back, straining upward towards a vision, or downward in suppressed anger . . . [they] have truly become the icons of that period of our history, a period when the black Jamaican was indeed aroused, ready for a new social order, demanding his place in the sun." (Boxer: 1989)

Edna Manley

A significant concordance of events highlights these years 1937 and 1938, the period of proletariat unrest in Kingston, of the Frome riots, the period also of Edna Manley's first exhibition of sculpture (1937), and the emergence of Albert Huie, Carl Abrahams and John Dunkley, three of Jamaica's great painters. They felt, experienced, portrayed the emotions, desperation, frustrations, hopes, visions of the people. Edna Manley's "Negro Aroused" and John Dunkley's dark-grey landscapes of never-ending roads, a world with neither dawn nor noonday, its landscape of truncated trees, of soul-yearnings and dreams, Carl Abrahams' "Last Supper", were all memory and prophecy, effort and vision, self-discovery and racial affirmation, pain and triumph. The great collection of the National Gallery of Jamaica presents a moving, often apocalyptic, always uplifting portrait of the Jamaican people during this period. Carl Abrahams, Karl Parboosingh, Alvin Marriott, the revivalist preacher Mallica Reynolds, known as "Kapo", Sydney McLaren and Cecil Baugh, the potter, are among the honoured names of the men and women who in one generation told the story of the Jamaican people in vivid splendid works of art.

John Dunkley

The message went deep. It was Africa confronting Europe with a deeply religious sense of the world and of man's relationship with God, which we find especially in the work of the "intuitive painters", members of "a whole

Kapo

undercurrent of untutored art in Jamaica that could not be ignored as the isolated primitives which critical opinion has made them out to be". (Boxer: 1989) The work of Kapo, for example, commanded international attention and admiration. In Boxer's words, Kapo's first important painting (1947) was:

An image of Christ, a black Christ seated on the shore of the Sea of Galilee. Shortly afterwards he abandoned painting and produced between 1948 and 1967 a remarkable collection of works that have few equals among Jamaican, indeed Caribbean, carvers in wood. The inspiration for these carvings came out of Revivalism: the works are imbued with the movement, the rhythms, the whole intense emotionalism of this religion that is at once African and Christian. (Boxer: 1989)

Ralph Campbell

Alongside the artists of this period moved the poets and novelists, George Campbell, Vic Reid, Roger Mais, John Hearne and Andrew Salkey, who joined their fellow West Indians of the period, George Lamming, Vidia Naipaul, Jan Carew, Edgar Mittelholzer, Arthur Seymour and others in founding a West Indian literature that was soon recognised as a significant contribution to world literature.

The range of artistic achievement was wide. It brought together educated middle-class, white Edna Manley, working-class African-Jamaicans, all meeting as Jamaicans, all driven by the urge to portray the land and the Jamaican experience.

The range of achievement extended to setting and implementing national goals, to areas of scholarship and scientific research on the one hand, and, on the other, it included the founders of a messianic group that came to be called Rastafarians. It was Sir Herbert McDonald's vision and his insistence on building a national stadium and sports arena that made it possible for Jamaica to host the Central American and Caribbean Games in 1962, the British Empire and Commonwealth Games in 1966, thus also providing the country with a venue for accommodating national events of great size.

Vic Reid

Of the scholars and scientists, Thomas Philip Lecky deserves special mention. Early in the 1920s he entered the Farm School, where he became so interested in livestock and so skillful in dealing with cattle that his fellow-students called him "Cow Bredda". Determined to breed a special kind of cattle suited to Jamaican conditions, he became Livestock Officer at Hope, equipped himself by studying at the Universities of McGill, Toronto and Edinburgh, continued his experiments over many years and at last, in the 1950s, established a new breed of cattle, the Jamaica Hope, an animal slightly bigger than a Jersey that yielded a good supply of milk and beef. Lecky did with cattle what J. R. Bovell did in Barbados by propagating new and better varieties of sugar cane and what J. B. Sutherland did for Jamaica by breeding the Lacatan variety of banana.

T. P. Lecky

The Rastafarians draw their inspiration chiefly from the Bible – the Old Testament especially – and an American publication, *The Sixth and Seventh Books of Moses*. Their story brings together despised black men in Back O' Wall, the Emperor Haile Selassie and a worldwide musical explosion that featured Bob Marley.

Rex Nettleford reminds us that the Rastafarian Movement was yet another form of the African-Jamaican's protest against a society in which:

> The sounds and pressure of poverty continued to be underlined in clear colour, the Jamaican of unmistakably African descent decidedly relegated to the base of the society. All the responses known to Jamaican history were invoked by the Rastafarian . . . For in Rastafarianism are to be found such old responses as psychological withdrawal, black nationalism, apocalyptic exultation and denunciation tied to a bold assertion of a redemptive ethic as aid to liberation and relief from suffering. (Nettleford: 1973)

In 1930 Ras Tafari, great-grandson of King Saheka Selassie of Shoa, was crowned Negus of Ethiopia in St George's Cathedral, Addis Ababa. The young king took the name Haile Selassie (Might of the Trinity), as well as other titles, King of Kings and the Lion of Judah, which put him in the legendary line of descent from King Solomon.

Many followers of Marcus Garvey saw this as a revelation from God. Some recalled that years earlier, just before leaving for the United States, Garvey was reported to have said, "Look to Africa for the crowning of a Black King. He shall be the Redeemer." The words "came echoing like the voice of God. Possessed by the spirit of this new development, many Jamaicans now saw the coronation as a fulfillment of biblical prophesy and Haile Selassie as the Messiah of African redemption". (Barrett: 1977)

Garvey thought and dreamed Ethiopia. The "Universal Ethiopian Anthem" began with the words "Ethiopia, thou land of our fathers", and he never wearied of declaring:

> We negroes believe in the God of Ethiopia, the Everlasting God – God the Son, God the Holy Ghost, the one God of all ages. This is the God in whom we believe but we shall worship him through the spectacles of Ethiopia; and, as Scripture foretold, Ethiopia shall once more stretch forth its hands to God.

Garvey's message lived on after him. He is for many Rastafarians a great prophet, and for some none other than John the Baptist incarnate: "There can be no doubt that Garvey's Back to Africa Movement set the stage for the rise of Rastafarianism." This was the glory that filled the mind of Leonard Howell, who had served in the Ashanti war of 1896, had learned several African languages and had returned to Jamaica some time after the coronation, convinced that Haile Selassie was the messiah of the black people. He began his ministry amid the slums of West Kingston. He was joined later by three other preachers, Joseph Hibbert, Robert Hinds and Archibald Dunkley. They built up a small but faithful membership.

Somehow the name "Ras Tafari" and not "Haile Selassie" came to be adopted, "Ras" being in Amharic a title equivalent to the English "Duke" and "Tafari" being the king's family name. His name, Haile Selassie, is used in their ritual, in prayers and songs. The name "Jah", which is also reverenced, is probably a shortened form of "Jehovah".

By 1933 Howell and his followers were ready with their redemptive message of Haile Selassie as the Supreme Being and only ruler of black people. The question is not whether or not they were right in their belief. This is what they believed and in the strength of that belief they placed Africa at the centre of Jamaican concerns.

The year 1935 was one of great distress for the Rastafarians, for it saw Mussolini's brutal, unprovoked attack on Ethiopia. Jamaicans in general were angered at this assault, and they welcomed the founding in New York two years later of the Ethiopian World Foundation to work for the unity and solidarity of the black people of the world. By 1938 several local groups were established in Jamaica.

In the meantime, the Rastafarians held together and began to grow in numbers, despite harassment and hardship. Leonard Howell and some hundreds of his followers settled a derelict and desolate estate, Pinnacle, near Sligoville. The police raided Pinnacle in 1941 and arrested a number of Rastafarians. During those difficult years the Brethren developed their community-style of living, proclaimed their identity by wearing dreadlocks and solidified the movement notwithstanding police harassment. Some time before his death, other leaders succeeded Howell.

Confrontation, not flight to the hills, became the mood. In March 1958, for the first time in local history, members of the Rastafarian cult were having what they called a "Universal Convention" at their headquarters, the Coptic Theocratic Temple in Kingston Pen. Hundreds of Rastafarians, men and women, attended the convention. On 24 March, reported the *Star*,

> The City Kingston was 'captured' near dawn on Saturday by some 300 . . . men of the Rastafarian cult along with their women and children. About 3:30 a.m. early market goers saw members of the Rastafarian Movement gathered in the centre of Victoria Park, with towering poles atop of which fluttered black flags and red banners, and loudly proclaiming that they had captured the city . . . When the police moved toward them a leader of the group with his hands uplifted issued a warning to the police: 'Touch not the Lord's anointed' . . . the police finally moved them.

Later that year Old King's House in Spanish Town was "captured" in the name of the Negus of Ethiopia. The police replied by enforcing the Jamaica Dangerous Drugs Law, arresting members of the cult, shaving their heads and generally harassing them. A sociologist of the University of the West Indies urged in the press that "the aspiration of a social group are not to be disregarded by an attitude of angry contempt for its personal and private habits . . . For in the long run the type of Prince Emanuel [a Rastafarian leader] may have more to do with the West Indies future than the type of Lord Hailes" [former Governor-General of the West Indies].

In 1959 the Rev. Claudius Henry, another messianic leader, was charged with planning a military takeover of Jamaica. He was convicted of treason and sent to prison for six years. Claudius Henry's son Ronald and a small band of guerrilla fighters were later captured in the Red Hills in an operation in which two British soldiers were killed. The rebels were sentenced to death. There is no evidence that the Rastafarians were linked with Claudius Henry.

At this point some of the leading Rastafarian brethren, disturbed at the turn events had taken, and at the harm that Henry's rebellious acts had done to their cause, asked the university to enquire into their doctrines, grievances and conduct, and to report on them to the government. The Nettleford-Smith-Augier report, undertaken and completed in a month, marks a turning point in the history of Rastafarianism. "The study not only revealed the socio-economic conditions of the movement to the general public, but also, for the first time, articulated the history and doctrine of the movement." The report found that the great majority of Rastafari brethren are peaceful citizens who do not believe in violence. Rastafarian doctrine is radical in the broad sense that it is against the oppression of the black race, much of which derives from the existing economic structure.

The report highlighted the social cleavages in Jamaican society, many of which were caused by the colonial system of education. Upper-class Jamaicans, and many in the middle class, being products of the secondary schools, looked at the black working class through European eyes. The report reminds us that cultural development requires not only institutional underpinning such as the Institute of Jamaica, the national stadium and the arena provided, but also the support of scholarship, analysis and research. It draws strength from both vision and intellectual rigour. By 1960 the young University of the West Indies was beginning to contribute to the cultural movement through active, talented groups, such as the University Singers, University Players and highly gifted students such as Slade Hopkinson, future Nobel Prize winner Derek Walcott, Rex Nettleford and Archie Hudson Phillips. Alongside these were the scholars of the recently founded Institute of Social and Economic Research, the Institute of Education and the faculties of the Social Sciences, the Arts, Natural Sciences and Medicine. A number of young scholars were already making their mark, among them M. G. Smith, Norman Girvan, Alister McIntyre, Elsa Goveia, not scholars in isolation but men and women involved in West Indian research and in nation-building. With them were visiting scholars such as the Jamaican, Fred Cassidy, whose *Jamaica Talk* and *A Dictionary of the Jamaican Language*, written jointly with Robert Le Page, demonstrated the historical and aesthetic value of the folk-language. Sociological and economic research revealed how British colonial policy lived on in the educational system and being divisive hindered it from becoming a unifying force.

The second phase of the Rastafarian movement began in the 1960s, when along with the women's movement it became a transforming cultural force. At this point we will pause to join the young Jamaican nation in its celebration of independence and in its welcome to two royal visitors.

In July 1962, from Holland Point to Negril, from Old Harbour Bay to

Port Maria, Jamaicans made ready to celebrate their achievement of independence. Black, green and gold: these are the strong vibrant colours of Jamaica's flag, black for Africa, an affirmation of racial identity; green, a token of ever-springing hope; gold for the sun's life-giving energy.

At midnight on 5 August 1962 the Union Jack was lowered, the flag of Jamaica was raised officially for the first time and the words of Jamaica's national anthem echoed through the streets and across the fields, not a battle cry like the *Marseillaise* but the prayer of a small, newly independent nation for guidance and protection for themselves and for "Jamaica, land we love".

> Eternal Father, bless our Land,
> Guide us with Thy Mighty hand
> Keep us free from evil powers
> Be our guide through countless hours
> Through our leaders great defender
> Grant us wisdom from above.

On 6 August 1962, at the first session of Jamaica's parliament, the constitutional documents were handed to the prime minister, Alexander Bustamante, by Princess Margaret who, on behalf of the Queen, wished the new nation well. It was a solemn occasion. With that act Jamaica moved from the protection of the British Crown and stood alone, shaper of her own future.

The most moving ceremony was the lowering of the Union Jack and the hoisting of the black, green and gold flag in the national stadium at midnight. Next morning at the ceremony in Gordon House, Norman Manley in a brief speech, gave depth to the occasion when he reminded the nation:

> We here today stand surrounded by an unseen host of witnesses, the men who in the past and through all our history strove to keep alight the torch of freedom in this country. No one will name them today but this house is in very deed their memorial and they are with us in spirit in these great days and they too moved through the door which opened into our new future only one day ago.
>
> And what of the future? We have come to independence prepared and ready to shoulder our new responsibilities and united I believe in one single hope that we may make our small country a safe and happy home for all our people. (Nettleford: 1971)

"For all our people": that was the test and the challenge. The cultural revolution pointed the way to go. So did a second royal visit, that of Haile Selassie, which took place for four days from 21 April 1966. Princess Margaret's visit signified the withdrawal of Britain. The visit by the

Emperor of Ethiopia underscored Africa's role in the Caribbean and revealed that the contacts with the true motherland had been kept open by the ancestors.

> Their souls shuttle
> still the secret paths of ocean
> connecting us still, the current unbroken
> the circuits kept open. (Chamberlin: 1993)

Haile Selassie went to Trinidad at the invitation of the Prime Minister, Eric Williams, and continued on to Jamaica at the invitation of a group of African nationalists, among them Dr M. B. Douglas, who wrote:

> There were no less than 100,000 people at the airport to meet him. The Rastafarians numbered at least 10,000. As soon as the plane had come to a stop, the Rastafarians responded with a roar of joy and surged out on the tarmac, each one pushing to get a touch of the plane. When the Emperor saw the people, the Rastafarian flags, the cheering and singing, he wept.
>
> The crowd was so thick around the plane that the Emperor was unable to get out for close to thirty minutes . . . Then the crowd followed instructions to make way and the Emperor got into a car and rode off to King's House, but by this time all the official plans for the welcome ceremony had been cancelled.
>
> The Rastafarians were not interested in protocol . . . their explanation was "This is our day: This is our God. It is him we come to see. It is we who welcome him."

The Rastafarian papers told how for the first time Rastafari brethren were officially invited to King's House: "Glory be to the visit of Emperor Haile Selassie. Although we were born here, the privilege was never granted to us until April 21, 1966. The Rases were there, the aristocrats were there . . . It took Ras Tafari in person to occasion the reality 'that all men were created equal'. And, declared another, 'The emperor's coming lifted us from the dust and caused us to sit with princes of this country.'" (Barrett: 1977)

Haile Selassie is said to have given some of the brethren instructions not to seek to emigrate to Ethiopia until they had liberated the people of Jamaica and that the day of his arrival should be celebrated each year. Following on these instructions the Rastafarians began to adjust to Jamaica as home. In so doing they set in motion a wave of new industries, the most remarkable and important being music, especially the Rastafari drumbeat originated by Count Ossie, in the early years a member of the movement.

Rastafarian musicians and singers, "Toots" Hibbert among them, ventured into world markets with their tunes and songs. By 1968 Hibbert's "Do the Reggae" was taking the market. Within a year or two Bob Marley was making reggae the world's favourite beat. His performances were intensely moving:

> A spasm of frenzied joy greeted Bob Marley as he jumped, spun, and shook his dreadlocks in front of the audience. With raised hands, in true Rastafarian style, he psyched his audience with his familiar yell, "Yeah". The audience responded "Yeah". Then reverently he . . . with bowed head and drooping dreadlocks, invoked the god of Rastafarianism, "Jah" and . . . concluded the invocation with the chant "One Lord, and One God in Mount Zion. (Barrett: 1977)

Leonard Barrett described Reggae as "Africa, Jamaica, soul, nature, sorrow, hate and love all mingled together. It sprang from the hearts of Africa's children in 'Babylon' – Jamaica. It is liminal music that sings of oppression in exile, a longing for home, or for a place to feel at home." Marley stamped his personality on reggae until the sound became identified with the Rastafarian movement. Reggae music, now a multimillion dollar business, derives from that unique sect whose music is an inseparable and expressive ingredient. (Barrett: 1977)

In this period also the Rastafarian "dub" poet, joined the other Jamaican writers of the 1960s and 1970s. The term "dub poetry" was promoted early in 1979 by Oku Onuora (the former Orlando Wong), to identify work then being presented . . . by Oku himself, Michael Smith and Noel Walcott. "The dub poem," Oku said, "is not merely putting a piece of poem pon a reggae rhythm; it is a poem that has a built-in reggae rhythm (so to speak) backing, one can distinctly hear the reggae rhythm coming out on the poem." (Morris) One of the earliest of these poets was Jimmy Cliff, with defiant songs that are social commentary and angry protest.

> And I keep on fighting for the things
>   I want
> Though I know that when you're dead
>   you can't
> But I'd rather be a 'free man' in the grave
> Than living as a puppet or a slave.

To this group of poets belong also Peter Tosh, Mutabaruka and Michael Smith with their vivid images of the lonely Rastafarian attacking oppressive "Babylon".

I an I alone
Ah trod tru' creation,
Babylon on I right,
Babylon on I left
Babylon in front of I
an Babylon behind I
an I an I alone in de middle
like a Goliat wid a sling shot.

The message was the same as that which the working-class women of the Sistren Theatre Collective were delivering in the 1970s, for they also added important new dimensions to the cultural revolution movement by making drama and literature a passionate protest, a lightning flash revelation of the searing effects of social injustice.

Throughout our story, whether it had to do with economic growth, industrialisation or the demand of an oppressed group for social change, we have identified the colonial system of education as a major impediment to social and cultural development. The story of the working-class Jamaican women confirms this conclusion. For example, in education the role of women in Jamaican history is totally ignored. Nowhere do we see more clearly than in *Lionheart Gal*, the destructive effect of a system of education that marginalised the human being and inculcated the acceptance of circumscribed horizons. *Lionheart Gal*, a collection of the life stories of 13 working-class and two middle-class Jamaican women, has to do with the period between 1940 and 1980. The passage quoted below is from "My Own Two Hand". These stories, as the editor points out, "attest to the fact that, when women select their own creative organizational forms, they begin to build a base from which they do transform their own lives. But this transformation is only secure in so far as it is guaranteed by the power relations in the whole society". (Sistren with H. Ford Smith: 1986) Sistren and the women's movement challenge the structure and value systems of traditional Jamaican society. They also reveal the inner lives of many Jamaican women, their loneliness, the intolerable mental strain that results from a lack of stable family life and of regular employment, and the degradation of labour. The women who speak here like the Rastafarians, and like the liberation fighters of earlier generations, are leaders against oppression. They display the strength of will, the leadership, the refusal to accept defeat that are at the heart of the history of the Jamaican people.

Baldwin help me to di building, but a me head it. Sometime when me an him quarrel, him no go. Ah haffi go myself, mix di mortar and put di block. Ah haffi help myself and do di work. When me an' him no quarrel, him go and structure di work an' do it.

Di house is made of wood and concrete. It is not like one a dem lickle concrete box dat dem have nowadays for poor people to live in. It is not big. So it fit right against di mountin side. It have plenty window to let in light and air. We plant up di land around it, so we have banana and odder fruit and vegetable.

Building di house mek me feel proud of meself for me never wait pon no man fi do it. If Baldwin say him cyaan do something me find anodder way out, but me nah siddung an wait pon him. Me tek me own decision and me stick to it. Baldwin and me have an understanding. Him know dat nowadays me tek me own initiative and depend pon meself and tru dat, him haffi respect me. (Sistren with H. Ford Smith: 1986)

Another selection from *Lionheart Gal* reveals the same strength, the same belief that "without a reality we shall emerge from captivity", the same struggle against a hostile social environment, the same loneliness and the same ennobling spirit.

The gap between the two Jamaicas remains wide, but there were times when great events brought both groups together so that they thought in terms of Jamaica, and of being Jamaicans and even West Indians. In cricket our bowlers, batsmen and wicketkeepers revealed the cohesive national power of great achievement. So did our distinguished male and female athletes, among them Donald Quarrie, the first male sprinter from any country to make five Olympics and gain a medal in each of the five; and in the decade of the 1980s the women athletes came into their own. For the first time they outperformed or equalled the men. Among them were Grace Jackson and Merlene Ottey, the sprint queen. Merlene won a gold medal in the World Championships at Stuttgart in 1993 and confirmed her claim as one of the world's great female short-distance runners.

Merlene Ottey

Her achievement bound all Jamaicans together in pride and in rejoicing. Nationhood was no longer a cold, remote concept. Our athletes transformed it into the warm relationship of kinsfolk. To this decade of the 1980s also belong three boxers, Trevor Berbick, Lloyd Honeygan and the remarkable Mike McCallum, who in 1986 held three world titles in boxing at the same time.

World-class achievements such as these provide Jamaicans with their own models of performance and achievement. The story would have been remarkable if it had been in one or two areas of activity only, such as sports and athletics, but it covers a wide cultural spectrum including painting, sculpture, literature, music and dance. The achievements derived from the

Rex Nettleford

great mass of the people, who were drawing on their creative gifts, setting new standards, breaching the old barriers of colour and race. The story of this cultural movement is told in *Jamaica in Independence*, edited by Rex Nettleford, who refers to the continuity of effort made possible by the understanding and support of political leaders such as Norman Manley, Edward Seaga and Michael Manley, as well as by the strength of voluntary associations that, like tributaries, enlarged the main stream.

Voluntary organisations reinforced the ongoing work of the educational authorities and the Institute of Jamaica and Jamaica Welfare Ltd (now the Jamaica Social Development Commission), to foster a spirit of self-help and self-esteem in rural areas. The 1920s and 1930s witnessed the development of competition among the performing arts with the founding of the Poetry League of Jamaica (1923), the Musical Society of Jamaica (1926) and the Jamaica Arts Society (1937). The Little Theatre Movement (LTM) came into existence in 1941, the Jamaica Library Service in 1949 and the National Dance Theatre Company of Jamaica (NDTC) in 1962. Henry and Greta Fowler, founders of the LTM, established the annual national pantomime which is now over 50-years-old.

NDTC

The NDTC, founded by Rex Nettleford and Eddie Thomas, has become a company of international repute.

In 1955 the work of the Jamaica Welfare Ltd in the country parts, received a special boost when Louise Bennett, a young charismatic woman, recently returned from drama school in England, joined the staff. She was at one with the heart and soul of the Jamaican people, and a comic muse inspired her poetry, music and song. Wherever she went she established an immediate rapport with the people. Miss Lou's use of the dialect on stage, platform and in print, has helped the Jamaican dialect to gain acceptance at all levels of society. Her work as folklorist, writer and commedienne has established her as perhaps the most authentically Jamaican of all performing artists of her generation.

Louise Bennett
Coverly

The year 1955 also witnessed the staging of the first Jamaica National Festival of Arts. It was islandwide and year-long, and formed part of the celebrations to mark the tercentenary of the association of Jamaica with Britain. It was the fact of being a national festival that made the observance national as distinct from being colonial. The task of mounting the festival was given to a young civil servant, Wycliffe Bennett, who had proposed the idea. The festival discovered and displayed artistic talent which was distributed randomly in the society. It came at the right time and helped develop a conscience for ideal beauty among the people.

A second festival was held in 1958. Then, in April 1963, Edward Seaga, Minister of Development and Welfare, put the festival on a permanent footing. It became an annual event on "the creativity of the nation – a national stage where Jamaicans from all walks of life would have the opportunity to create their own brand of artistic expression, reflecting their life history and their life styles". (Seaga)

Nettleford noted: "Jamaica stands out among newly independent, third world countries in its efforts to provide for itself an institutional structure for cultural development in independence . . . The contact with the young . . . was guaranteed by pulling together in 1965 under the umbrella of . . . the Festival Commission, [which was] broadened in concept in the 1970's to become the Jamaica Cultural Development Commission (JCDC)." (Nettleford: 1978) JCDC's extensive programmes of training were developed along with national contests in song, dance, speech and drama. Leaders in the movement included Wycliffe Bennett and Hugh Nash.

Barrington
Watson

The years saw also an impressive broadening and deepening of artistic activity among a new generation of painters, sculptors and potters such as Barrington Watson, Eugene Hyde, Osmond Watson, Gloria Escoffery, Judy MacMillan, Colin Garland, Christopher Gonzales, Fitzroy Harrack, Alexander Cooper, Karl Craig and Cecil Baugh's outstanding successors Gene Pearson and Norma Harrack. The story is the same in the dance, in the plays of Trevor Rhone, in the works of women writers such as Lorna Goodison and Olive Senior. In these decades of the 1970s and 1980s, the cultural movement changed in mood, leaving behind the early fervour of self-discovery and the anger at anti-colonialism and turning to the essential task of interpreting and claiming as a matter of right the experience of the Jamaican people. Lorna Goodison's work reveals this new mood of identification.

So does Pam Mordecai's anthology *From Our Yard*, which reflects the very significant developments taking place in Jamaican society. The press and the media helped to bring this change about. Through radio and TV the journalists and broadcasters have brought Jamaicans into closer, more personal contact with each other. The talk shows, "Public Eye" among them, are building on strong foundations laid by the journalists, commentators, analysts and editors of the longer established print media. Among the print journalists of great influence were Theodore Sealy, Ulric Sommonds, L. D. "Strebor" Roberts, Jack Anderson, Aimee Webster-DeLisser, Evon Blake, Vic Reid, John Maxwell, Hector Bernard, J. C. Proute, Morris Cargill and Peter Abrahams. The talk-show hosts and presenters on radio and television have included Lindy Delapenha, Ronnie Thwaites, Barbara Gloudon, Wilmot Perkins and Dennis Hall. These introduced a greater degree of transparency and accountability into Jamaican public life and conduct. This daily frank interchange of views gives life to democracy and independence. In a young nation with so long a history of racial, economic and political division, this daily continuing discussion has reinforced the opportunities for giving meaning to the concept of nationhood.

Islandwide networks of minibus operators and transistor radios have, in Carl Stone's words, "laid the base for the emergence of genuinely national public opinion among the majority classes although a certain level of parish and country regionalism still persists in the western end of the island".

The private sector has also played an increasingly important role by modernising the nation's industrial and commercial sector and by bringing the business community out of the parochialism of the colonial period by developing a network of global contacts and by setting an example of civil responsibility.

The change in attitude between the expatriate business leadership of the 1930s and that of the post-independence period is striking. Jamaican industrialists, manufacturers, entrepreneurs, financiers and professional groups have established a tradition of public philanthropy by setting up charitable foundations, taking a close interest in cultural activities, in promoting athletics, sport, games, scholarly and literary undertakings, as well as through the service clubs with their encouragement of self-help and of sensitivity to community needs. Their support of the University of the West Indies, of the College of Arts, Science and Technology (University of Technology), of schools, of teaching and research programmes has been of major importance in strengthening social cohesion and increasing educational and economic opportunity. Furthermore, by advice and by their specialised knowledge and expertise, they influence the development of a harmonious relationship between the public and private sectors.

A rapidly growing proletariat, a more sophisticated and consumer-oriented public demands more goods and services; an increasingly large group puts economic betterment first and foremost. The task of nation-building was formidable. Norman Manley minced no words about that when he called for the development of a national spirit and of a system of education that would strengthen the nation. He declared: "You have got to make up your minds as to whether you believe that this country can aim at the great adventure of being fit for achieving self-government . . . This country can only become worthwhile if all the discordant and disunited elements in it can be knitted into a new unity and that can only be brought about by the development of a national spirit." (Nettleford: 1971)

The appeal was made to the teachers of Jamaica in 1939. Norman Manley asked them, "Have we ever in Jamaica inculcated in the children in our schools a spirit which believes that the Jamaican is a fine person?

That he is a laudable person? That the Jamaican has a great future before him?" (Nettleford: 1971)

The questions were asked more than half-a-century ago. Their continuing relevance compels us to look critically at the Jamaican system of education. Our guide is one of Jamaica's best-known educators, Errol Miller. In his essay, "Educational Development in Independent Jamaica", Miller pointed out:

> The most fundamental change to date has been in the size of the system. The educational system is now bigger than it ever was in the colonial period . . . there is evidence that educational standards have improved since independence . . . not only has the educational system expanded in the Independence period but expansion has been accompanied with qualitative improvements as well. Not only has more been produced but at a better standard. (Miller: 1989)

He pointed out, however, that in certain vital areas the colonial patterns continued of prejudice against primary students, anglicisation, devaluation of the achievements of teachers, students and schools, and a sense of cross-purpose in the expectations of the providers and the participants.

A devastating section follows:

> In a real sense the ideas that have informed educational developments in independent Jamaica have been those that were formulated by the colonial administration in the 1940's. Very little new thinking has taken place. B. H. Easter (expatriate Director of Education in the

Prime Ministers of Jamaica since Independence, from left to right: Alexander Bustamante (1962–67); Donald Sangster (Feb. 1967–April 1967); Hugh Shearer (1967– 72); Michael Manley (1972-80, 1989–92); Edward Seaga (1980– 89); P. J. Patterson (1992–)

early 1940's) still directs Jamaican education. This probably explains why what has been accomplished has not differed much from the objectives that guided educational provision in the colonial past.

The racist assumptions and divisive notions remained embedded in the system of education, because up to the 1940s, even those of us who were nationalists knew only the imperialist ver-sion of Jamaica's history. Without realising it, we looked at our society through British eyes because we had at the time no intellectual focus of our own.

Today the first step is for the nation to recognise that the existing deep social cleavages and antagonisms can only be resolved by strengthening the sense of national unity. This calls for the fundamental educational reform of which Errol Miller spoke. By projecting Eurocentric values and attitudes, the existing system of education weakens Jamaica's drive for economic growth, reinforces the traditional social cleavages, erodes the African-Jamaican's sense of a racial identity, denies Africa her place of centrality as motherland, denigrates the historic African-Jamaican achievements of the defeat of slavery and of the white planter oligarchy, and leaves the significance of the national symbols in doubt. National symbols generate powerful emotional and creative forces, but they do not permit of ambiguity.

The immediate challenge is for African-Jamaicans to claim their past with its record of heroic uprisings against European oppression, to claim their African heritage and to draw on today's achievements as a source of empowerment. It is out of our deep feeling about Jamaica and the Jamaican people that a better, happier Jamaica will come, out of our own faith in ourselves and our country, out of our own conviction about its future, out of our own minds, out of our own will.

The guiding principles for revitalising the Jamaican nation and making the educational system a source of inspiration begin with the affirmation that Jamaica is predominantly a black nation whose ancestral motherland is West Africa. The only way to destroy the psychosocial controls instituted by European imperialism is to set the historical record straight. This is the self-liberation of which Garvey spoke. Once this has been accomplished, the nation will find a perennial source of strength in its past.

The nation must enlist the help of its visionaries and achievers – be they poets, sculptors, athletes, priests and clergymen, business men, politicians – in order to make Jamaica's record known to its people. Achievement is infectious. Development is a state of mind. Let the walls of every school in Jamaica carry visual reminders of our great heritage, with portraits of the national heroes and other pathfinders.

The private sector of Jamaica, corporations, foundations and service clubs, have played a role in enriching the quality of Jamaican life and in building self-esteem. They have established a tradition of memorialising historic achievements by commissioning artists to create murals that give a feeling of completeness to their finest buildings. By their generous support of sports and athletics they have opened up opportunities for achieving international and world records. This knitting together of commercial, industrial and manufacturing organisations with the interests and advancement of the Jamaican people is a significant indicator of the growing strength of nationhood.

Religion remains at the centre of national life. Church and school, parson and teacher, working with their church leaders, continue to build into the social fabric a tradition of democratic self-government which they began when colonial rule was authoritarian. In addition they enunciate the principle that power should always be based on morality. They strengthen the trends toward self-help and voluntarism that provide the folk with the labour and capital they need in times of emergency. Through the outreach work of all the religious bodies, the sacrificial service of the ghetto priests and sisters, and through a network of religious societies and clubs, the various religious bodies continue to shape the life of Jamaica.

In this period of crisis Jamaica depends more than she has ever done on the intellectual and moral quality of her people, on their wisdom and patriotism. The times call for a renewing and deepening of religious commitment as well as for greater intellectual effort. In consequence, educational reform should give high priority to inculcating ethical principles and moral values.

Yesterday reminds us that our West African ancestors were captives in small crowded ships on a lonely ocean. "Shipmates" was the word that held them together and gave them hope. Today, we and all mankind are shipmates on a small spaceship – fragile, destructible, planet earth. The onward-rushing third millennium beckons us to greatness of vision in transforming our two Jamaicas into a united, vibrant nation fitted by its record of cultural achievement to contribute significantly to the unity and happiness of our shipmates.

Select Bibliography

Abolition of Slavery Act, 1833. Will. IV. Cap. LXXIII.

Abrahams, Peter "The blacks", in *African Treasury* ed. by Langston Hughes, (New York: Pyramid Books, 1969).

Anti-Slavery Reporter, 2 May 1859.

Armstrong, Douglas V. *The old village and the great house: An archaeological and historical examination of Drax Hall Plantation, St. Anns Bay, Jamaica*, (Urbana: University of Illinois Press, 1990).

Atkins "A Voyage to Guinea, 1735", in *Caribbean generations: A CXC history source book*, ed. by Shirley Gordon, (Kingston: Longman Caribbean, 1986).

Baugh, Edward "Sometimes in the middle of the story", in *Come Back to me my Language*, ed. by J. E. Chamberlain, (University of Illinois Press, 1993).

Barrett, Leonard *The Rastafarians: the dreadlocks of Jamaica*, (Kingston: Heinemann & Sangster's Bookstores Ltd, 1977).

Beckford, George *Persistent Poverty: Underdevelopment in plantation economies of the third world*, (London: Oxford University Press, 1972).

Beckford, William *A Descriptive Account of the Island of Jamaica* 2 vols, (London, 1790).

Bell, K. N. & Morrell, W. P. Slavery and the Plantation System. Select Documents on British Colonial Policy 1830-1860, mimeo.

Berlin, I. *Against the Current: Essay on the History of Ideas*, (Oxford: Clarendon Press, 1981).

Bernáldez, Andrés *Historia de los Reyes Católicos, Don Fernando y Doña Isabel* 2 vols, (Seville, 1870).

Black, C. V. *A New History of Jamaica* (Kingston: William Collins Sangster Jamaica Ltd, 1973).

Blanchard, P. *Democracy and Empire in the Caribbean*, (New York, 1947).

Bleby, Henry *Death Struggles of Slavery* . . . 2nd edn, (London, 1868).

Blome, Richard *Description of the Island of Jamaica*, (London: T. Milbourne, 1672).

Boxer, David *Edna Manley, Sculptor*, (Kingston: National Gallery of Jamaica & Norman Manley Foundation, 1989).

Bradford, Ernle *Christopher Columbus*, (New York: Viking Press, 1973).

Brathwaithe, Edward *The Development of Creole Society in Jamaica, 1770-1820*, (Oxford: Clarendon Press, 1971).

—— *Masks*, (Oxford University Press, 1968).

Braudel, Fernand *Civilization and Capitalism, 15th to 18th Century* 3 vols, (New York: Harper & Row, 1982-84).

Bridenbaugh, Carl & Roberta *No Peace Beyond the Line*, (New York: Oxford University Press, 1972).

Brodber, Erna "Oral Sources and . . . Social History . . .", *Jamaica Journal* 16:4 (1983).

Bryan, Patrick *Leisure and Class in Late Nineteenth Century Jamaica*, (Kingston: Department of History, University of the West Indies, 1987).

Buxton, Thomas F. Meeting of Abolitionists, 12 May 1832.

Callendar of State Papers, HMSO 1663.

Campbell, George *First Poems*, (London: Garland Publishers, 1981).

Campbell, Mavis *The Dynamics of Change in a Slave Society; a sociopolitical history of the free coloured of Jamaica, 1800-1865*, (New Jersey: Associated Universities Press, 1976).

Carlyle, Thomas "Occasional Discources on the Negro Question", *Frazer's Magazine* (1849).

Carmichael, A. C. *Domestic Manners and Social Conditions of the White, Coloured and Negro Population of the West Indies* 2 vols, (London: Whittaker, Treacher Company, 1883).

Carnegie, James *Great Jamaican Olympians*, (Kingston Publishers, 1996).

Caseate, Frank *Jamaica Talk*, (London: Macmillan, 1961).

Caseate, F. & LePage, R. B *Dictionary of Jamaican English*, (Cambridge University Press, 1967).

Chamerlain, J. E. *Come Back to me my Language*, (University of Illinois Press, 1993).

Chevannes, Barry *Rastafari: Roots and Ideology*, (Kingston: The Press, 1995).

Child, Joshua *A New Discourse of Trade . . .*, (London: J. Hodges etc., 1740).

Clarke, Colin *Kingston, Jamaica: Urban Development and Social Change 1692-1962*, (Berkley: California Press, 1975).

Clarke, Edith *My Mother who Fathered me*, (London: Allen & Unwin, 1957).

Clarkson, Thomas *The History of the Rise, Progress and Accomplishment of the Abolition of the African Slave Trade* 2 vols, (London Reese & Orme, 1808).

Colón, Don Pedro *The Petition of Don Pedro Colón de Portugal y Castro, Duke of Veragua and la Vega, Marquis of Jamaica to Her Royal Highness Mariana of Austria, Queen Regent of Charles II of Spain, for the Island of Jamaica 1672*, (Mill Press, 1992).

Cox, Oliver *Upgrading and Renewing a Historic City: Port Royal, Jamaica*, (Kingston: Jamaica National Heritage Trust, 1984).

Craton, Michael *Slavery, Abolition and Emancipation: black slaves and the British Empire*, (London: Longman, 1976).

Cronon, Edmund D. *Marcus Garvey: Black Moses*, (University of Wisconsin Press, 1955).

Cumper, George "Labour Demand and Supply in Jamaican Sugar Industry 1830-1950", *Social & Economic Studies* 2:4 (1954).

Cundall, Frank & Pietersz, J. *Jamaica Under the Spaniards*, (Kingston: Institute of Jamaica, 1919).

Curtin, Philip D. *The Atlantic Slave Trade*, (University of Wisconsin Press, 1969).

—— *Two Jamaicas*, (Harvard University Press, 1955).

Dallas, R. C. *History of the Maroons*, (London: Longman & Reese, 1803; Frank Cass 1968).

da Veiga Pinta, Francoise & Carreira, A. "Portuguese participation in the slave trade . . ." in *African Slave Trade from the Fifteenth to the Nineteenth Century*, (Paris: UNESCO, 1979).

Davidson, David "Negro Slave Control and Resistance in Colonial Mexico, 1519-1650" in *Maroon Societies: rebel slave communities in the Americas,* (Garden City, New York: Anchor Press, 1973).

Dawes, Neville *Prolegomena to Caribbean Literature,* (Kingston: Institute of Jamaica for the African Caribbean Institute, 1977).

Dennes, Jona Letter to Spencer Compton 14 August 1683, (Spencer Compton Papers, 1675-1765).

Dictionary of Modern Thought, (New York: Harper & Row, 1977).

Diop, C. A. *The African Origin of Civilization: Myth or Reality,* (Westport: Lawrence Hill, 1974).

Downing, G. Letter to his Cousin. 1645.

Durant-Gonzales, Victoria *The Role and Status of Rural Jamaican Women: Higglering and Mothering.* (Ann Arbor: UCLA Microfilms, 1976).

Eden, R. *The History of Trauayle in the West and East Indies: The first book of the Decades of the Ocean Written by Peter Martyr of Angieria Milenoes, Counfaylour to the Bishop of Rome Leo X,* (London, 1577).

Edwards, A. *Marcus Garvey 1887-1940,* (London: New Beacon Publications, 1967).

Edwards, Bryan *The History, Civil and Commercial, of the British Colonies in the West Indies* 2 vols, (London: J. Stockdale, 1793).

Edwards, Paul ed. *Equiano's Travels 1789,* (London: Heinemann, 1967).

Espiñoza, Antonio V. *Compendio y Descripción de las Indias Occidentáles . . .,* (Washington, 1948).

Esquemeling, John *The Buccaneers of America,* (Amsterdam, 1678).

Fage, J. D. *A History of West Africa,* (London: CUP, 1969).

Forde, C. Daryll *Introduction to African Worlds,* (Oxford University Press, 1954).

Froude, James A. *The English in the West Indies,* (London: Lingmans, Green & Co, 1887).

Gibbs, J. ed. *Peoples of Africa,* Abridged, (New York: Holt, Rinehart & Winston, 1978).

Girvan, Norman *Working Together for Development,* (Kingston: Institute of Jamaica, 1993).

Gordon, Shirley ed. *Caribbean Generations,* (Kingston: Longmans Caribbean, 1986).

Great Britain. *Jamaica. Royal Commission 1866,* Report.

Guerra y Sánchez, J. M. *Historia de la Nación Cubana* 10 vols (Havana, 1952).

—— *Sugar and Society in the Caribbean,* (New Haven: Yale University Press, 1964).

Hall, Douglas. *Free Jamaica, 1838-1865: An Economic History,* (New Haven: Yale University Press, 1959).

—— "Diary of a Westmoreland Planter", *Jamaica Journal* 21:3; 21:4 (1988); 22:1 (1989).

Hamilton, D. L. "Simon Benning, Pewterer of Port Royal", in *Test-aided Archaeology,* ed. by B. J. Little (Boca Raton: CRCP,1992).

Haring, C. H. *The Spanish Empire in America,* (New York: Harcourt, Brace and World, 1963).

—— *Blacks in Bondage,* vol 1 (Kingston: Insitutue of Social and Economic Research, University of the West Indies, 1985).

Hart, Richard *Slaves who Abolished Slavery* vol 2 *Blacks in Rebellion* (Kingston: Social & Economic Research, University of the West Indies, 1985).

Hart, Ansell *The Life of George William Gordon,* (Kingston: Institute of Jamaica, 1972).

Hausheer, R. "Introduction", in *Against the Current: essays in the history of Ideas* ed. by Isaiah Berlin, (Penguin Books, 1982).

Hearne, John "Landscape with faces", in *Ian Fleming Introduces Jamaica*, (Kingston: Sangster's Bookstores, 1965).

Heuman, Gad J. *Between Black and White: Race, Politics and the Free Coloureds in Jamaica 1792-1865*, (Westport: Greenwood Press, 1981).

Hickeringill, Edmund *Jamaica Viewed, with all its ports, harbours ...*, (London, Pr. for John Williams 1661).

Higman, B. W. *Jamaica Surveyed*, (Kingston: Institute of Jamaica, 1988).

—— *Slave Population and Economy in Jamaica 1807-1834*, (Cambridge University Press, 1976).

Hill, R. A. ed. *The Marcus Garvey and Universal Negro Improvement Association Papers* 10 vols, (UCLA Press, 1983-85).

—— *Marcus Garvey: Life and Lessons*, (UCLA Press, 1987).

Hinden, Rita *Fabian Colonial Essays*, (London: Allen & Unwin, 1945).

Holt, T. C. *The Problem of Freedom: Race, Labour, and Politics in 1832-1938*, (Kingston: Ian Randle Publishers, 1992).

Holzberg, C. S. *Minorities and Power in a Black Society. The Jewish Community of Jamaica*, (Maryland: N. S. Publishing Co, 1987).

Hughes, Langston ed. *An African Treasury*, (New York: Crown Publishers, 1960).

Ikake, Ibrahim in *The African Slave Trade from the Fifteenth to the Nineteenth Century*, (Paris: UNESCO, 1979).

Inikori, Joseph "The Atlantic Slave Trade", in *The African Slave Trade from the Fifteenth to the Nineteenth Century*, (Paris: UNESCO, 1979).

Jacobs, H. P. *Sixty Years of Change 1806-1866*, (Kingston: Institute of Jamaica, 1973).

Jamaica Government. Laws of Jamaica 1831.

Jamaica. Royal Commission. Minutes of Evidence . . . 1866.

Jefferson, O. *The Post War Development of Jamaica*, (Kingston: Institute of Social & Economic Research, 1972).

Jones, A. Creech *Fabian Colonial Essays*, (London: Allen & Unwin, 1945).

Journals of the Assembly of Jamaica 1664/5. St. Jago de la Vega . . ., (A. Aikman, 1811).

Katzin, M. F. "Higglers of Jamaica". Ph.D. Thesis, University of the West Indies, Mona 1959.

Kennedy, Paul *The Rise and fall of the Great Powers . . . from 1500-2000*, (New York: Random House, 1987).

Kerr, Madeleine *Personality and Conflict in Jamaica*, (London & Kingston: Collins, 1963).

King, in *Maroon Societies: Rebel Slave Communities in the Americas*, (Johns Hopkins University Press, 1979).

Knibb, William *Address at Spitalfields Chapel*, (London, 1832).

—— Jamaica. Speech . . . before the Baptist Missionary Society in Exeter Hall, 28 April 1842.

Knight, R. A. L. *William Knibb, Missionary and Emancipator*, (London: Carey Press, 1948).

—— *Liberty and Progress: A short history of the Baptists of Jamaica*, (Kingston: The Gleaner Company, 1938).

Kopytoff, B. K. "The Maroons of Jamaica" Ph.D. Thesis, University of the West Indies, Mona, 1974.

Krawath, Fred F. *Christopher Columbus, Cosmographer. A history of metrology, Geodesy, Geography and Exploration from Antiquity to the Columbian Era*, (California: Landmark Enterprises, 1987).

Lalla, B. & D'Costa, J. Language in Exile, (University of Alabama Press, 1990).

Lamming, George *In the Castle of my Skin*, (New York: Collier Books, 1983).

Las Casas, Bartolomew *History of the Indies Bk. III. 1559*, (Madrid, 1875).

Latrobe, J. C. *Negro Education in Jamaica, 1837*, (Ordered by the House of Commons, 1838).

Leslie, Charles *A New and Exact Account of Jamaica ...*, (Edinburgh: R. Fleming, 1739).

Levy, Jacqueline "The Economic role of the Chinese in Jamaica. The Grocery Retail Trade", *Jamaica Historical Review* XV (1986).

Lewis, Gordon *The Growth of the Modern West Indies*, (London: Modern Reader Paperbacks, 1968).

Lewis, M. G. *Journal of a West India Proprietor*, (London: Murray, 1834).

Lewis, Rupert *Marcus Garvey: Anti-Colonial Champion*, (London: Karia Publishing, 1987).

Lewis, R, & P. Bryan eds *Garvey: his Work and Impact*, (Kingston: Institute of Social and Economic Research & Department of Extra-Mural Studies, University of the West Indies, 1988).

Ligon, Richard *True and Exact History of the Island of Barbados . . .*, (London, 1657).

Lloyd, P. C. "The Yoruba of Nigeria", in *Peoples of Africa*, ed. by James L Gibbs (New York: Holt, Rhinehart and Winston, 1965).

Long, Edward *The History of Jamaica . . .*, (London: T. Lowndes, 1774).

Lumsden, Joyce "Robert Love and Jamaican Politics", Ph.D. Thesis, University of the West Indies, Mona 1987.

Mair-Mathurin, Lucille "Women Field Workers in Jamaica during Slavery", Elsa Goveia Memorial Lecture, Mona, 1986.

—— "A Historical Study of women in Jamaica from 1655-1844" Ph.D. Thesis, University of the West Indies, Mona, 1974.

—— *The Rebel Woman in the British West Indies During Slavery*, (Kingston: Institute of Jamaica for the Afro-Caribbean Institute of Jamaica, 1975).

Manley, Norman "Foreword", in *Three Novels of Roger Mais*, (London: Jonathan Cape, 1966).

Mannix, D. *Black Cargoes: A History of the Atlantic Slave Trade 1518-1865*, (London: Longmans, 1962).

Mansingh, L. & Mansingh, A. "Indian Heritage in Jamaica", *Jamaica Journal* 10: 2, 3, 4 (1976).

Marsala, V. J. *Sir John Peter Grant ... 1866-1874*, (Kingston: Institute of Jamaica, 1972).

Marsden, Peter *An Account of the Island of Jamaica*, (Newcastle, 1788).

Mayes, Philip *Port Royal Jamaica. Excavations 1969-1970*, (Kingston: Jamaica National Trust Commission, 1972).

Mbiti, John S. *Concepts of God in Africa*, (London: SPCK 1970).

McKay, Claude *Banana Bottom*, (New York: Harper & Row, 1961).

—— *The Dialect Poetry of Claude McKay*, (New York: Books for Libraries Press, 1972).

Miller, Errol "Educational Development in Independent Jamaica", in *Independence Essays on the Early Years,* (Kingston; London: Heinemann Publishers & James Currey Ltd, 1989).

Mintz, Sidney *Caribbean Transformations*, (Chicago: Aldine Press Co, 1974).

Morrissey, M. *Slave Women in the New World*, (University of Kansas Press, 1989).

Murray, R. N. ed. *J. J. Mills, His own Account of his life and Times Jamaica*, (Kingston: Collins & Sangster's 1969).

Nettleford, Rex *Caribbean Cultural Identity: The case of Jamaica,* (Kingston: Institute of Jamaica, 1978).

—— *Manley and the New Jamaica,* (London: William Clowes & Sons, 1971).

—— ed. *Manley in the New Jamaica. Selected Speeches & Writings 1938-1939,* (London: Longman Caribbean, 1971).

New York Times, 16 January 1992

Nicholls, David "The Syrians of Jamaica", *The Jamaican Historical Review* XV (1986).

Nugent, George Report to Colonial Office 20 February 1802.

Nugent, Maria *Lady Nugent's Journal,* (Kingston: Institute of Jamaica, 1939).

O'Connell, R. L. *Of Arms and Men . . .,* (New York: Oxford University Press, 1989).

Ogilvie, D. L. *History of the Parish of Trelawny,* (Kingston, 1954).

Oldmixon, John *The British Empire in America,* (London, Printed for John Nicholson . . . 1708).

Olivier, S. Lord *Jamaica the Blessed Island London,*: (Fisher & Faber Ltd, 1936).

—— *The Myth of Governor Eyre,* (London: Hogarth Press, 1933).

Olsen, Fred *On the Trail of the Arawaks,* (University of Oklahoma Press, 1974).

Padrón, Moráles *Spanish Jamaica,* (1952).

Parboosingh, I. S. "An Indo-Jamaican Beginning . . .", *Jamaica Journal* 18:2 (1985).

Parrent, J. M. & Parrent, M. B. Columbus Caravels Archaeological Project . . ., Report 1993, mimeo.

Parry, J. H. & Sherlock, P. M. *Short History of the West Indies,* (London: Macmilllan, 1987).

Patterson, H. O. *The Sociology of Slavery: An analysis of the origins, development and structure of Negro slavery in Jamaica,* (N. J. Rutherford; Fairleigh: Dickenson University Press, 1969).

Pawson, M. & Buisseret, D. *Port Royal, Jamaica,* (Oxford University Press, 1975).

Phillippo, J. M. *Jamaica: Its Past and Present State,* (London, 1843).

Polianyi, K. The *Great Transformation* (New York & Toronto: Farrar and Rinehart, 1944)

Price, Richard. ed. *Maroon Societies: Rebel Slave Communities in the Americas,* (New York: Doubleday, 1973).

Rhys, Ernest *The Growth of Political Liberty.* (London: Everyman's Library, 1921)

Roberts, G. W. *The Population of Jamaica,* (Cambridge University Press, 1957).

Roberts, W. A. *Jamaica: the Portrait of an Island,* (New York: Coward-McCann, 1955).

—— *Six Great Jamaicans,* (Kingston: Pioneer Press, 1951).

Robotham, Don *"The Notorious Riot" The Socio-Economic and Political Bases of Paul Bogle's Revolt,* Kingston: Institute of Social and Economic Research, No. 28, 1981 University of the West Indies.

Roland, J. G. ed. *Africa. An Anthology of African History,* (1974).

—— ed. *Africa, the Heritage and Challenge,* (Pace Coll.: Fawcett Publications, 1974).

Rossiter, C. *The First American Revolution,* (New York: Harvest Books, Harcourt Brace, 1956).

Roughley, T. *The Jamaica Planter's Guide . . .,* (London: Longman, Hurst, Reese, Orme & Brown, 1823).

Rouse, Irving *The Tainos: Rise and Decline of the People who Greeted Columbus,* (New Haven: Yale University Press, 1992).

The Royal Gazette, 21-28 January 1832.

Russell, Horace "The Missionary Outreach of the West Indian Church to West Africa in the Nineteenth Century With Particular Reference to the Baptists", Ph.D. Thesis Oxford University, 1972.

Ryman, Cheryl "Jonkonnu a neo-African Form", *Jamaica Journal* 17:1 & 17:2 (1984).

Satchell, V. *The Jamaican Peasantry 1866-1900*, (Kingston: Department of History, University of the West Indies, 1983.

—— *From Plots to Plantations: land transactions in Jamaica, 1866-1900*, (Kingston: Institute of Social and Economic Research, University of the West Indies, 1990).

Schama, Simon *Citizens*, (London: Penguin, 1989).

Sedeno, Jacinto *Description of Jamaica*, (Santa Domingo: Archive de Indias, n.d.) (Government of Jamaica 1639-40).

Senior, B. M. *Jamaica, as it was, as it is, and as it may be . . . also an Authentic Narrative of the Negro Insurrection in 1831*, (New York: Negro Universities Press, 1969).

Senior, Olive "The Panama Railway", *Jamaica Journal* 44 (1980).

—— "The Colon People. Part I", *Jamaica Journal* 11:3 (1977).

—— "The Colon People. Part II", *Jamaica Journal* 42 (1978).

Sewell, William G. *The Ordeal of Free Labour in the British West Indies*, (New York: Economic Classics, 1968).

Shepherd, Verene *Transcients to Settlers: The Experience of Indians in Jamaica, 1845-1950*, (Peepal Tree Publications, 1994).

—— "Transcients to Citizens: The Development of a settled East Indian Community", *Jamaica Journal* 18:3 (1985).

Sheridan, Richard *The Development of the Plantations to 1750*, (Caribbean Universities Press, 1970).

Sherlock, Philip *Norman Manley, a Biography*, (London: Macmillan, 1980).

Simmonds, Lorna "Slave Higglering in Jamaica 1780-1834", *Jamaica Journal* 20:1(1987).

Sistren, with H. Ford Smith *Lionheart Gal*, (London: The Women's Press, 1986).

Sloane, Hans *A Voyage to the islands, Madera, Barbados, Nieves, S. Christopher and Jamaica with the Natural History of the Herbs and Trees . . .* 2 vols, (London, 1707).

Smith, John (Demerara). Letter to the London Missionary Society, 1823.

Smith, M. G. *The Plural Society in the British West Indies*, (Kingston: Sangster's Bookstores, 1974).

Smith, M. G., Augier, Roy, Nettleford, Rex *The Rastafari Movement in Kingston Jamaica*, (Kingston: Institute of Economic and Social Research, University College of the West Indies, 1960).

Sohal, H. S. "The East Indian Indentureship System in Jamaica 1845-1917" Ph.D. Thesis, University of Waterloo, 1979.

The Spencer Compton Papers, 1675-1765.

The Star Newspaper, 8 August 1936.

Stedman, T. G. in *Maroon Societies: Rebel Slave Communities in the Americas*, (Baltimore Johns Hopkins University Press, 1973).

Stewart, John *An Account of Jamaica and its inhabitants*, (London: Longman, Nurse, Reese & Orme, 1808).

Suicke, J. B. Letter to the Earl of Belmore, 25 May 1832

Thompson, E. P. *Making of the English Working Class*, (London: Gollanz, 1963).

Times Atlas of World History, (London, 1984).

Trollope, A. *The West Indies and the Spanish Maine*, (London: Chapman & Hall; Frank Cass, 1968).

Tuchman, B. *The Proud Tower*, (New York: Macmillan, 1966).

Udeagu, Onyenaekeya *An African Treasury*, (New York: Crown Onyenaekeya Publishers, 1960).

Underhill, E. B. *The Tragedy of Morant Bay . . .*, (London: Alexander & Shapherd, 1895).

Waddell, Hope *Twenty-Nine Years in the West Indies and Central Africa . . . 1829-1858,* (London: Nelson, 1863).

Walker, D. F. *The Call of the West Indies,* (London: Cargate P. 1930).

Wallace, & Hinds *Our West African Heritage,* (Kingston: African Caribbean Institute of Jamaica, 1989).

Ward, W. E. F. *History of Ghana,* (New York: Praeger, 1963).

West Indies Royal Commission Report, HMSO, 1884).

West Indies Royal Commission 1938-1939, HMSO, 1945.

West India Royal Commission, Report. 1897, HMSO.

West Indies Sugar Commission 1929-1930 Report 2 vols HMSO, 1930.

Westphal, A. *The Breaking of the Dawn or Moravian Work in Jamaica, 1754-1904,* (Belfast, 1904).

Williams, *Eric Capitalism and Slavery,* (University of North Carolina Press, 1944).

—— *Documents of West Indian History 1492-1655,* (Port-of-Spain: PNM Publishing Co. 1963).

—— *Forged from the Love of Liberty: Selected Speeches of Dr. Eric Williams.* (Port-of-Spain: Longman Caribbean, 1981).

Woodhouse, A. S. P. *Puritanism and Liberty,* (Chicago University Press, 1951).

Wynter, Sylvia "Bernardo de Balbuena . . . 1562-1627", *Jamaica Journal* 3:3; 3:4 (1969); 4:1; 4:3 (1970).

Yin, Lee Tom, ed. *The Chinese in Jamaica,* (Kingston: 1963).

Index of Names

Abraham, 36, 37-38
Abrahams, Carl, 392
Abrahams, Peter: on tribal
 society, 28, 29
Accompong, 136
Allan, Edris, 360
Alves, Bain, 247
Archbould, Henry, 85, 86
Azikiwe, Nnamdi, 15

Bailey, Amy, 359
Baker, Lorenzo Dow: and Boston
 Fruit Company, 275; strategy
 of, 278; views of, 279
Baker, Moses, 39, 203; signifi-
 cance of, work of, 180-181,
 182
Balcarres, earl of, 145-149
Ballard, Thomas, 85
Barham, Joseph, 179
Barrett, Samuel, 217, 222
Barry, Samuel, 85
Baugh, Cecil, 394
Beckford, Peter, 155
Beckford, William, 4, 158;
 quoted, 32
Beeston, William, 86, 87
Benham, F. C., 379
Bennett, Louise: and Jamaican
 dialect, 405
Bennett, Wycliffe, 405
Berbick, Trevor, 403

Berlin, Isaiah: on Eurocentricity,
 12-13
Bernáldez, Andres, 64
Bleby, Henry, 213; on execution
 of Sam Sharpe, 227
Bligh, William: and West Indian
 food supply, 192
Blome, Richard: *Description of
 the Island of Jamaica*, 88
Bogle, Paul, 4, 246; capture of,
 259; as deacon, 249; descrip-
 tion of, 247; hanging of, 259;
 and military training of follow-
 ers, 255; stature of, 252; and
 unofficial court system, 255;
 and walk to Spanish Town,
 257
Bolas, Juan de, 73, 81
Bolívar, Simón, 16
Borrowes, Alfred, 296
Bougainville, Captain Antoine
 de, 192
Boukman, 185, 186
Brathwaite, Edward Kamau:
 poems of, 102, 103-106
Bridges, Rev. William, 222
Briere, Jean: quoted, 3
Brown, Rev. Ethelred, 373
Brown, Everald, 202
Brown, G. Arthur, 383
Brown, Sam: on social conditions
 in Kingston, 351, 356

Buie, Theodore, 253
Burchell, Thomas, 241
Burke, Eddie, 360
Burke, Edmund, 161
Burke, Lilly Mae, 360
Bustamante, Alexander: activities
 of, 364, 366-367; as chief
 minister, 374; and Jamaica
 Labour Party, 5; and Jamaica
 Workers' and Tradesmen's
 Union, 364; and labour
 movement, 5-6, 248, 363,
 368; Norman Manley on, 375-
 376; release of, 367
Bustamante, Lady Gladys, 360
Buxton, Thomas Fowell, 208

Cadbury, George, 383
Calder, Vassal: and criticism of
 Robert Love, 288-289
Campbell, Charles, 285
Campbell, George: quoted, 6-7,
 19
Campbell, Ralph, 392
Candler, John: on industry of the
 peasants, 242-243
Cardwell, Edward, 254
Carlyle, Thomas: *Discourse on the
 Negro Question*, 12
Carney, Arthur, 360
Cartwright, Edmund, 189
Césaire, Aimé, 15

Chamberlaine, Richard, 241
Christophe, Henri, 186, 188
Clarke, Colin: *Kingston, Urban Change and Reform*, 352-353
Clarke, Edith: *My Mother Who Fathered Me*, 275
Clarke, Rev. Henry, 236
Clarke, Samuel, 4
Clarkson, Thomas, 179
Cliff, Jimmy: quoted, 401
Columbus, Christopher, 20; arrival of, in the Bahamas, 55; arrival of, in Hispaniola, 63; encounter with Tainos in Jamaica, 64-67; first encounter with Indians, 55; and settlement of the Indies, 56-57; voyages of, 54-57
Columbus, Diego, 67
Cook, Captain James, 192
Coombs, A. G. S.: and Jamaica Workers' and Tradesmen's Union, 364
Cortés, Hernando, 61
Cox, Sandy, 247; and National Club of Jamaica, 297
Craskell, Thomas, 145
Craton, Michael: on slave punishment, 14
Cromwell, Oliver: and Western Design, 78, 84
Cubah ("Queen of Kingston"), 144
Cudjoe, 4, 136, 137; peace treaty of, 140-141
Cuffy, 136
Cugnet, Nicolas, 189
Cumper, George, 5
Cundall, Frank, 392
Cuneo, Michele de, 58
Curtin, Philip: and census of African slave trade, 93; *The Atlantic Slave Trade*, 14

Daley, Henry, 392
Daley, James, 248
Danquah, J. B., 312
Davis, Henrietta Vinton, 312
Dawes, Neville: *Prolegomena to*

Caribbean Literature, 337; on attitudes to Africa, 337
D'Costa, Alfred: and bauxite, 380
Dehaney, 39
DeLisser, H. G.: and perceptions of Africa, 17
Dendy, Walter, 240
Dessalines, Jean Jacques, 186, 188; assassination of, 189; as emperor of Haiti, 189
Diaz, Bartholomew, 54
Diop, Birago: quoted, 27
Dixon, Alexander, 288, 297
Dom Alfonso, 120
Domingo, W. A., 300, 350
Dove, Thomas, 39, 216, 220
Dowdy, Chester, 360
D'Oyley, Edward, 81, 84
Drake, Francis, 78-79
Drax, Charles, 155
Drax, James, 91
Drax, William, 155
Drummond, Andrew, 243-244
DuBois, W. E., 299, 300
Dunkley, Archibald, 396
Dunkley, John, 363, 392
Edward VII: funeral of, 267-268
Edwards, Bryan: and perception of Africans, 31
Ellis, George, 165
Equiano, Olaudah: account of enslavement of, 123-124, 125-126
Esquivel, Juan de, 59, 67; conduct of, 70
Evelyn, Linden H., 239
Eyre, Governor Edward: and call for abolition of Jamaican Assembly, 264-265; Gordon's attack on, 253

Fairclough, O. T., 350; and formation of People's National Party, 368
Farquharson, May, 359
Foot, Sir Hugh, 265
Foster, William, 179
Francis, Sybil, 360

Froude, J. A.: on civilising mission of Europeans, 266; quoted, 12

Gama, Vasco da, 54
Garay, Francisco de, 69, 70
Gardner, Robert, 216, 220
Garvey, Amy Jacques, 307
Garvey, Marcus, 3, 11, 247; achievements of, 314-315; activities of, in Jamaica, 308-313; and advocacy of social change, 310; on Africa, 17, 18; on black history, 10; and the *Black Man*, 308; in Central America, 298; challenge of, to the peasantry, 5; death of, 314; debate with Otto Huiswood, 311; and decolonisation, 295; deportation of, 307; efforts to intimidate, 302; and Harlem Renaissance, 300; impact of, 292-293; influence of Robert Love on, 291, 297; life of, 296-302, 304-314; and local elections, 310; migration of, to Britain, 313; and the *New Jamaican*, 308; and People's Political Party, 309; as publisher, 301; on race consciousness among Jamaicans, 294-296, 362; research on, 20; return to Jamaica, 307-308; and School of African Philosophy, 313-314; trial and imprisonment of, 306-307; as universalist, 296
Girvan, Norman: *Working Together for Development*, 360
Girvan, Thom, 360
Goodison, Lorna, 406; on history, 194
Gordon, George William, 4, 246; attack on Governor Eyre, 253; and efforts to encourage voting, 253; hanging of, 260; letter to his wife, 260, 262; life of, 248-249; religious conviction of, 249

Gordon, Joseph, 248
Grant, Governor Sir John Peter: work of, 265
Grant, St William: release of, 367
Guthrie, Colonel: and negotiations with Cudjoe, 140

Hannan, W. B., 286
Hargreaves, James, 177, 189
Hart, Richard: *Blacks in Rebellion*, quoted, 8-9
Harvey, Thomas, 239
Hazlitt, William, 179
Headley, George: record of, 391
Hearne, John, 158-159
Henry, Rev. Claudius, 397
Hibbert, George, 167
Hibbert, Joseph, 396
Higman, Barry, 31; *Jamaica Surveyed*, 152
Hill, Frank, 350
Hill, Ken, 350
Hill, Richard: and Underhill meetings, 255
Hill, Robert: and research on Garvey, 20, 296
Hinds, Robert, 396
Honeygan, Lloyd, 403
Hope, Richard, 86
Hope, Roger, 85, 153
Howell, Leonard, 396
Hughes, Langston, 3
Huie, Albert, 392
Huiswood, Otto: debate between Garvey and, 311
Hylton, Edward, 213

Inikori, Joseph: *The Slave Trade and the Atlantic Economies*, 124-125; on capitalism and slavery, 161
Issa, Abe: and tourism promotion, 381
Jackson, Grace, 403
Jackson, Richard Hill, 285
Jacobs, H. P., 350
James, C. L. R., 15, 161; *Black Jacobins*, 19

James, Edith Dalton, 359
James, John, 145
James, Captain Montague, 146
Jefferson, Thomas: and the American Declaration of Independence, 184
Johnny, 136
Johnson, 39
Johnson, William, 214
Jordon, Edward, 259

Kapo, 202, 394
Kenyatta, Jomo, 15; influence of Garveyism on, 302; and the Mau Mau, 28-29;
Kerr, Madeleine: on society and personality development, 354
Ketelhodt, Baron von, 258; death of, 259
King, Johannes, 130-131
King, Martin Luther, 3, 15
Kishee, 136
Knibb, Mary Morris, 359
Knibb, William, 216, 224-225, 236; arrival of, in Jamaica, 207-208; and development of free villages, 239; testimony of, regarding Western Uprising, 214

Lamming, George: on black consciousness, 294-295; *In the Castle of my Skin*, quoted, 1; quoted, 11
La Renteria, Pablo de, 67
Las Casas, Bartolome de, 67-68
Lascelles, Daniel, 31
Lecky, T. P.: and livestock development, 395
LeClerc, General Charles, 188
Leslie, Charles, 151-152
Lewis, Bernard, 392
Lewis, M. G. "Monk": on death of children in Jamaica, 193-194; on slave family, 14
Lewis, Rupert: and research on Garvey, 20, 296
Lewis, W. Arthur: on social conditions in the West Indies, 351-352; *Theory of Economic*

Growth, 377; on West Indian economic policy, 379
Lincoln, Abraham, 16
Lightbourne, Robert: and industrialisation programme, 382
Linton, 39
Lisle, George, 39, 203; significance of work of, 180-181, 182
Locke, Alain, 3
Long, Edward, 77, 167
Long, Samuel, 30, 87
Longbridge, Gladys. *See* Bustamante, Lady Gladys
L'Ouverture, Toussaint, 16; role of, in St Domingue revolution, 187-188
Love, Robert, 247; anti-colonial views of, 285; career of, 283-285; contribution of, to national movement, 11; death of, 291; influence of, on Marcus Garvey, 291; in Kingston City Council, 288; in Legislative Council, 288; and People's Convention, 286; on political representation, 287; and support of black representation in government, 283; and support for Pan-Africanism, 291; on tax structure, 287
Lowry, Somerset (Earl of Belmore), 220
Lunan, Henry: and payment for lot, 237
Lusan, Carmen, 360
Lynch, Thomas, 86
Lyttleton, Sir Charles, 81

Maclaren, James, 252; and walk to Spanish Town, 257
Mais, Roger: *Brother Man*, 351
Manikongo Garcia, 121
Manley, Edna: first exhibition of, 393; and Jamaican art movement, 392-393; "Negro Aroused" of, 6

Manley, Norman: on
  Bustamante, 375-376; and
  campaign for universal adult
  suffrage,
5-6, 247; in dock workers
  dispute, 1938, 365-367; on
  national unity, 8, 362-363;
  and People's National Party, 6,
  368; quoted, xii
Marley, Bob, 395, 401
Marriott, Alvin, 394
Marson, Una: in Jamaican
  cultural revolution, 338, 344-
  345; and social concern, 360;
  women in the work of, 345
Martyr, Peter, 71-72
Mazuelo, Pedro de: and sugar
  making, 74
Mbiti, John, 20; on African
  concept of time, 207
McCallum, Michael, 403
McDonald, Sir Herbert, 395
McKay, Claude, 3; *Banana
  Bottom*, 338, 339-344; on
  banana, 276; and Harlem
  Renaissance, 300; in Jamaican
  cultural revolution, 338
McKenley, Herb, 391-392
Medina, Juan de, 71
Mico, Lady: and Mico
  Institution, 240
Miller, David, 393
Miller, Errol: on education
  system, 408
Mills, Don, 383
Mills, Gladstone, 383
Modyford, Thomas, 84, 157
Moncrieffe, Benjamin Scott, 166
Moncrieffe, Peter, 166
Monk, George, 85
Moody, Harold, 351
Mordecai, John, 383
Morgan, Henry, 85
Moses, 36, 38-39
Moton, Major Robert, 299
Musgrave, Sir Anthony, 392
Mutabaruka, 401

Nanny, 4, 137

Nanny Grigg, 204
Nettleford, Rex: *Jamaica in
  Independence*, 404; *Manley and
  the New Jamaica*, 378; and
  NDTC, 405
Nkrumah, Kwame, 15
Nugent, George, 167
Nugent, Lady Maria, 153, 154,
  158, 166
Nzinga, Queen, 121

Oge, 184
Olivier, Lord, 265
Onuora, Oku: and dub poetry,
  401
Ortiz, Fernando: *Cuban
  Counterpoint*, 275
Osei Tutu: and Ashanti political
  development, 110, 112
Ottey, Merlene, 403
Ovando, Nicolas de, 57

Padmore, George, 15
Palache, J. T., 285
Parboosingh, Karl, 394
Parks, Rosa, 15
Patterson, Orlando: on colonial-
  ism, 13
Penn, Admiral William, 78
Phibbah, 170
Phillippo, Rev. James, 249; and
  establishment of free villages,
  237
Pink, John H., 155
Pizarro, Francisco, 61
Porras, Francisco, 66
Pottinger, David, 393
Price, Charles, 288
Pringle, John: and tourism
  promotion, 380

Quao, 136
Quarrie, Donald, 403
"Queen's Advice", 257

Ramsay, James, 179
Reid, V. S.: *New Day*, 19, 207
Reynolds, Mallica. *See* Kapo
Rhodd, Ethlyn, 359

Rhone, Trevor, 406
Richardson, Egerton, 383
Rigaud, Pierre de, 188
Roberts, George, 280
Roberts, W. Adolphe, 282, 350;
  Six Great Jamaicans, 285
Rodney, Walter, 102-103
Rousseau, Jean-Jacques, 177;
  influence of, 183-184
Rowe, John, 203

Sargon: of Kish, 36
Seaga, Edward: and festival of
  arts, 405-406; on social classes,
  385
Sedeño, Jacinto, 75
Selassie, Haile, 19; visit of, to
  Jamaica, 399, 400
Senior, Olive, 406
Sewell, William, 6
Sharp, Granville, 178-179
Sharpe, Sam, 4, 39, 128; and
  campaign for strike, 214;
  execution of, 227; role of, in
  Western Liberation Uprising,
  213-214, 226; significance of,
  212-213; surrender of, 220
Simpson, H. A. L., 297
Sligo, marquis of: and freeing of
  slaves, 234
Slim and Sam: and social
  commentary, 355-356
Smicle, Josiah, 288
Smith, Adam, 177
Smith, John: imprisonment of,
  205
Smith, M. G.: on cultural differ-
  ences in Jamaica, 354; *Plural
  Society*, 351
Smith, Michael, 401
Somersett, James, 178
Sonthonax, Leger Felicite, 185
Stedman, T. G.: on maroon
  warfare in Suriname, 130-132
Steibel, George, 285
Stewart, Margery, 360
Stokes, Luke, 85
Stone, Carl: on industrialisation
  in Jamaica, 384-385

GENERAL INDEX

Aboukir: Taino artefacts near, 44
Abolition of the Slave Trade Act (1807), 180
Absenteeism: of Jamaican proprietors, 94, 159; and ownership of office, 160-161
Africa: artistic tradition of, 22; as cradle of mankind, 22; effect of partitioning of, 268-269; folklore of, 9; impact of slave trade on life in, 102-103; ironworking in, in antiquity, 22; Jamaican perceptions of, 17-18; Marcus Garvey on, 17; partitioning of, 266-267; place of, in civilisation, 20-24; religion in, 26-27; retentions of, in Jamaica, 2, 316; tribal society in, 28, 29; tribes of, 24, 26; and use of history, 9; visit of Bush Negro chiefs to, 18; white perceptions of history of, 20
African Communities League, 298
African society: features of, 26-29
Africans: and concept of justice, 247; and creation of democratic society in the Americas, 41; enslavement of, by Spanish, 73; and injustice of plantation society, 94-95; in Jamaica, at time of British conquest, 77;

and kinship, 28; in liberation movements in plantation America, 15-16, 81, 84; mortality rate of, 93; music and, 97; and prayer, 26-27; recruitment of, 317-318; and religion, 94-97; and resistance to English invaders, 80; and slavery, 116-118
Agriculture: stigma attached to, 245
Akan-Ashanti people, 110, 112; characteristics of, 134; and the slave trade, 133-134
Aluminium: development of, in Jamaica, 379-380
Anansi: in West African tradition, 197
Anti-colonial movement, 267; in Jamaica, 272
Anti-slavery society: public interest in, 180; work of, 179-180
Apprentices: treatment of, 234-235
Apprenticeship: system of, 230
Aqueduct: at Mona and Hope Estates, 154
Arawakan: as language of the Caribs and Tainos, 43
Art movement: growth of Jamaican, 392-394; new generation of artists in, 406
Asia: and colonisation of New World, 42

Assembly. *See* House of Assembly
Atlantic Age: explained, 51-52; Genoa and, 53, 54
Atlantic Slave Trade, Philip Curtin, 14
Aztecs: and geometry, 43; and mathematics, 43; and zero concept, 43

Back to Africa movement, 305
Bahamas, the: arrival of Columbus in, 55
Bamboo Pen, 163
Banana: export of, 271; Lacatan variety, 395; in life of the peasant, 276-277; in Port Antonio, 277-278; rise in trade, in Jamaica, 275-279
Banana Bottom, Claude McKay, 338, 339-344; message of, 342-343; significance of, 339
Bank of Jamaica, 383
Baptist Church: native, 180
Baptist Missionary Society, 39; arrival of, in Jamaica, 203; founding of, 178
Barbados: slave uprisings in, 204; transformation of, by sugar manufacturing, 91-92
Bauxite: in Jamaica, 379-380
Beach Control Authority, 381
Benham Spring, 166
Bible, the: and African-Jamaicans, 39

Birmingham, 239

Black Cross Navigation and Trading Company: establishment of, 307

Black electorate: mobilisation of, 283

Black Jacobins, 189

Black Jacobins, C.L.R. James, 19

Black Power movement, 15

Black proletariat: beginnings of, 273, 280; growth of, in Kingston and St Andrew, 350

Black Star Line: formation of, 305-306

Blackman, the, 308; folding of, 313

Blacks: challenge to, 409-411; disparity in number between whites and, 160; occupations of, in Kingston, 353; and perception of self determination, 369

Bluefish Caves, Yukon: archaeological finds at, 42

Bog Estate: renaming of, 278

Boston Guardian: tribute of, to Garvey, 314

Boston Fruit Company: formation of, 275; merged, 278

Boundbrook, 278

Boxing: Jamaicans in, 403

Brazil: maroon settlement in, 129

Britain: retentions of, in Jamaica, 2; and use of history, 9-10

British and Foreign Bible Society, 178

Brother Man, Roger Mais, 351

Buccaneers: activities of, 84-85; at Port Royal, 84

Burrowfield Pen, 166

Bush Negroes: of Suriname, 15, 130-132; visit of chiefs of, to Africa, 18. *See also* Maroons

Bustamante Industrial Trade Union: formation of, 367

Cabinet: institution of, in government system, 374

Calabar College: and training of ministers, 241

Cape of Good Hope, 54

Capitalism and Slavery, Eric Williams, 19

Caribbean Basin: americanisation of, 270

Caribs: settlement of, 43

Carpenter's Mountain, Manchester: Taino artefacts in, 44

Carrion Crow Hill, 139

Carvings: of the Tainos, 2

Cassava: export of, by Spanish, 69

Catholic Church: and slavery, 68

Census: of 1611, 74, 75; of African slave trade, 93

Central Bureau of Statistics, 383

Central Planning Agency, 383

Chapels: destruction of, 222

Chartist Movement, 211

Cherry Garden Estate, 248

Children: mortality rate of, in Jamaica, 193-194; skills training for, 244-245

China: civilisation of, 61-62

Chinese: attitude of black Jamaicans toward, 331; immigration of, to Jamaica, 327, 328; in Jamaica, 7; as labourers, 327; occupations of, 330; in retail trade, 328, 330; and riots in the 1930s, 331; savings scheme of, 329; traditional values of, 332-333

Christianity: conversion of Indians to, 70, 71

Church, Spanish: building of, 71-72

Church of England: reform movement in, 178

Civil disabilities: removal of, in Jamaica, 229-230

Civil Rights Act (US), 15

Civil service: modernisation of, 383

Clapham Sect: and establishment

of Sierra Leone, 179-180

Class: composition of the Jamaican ruling, 13; consciousness of, in Jamaica, 389-390; gap among social, 386; insensitivity to, in Jamaica, 386;

Cocoa: cultivation of, by early settlers, 88

Codex Montezuma, 43

College of Arts, Science and Technology, 314

Colonial Church Union, 223; formation of, 222

Colonial development fund: establishment of, 368

Colonialism: beginning of, in Jamaica, 30; culture and release from, 337-338; effect of, on the Caribbean, 10-14, 32; Eric Williams on, 13; Orlando Patterson on, 13

Colour: gradations of, 12; prejudice, in Jamaica, 192; and social change, 374

Communication: developments worldwide, 270

Community organisation: of the peasantry, 357

Compensation: for slave owners, 230

Constitution: criticism of 1944, 373; granting of, in 1944, 370

Co-operation: methods of, among black Jamaicans, 6

Cornwall Courier, 217, 218

Coromanti people: characteristics of, 134; role of, in struggle for freedom, 142-144

Cotterwoods, 139

Cotton industry: development of, 189

Court system: organised by Bogle, 255

Craftsmanship: of the Tainos, 71, 72

Cricket: performance of West Indians in, 391

Crooked Spring, 216

Ex-slaves: and land ownership, 236-238; treatment of, by planters, 235-238

Fabian Society: establishment of, 286
Family: of Africans, 335; concept of, under slavery, 14; of Middle Eastern immigrants, 335
Farming: in Spanish Jamaica, 69
Federation: in the West Indies, 386
Festival of arts: Edward Seaga and, 405; staging of national, 405; Wycliffe Bennett and, 405
Festivals: of East Indians, 325-326
Firestone: in Liberia, 309
Fletcher's Land, 280
Florence Hall: protest at, 253
Folk songs: of Jamaica, 99
Folk tales: origin of, 197
Food: shortage of, in the late eighteenth century, 191-192; William Bligh and, 192
Food and Agriculture Organisation, 377
Franchise Act: literacy clause in, 283; requirements of, 251
Free blacks: in plantation society, 159
Free coloureds: in plantation society, 159
Free persons: registration of, 160
Free villages: chapels in, 240; establishment of, 237; layout of, 239-240; spread of, 241-242
Freedom: maroons and, 141-142; Sunday market and, 162; as theme in history, 128
Freedom fighters: in the Americas, 3-4
French Revolution, 184
Friendly societies: Robert Love on, 290
Friends of the Blacks, 184

Friendship, 166
Frome: riots in, 365
Fulani, 24

Genoa: and the Atlantic Age, 53, 54
Geometry: and the Incas and Aztecs, 43
Germans: settlement of, in Jamaica, 317
Ghana: and connection to Jamaica, 101; history of, 106-108
Ginger, 88
Global Age, 270
Goshen Pen: described, 165
Government: constitutional reform, in 1944; of Jamaica, in mid seventeenth century, 86, 87; representative, in Jamaica, 87, 282
Government policy: shaping of, 5
Great houses: in Jamaica, 151
Griot: in African society, 207
"Ground": meaning of, 164
Guanaboa Vale, 80
Guerrilla warfare: maroons and, 132
Guinea grass: introduction of, 165
Guys Town, 139

Haiti: independence of, 15; revolution in, 184-189
Hammocks: in Spanish Jamaica, 69
Hannah Town, 280
Harlem Renaissance: Garvey and, 300; Claude McKay and, 300
Haughton Court, 166
Hayes, Clarendon: East Indians in, 323
Hereditaments tax, 251
Hides, 88
Higglering: features of, 174-175
Higglers: slave, 170; urban slaves as, 173; and West African trading tradition, 170-171

Hispaniola: arrival of Columbus at, 63; sugar industry in, 57
Historians: perspective of, 51
History: African use of, 9; British colonial, and self-perception of Jamaicans, 10-11; British use of, 9-10; Derek Walcott on, 194; and empowerment, 9-10; Jamaican attitude to, 10; Lorna Goodison on, 194; white perceptions of African, 20
Holland, 166
Hope Estate, 153; aqueduct at, 154; described, 154
Hope River: and water supply, 154
Horse racing: at Drax Hall, 166
Hosay: celebration, 325-326
House of Assembly: establishment of, in Jamaica, 86, 87; first meeting of, 86, 87; power of, 251; response of Barbadian, to Crown colony rule, 264; on slavery, 209
Hymns: role of, in life of slaves, 201-202

Ibo people, 24, 110; values of, 114
Immigration: from China, 327; from Europe, 317; from India, 318; from the Middle East, 333-334
Immigration law: amendments to, 329-330; and literacy, 330
Imperialism, 78; fight against, by non-whites, 267; growth of US, 270; spread of, 266
In the Castle of my Skin, George Lamming: quoted, 1
Incas: empire of, 42-43; and geometry, 43; and mathematics, 43
Indenture system: slavery and, compared, 127; on sugar plantations, 317
Independence celebrations: in Jamaica, 398-399

324-325; of slaves, 173; of Lebanese, 334

Office: ownership of, 160-161

Old Harbour: growth of, 243

Orde Brown Inquiry: into labour conditions in Jamaica, 367

Orogrande Cave, New Mexico, 42

Palenques, 81

Palmares Republic, 15, 129

Pan-Africanism: support of, by Robert Love, 291

Panama Canal: building of, 270, 274

Papine Estate, 153; reservoir at, 154

Passage Fort, 167

Peace treaty: negotiation of by maroons, 129-131; of Quao, 141; terms of Cudjoe's, 140-141

Peasantry: challenge to, of banana plantations, 281; community organisation of, 357-358; development of, 5; economic conditions of, 4-5; education, and mobility of, 240; and emigration, 5; industry of, 242-243; self-reliance of, 244; taxation and the, 252; and voting, 242

Pen, 157; difference between plantation and, 164; meaning of, 163

People's Convention: of Robert Love, 286

People's National Party (PNP): launching of, 368; and movement for self-government, 372-373

People's Political Party: formation of, 309; manifesto of, 309-310

Performing arts: development of, in Jamaica, 404

Petition: to the queen on conditions in Jamaica, 255-256; response to, 257

Pette River Bottom: described, 142

Pimento, 69, 88, 165-166

Piracy, 85

Place names, 142; origin of, 85

Plantation economy: decline of, 233; and transformation of Caribbean society, 92-93

Planters Bank, 233

Plants: folk names of, 171-172; importance of, as food, 171-172

Plural Society, M. G. Smith, 351

Pocomania. *See* Pukumina

Poetry League of Jamaica, 404

Political consciousness: growth of, 280, 372

Political power: and land ownership, 279-280

Political revolution: effect of, in 1930s, 390

Poll tax, 251

Population: distribution of, in late nineteenth century, 271; of Jamaica, 93; slaves in Spanish Jamaica, 75; of Spanish Jamaica, 74-75

Port Antonio, 138

Port Royal: buccaneers at, 84; earthquake at, 1692, 85

Portugal: and African slave trading, 118-121; role of, in world expansion, 52-54

Porus, 66, 80; establishment of, 243-244

Prayer: Africans and, 26-27

Private sector: role of, in modern Jamaica, 407

Prolegomena to Caribbean Literature, Neville Dawes, 337

Property laws: protest against, 253

Prospect, 166

Protector of Immigrants: appointment of, 318

Proverbs: in Jamaica, 196

Provision grounds, 157; Crossman Commission's remarks on, 274; development of, at

Vineyard Pen, 169-170; role of, on plantation, 171; symbolism of, to slaves, 170

Public opinion: encouragement of, 406-407

Puerto Rico: development of, 386-387; model of industrialisation in, 379

Pukumina: African influence in, 358

Quakers: and anti-slavery society, 179

"Quashie": meaning of, 6

Quilombos, 129

Race: issue of, in Jamaica, 389-390

Race consciousness: Garvey and, 294-296, 362; and national development, 295, 337

Race discrimination: in the British colonies, 192; in plantation society, 159, 160

Rastafarian movement: and Africa, 296; beginnings of, 395-398; and development of Jamaican music, 400-402; and perception of Marcus Garvey, 396; report on, in 1960, 398; role of, 395

Reggae music: and Rastafarians, 401

Registration: of free persons, 160

Religion: in Africa, 26-27; and African-Jamaican slaves, 39; intolerance of non-Christian, 321; role of women in traditional, 358

Repartimiento system, 70

Requirimiento system, 70-71

Retreat Pen: free village of, 239

Revival Zion: African influence in, 358

Revivalism: African influence in, 358

Rice planting: by East Indians, 324

DATE DUE
